The Daily CRICKET YEAR BOOK 87

Michael Melford
Wendy Wimbush

Consultant Editor Michael Melford
Statistics Wendy Wimbush
Special articles E.W. Swanton, Vic Marks
Other contributors
Rajan Bala (India), Mike Beddow,
Tony Cozier (West Indies), Rachael Flint, John Fogg,
David Green, Neil Hallam, Derek Hodgson, Doug
Ibbotson, David Leggat (New Zealand), Michael
Owen-Smith (South Africa), Qamar Ahmed (Pakistan),
D.J. Rutnagur, Mike Selvey, Alan Shiell (Australia),
Sa'adi Thawfeeq (Sri Lanka), A.S.R. Winlaw.

Editor: Norman Barrett
Illustrators Dennis Curran, Nick Robertson (cover)

Acknowledgements Thanks are due to David
Armstrong and Mike Gear for supplying the
statistics for the Minor Counties and Second XI
championships, respectively, and to the TCCB for
making the first-class fixtures available. The English
Schools' Cricket Association material was kindly
supplied by Cyril J. Cooper.

The photographs appearing in this book are reproduced
by permission of Adrian Murrell/All-Sport, Bill Smith,
Syndication International, Patrick Eagar, Bob Thomas,
Keystone, Sport & General, Michael Pattison,
Mike Powell/All-Sport, and Peter Sheppard/Cheshire
Press Photos.

The editors particularly wish to thank Radford
Barrett, Daily Telegraph Sports Editor, for his
generous help.

Published by Telegraph Publications
135 Fleet Street, London EC4P 4BL

First Published 1986
© Daily Telegraph 1986

ISBN 0-86367-045-8
ISBN 0-86367-031-8 Pbk

Conditions of Sale:
This book is sold subject to the conditions that it shall
not, by way of trade or otherwise, be lent, re-sold,
hired out or otherwise circulated without the
publisher's prior consent in any form of binding or
cover other than that in which it is published.

Printed in Great Britain
by Redwood Burn Limited, Trowbridge, Wiltshire.
Typeset by Thomas/Weintroub Associates, Wembley.

Contents

- 4 Foreword, by W.F. Deedes
- **9 Looking Back**
- 10 Changing Times, Changing Standards by Michael Melford
- 15 Spinners in Decline by Vic Marks
- 18 Daily Telegraph Schools Cricket Awards by D.J. Rutnagur
- 19 Daily Telegraph Cricketers of the Year, by E.W. Swanton
- 21 Looking Back on a Legend (D.S.C. Compton) by E.W. Swanton
- 22 Happy 80th, Leslie Ames by E.W. Swanton
- **23 England's Winter Tour**
- 24 England in West Indies
- **37 Overseas Cricket 1985-86**
- 38 Sri Lanka v India
- 45 Pakistan v Sri Lanka
- 52 Australia v New Zealand
- 59 Australia v India
- 66 New Zealand v Australia
- 73 Sri Lanka v Pakistan
- 80 Benson & Hedges World Series Cup
- 83 Pakistan v West Indies (1-day)
- 84 Sri Lanka v England 'B'
- 86 South Africa v Unofficial Australians
- 87 Other Overseas Results
- 88 Cricket in Australia
- 92 Cricket in South Africa
- 96 Cricket in West Indies
- 98 Cricket in New Zealand
- 100 Cricket in India
- 103 Cricket in Pakistan
- 105 Cricket in Sri Lanka
- **107 Tours to England 1986**
- 108 India in England
- 132 New Zealand in England
- **157 English Season 1986**
- 158 Britannic Assurance Championship
- 162 Review of the Counties
  - 162 Derbyshire
  - 164 Essex
  - 166 Glamorgan
  - 168 Gloucestershire
  - 170 Hampshire
  - 172 Kent
  - 174 Lancashire
  - 176 Leicestershire
  - 178 Middlesex
  - 180 Northamptonshire
  - 182 Nottinghamshire
  - 184 Somerset
  - 186 Surrey
  - 188 Sussex
  - 190 Warwickshire
  - 192 Worcestershire
  - 194 Yorkshire
- 196 Oxford and Cambridge
- 199 First-Class Averages
- 207 Benson & Hedges Cup
- 210 NatWest Bank Trophy
- 213 John Player League
- 215 Second XI Competition
- 217 Minor Counties
- 219 England YC v Sri Lanka YC
- 220 ICC Trophy
- 222 Village and Club Cricket
- 223 Schools Cricket
- 225 Women's Cricket
- **227 Extras**
- 228 Test Career Records
- 235 Guide to Newcomers
- 239 Obituary
  - 242 Jim Laker
  - 243 Bill Edrich
- **245 Looking Forward**
- 246 England on Tour 1986-87
- 247 The 1987 Season
- 248 Fixtures 1987

Foreword

On a sunny afternoon during Canterbury cricket week this year, sitting most comfortably in one of the tents and idly observing two heavily armoured batsmen playing medium-pace bowling, a question occurred to me: what are they frightened of?

Canterbury week has drawn me off and on for so many years that I can remember Augusts when Kent played seven amateurs in the side there. They batted bare-headed, or capped if the sun was falling, against the best fast bowling that other counties could muster. Their professional brothers did the same.

I remember Leslie Ames scoring his century of centuries there against quickish stuff on a green wicket from J.J. Warr of Middlesex. He looked totally assured in a county cap.

Yet in the 1986 cricket season, a newspaper reported just before Canterbury week, 29 professional cricketers had broken fingers during the summer. That is 10 per cent of the labour force.

Keith Fletcher of Essex was asked by the *Daily Mail*, after breaking one of his fingers, to explain these injuries. He thought there were more fast bowlers around. He added: 'Too many umpires are letting fast bowlers get away with too much short-pitched bowling. Only Dickie Bird and Alan Whitehead have a reputation for being strict about bouncers. Too many others prefer an easy life.'

Challenging words, and a good opening statement on which to begin the debate on my idle question: what are they frightened of?

At least Keith Fletcher's remarks dispose of the notion that bumpers are a West Indian monopoly. With a battery of four very fast bowlers against the MCC last winter — and on some pretty indifferent wickets — they took the art of intimidation a stage farther than anyone else has been able to do.

But the idea, which is prevalent in cricket-talking circles, that, if the West Indians could be persuaded or compelled to cool it, the problem would go away, is wide of the mark. They simply make most use of 'hot' bowling.

History, I fear, is against us. In truth, innocence was lost in the Garden of Eden when the serpent tempted Douglas Jardine in 1933. Endowed with the gifts of Larwood and Voce and confronted with Australian batsmen such as Ponsford, Woodfull, and Bradman, he evolved the strategy of bowling fast at the batsmen's bodies with a loaded leg field.

At the time I had to report for a London newspaper some of the fearful repercussions at this end. It seemed to me then that no matter how the row finished up, nothing would ever be quite the same again.

True, it was some years before the armoured batsman arrived; but the fuse had been lit. That fine English gentleman and Oxford Harlequin had released an explosive force. It was cricket's Hiroshima.

So the question that logically follows now is: can we get an arms agreement? As in arms talks, there is no lack of ideas on what might be done, only a marked absence of resolution.

Keith Fletcher's approach of planting more responsibility on the umpire has many supporters, but they do not include me. Umpires are expected to do their work logically and objectively. Once an umpire is called upon to decide what a bowler has in his mind; to determine whether he is intentionally bowling dangerously, he is taken into the realm of the subjective.

In theory, umpires have redress now. They can warn the bowler once; warn a second time and inform the bowler's captain and the square leg umpire, and finally warn the bowler off. The number of times that has happened qualifies for whatever is the opposite of the *Guinness Book of Records*. Imagine, incidentally, an umpire in the West Indies faithfully carrying through that procedure. He would need solid police protection for himself, his home, and his family.

One or two experienced judges of the game, including Jim Swanton, see a need for closer definitions if the umpire's judgement is to remain objective. They advocate a chalk or tape line across the pitch, bowling short of which constitutes a bumper.

That keeps the umpire in a sensible position, but it radically alters the character of the game. Furthermore, the artificial fixed line assumes that all cricket pitches are equal, like billiard tables; but we know very well that some are more equal than others. The bouncer will do one thing at Grandford, another at Mudford.

A more indirect but wholly legitimate approach would be to get much tougher on the over-rate. Bumpers apart, a battery of fast bowlers working at something like 12 overs an hour in order to conserve energy represents extraordinarily dull cricket.

The over-rate in much competitive cricket today compared with earlier years is deplorable, bad for cricket, unfair to cricket watchers, and indefensible. A minimum over-rate, strictly enforced and with suitable penalties attached, would handicap the side that put their strength into a battery of field guns. It would foster more spinners and it would be good for the game.

In one discussion about bumpers, I entered the responsibility of captains. Why should an umpire be held entirely responsible for fair play? Why should he alone have to decide what constitutes dangerous and therefore unfair bowling, while the captain of the fielding side stands idly by?

Is a captain not responsible for the conduct of his side? Suppose, as may happen one day soon, someone is killed by a bumper. Is the captain of the bowling side not to feel a scintilla of guilt?

My observation in friendly, cricket-loving company was received with mocking laughter. They fell about. 'And what,' they asked, 'do you suppose would be the fate of a captain who discouraged his side from winning by every means at their disposal?'

Sensing that I was on the verge of an important discovery, I persisted. 'You think,' I replied, 'that a strong captain would not be respected for that?' 'That is not the *point*,' they said. 'He would be costing his side *money*.'

And there, Watson, I think that our friends may have pointed us in the right direction. The game is up. If Mrs Hudson will be kind enough to summon a hansom cab, we may be able to bring this little matter to a swift and satisfactory conclusion.

Harking back to Canterbury, the alma mater of my cricket, when years ago I watched bareheaded batsmen flicker to and fro, there was nothing at stake except a place up or down the championship table.

If you lost a sporting game, some discerning judge like Johnny Woodcock or Jim Swanton wrote that both sides had done the game a power of good, losers no less than winners. Nobody stood to win or lose £1,000 a head.

The stakes have risen steadily. Great benefits result. Today's professional is far removed from the penurious fellow whom Lord Harris and the ilk bossed about the field; who earned a salary from his county when he had been granted a cap; a fee if he got a place in the MCC side for a Test match — and who had usually to look for winter work.

Those who work for Mr Kerry Packer's circus in Australia are well rewarded, and for good measure their wives and children are encouraged to join the caravan. The stakes are substantial. All sponsors — and cricket now depends heavily on sponsors — offer good stakes. The keener the contest, the better for their trade name.

But in a game like cricket, because it is such a wonderful reflection of the human condition, nothing is gained here without a corresponding loss elsewhere.

If bumpers help a side to win the sort of stake that sponsored tournaments carry today, then bumpers are OK. And woe betide the umpire (who is not going to be in the share-out) who declares that it is not OK. Yes, we are engaged in arms talks. Lots of ideas, but no marked resolution to take steps that would lose an advantage.

That is why Keith Fletcher is being less than fair when he lays blame for dangerous bowling on the umpire who opts for an easy life. The modern umpire, without our realizing it, has become a croupier. 'Money, thou bane of bliss and source of woe,' as George Herbert observed.

But to put it all down to money is too simplistic by half. Because cricket does indeed reflect the human condition, it cannot wholly isolate itself from a society that has become more violent in so many other respects.

This epidemic, I have no doubt, troubles apostles of rugby league no less than lovers of cricket. It torments the Football Association. A national game like cricket carries the burden of reflecting national vices, as well as virtues.

Bumpers are not a little wart on the game that surgeons of ICC or MCC can skilfully remove in a painless operation. Bumpers are part of what we have become, part of what we are.

In her study of the 14th century, *A Distant Mirror*, Barbara Tuchman, the American historian, seeks to draw certain striking parallels between that grim century and our own 600 years later.

A comparison of the human condition in Europe after the Black Death of 1348-50 and the two world wars of 1914 and 1939 shows that many of the social phenomena that disturb us now prevailed then: social unrest, depraved morals, industrial indolence, frenetic gaiety, luxury, debauchery, greed, avarice, maladministration, decay of manners.

Men behaved with inane savagery towards each other, and inflicted unspeakable cruelties. In the calamitous 13th century men also wore armour when engaged in certain sports. It did not always save them from being hacked to death.

Barbara Tuchman would see nothing unusual in 29 broken fingers in the course of a single cricket season in this 20th century. She would probably reckon they got off lightly!

Looking back

Changing Times, Changing Standards

In a year the mood has changed completely. Twelve months ago English cricket could congratulate itself, not only on regaining the Ashes but on the dashing batting that had made it possible; on the signs, too, that the dearth of top-class bowlers might soon be ending. Yet at the end of the 1986 season, England had suffered eight defeats in their last 11 Test matches and had not won one. Those who relish the opportunity to condemn players, administrators, and anyone else in sight when England lose a Test match leapt into action again and again. It is always easier to knock than to applaud. But how has the let-down come about, especially after the high hopes of autumn 1985?

One reason obviously is that a side that has been knocked about on not very good pitches by as formidable a force as West Indies were in 1985-86 does not recover its stride and confidence quickly. Another is an overestimate of the strength of the 1985 Australians. They were, perhaps, not the prestigious victims of earlier days; not quite. But more to the point is that standards in India and New Zealand have risen so sharply in recent years that the old assumption they they will be a push-over in England is no longer valid.

Perhaps both came at a time when they were on the crest of a wave. Certainly New Zealand's resources in the past have not been able to sustain a successful run for long, and they will soon face the harsh facts of life after Hadlee. But even allowing for the ups and downs that affect all countries (all, that is, except the modern West Indies), their playing standards and their depth of talent seem to have appreciated. Why should this be?

It is fair to say that there is now more money in sport worldwide, and that that has benefited the 'developing' cricket countries more than the established ones. There is a parallel in football. England have not noticeably advanced much since Stanley Matthews and others were limited to £25 a week, but Middle Eastern and other countries, now able to afford more thorough coaching and better facilities than before, have closed the gap on them.

At the heart of the change is the aeroplane, which in the last quarter of a century has provided cricketers with more frequent opportunities to test their strength internationally and to keep abreast of current trends. Most importantly, tours of England have been greatly simplified for visiting teams in two ways.

One is by the covering of pitches, so that they no longer find themselves on wet pitches that are totally strange to their batsmen and indeed their bowlers. The other is the institution from the mid-1960s of the short tour, which means that tours to England take place more frequently, every four or five years instead of sometimes as much as every nine. Players are now more likely to use the experience gained on one tour to do better on the next.

A third factor cannot be ignored. England, by opening its domestic game to overseas players to the extent that it did in the late 1960s, invited present or future opponents to come and absorb at length English conditions. In New Zealand's case, John Wright, Martin Crowe, and Richard Hadlee must surely have been the more effective for the years of experience playing for their counties.

So it is no dishonour — no 'humiliation' in the popular phrase — for England to lose to opponents of the calibre of India and New Zealand in 1986. But there are two other factors that are disquieting, one illustrated by the loss of form of Richard Ellison, the other deriving from an assessment of the comparative standards of youth cricket at international level.

In 1985, nothing was more heartening and more overdue than the emergence of Ellison as a swing bowler capable of turning matches — for example, by his 4 wickets in 15 balls one evening at Edgbaston and his 17 wickets at 10 apiece in the last two Tests. His bowling success was all the more welcome because he is a late-order batsman of spirit and power, and this is one area where England have been less well equipped than their opponents in recent years.

Is one to believe that at the age of 26 he had lost his flair altogether? There certainly have been good bowlers who lost their nerve or control to the extent that, when they ran up, gully or even the square-leg umpire had to be prepared to take cover. Just as golfers can putt perfectly well on the drawing-room carpet but are struck down by an impossible twitch on the green, so bowlers can lose all control of length and direction on the field while having no problem at the nets.

Ellison's case seems to be more subtle. Many bowlers have temporary losses of form but overcome them by going on bowling until they work them off. Now I suspect that this may not always happen. There is often another good bowler, perhaps an overseas bowler, on hand who will mop up the wickets which should have fallen to his out-of-form colleague. This the excellent Alderman clearly did for Kent in 1986, no doubt to their relief. The snag, however, is that, when this happens, the ailing bowler gets no chance to restore his shattered confidence in the best possible way, which is by taking wickets.

England did record one victory this season — in the Under-19 series. After draws in the first two matches against Sri Lanka, they had a spectacular win in the third after having been in danger at one time of following on. But that is not any cause for long-term jubilation. For much of the series Sri Lanka, who included three players with Test match experi-ence, had the better of things, which is in accord with what similar England Under-19 sides have found in the past.

Nowadays entry into county teams for the best young cricketers can happen at a much younger age than was once the case. Many of them look very good players and everyone is delighted with them with an eye to the future. But when they come up against Young Australia or Young West Indies they look immature compared with the opposition. I remember one captain of an England youth side to West Indies telling me twenty-odd years ago that his greatest shock had been discovering that his victorious opponents were not the same age, 18 or 19, as his side, but were only 15 or 16.

The work and organization of youth cricket and representative schools cricket, difficult though it is in Britain, seems to me to be extremely efficient nowadays, but the NCA and their representatives are still up against the physiological problem that English cricketers develop later than others, presumably partly because of the climate. To some extent, this disadvantage has been offset by the extra experience gained by young players who go on winter coaching and playing visits to South Africa, Australia, and New Zealand. But 22 is still much older in, say, Australia than it is in England. In an era when the average age of Test cricketers is lower than it was, no wonder therefore if the representative sides of other countries often have a more mature look about them than England's.

Off the field. The year has not been a lucky one for English cricket off the field either. The rejection by Bangladesh and Zimbabwe of the England 'B' team, and the fact that it took place when the side were just about to depart from London Airport, was no help to international harmony, though the main sufferers were the cricketing communities of the two countries concerned. Yet Zimbabwe and Bangladesh teams were allowed by their governments (and by the ICC) to come to England to play in the ICC Trophy. While governments use cricket to make political points and their cricket administrators are forced to comply, the standing of the International Cricket Conference is unlikely to rise very high.

In any case, what authority could the ICC have against such persistent criticisms of cricketers as were levelled by Caribbean politicians at Graham Gooch long after he had, as it were, served his sentence for making an unofficial tour of South Africa?

It was no help to the maintenance of the game's peace and dignity that one of its most flamboyant modern figures, Ian Botham, and his pursuant Press should have had an active year. His walk for charity from John o'Groats to Land's End reflected much credit on cricket and cricketers. His admissions of past drugtaking led to a three-month suspension from first-class cricket and a split in public opinion. On the one side, it was held that he should not be picked for England when he had set such a deplorable example and furthermore made no great contribution to team discipline. On the other hand, a probably larger and certainly more vocal body of opinion pointed to his matchwinning potential with the bat, the occasional flashes of his old brilliance with the ball, and his attractiveness as a player to a huge public. Somewhere in between these two strongly held views, the TCCB had to do their best to be fair to all sides and to maintain order within the law of the country.

Near the end of the season, a further schism developed in Somerset when the committee, seeking to do something to revive a side that had finished bottom and then bottom but one in the Championship in successive years, decided to take action. They were lucky enough to have one of the world's best young players, the New Zealander Martin Crowe, keen to join them, and they saw in his runs, to which would be added some wickets and a harmonious disposition in the dressing-room, a foundation of long-term success. They thus took the decision very reluctantly to dispose of the services of Viv Richards and Joel Garner, who were still two of the world's leading players but who had not been able to arrest the decline of recent years and were unlikely anyway to be available in 1988 when there was a West Indian tour of England due. With what kindness and diplomacy this decision was conveyed to the players is not known.

At once, sides were taken, with Botham threatening his resignation if the West Indians were allowed to go and later with the captain Peter Roebuck aligning himself with the committee decision.

There were rows in the old days, but they could be conducted fairly discreetly without the enterprise of the modern media. This, moreover, is the age of the 'quote' — when the opinion of the writer is often overshadowed by the words of a participant which may be uttered in the heat of the moment and may or may not make sense.

It is an age when a body such as the TCCB has an unenviable job in trying to uphold the game's reputation without inhibiting the players too harshly. This manifested itself in the TCCB's decision to ban players on the coming tour of Australia from writing in newspapers during the tour as they had been allowed to do in recent years. It is, of course, an age when the manager of a touring side needs not only the wisdom of Solomon but of Solomon at the very top of his form.

Too much cricket. Much is heard of the excessive amount of cricket played nowadays. In England, the problem is not so much the amount played — this is little if any more than when the Championship was of 32 matches — but that it can sometimes be seven days a week, entailing a lot of travelling and awkward journeys, especially at week-ends. The real surfeit of cricket comes in the seemingly unending string of tours, especially those short, condensed, and doubtless exhausting tours such as the one undertaken by Australia in India in September and October 1986. Starting five days after they left Melbourne out of season, the Australians' schedule was for three five-day Tests, six one-day internationals, and three other three-day matches, all inside seven weeks. This immediately preceded a six-month home season.

It is not exactly new. When England, on the way home from Australia, stopped in Bombay in February 1980 to play a jubilee Test match, it was the 13th Test played by the Indians that season — and was played for their part in a somewhat festive end-of-term mood. England won easily.

The idea that players are being forced to play too much by greedy Boards is not strictly true. The players are interested in the financial rewards, too. In England, certainly, until the advent of Packer in 1977, the TCCB laid down that one winter in four should be kept clear of tours, providing the best players with a complete rest from cricket. That was abandoned in the years that followed. But few decisions concerning players are taken by the TCCB without the active support of the Cricketers' Association, and it is a fair guess that if it were the players' wish, the programme would be pruned accordingly.

Enough has been written in this review in other years about short-pitched bowling, and possible remedies, for nothing to be added here. But just imagine you had been away for thirty years, stand back from it all and look at the impersonal helmets, the visors, the rib and thigh protectors, the strapping on the forearm, the abdominal protectors for close fielders, the time-wasting while all this equipment is put on, the time-wasting while the ball flies far over the batsman's head — just look at all this and ask yourself 'What has happened to a graceful, charming, skilful game?'

The answer may be: 'The game has been made safer for the players.' If that is so, hooray! But has it? Once a number eleven was equipped with a helmet, he apparently became a fair target for the bouncer. Is that making the game safer?

Spinners in Decline
by Vic Marks

In 1986 the TCCB selected an under-25 side to play the New Zealanders at Edgbaston. They chose an impressive array of cricketers, but one name stood out, Peter Such of Nottinghamshire; for he was plucked not from the first team at Trent Bridge but from the anonymity of second-team cricket at Worksop. Peter Such is an accomplished off-spinner, but his selection highlighted the dearth of young spin bowlers in county cricket. While the TCCB XI's middle-order batsmen, Robert Bailey and James Whitaker, might have been musing over the possibility of an Australian tour, Peter Such must have been dreaming of no more than an extended run in Nottinghamshire's first team.

It is becoming increasingly difficult for a young spin bowler to establish himself in country cricket, particularly if he is a specialist in the Pocock mould. Admittedly, one reason is the longevity of his rivals. A quick survey of the 25 spinners playing on a regular basis in 1986 reveals that only 6 were under the age of 30, while 10 were over 35. A receding hairline, occasionally coupled with an expanding waistline, has never seemed to hamper the spinners' effectiveness. Indeed such signs of maturity are often deemed to be a positive advantage; that well-worn, omniscient glare down the wicket sometimes gives the impression that those two straight sixes just conceded are all part of the master plan.

There are, however, several other factors contributing to the paucity of young spinners and the general decline of spin bowling. In 1980 it was decided that wickets should be covered from the elements at all times. This was a perfectly logical decision; it was the rule in Test cricket and it was palpably fairer that both sides should bat on a similar surface. In the late seventies the team winning the toss and batting first during one of those rather frequent 'unsettled' spells would usually win the game, as their opponents struggled to cope with the vagaries of a wet wicket later in the match. However, this decision robbed spinners of 20-30 wickets a year; often the wet wickets would not respond to the faster bowlers, but the spinners could make the ball jump and turn to devastating effect. Kent gleefully carried Derek Underwood around with them like an umbrella — just in case of rain.

With the abolition of uncovered wickets, ambitious county captains became frustrated by the high proportion of draws, as ordinary sides often managed to stifle a game if they batted diligently on unresponsive surfaces.

Their solution has been quietly to instruct their groundsmen to prepare 'result' wickets; very often this has involved leaving plenty of grass on the pitch to improve their seamers' chances of success so that spinners have sometimes become superfluous. Moreover, during the last decade the West Indians have dominated world cricket by using a battery of high-class fast bowlers in rotation, and it is hardly surprising that at county level clubs have tried to emulate them.

Fortunately for the spinner — and the game — this strategy has not been entirely successful; the best Championship sides have found that they need a balanced attack. The 1986 season provides us with a good illustration.

16 LOOKING BACK / SPINNERS IN DECLINE

Gloucestershire's Championship hopes floundered once Courtney Walsh finally stopped taking wickets, whereas Essex, whose early-season success was based upon the seam bowling of Lever, Foster, and Pringle, were able to produce their final trump card midway through the summer in the form of John Childs, ironically once of Gloucestershire, who was sagely supported by David Acfield. The English season is too arduous to rely solely on pace for success, which is the only legitimate argument I can summon for justifying the volume of cricket we are required to play. Even so, the spinner is becoming an endangered species.

The advent of one-day cricket has often been cited as the cause of 'the decline of English batsmanship'. However, I believe that it has damaged the quality of our bowling to a far greater extent. In the fifties and sixties the great English bowlers, such as Titmus, Laker, Lock, Cartwright, and Shackleton, presumably rediscovered their optimum length in a net every April, and they persevered with it without interruption each year until the conkers started falling. Minor adjustments might be made for individual players, but basically there was one place to bowl — a good length at off-stump.

Now every Sunday evening, when once the likes of Titmus and company were returning from the golf course, Magnums and Jumbos are flying through the air like helicopter rotors, and captains around the country are beseeching their bowlers to bowl anything but a good-length ball at off-stump. Such deliveries give the batsmen too much room to swing their bats as they search for that elusive matchwinning six over mid-wicket. Spinners are asked to attack leg-stump as quickly as possible — in complete contrast to the requirements of Saturday and Monday. Even Norman Gifford admits that it is hard to make the adjustment, so what chance has Keith Medlycott or Richard Illingworth? I'm sure that it is no coincidence that Nick Cook, while at Leicester, just like John Childs this year, was most successful when he wasn't playing regular limited-overs cricket.

Another side-effect of the one-day game is that batsmen have altered their approach to playing spinners; unfortunately, they have discovered that smashing the ball over the top of mid-off or mid-wicket is rather a good shot. Pat Pocock's career has coincided with this change in technique. He observes that modern players are no longer as adept at manipulating the ball between the fielders but they are much better at hitting boundaries. In the sixties, top-class batsmen, such as Cowdrey and Graveney, preferred to stroke the ball along the ground; their modern counterparts, say Gatting and Lamb, loft the ball over the infield without any hesitation or apparent risk. The rapid improvements in bat design and manufacture, as well as the current preference for 3-pound cudgels, have meant that mishits can now carry for six. The sense of injustice is bewildering for the spinner, who feels like an old Scottish distiller watching his prize whisky being doused with ice and water and swallowed in one gulp.

My venerable Somerset colleague Brian Rose had made a similar observation. He says that when he began his career he feared the prospect of batting against Titmus, Allen, and Mortimore more than any other type of bowler; he could not envisage where he might sneak a run against them. However, over the last decade, the proliferation of fast bowlers, even if very few of them have been English, has meant that the source of a batsman's fear has been monopolized by the pacemen. Understandably, any sane cricketer would be more frightened of being banged on the head by a bumper than being humiliated by a guileful left-arm spinner.

Increasingly, spinners have become light relief between the barrage. I have often experienced a sinking feeling playing for Somerset when replacing Joel Garner in the attack. The batsmen, while trying to disguise their relief, summon the 12th man to collect their helmets, which are replaced by that faithful remnant of the sixties, the county cap. Suddenly, they look as if they are about to enjoy batting, like a nomad who has just discovered an oasis in the desert.

So it is scarcely surprising that tomorrow's bowlers strive to be fast, having been nurtured on West Indian success on TV and the demands of limited-overs cricket at every level of the game. Pat Pocock recalls taking 5 for 102 from 20 overs in his first club game and everyone was delighted. Today, a club captain might be vilified by his colleagues for such an extravagance; run-rates, bonus points, and league tables now dominate cricketers' thoughts even at club level. Spinners can be an unnecessary risk.

Can the decline be arrested? Well, at least the 1986 performances of Childs, Maninder Singh, Edmonds, and Emburey demonstrated that the spinner is not yet redundant. But who are going to replace them? The legislators, unless they accede to the growing lobby in favour of a return to the lottery of uncovered wickets, seem powerless to act.

Probably the only practical solution lies with the much harassed groundsman. He must provide true, even-bouncing wickets that encourage the fast bowlers on the first morning, the batsmen on the second, and the spinners on the third. This is asking a great deal, but recently Harry Brind's Test wickets at the Oval have satisfied these requirements admirably, giving every department of the game a fair chance. Even a leg spinner — remember them? — would have enjoyed bowling there.

Without this type of surface, cricket as a spectacle will decline along with the spinner's role, and the legislators in helpless desperation will be driven to extreme measures, such as demanding 130 overs per day along with more punitive fines. This, they might surmise, would make spin bowlers a financial necessity; more likely it would lead to the first general strike by the Cricketers' Association. Let's hope instead that 1987 sees a general improvement in the standard of cricket wickets, resulting in a steady resurgence in the spinner's craft.

Daily Telegraph Schools Cricket Awards
by D.J. Rutnagur

Alive to the large following commanded by its coverage of junior cricket, the *Daily Telegraph* last season made a further declaration of its interest in the game at its grass roots by sponsoring awards for schoolboy cricketers.

Four awards were established: for the highest scoring batsmen and the main wicket-takers in categories of under-15 and under-19. Each winner received a trophy as a lasting memento of his achievement, while his school was presented with cricket equipment worth £1,000, the awards being made at separate ceremonies at the winners' schools.

This sponsorship was conceived during the euphoria that prevailed after the recovery of the Ashes in 1985. By the time its mechanics were finalized, however, the need for incentives for schoolboy cricketers became even more urgent as, meanwhile, England were trounced 5–0 in the Caribbean. Against this background, the *Daily Telegraph* saw it appropriate to announce the scheme on St George's Day. The major trophies of English cricket all stayed South in 1986. But Lancashire and Yorkshire will no doubt draw hope from the fact that, between them, they won three of the four awards, the exception being the under-19 bowler.

Various matches played under the jurisdiction of the English Schools Cricket Association and the Headmasters Conference were taken as the basis for the awards. Purists will appreciate that limited-overs games were not counted. In the under-19s, Michael Atherton, three years captain of Manchester Grammar and also captain of England Schools in 1985, missed a large part of the schools' season because of a fractured thumb. Yet, he scored more than 600 runs and, with his leg-breaks, took above 50 wickets. Atherton's performance made a good case for the addition of an all-rounder's award in the future. Had Atherton played a full season he could not only have been a threat to his schoolmate, **Mark Crawley**, who finished top among the under-19 batsmen, with 1,652 runs, but could also have challenged the winning bowler, off-spinner **James Boiling** (Rutlish), from Surrey.

Crawley, the winning batsman, is bound for Oxford and the Parks, where reinforcements are badly needed. He finished 126 runs ahead of Neil Stanley, of Bedford Modern. Among the under-19 bowlers, Boiling was a runaway winner, with 94 victims to 60 claimed by James Nuttall (Pocklington).

Connoisseurs of spin bowling will rejoice in the triumph of Boiling. His large bag included a clean sweep of all 10 against Wallington. Boiling aspires to play professionally, but his first priority is a history degree.

The under-15 awards were most keenly contested. **Paul Simmonite** (SS Fisher & Thomas More HS), who may well wear the Red Rose of Lancashire one day, and Simon Lister (Tadcaster GS) finished only 19 runs apart, while a mere five wickets separated two bowlers from Yorkshire, **Paul Stelling** (Brigshaw), who has already propelled the new ball for England Schools, and Jeremy Batty (Bingley GS).

Daily Telegraph Cricketers of the Year
by E.W. Swanton

Here goes for the fifth annual selection of *Daily Telegraph* correspondents of their respective Cricketers of the Year. In beginning with the joint choice by Michael Melford and me of **John James Whitaker**, I should, first wish him better fortune in the coming year than our English nomination R.T. Robinson of Notts has enjoyed in 1986. There are so many more batsmen nowadays playing county cricket who are broadly equal both as to merits and limitations than used to be the case that Whitaker flew with the team to Australia without having had the chance to show his quality in Test cricket. This may possibly have worked to his advantage. Yet on his record his tour selection seemed fair enough, and it was warmly applauded by those who have seen most of him. Like so many aspiring cricketers today, Whitaker armed himself for the future with university qualifications before throwing in his lot with Leicestershire. Thus, at the age of 24, he has had only three full county seasons. He is in consequence relatively mature in spirit as well as in physique and batting technique. His position in second place in the first-class averages with 66.34 for 1,526 runs scored is all the more impressive considering that he missed five weeks in mid-season re-covering from having both hands broken by Malcolm Marshall. In Uppingham he comes from a famous cricket stable.

Alan Shiell from Adelaide describes **Allan Border** as 'the only choice' for Australia, a fact abundantly confirmed by figures, apart from his qualification as Test captain. Australia's stock is not high (writing, of course, before the Test series against England starts), which has added to Border's responsibilities. In the nine Tests over the period he made 866 runs, including four hundreds, at 61.85. He also led Queensland for the second year running to the very brink of what would have been their first-ever capture of the Sheffield Shield, averaging 94.66. He won the umpires' Shield Cricketer of the Year award in what must almost have been a one-horse race. As if that were not sufficient endeavour, Border, after a slow start, played a considerable part in Essex's Championship victory.

In the light of recent unhappy events in Somerset, Tony Cozier's choice of **Joel Garner** as the West Indian Cricketer of the Year has a special significance. What with a knee operation and an infection that cost him 1½ stone in weight, there was doubt about his fitness for the West Indian season. However, 'his elevation to the Barbados captaincy for the first time appeared to be an important stimulus,' and he enjoyed an outstanding season. 'He committed himself completely to the Barbados captaincy and led them to their 12th Championship in the 20 seasons of the Shell Shield... He was an influential motivator of the younger players.' That makes good reading, as do his record Shell bag of 28 wickets and the fact of his heading the Test bowling against England with 27 wickets at 16 runs apiece. At 34, the Big Bird seems to have plenty of wing-flapping in him yet.

Equally in his mid-30s, **Richard John Hadlee** of New Zealand must have been the most unquestioned choice of all. As David Leggat points out, his bowling has conquered Australia twice and England once. He has brought his tally of Test wickets to 315 — only three men can better that — and he is assuredly not done with yet. His forceful batting has won many a match and saved some, too. Moreover, he is a model for the young cricketer in several respects, in his action, in the moderate length of his run-up, and in that he is a fair bowler who does not descend to intimidation.

Another great cricketer steps on to the rostrum for India, **Sunil Manohar Gavaskar**. Rajan Bala underlines his transcendent career figures, his record number of Tests, of Test runs, and of Test hundreds. Will he reach 10,000 in Tests? He may well do so, though with a lower average than such men as Sobers, Hammond, Barrington, and Hutton, while Bradman soars above all. However, younger Indians are now forcing attention — for instance, Vengsarkar and Amarnath, both of whom contributed distinctly more than Gavaskar to the defeat of England last summer.

If Gavaskar's selection for this year is surely at least arguable, what can a reviewer from a distance say of Qamar Ahmed's nomination of **Rizwan-uz-Zaman**, who, though he had an outstanding first-class season, has failed to catch the selectors' eye since he made three Test appearances with indifferent success back in 1981? However, I can only quote the citation: 'My man of the year is, of course, Test discard, opener Rizwan-uz-Zaman who plays for PIA and Karachi. In eight first-class matches, he scored 1,198 runs at an average of 92.15, his highest score being 175. He hit five centuries and five half-centuries. His batting helped Karachi win the Patron's Trophy and the Quaid-e-Azam Trophy.'

The Sri Lankan choice of Sa'adi Thawfeeq is by contrast unexceptionable — **Arjuna Ranatunga**. He was blooded aged only 18 in his country's first Test five years ago, since when he has developed, under the coaching of Sir Garfield Sobers no less, to the point of averaging 79 in the home series against Pakistan's strong attack.

Kenneth McEwan, of Western Province, was the top batsman in the 1985-86 Currie Cup, and made a match-winning 102 off 81 balls in the Benson & Hedges night series final to help bring off an exciting win by 12 runs. Michael Owen-Smith's naming of McEwan will be a welcome reminder to Essex supporters of the popular overseas cricketer who had so much to do with the county's several successes during his decade of service, 1974-83.

Looking Back on a Legend
by E.W. Swanton

Fifty Whitsuntides ago at Lord's a captivating piece of cricket took place, the recollection of which I believe will still remain clear in the memories of those present. And as there were some 15,000 of us present in 1936, the presumption is there are quite a few left, in various stages of dotage no doubt.

That there are many younger members of the Denis Compton fan club who first saw and read about this most charismatic of cricketers in the decade following the war is certain.

Middlesex were engaged against Sussex, as always over the Bank Holiday. On the Monday they were being hard-pressed to gain a first innings lead against the modest Sussex score of 185, when the youthful Compton (D.) came in last to join G.O. Allen, with 24 runs needed.

Denis and I earlier in the week had made about a hundred in partnership for Middlesex 2nd XI against Kent 2nd XI at Folkestone, and I claim no credit for telling R.W.V. Robins on returning to Lord's that I had seen an altogether exceptional young batsman. Now here he was, aged 18 only a few days before, making his first first-class appearance at a quite taxing moment.

The well-known exchange as the young tyro joined the seasoned Test cricketer is right in character. Maurice Tate on a fresh pitch could still be a difficult proposition; and he had already taken six wickets. As Denis passed him Gubby said: 'This chap comes off much quicker than you expect. Whatever you do, play forward.' 'Yes, sir.' The first ball was dead on a length, and, beating Denis's back stroke, passed an inch or two over the stumps before landing in Tich Cornford's gloves. An emphatic rebuke from the other end was meekly received, and thereafter all went well. The target was passed before the MCC ground-staff boy from Hendon was leg before to Jim Parks for 15.

Apart from the Folkestone match Denis had hitherto made no stirring impact, although Archie Fowler, the head coach at Lord's, had always seen the potential. Now, under Walter Robins' shrewd and not over-gentle care he blossomed. Three weeks later came his first hundred, at Northampton. By the end of the season, with 1,000 runs to his name, he had become the youngest cricketer to win a Middlesex cap, and only narrowly missed selection for the MCC tour of Australia.

He was just 20 when in June 1938 at Trent Bridge in his first Test against Australia he made a sparkling 102, and next followed it in the Lord's Test by taking out his bat for 76 on a rain-affected, difficult pitch, saving his side in the process. No-one who watched this latter innings could have doubted either his temperament or the touch of genius that set him apart.

When batting was easy he sometimes tempted fortune too far. But against the best bowling when the situation was critical he was as rigidly orthodox as his great contemporary, Len Hutton.

Whatever his mood, he had the crowd in the hollow of his hand. They shared his evident enjoyment of whatever he was doing, and when in the immediate post-war years runs came in an unceasing stream, there grew a 'golden boy' image that could well have spoiled one who had been brought up in a lesser school than that of the MCC and Middlesex professionals of his day.

As it was, neither Denis's modesty nor his instinctive good sportsmanship were ever at risk. Would that as much could be said of a few of those on whome the spotlight has fallen since!

Extract from *The Daily Telegraph*, 21 May 1986.

Happy 80th, Leslie Ames
by E.W. Swanton

Cricket is seldom forgetful of its favourite sons. Even so, it is a signal mark of the affection in which Leslie Ames is held that his 80th birthday should be marked by celebration dinners and a reception at the House of Lords.

Les is the fittest 80 imaginable, a blessing he attributes to a daily diet of walking, whether on the links at Deal or the nine miles from his Canterbury home to his native village of Elham.

Let me then note a few of the Ames milestones, beginning with his first visit, aged 8, to the Canterbury Week with the family the day before war was declared in 1914. When Arthur Fielder bowled Vallance Jupp of Sussex he broke the stump, and Les plainly recalls the umpire having to fetch a new one.

Les learned his cricket at Elham, a strong side playing on a good pitch and rarely beaten. In the post-war years it was said among opponents that the young kid hits you all over the place, then either father bowls you out or grandfather gives you out. The crucial milestone was the day at Hythe when Gerry Weigall, the Kent coach, told him after he had seen him bat, that if he had ambitions to be a professional he must be 'double-barrelled', and promptly made him keep wicket, which he had only ever done occasionally at Harvey Grammar School, Folkestone. A place on the Kent staff soon followed, and he was only 19 when in the Tunbridge Wells Week he made 35 in his first innings for Kent.

The following year, 1927, he became the regular keeper, made 1,200 runs and scored the first of his 102 hundreds. *Wisden* thought he would soon be playing for England, and so he was. He played in 47 Tests before Hitler brought the sequence to an end, by which time his record among the world's wicket-keeper batsmen was one to which only Alan Knott (subsequently) could hold a candle. He did not keep after the war, Kent having found a promising lad called Godfrey Evans.

A milestone with a personal touch: I broadcast the Middlesex match in the 1950 Canterbury Week and happened to be on the air at the moment he reached his 100th hundred. Les was in his favourite role, chasing runs against the clock, and one can see him now going yards down the pitch to Jack Young and Jim Sims and hitting them sweetly past extra-cover. He made 131 out of 211 in two hours, and Kent won by four wickets and seven minutes.

It was his fifth 100 of the summer, and there seemed surely more in the bag. But in the first match of 1951 his back 'went' badly. That was the end, the Kent Committee being thus frustrated in their intention to offer him the captaincy in 1952.

Since then Les Ames's service to the game (rewarded with the CBE) is a saga on its own: for 17 years secretary-manager of Kent before becoming the Club's President; Test selector; manager of three MCC teams abroad; first professional elected to the MCC Committee. To each post he has brought the virtue of plain-spoken, completely unprejudiced good sense.

When exactly 10 years ago, I saluted L.E.G Ames in these pages on his 70th birthday, I mentioned that the E. stood for Ethelbert, an old family name. Now, Ethelbert was King of Kent for 56 years, AD 560-614. Well, it is 56 years since our Kentish Ethelbert first played for England — and he's still going strong.

Extract from *The Daily Telegraph*, 2 December 1985

England's winter tour 1985-86

England in West Indies

It was not just the second successive 5–0 defeat at the hands of West Indies which made England's tour of the Caribbean early in 1986 such a melancholy affair, but the total one-sidedness of every Test match. At no stage did David Gower's side look like winning one. Only on the last day of the tour were they in sight of earning a draw. There seemed to be an acceptance of forthcoming defeat unprecedented in an England side, and all the more disappointing because this tour took place at a time when, after victories in India and against Australia at home, the standard of English cricket at Test level seemed to be rising. To the failures on the field could be added off-the-field allegations and political protests which made this even less like the happy, relaxed Caribbean cricket tours of the 1930s.

It is only fair to list the difficulties with which the England party had to grapple. The main obstacle to cricketing success had always seemed likely to be the modern West Indian dreadnought of four fast bowlers. Hopes that such as Holding and Garner might be in decline proved ill-founded, and the team was if anything strengthened by the arrival of the very fast and menacing Patrick Patterson. Marshall bowled as well as ever, Courtney Walsh was an able deputy, if required — which was very little, for the standard of fitness of the West Indian fast bowlers remained extremely high. It was confirmed once again that though individually they may not be invincible, as a quartet they pose problems seldom met before in cricket. The batsman has no respite, has so few chances of playing normal fluent strokes that he loses timing, confidence and sometimes patience. He is driven to play strokes which in normal times he would either eschew or execute better.

The many pitches of uneven bounce greatly favoured the West Indian fast bowlers. England, for their part, were especially undermined by the poor pitches of the preliminary matches, the particularly bad, even dangerous pitch for the first Test in Jamaica, and the general lack of good practice facilities.

The most compelling evidence of the low quality of the pitches lies in the fact that in the first four Tests, against often moderate English bowling, only two West Indian 100s were made. In the same Tests, 79 out of the 80 England wickets fell to fast bowlers, the other to a run-out. Not a single first-class 100 was made by an English batsman on the tour.

Off the field the tour was always threatened by the glut of reporters and photographers not primarily concerned with the cricket. These were attracted by the frequent pre-tour threats to England's visit caused by anti-apartheid elements in the Caribbean and focusing on Graham Gooch for his part in the 1982 visit of an English team to South Africa. In the event, the demonstrations against the tour were of a minor nature and the news correspondents had more time to devote to such features as allegations of impropriety against Ian Botham, Gower's private life, and Gooch's understandable resentment of unwelcoming words by the Antiguan foreign minister, all items unlikely to contribute to the harmony and enjoyment of a tour.

A further major handicap under which England laboured was the loss for most of the tour of Mike Gatting, who, when struck down by the first of two fractures, was the batsman most in form and the one most likely to provide a combative answer to the fast bowlers.

Of the other batsmen, Gower, recovering from a poor start, offered increasingly stiff resistance as the tour progressed. Gooch's 129 not out, which won the second one-day international off the last ball, was the brightest spot of the tour, though the rest of the one-day series, lost 3–1, was no less one-sided than the Test series.

If the disrupted batting, admittedly faced with a fearsome task, was not marked by any great fighting spirit, the fielding was also well behind that of West Indies, and the bowling not good enough or accurate enough to make the most of the few opportunities which occurred, such as those in the second Test, in Trinidad. There were signs early on that England had at last found a genuine fast bowler in Greg Thomas, but even his undoubted improvement faltered as the tour atmosphere became ever less helpful.

It was hard to think of English players left at home who might have been more successful, though Slack, a reinforcement before the Second Test, played well enough on occasions to suggest that he should have been included originally in the light of pre-tour fears that Robinson might have technical weaknesses against the fastest bowling.

When any team fails to do itself justice, there are doubts cast upon the captaincy. Here, the critical eye ranged also to Bob Willis, the assistant-manager, whose responsibility it was to arrange worthwhile net practice, and to the TCCB, who have long experience of trying to arrange suitable practice facilities and suitable itineraries for their touring teams. Teams coming from an English midwinter always need at least a month to reach their best form. When they have only three first-class matches before the first Test, and scarcely a sight of a decent pitch, it provides an ominous start to any tour.

Whatever happened, England would not have won this series against an immensely formidable West Indian side. The really disquieting factor was that they did so much worse than New Zealand, who did at least draw two out of four Tests in the Caribbean 12 months before. It did at least leave an intriguing question-mark about the outcome of England's home series in 1986 against India and New Zealand.

First Test: Kingston, Jamaica, 21, 22, 23 February.
West Indies won by 10 wickets.

Deprived, by the first injury to Mike Gatting (a broken nose), of their most effective batsman so far, England had little answer to the pace of Marshall, Garner, Patterson, and Holding on a pitch of variable bounce. Having been bowled out before tea on the first day, they did at least make West Indies work hard for their runs, Thomas, in his first Test, and especially Ellison bowling promisingly. But West Indies' middle batting produced a lead certain to make the match safe, and England's second innings, against a wealth of short-pitched bowling on an often dangerous pitch, was no improvement on the first. Though Willey batted with much courage for his 71 on the third afternoon, West Indies needed to bowl only 43 overs — and only 89 in the match.

Second Test: Port-of-Spain, Trinidad, 7, 8, 9, 11, 12 March.
West Indies won by 7 wickets.

England went into the second Test heartened by their one-day win and by the prospect of a slower pitch. However, having been put in, they failed to develop a dashing, if speculative, third-wicket stand of 106 between Gower and Lamb, and, in answer to their total of only 176, West Indies reached 67 for 1 that night. A fine innings by Richardson took West Indies ahead next day, but at 198 for 1 Emburey and Edmonds bowled together for the first time, and the innings declined before them, reaching 399 only when Marshall sustained the tail with some controlled hitting on the third morning.

At 168 for 3 that evening, England were not out of the match, but the only significant resistance after the rest day came in a remarkable last-wicket stand of 72 between Ellison and Thomas, which held West Indies up for 2½ hours. West Indies, still needing 17 of the 93 required, had to return on the fifth morning to finish the match.

Third Test: Bridgetown, Barbados, 21, 22, 23, 25 March.
West Indies won by an innings and 30 runs.

England faced the third Test with the minimum of confidence, for Gatting, returning from London with one fracture repaired, at once suffered another, a broken thumb, and Ellison was also not fit. They chose to field, but the pitch did little on the first day for their bowlers and, worse still, deteriorated afterwards.

On the first day, when West Indies scored 269 for 2 off 81 overs, Richardson played brilliantly to make 78 of the first 100 added for the second wicket with Haynes. He was out early on the second day when England won back lost ground by taking the last 8 wickets for 149. On one of their few good days, they finished at 110 for 1 despite the early loss of Robinson.

The partnership between Gooch and Gower soon ended next morning, and the innings became a struggle which never promised to avoid the follow-on. Before tea, Richards, with a rest day to come for his bowlers, enforced it, and after an opening stand of 48 dominated by Robinson, 6 second innings wickets were taken for 132. Before lunch on the fourth day the match was over and West Indies had won the series.

ENGLAND IN WEST INDIES 1985-86 27

Fourth Test: Port-of-Spain, Trinidad, 3, 4, 5 April.
West Indies won by 10 wickets.

The England selectors gave deep thought to their next team before they picked Botham, who had done little so far with bat or ball. Eventually they left out Ellison and, having found an unexpected amount of grass on the pitch, also omitted Edmonds. Unlike its bare neighbour used for the second Test, this pitch allowed a lot of movement and became erratic in bounce.

The match followed a familiar pattern. England, having been put in, were bowled out on the first day, Smith, in his first Test, Lamb and Botham making over half of the 200 total. Though Thomas was not accurate enough to bother them, West Indies had problems next day against Emburey, Foster, and eventually Botham, who finished with 5 wickets in a Test innings for the 26th time.

On the third morning, England batted again only 112 runs behind. Gooch, hooking, was caught off Marshall's third ball and there was little further resistance against the four fast bowlers, who were sometimes bowling the equivalent of fast off-breaks or leg-breaks. The match was over soon after tea.

Fifth Test: St John's, Antigua, 11, 12, 13, 15, 16 April.
West Indies won by 240 runs.

Though Mike Gatting was fit to play in his first Test of the series — on the slender preparation of an hour's batting in the middle in the previous seven and a half weeks — England were beyond reviving by now. They did take the final Test into the last hour of the last day, but in the second innings were as completely outplayed as at any time in the series.

Gower put West Indies in on a pitch which started damp, and the middle days of the match played better than any other in the series. This time the West Indies later batsmen did the damage, Marshall, Harper, and Holding hitting powerfully to make 183 for the last 4 wickets. Against a total of 474, Gooch and Slack made 127 in England's best opening stand of the tour, and Gower, though suffering from a bruised wrist, played the first of two defiant innings. His 90 was England's highest first-class score of the tour.

In the second innings, begun on the fourth morning after Gower had ensured that the follow-on was saved, Richards, with many devastating strokes, scored the fastest ever Test 100 — in 56 balls — and declared in time for his bowlers to take two wickets that evening. On the last morning, Gooch reached his second 50 of the match, and the nightwatchman, Ellison, stayed with him for nearly two hours. But with the fast bowlers now adding to their menace with the occasional shooter, Gower's three-hour defence was not enough to earn a draw.

West Indies v England 1985-86 1st Test
West Indies won by 10 wickets
Played at Sabina Park, Kingston, Jamaica, 21, 22, 23 February
Toss: England. Umpires: D.M. Archer and J.B. Gayle
Debuts: West Indies – C.A. Best, B.P. Patterson; England – D.M. Smith, J.G. Thomas

England

G.A. Gooch	c Garner b Marshall	51	b Marshall	0
R.T. Robinson	c Greenidge b Patterson	6	b Garner	0
D.I. Gower*	lbw b Holding	16	c Best b Patterson	9
D.M. Smith	c Dujon b Patterson	1	(7) c Gomes b Marshall	0
A.J. Lamb	b Garner	49	c sub (R.A. Harper) b Patterson	13
I.T. Botham	c Patterson b Marshall	15	b Marshall	29
P. Willey	c Dujon b Holding	0	(4) b Garner	71
P.R. Downton†	c Dujon b Patterson	2	c Haynes b Holding	3
R.M. Ellison	c Haynes b Patterson	9	b Garner	11
P.H. Edmonds	not out	5	lbw b Patterson	7
J.G. Thomas	b Garner	0	not out	1
Extras	(NB5)	5	(B5, NB3)	8
		159		**152**

West Indies

C.G. Greenidge	lbw b Ellison	58
D.L. Haynes	c Downton b Thomas	32	(1) not out	4
J. Garner	c Edmonds b Botham	24
R.B. Richardson	lbw b Botham	7	(2) not out	0
H.A. Gomes	lbw b Ellison	56
C.A. Best	lbw b Willey	35
I.V.A. Richards*	lbw b Ellison	23
P.J.L. Dujon†	c Gooch b Thomas	54
M.D. Marshall	c sub (J.E. Emburey) b Ellison	6
M.A. Holding	lbw b Ellison	3
B.P. Patterson	not out	0
Extras	(B2, LB4, NB3)	9	(NB1)	1
		307	(0 wkt)	**5**

West Indies

	O	M	R	W	O	M	R	W
Marshall	11	1	30	2	11	4	29	3
Garner	14.3	0	58	2	9	2	22	3
Patterson	11	4	30	4	10.5	0	44	3
Holding	7	1	36	2	12	1	52	1
Richards	1	1	0	0				
Richardson	1	0	5	0				

England

	O	M	R	W	O	M	R	W
Botham	19	4	67	2				
Thomas	28.5	6	82	2	1	0	4	0
Ellison	33	12	78	5				
Edmonds	21	6	53	0				
Willey	4	0	15	1				
Gooch	2	1	6	0				
Lamb					0	0	1	0

NOTE: Lamb bowled a no-ball.

Fall of Wickets

Wkt	E 1st	WI 1st	E 2nd	WI 2nd
1st	32	95	1	–
2nd	53	112	3	–
3rd	54	115	19	–
4th	83	183	40	–
5th	120	222	95	–
6th	127	241	103	–
7th	138	247	106	–
8th	142	299	140	–
9th	158	303	146	–
10th	159	307	152	–

West Indies v England 1985-86 2nd Test
West Indies won 7 wickets
Played at Queen's Park Oval, Port-of-Spain, Trinidad, 7, 8, 9, 11, 12 March
Toss: West Indies. Umpires: D.M. Archer and C.E. Cumberbatch
Debuts: West Indies – T.R.O. Payne; England – W.N. Slack

England

G.A. Gooch	c Best b Marshall	2	lbw b Walsh	43
W.N. Slack	c Payne b Marshall	2	run out	0
D.I. Gower*	lbw b Garner	66	b Walsh	47
P. Willey	c Payne b Patterson	5	b Marshall	26
A.J. Lamb	c Marshall b Garner	62	lbw b Walsh	40
I.T. Botham	c Richardson b Marshall	2	c Payne b Marshall	1
J.E. Emburey	c Payne b Garner	0	c Best b Walsh	14
P.R. Downton†	c Marshall b Walsh	8	lbw b Marshall	5
R.M. Ellison	lbw b Marshall	4	lbw b Marshall	36
P.H. Edmonds	not out	3	c Payne b Garner	13
J.G. Thomas	b Patterson	4	not out	31
Extras	(LB4, NB14)	18	(B20, LB11, W1, NB27)	59
		176		**315**

West Indies

C.G. Greenidge	c Lamb b Thomas	37
D.L. Haynes	st Downton b Emburey	67
R.B. Richardson	c Downton b Emburey	102
H.A. Gomes	st Downton b Emburey	30
C.A. Best	b Edmonds	22
I.V.A. Richards*	c Botham b Edmonds	34
T.R.O. Payne†	c Gower b Emburey	5
M.D. Marshall	not out	62
J. Garner	c Gooch b Emburey	12
C.A. Walsh	c Edmonds b Thomas	3
B.P. Patterson	c Gooch b Botham	9
Extras	(LB11, W1, NB4)	16
		399

c Lamb b Edmonds		45
not out		39
c Gooch b Emburey		9
b Emburey		0
not out		0
(LB2)		2
(3 wkts)		**95**

West Indies	O	M	R	W	O	M	R	W
Marshall	15	3	38	4	32.2	9	94	4
Garner	15	4	45	3	21	5	44	1
Patterson	8.4	0	60	2	16	0	65	0
Walsh	6	2	29	1	27	4	74	4
Richards					7	4	7	0
Gomes					1	1	0	0

England	O	M	R	W	O	M	R	W
Botham	9.4	0	68	1				
Thomas	20	4	86	2	5	1	21	0
Ellison	18	3	58	0	3	1	12	0
Edmonds	30	5	98	2	12.3	3	24	1
Emburey	27	5	78	5	10	1	36	2

Fall of Wickets

Wkt	E 1st	WI 1st	E 2nd	WI 2nd
1st	2	59	2	72
2nd	11	209	82	89
3rd	30	242	109	91
4th	136	256	190	–
5th	147	298	192	–
6th	148	303	197	–
7th	153	327	214	–
8th	163	342	214	–
9th	165	364	243	–
10th	176	399	315	–

West Indies v England 1985-86 3rd Test
West Indies won by an innings and 30 runs
Played at Kensington Oval, Bridgetown, Barbados, 21, 22, 23, 25 March
Toss: England. Umpires: D.M. Archer and L.H. Barker
Debuts: nil

West Indies

C.G. Greenidge	c Botham b Foster	21
D.L. Haynes	c Botham b Foster	84
R.B. Richardson	lbw b Emburey	160
H.A. Gomes	c Gower b Thomas	33
I.V.A. Richards*	c Downton b Thomas	51
C.A. Best	lbw b Foster	21
P.J.L. Dujon†	c sub (W.N. Slack) b Botham	5
M.A. Holding	b Thomas	23
M.D. Marshall	run out	4
J. Garner	c Gooch b Thomas	0
B.P. Patterson	not out	0
Extras	(B2, LB9, W3, NB2)	16
		418

England

G.A. Gooch	c Dujon b Garner	53	b Patterson	11
R.T. Robinson	c Dujon b Marshall	3	b Patterson	43
D.I. Gower*	c Dujon b Marshall	66	c Marshall b Garner	23
P. Willey	c Dujon b Marshall	5	lbw b Garner	17
A.J. Lamb	c Richardson b Marshall	5	c & b Holding	6
I.T. Botham	c Dujon b Patterson	14	(7) c Dujon b Garner	21
P.R. Downton†	lbw b Holding	11	(8) c Dujon b Holding	26
J.E. Emburey	c Best b Patterson	0	(9) not out	35
P.H. Edmonds	c Richardson b Patterson	4	(6) lbw b Garner	4
N.A. Foster	lbw b Holding	0	c Richardson b Holding	0
J.G. Thomas	not out	4	b Patterson	0
Extras	(B4, LB8, W2, NB10)	24	(B1, NB12)	13
		189		**199**

England	O	M	R	W	O	M	R	W
Botham	24	3	80	1				
Thomas	16.1	2	70	4				
Foster	19	0	76	3				
Edmonds	29	2	85	0				
Emburey	38	7	96	1				

West Indies	O	M	R	W	O	M	R	W
Marshall	14	1	42	4	13	1	47	0
Garner	14	4	35	1	17	2	69	4
Patterson	15	5	54	3	8.4	2	28	3
Holding	13	4	37	2	10	1	47	3
Richards	3	0	9	0	4	1	7	0

Fall of Wickets

Wkt	WI 1st	E 1st	E 2nd
1st	34	6	48
2nd	228	126	71
3rd	286	134	94
4th	361	141	108
5th	362	151	108
6th	367	168	132
7th	406	172	138
8th	413	181	188
9th	418	185	188
10th	418	189	199

West Indies v England 1985-86 4th Test
West Indies won by 10 wickets
Played at Queen's Park Oval, Port-of-Spain, Trinidad, 3, 4, 5 April
Toss: West Indies. Umpires: C.E. Cumberbatch and S. Mohammed
Debuts: nil

England

G.A. Gooch	c Richards b Garner	14	c Dujon b Marshall		0
R.T. Robinson	c Marshall b Garner	0	b Garner		5
D.I. Gower*	c Dujon b Garner	10	lbw b Patterson		22
D.M. Smith	c Greenidge b Patterson	47	lbw b Holding		32
A.J. Lamb	b Holding	36	b Patterson		11
I.T. Botham	b Holding	38	c Gomes b Marshall		25
P. Willey	c Richardson b Garner	10	lbw b Marshall		2
P.R. Downton†	c Garner b Marshall	7	not out		11
J.E. Emburey	c Haynes b Marshall	8	b Holding		0
N.A. Foster	c Richards b Holding	0	b Garner		14
J.G. Thomas	not out	5	b Garner		0
Extras	(B1, LB2, W1, NB21)	25	(B5, LB7, NB16)		28
		200			**150**

West Indies

C.C. Greenidge	lbw b Emburey	42
D.L. Haynes	c Botham b Foster	25
R.B. Richardson	b Emburey	32
H.A. Gomes	c Downton b Foster	48
I.V.A. Richards*	lbw b Botham	87
P.J.L. Dujon†	c Downton b Botham	5
M.D. Marshall	b Emburey	5
R.A. Harper	lbw b Botham	21
M.A. Holding	b Botham	25
J. Garner	not out	5
B.P. Patterson	c Downton b Botham	3
Extras	(LB10, W3, NB1)	14
		312

(1) not out 17
(2) not out 22

(0 wkts) **39**

West Indies

	O	M	R	W	O	M	R	W
Marshall	23	4	71	2	10	2	42	3
Garner	18	3	43	4	9	3	15	3
Patterson	10	2	31	1	9	1	36	2
Holding	14.4	3	52	3	10	1	45	2

England

	O	M	R	W	O	M	R	W
Botham	24.1	3	71	5	3	0	24	0
Thomas	15	0	101	0				
Foster	24	3	68	2	2.5	0	15	0
Emburey	27	10	62	3				

Fall of Wickets

Wkt	E 1st	WI 1st	E 2nd	WI 2nd
1st	8	58	0	–
2nd	29	72	30	–
3rd	31	111	30	–
4th	123	213	75	–
5th	124	244	105	–
6th	151	249	109	–
7th	168	249	115	–
8th	181	299	126	–
9th	190	306	150	–
10th	200	312	150	–

West Indies v England 1985-86 5th Test
West Indies won by 240 runs
Played at St. John's, Antigua, 11, 12, 13, 15, 16 April
Toss: England. Umpires: L.H. Barker and C.E. Cumberbatch
Debuts: nil

West Indies

C.G. Greenidge	b Botham	14		
D.L. Haynes	c Gatting b Ellison	131	(1) run out	70
R.B. Richardson	c Slack b Emburey	24	(2) c Robinson b Emburey	31
H.A. Gomes	b Emburey	24		
I.V.A. Richards*	c Gooch b Botham	26	(3) not out	110
P.J.L. Dujon†	b Foster	21		
M.D. Marshall	c Gatting b Gooch	76		
R.A. Harper	c Lamb b Foster	60	(4) not out	19
M.A. Holding	c Gower b Ellison	73		
J. Garner	run out	11		
B.P. Patterson	not out	0		
Extras	(B2, LB11, W1)	14	(B4, LB9, W1, NB2)	16
		474	(2 wkts dec)	**246**

England

G.A. Gooch	lbw b Holding	51	lbw b Holding	51
W.N. Slack	c Greenidge b Patterson	52	b Garner	8
R.T. Robinson	b Marshall	12	run out	3
D.I. Gower*	c Dujon b Marshall	90	(5) c Dujon b Harper	21
A.J. Lamb	c & b Harper	1	(6) b Marshall	1
M.W. Gatting	c Dujon b Garner	15	(7) b Holding	1
I.T. Botham	c Harper b Garner	10	(8) b Harper	13
P.R. Downton†	c Holding b Garner	5	(9) lbw b Marshall	13
R.M. Ellison	c Dujon b Marshall	6	(4) lbw b Garner	16
J.E. Emburey	not out	7	c Richardson b Harper	0
N.A. Foster	c Holding b Garner	10	not out	0
Extras	(B5, LB6, NB40)	51	(B10, LB10, W2, NB21)	43
		310		**170**

England	O	M	R	W	O	M	R	W
Botham	40	6	147	2	15	0	78	0
Foster	28	5	86	2	10	0	40	0
Ellison	24.3	3	114	2	4	0	32	0
Emburey	37	11	93	2	14	0	83	1
Gooch	5	2	21	1				

West Indies	O	M	R	W	O	M	R	W
Marshall	24	5	64	3	16.1	6	25	2
Garner	21.4	2	67	4	17	5	38	2
Patterson	14	2	49	1	5	3	29	0
Holding	20	3	71	1	16	3	45	2
Harper	26	7	45	1	12	8	10	3
Richards	2	0	3	0	3	1	3	0

Fall of Wickets

Wkt	WI 1st	E 1st	WI 2nd	E 2nd
1st	23	127	100	14
2nd	63	132	161	29
3rd	137	157	–	84
4th	178	160	–	101
5th	232	205	–	112
6th	291	223	–	124
7th	351	237	–	147
8th	401	289	–	166
9th	450	290	–	168
10th	474	310	–	170

Test Match Averages: West Indies v England 1985-86

W. Indies: Batting/Fielding	M	I	NO	HS	R	Avge	100	50	Ct/St
D.L. Haynes	5	9	3	131	469	78.16	1	3	3
I.V.A. Richards	5	6	1	110*	331	66.20	1	2	2
R.B. Richardson	5	9	2	160	387	55.28	2	–	6
M.D. Marshall	5	5	1	76	153	38.25	–	2	4
C.G. Greenidge	5	6	0	58	217	36.16	–	1	3
H.A. Gomes	5	6	0	56	191	31.83	–	1	2
M.A. Holding	4	4	0	73	124	31.00	–	1	3
C.A. Best	3	4	1	35	78	26.00	–	–	4
P.J.L. Dujon	4	4	0	54	85	21.25	–	1	16/0
J. Garner	5	5	1	24	52	13.00	–	–	2
B.P. Patterson	5	5	3	9	12	6.00	–	–	1

Also batted: R.A. Harper (2 matches) 21, 60, 19* (2ct); T.R.O. Payne (1 match) 5 (5ct); C.A. Walsh (1 match) 3.

W. Indies: Bowling	O	M	R	W	Avge	Best	5wI	10wM
J. Garner	156.1	30	436	27	16.14	4-43	–	–
M.D. Marshall	169.3	36	482	27	17.85	4-38	–	–
C.A. Walsh	33	6	103	5	20.60	4-74	–	–
B.P. Patterson	118.1	18	426	19	22.42	4-30	–	–
M.A. Holding	102.4	16	385	16	24.06	3-47	–	–

Also bowled: H.A. Gomes 1-1-0-0; R.A. Harper 38-15-55-4; I.V.A. Richards 20-7-29-0; R.B. Richardson 1-0-5-0.

England: Batting/Fielding	M	I	NO	HS	R	Avge	100	50	Ct/St
D.I. Gower	5	10	0	90	370	37.00	–	3	3
G.A. Gooch	5	10	0	53	276	27.60	–	4	6
A.J. Lamb	5	10	0	62	224	22.20	–	1	3
D.M. Smith	2	4	0	47	80	20.00	–	–	–
P. Willey	4	8	0	71	136	17.00	–	1	–
I.T. Botham	5	10	0	38	168	16.80	–	–	4
W.N. Slack	2	4	0	52	62	15.50	–	1	1
R.M. Ellison	3	6	0	36	82	13.66	–	–	–
J.G. Thomas	4	8	4	31*	45	11.25	–	–	–
J.E. Emburey	4	8	2	35*	64	10.66	–	–	–
P.R. Downton	5	10	1	26	91	10.11	–	–	6/2
R.T. Robinson	4	8	0	43	72	9.00	–	–	1
P.H. Edmonds	3	6	2	13	36	9.00	–	–	2
N.A. Foster	3	6	1	14	24	4.80	–	–	–

Also batted: M.W. Gatting (1 match) 15, 1 (2ct).

England: Bowling	O	M	R	W	Avge	Best	5wI	10wM
J.E. Emburey	153	34	448	14	32.00	5-78	1	–
N.A. Foster	83.5	8	285	7	40.71	3-76	–	–
R.M. Ellison	82.3	19	294	7	42.00	5-78	1	–
J.G. Thomas	86	13	364	8	45.50	4-70	–	–
I.T. Botham	134.5	16	535	11	48.63	5-71	1	–

Also bowled: P.H. Edmonds 92.3-16-260-3; G.A. Gooch 7-3-27-1; A.J. Lamb 0.0-0-1-0 (1 no ball); P. Willey 4-0-15-1.

Statistical Highlights of the Tests

1st Test, Kingston. The match was won in two days and five hours. Patterson was the new destroyer, 4-30 and 3-44, in his first Test. Edmonds was among those hit, although only Greenidge had to retire hurt for three stitches when hit above the eye by Botham. In the West Indies 1st innings there were 6 lbw decisions for only the fourth time in Test history. Ellison took 5 wickets for the third time. In the second innings Willey passed 1,000 runs in his 22nd Test.

2nd Test, Port-of-Spain. The England second innings total was the highest with no fifty by a batsman. Extras (59) was top score for only the seventh time in history. In his 42nd Test Marshall dismissed Downton as his 200th wicket, the fastest of the six West Indian bowlers to achieve this feat. Richardson reached 1,000 runs in 17 Tests with his fifth hundred, off only 111 balls. Botham dismissed Patterson for his 50th wicket against West Indies. Emburey took 5 wickets for the fourth time.

3rd Test, Bridgetown. Gatting returned after having his nose broken by Marshall in a one-day international, but now found himself unable to take his Test place because of a broken thumb. The sixth consecutive win ensured that West Indies retained the Wisden Trophy, which they have held since 1973. Richardson again scored a hundred, this time the first fifty coming off 44 balls. Dujon's five catches in the innings equalled a West Indies record.

4th Test, Port-of-Spain. England succumbed on the third afternoon. Botham took 5 wickets for the 26th time, equalling Hadlee's record. In the process he bowled Holding for his 350th Test wicket, leaving himself only 6 to overtake Lillee. Richards passed 6,000 runs in his 81st Test, the 15th in the world. Greenidge passed 5,000 runs in his 70th Test, and Gomes 3,000 in his 53rd.

5th Test, Antigua. For the sixth time in history a series was lost 5-0. West Indies beat England for the 10th successive time, making 24 Tests since England had beaten them. The astonishing batting came from Richards with 110 not out off 58 balls, his 20th hundred coming from just 56 of them. The innings included 7 sixes and 7 fours. He had passed 2,000 runs against England in the first innings. Haynes scored his 8th hundred, Garner and Marshall ended the series with a record 27 wickets apiece in a series against England in West Indies. Robinson passed 1,000 runs in his 15th Test.

One-Day Internationals

18 February at Sabina Park, Kingston, Jamaica. WEST INDIES won by 6 wickets. Toss: West Indies. England 145-8 (46 overs) (M.D. Marshall 10-1-23-4). West Indies 146-4 (43.5 overs) (C.G. Greenidge 45). Award: M.D. Marshall (10-1-23-4).

4 March at Queen's Park Oval, Port-of-Spain, Trinidad. ENGLAND won by 5 wickets. Toss: England. West Indies 229-3 (37 overs) (I.V.A. Richards 82, R.B. Richardson 79*, D.L. Haynes 53). England 230-5 (37 overs) (G.A. Gooch 129*). Award: G.A. Gooch (129*).

19 March at Kensington Oval, Bridgetown, Barbados. WEST INDIES won by 135 runs. Toss: England. West Indies 249-7 (46 overs) (I.V.A. Richards 62, R.B. Richardson 62). England 114 (39 overs). Award: I.V.A. Richards (62 and 1 ct).

31 March at Queen's Park Oval, Port-of-Spain, Trinidad. WEST INDIES won by 8 wickets. Toss: West Indies. England 165-9 (47 overs) (R.T. Robinson 55; M.D. Marshall 9-0-37-4). West Indies 166-2 (38.2 overs) (D.L. Haynes 77*, I.V.A. Richards 50*). Award: J. Garner (9-1-22-3).

England Tour of West Indies 1985-86

First-Class Matches: Played 10; Won 1, Lost 7, Drawn 2
All Matches: Played 14; Won 2, Lost 10, Drawn 2

First-Class Averages

Batting and Fielding	M	I	NO	HS	R	Avge	100	50	Ct/St
M.W. Gatting	5	9	0	80	317	35.22	–	3	4
A.J. Lamb	8	16	1	78	438	29.20	–	4	5
D.I. Gower	8	16	0	90	447	27.93	–	3	4
G.A. Gooch	9	18	0	53	443	24.61	–	5	10
I.T. Botham	8	16	0	70	379	23.68	–	1	6
D.M. Smith	5	10	1	47	195	21.66	–	–	1
R.T. Robinson	9	18	0	76	359	19.94	–	2	4
W.N. Slack	4	8	1	52	134	19.14	–	1	3
P. Willey	7	14	0	71	259	18.50	–	2	3
R.M. Ellison	6	11	0	45	183	16.63	–	–	1
J.E. Emburey	7	12	2	38	165	16.50	–	–	4
P.H. Edmonds	7	12	4	20	118	14.75	–	–	2
P.R. Downton	8	16	3	26	134	10.30	–	–	10/5
J.G. Thomas	6	12	6	31*	57	9.50	–	–	5
N.A. Foster	7	12	2	14	60	6.00	–	–	2
L.B. Taylor	4	6	3	9	14	4.66	–	–	2

Also batted: B.N. French (2 matches) 0, 0, 9 (5ct/1st).

Bowling	O	M	R	W	Avge	Best	5wI	10wM
L.B. Taylor	93.3	17	259	13	19.92	3-27	–	–
P. Willey	81.4	17	162	8	20.25	2-38	–	–
N.A. Foster	180.3	33	583	23	25.34	6-54	1	–
R.M. Ellison	162.3	31	513	18	28.50	5-78	1	–
J.E. Emburey	239.2	56	648	21	30.85	5-78	1	–
P.H. Edmonds	233.4	43	590	18	32.77	4-38	–	–
J.G. Thomas	135	19	547	14	39.07	4-70	–	–
I.T. Botham	180.5	26	671	15	44.73	5-71	1	–

Also bowled: M.W. Gatting 3-0-15-1; G.A. Gooch 17-6-56-1; A.J. Lamb 0.0-0-1-0 (1 no ball).

Overseas cricket 1985-86

Sri Lanka v India

India's first official cricket tour of Sri Lanka will always be remembered as the one that brought the home country its first-ever Test victory. That most memorable moment in Sri Lanka's cricket history arrived on 11 September at the P. Saravanamuttu Stadium when fast bowler Rumesh Ratnayake held on to a return catch to dismiss Indian captain Kapil Dev. The wicket gave Sri Lanka a win by 149 runs and their first victory, in their 14th Test match.

A disillusioned Indian side never played together as a team. There was a clash in personalities between Kapil Dev and Sunil Gavaskar, with the latter preferring not to open but to play as a middle-order batsman. Thus India were never given the start they wanted. The opening partnerships in the series were 19, 23, 0, 39, 10 and 74. On the only occasion they got off to a good start, in the third and final Test at Asgiriya, Kandy, India hit their highest total of the series, 325 for 5 declared, but the opportunity came too late.

Sri Lanka's most senior batsmen, skipper Duleep Mendis and his deputy Roy Dias, earned their country an honourable draw and with it the first series triumph, by 1–0. Both made hundreds in a 216-run fourth-wicket stand. They also became the first to complete 1,000 runs in Tests for their country. For Mendis it was a personal triumph as captain. He not only led by example, but also had his best series with the bat, hitting 310 runs, with one hundred and three fifties.

Left-handed opener and wicket-keeper Amal Silva also had an outstanding series, setting a new world record of 22 dismissals for a three-Test series and hitting a century to set up the Test win. He also had nine victims in a Test on two successive occasions.

Arjuna Ranatunga and Ranjan Madugalle completed their maiden Test centuries in the first Test of the series at the SSC grounds, which Sri Lanka narrowly failed to win.

On seaming pitches it was the fast-medium bowlers who reaped a harvest of wickets, Ashantha De Mel, Rumesh Ratnayake, and newcomer Saliya Ahangama together captured 50 wickets, with Ratnayake setting up a Sri Lanka record for a three-Test series by taking 20 wickets at an average of 22.95 runs apiece.

The Indians were outplayed in every department and, as it is with modern-day captains, the blame for the defeat was placed on the umpires, rather than on the team's shortcomings. Mohammed Azharuddin and Laxman Sivaramakrishnan, who came with high reputations, had poor series. Azharuddin averaged 18.66 in six innings and not once crossed fifty, while 'Siva' played only one Test, which saw him go unrewarded while conceding 117 runs.

Mohinder Amarnath scored the only century of the series for India, in the final Test at Kandy, where India seemed to have the upper hand until the final day, when Mendis and Dias staged their superb rearguard action.

Sri Lanka v India 1985-86 1st Test
Match Drawn
Played at Sinhalese Sports Club Ground, Colombo, 30, 31 August, 1, 3, 4 September
Toss: India. Umpires: H.C. Felsinger and K.T. Francis
Debuts: Sri Lanka – F.S. Ahangama, E.A.R. De Silva; India – L.S. Rajput, S. Viswanath

India

L.S. Rajput	c Silva b Ahangama	32	c Silva b Ratnayake	61
K. Srikkanth	b Ratnayake	2	c Silva b Ratnayake	9
M. Azharuddin	c Silva b Ahangama	3	lbw b Ahangama	16
D.B. Vengsarkar	c Silva b De Mel	6	not out	98
S.M. Gavaskar	run out	51	c De Mel b Ratnayake	0
R.J. Shastri	c Silva b De Mel	9	lbw b Ratnayake	40
Kapil Dev*	c Silva b De Mel	36	c sub (S.D. Anurasiri) b Ratnayake	6
S. Viswanath†	c E.A.R. De Silva b De Mel	20	c Silva b Ratnayake	0
C. Sharma	c Silva b De Mel	38	run out	4
G. Sharma	not out	10	lbw b Ahangama	1
Maninder Singh	lbw b Ratnayake	0	b Ahangama	3
Extras	(LB5, W1, NB5)	11	(B4, LB3, NB6)	13
		218		**251**

Sri Lanka

S. Wettimuny	c Viswanath b C. Sharma	13
S.A.R. Silva†	c Azharuddin b C. Sharma	7	(6) not out	1
R.S. Madugalle	c & b Maninder	103	(5) not out	5
R.L. Dias	c Azharuddin b C. Sharma	4	(3) c Srikkanth b Kapil Dev	0
L.R.D. Mendis*	c Gavaskar b Maninder	51	(2) c Kapil Dev b C. Sharma	18
A. Ranatunga	b Shastri	111	(4) run out	15
P.A. De Silva	c Azharuddin b Shastri	33	(1) c Maninder b Kapil Dev	21
A.L.F. De Mel	c Viswanath b Kapil Dev	16		
R.J. Ratnayake	lbw b Kapil Dev	2		
E.A.R. De Silva	not out	1		
F.S. Ahangama	c Viswanath b Kapil Dev	0		
Extras	(LB5, NB1)	6	(LB1)	1
		347	(4 wkts)	**61**

Sri Lanka	O	M	R	W	O	M	R	W
De Mel	28	8	64	5	30	3	84	0
Ratnayake	24.2	8	64	2	41	10	85	6
Ahangama	23	3	60	2	27.3	10	49	3
E.A.R. De Silva	12	5	18	0	15	6	20	0
Ranatunga	10	8	7	0	6	2	6	0

India	O	M	R	W	O	M	R	W
Kapil Dev	30.4	8	74	3	4	0	36	2
C. Sharma	25	3	81	3	4	0	24	1
Shastri	34	9	70	2				
Maninder	40	12	82	2				
G. Sharma	15	6	35	0				

Fall of Wickets

Wkt	I 1st	SL 1st	I 2nd	SL 2nd
1st	19	18	23	38
2nd	30	29	54	39
3rd	47	33	130	44
4th	49	118	130	58
5th	65	262	188	–
6th	101	317	206	–
7th	143	342	206	–
8th	202	346	220	–
9th	218	346	229	–
10th	218	347	251	–

Sri Lanka v India 1985-86 2nd Test
Sri Lanka won by 149 runs
Played at P. Saravanamuttu Stadium, Colombo, 6, 7, 8, 10 11 September
Toss: Sri Lanka. Umpires: S. Ponnadurai and P.W. Vidanagamage
Debuts: Sri Lanka – C.D.U.S. Weerasinghe

Sri Lanka

S. Wettimuny	run out	19	c Rajput b Sharma	32
S.A.R. Silva†	c Viswanath b Shastri	111	c Vengsarkar b Kapil Dev	11
R.S. Madugalle	lbw b Sharma	54		
R.L. Dias	c Viswanath b Sharma	95	not out	60
L.R.D. Mendis*	c Shastri b Amarnath	51	not out	13
A. Ranatunga	lbw b Sharma	21		
P.A. De Silva	c Azharuddin b Sharma	2	(3) b Shastri	75
A.L.F. De Mel	lbw b Shastri	0		
R.J. Ratnayake	c Shivaramakrishnan b Shastri	7		
C.D.U.S. Weerasinghe	b Sharma	3		
F.S. Ahangama	not out	0		
Extras	(LB3, W4, NB15)	22	(B4, LB6, NB5)	15
		385	(3 wkts dec)	206

India

L.S. Rajput	c Silva b De Mel	0	lbw b De Mel	12
K. Srikkanth	c Mendis b Ahangama	64	lbw b Ratnayake	25
M. Azharuddin	c Silva b Ratnayake	0	c Silva b De Mel	25
D.B. Vengsarkar	c Ranatunga b Ratnayake	1	c Silva b Ratnayake	0
L. Shivaramakrishnan	c Wettimuny b Ratnayake	18	(9) c Silva b De Mel	21
S.M. Gavaskar	st Silva b Ranatunga	52	(5) c Silva b Ratnayake	19
M. Amarnath	c Ahangama b De Mel	60	(6) c De Silva b Ratnayake	10
R.J. Shastri	c Silva b Ahangama	17	(7) c Silva b Ahangama	4
Kapil Dev*	c Ratnayake b Ahangama	6	(8) c & b Ratnayake	78
S. Viswanath†	c Wettimuny b Ratnayake	7	lbw b Ahangama	0
C. Sharma	not out	4	not out	0
Extras	(B4, LB6, W1, NB4)	15	(LB2, NB2)	4
		244		198

India	O	M	R	W	O	M	R	W
Kapil Dev	32	10	69	0	20	4	73	1
Sharma	33	3	118	5	13	1	55	1
Shastri	45.3	11	74	3	13	4	41	1
Shivaramakrishnan	31	4	90	0	7	1	27	0
Amarnath	15	2	31	1				

Sri Lanka	O	M	R	W	O	M	R	W
De Mel	31	8	63	2	22	4	64	3
Ratnayake	25.1	5	76	4	23.2	6	49	5
Ahangama	18	3	59	3	14	3	56	2
Weerasinghe	16	7	28	0	3	1	8	0
Ranatunga	5	1	8	1	4	0	19	0

Fall of Wickets

Wkt	SL 1st	I 1st	SL 2nd	I 2nd
1st	74	0	46	39
2nd	169	1	48	39
3rd	229	3	180	41
4th	328	79	–	84
5th	368	88	–	84
6th	372	178	–	98
7th	375	218	–	98
8th	375	229	–	168
9th	379	238	–	169
10th	385	244	–	198

Sri Lanka v India 1985-86 3rd Test
Match Drawn
Played at Asgiriya Stadium, Kandy, 14, 15, 16, 18, 19 September
Toss: India. Umpires: D.P. Buultjens and M.D.D.N. Gooneratne
Debuts: Sri Lanka – B.R. Jurangpathy

India

R.J. Shastri	c Madugalle b De Mel	6		c Silva b Ahangama	81
K. Srikkanth	b Ahangama	40		lbw b Ahangama	47
M. Amarnath	lbw b Ahangama	30		not out	116
D.B. Vengsarkar	run out	62		lbw b Ahangama	10
M. Azharuddin	c Silva b Ahangama	25	(6)	b Ratnayake	43
S.M. Gavaskar	c Silva b Ratnayake	49	(7)	not out	15
Kapil Dev*	lbw b Ahangama	0	(5)	b Ranatunga	2
R.M. Binny	c De Mel b Ahangama	19			
C. Sharma	c Wettimuny b De Mel	11			
S. Viswanath†	c Silva b Ratnayake	4			
Maninder Singh	not out	0			
Extras	(LB1, W1, NB1)	3		(LB5, W4, NB2)	11
		249		(5 wkts dec)	**325**

Sri Lanka

S. Wettimuny	c Viswanath b Kapil Dev	34		c Vengsarkar b Sharma	5
S.A.R. Silva†	lbw b Binny	19		c Viswanath b Kapil Dev	2
R.S. Madugalle	c & b Binny	5		c Viswanath b Kapil Dev	10
R.L. Dias	c Viswanath b Sharma	8		run out	106
L.R.D. Mendis*	c sub (L. Shivaramakrishnan) b Maninder	53		c Gavaskar b Sharma	124
A. Ranatunga	c Vengsarkar b Maninder	38		b Sharma	0
F.S. Ahangama	c Gavaskar b Maninder	11			
P.A. De Silva	run out	8	(7)	not out	29
B.R. Jurangpathy	c Viswanath b Kapil Dev	1	(8)	lbw b Kapil Dev	0
A.L.F. De Mel	c Viswanath b Maninder	1	(9)	not out	9
R.J. Ratnayake	not out	0			
Extras	(LB4, NB16)	20		(B8, LB4, W4, NB6)	22
		198		(7 wkts)	**307**

Sri Lanka	O	M	R	W	O	M	R	W
De Mel	26.3	5	97	2	13	2	66	0
Ratnayake	26	5	88	2	23	2	97	1
Ahangama	24	7	52	5	27	6	72	3
Ranatunga	8	5	11	0	16	4	51	1
Jurangpathy					4	0	24	0
Madugalle					1	0	10	0

India	O	M	R	W	O	M	R	W
Kapil Dev	19	4	46	2	24	2	74	3
Binny	12	0	49	2				
Sharma	14	1	40	1	20	4	65	3
Shastri	6	2	28	0	24	5	57	0
Maninder Singh	12.3	4	31	4	34	11	99	0

Fall of Wickets

Wkt	I 1st	SL 1st	I 2nd	SL 2nd
1st	10	36	74	5
2nd	66	44	178	8
3rd	111	68	206	34
4th	161	80	211	250
5th	180	153	289	250
6th	180	173	–	266
7th	212	196	–	267
8th	241	197	–	–
9th	242	198	–	–
10th	249	198	–	–

India 1st innings C. Sharma (4) retired hurt at 237-7 and resumed at 242-9

Test Match Averages: Sri Lanka v India 1985-86

Sri Lanka

Batting and Fielding	M	I	NO	HS	R	Avge	100	50	Ct/St
L.R.D. Mendis	3	6	1	124	310	62.00	1	3	1
R.L. Dias	3	6	1	106	273	54.60	1	2	–
R.S. Madugalle	3	5	1	103	177	44.25	1	1	1
A. Ranatunga	3	5	0	111	185	37.00	1	–	1
P.A. De Silva	3	6	1	75	168	33.60	–	1	1
S.A.R. Silva	3	6	1	111	151	30.20	1	–	21/1
S. Wettimuny	3	5	0	34	103	20.60	–	–	3
A.L.F. De Mel	3	4	1	16	26	8.66	–	–	2
F.S. Ahangama	3	3	1	11	11	5.50	–	–	1
R.J. Ratnayake	3	3	1	7	9	4.50	–	–	2

Also batted: E.A.R. De Silva (1 match), 1* (1 ct); B.R. Jurangpathy (1 match) 1, 0; C.D.U.S. Weerasinghe (1 match) 3.

Bowling	O	M	R	W	Avge	Best	5wI	10wM
F.S. Ahangama	133.3	32	348	18	19.33	5-52	1	–
R.J. Ratnayake	162.5	36	459	20	22.95	6-85	2	–
A.L.F. De Mel	150.3	30	438	12	36.50	5-64	1	–

Also bowled: E.A.R. De Silva 27-11-38-0; C.D.U.S. Weerasinghe 19-8-36-0; B.R. Jurangpathy 4-0-24-0; R.S. Madugalle 1-0-10-0; A. Ranatunga 49-20-102-2.

India

Batting and Fielding	M	I	NO	HS	R	Avge	100	50	Ct/St
M. Amarnath	2	4	1	116*	216	72.00	1	1	–
S.M. Gavaskar	3	6	1	52	186	37.20	–	2	3
D.B. Vengsarkar	3	6	1	98*	177	35.40	–	2	3
K. Srikkanth	3	6	0	64	187	31.16	–	1	1
L.S. Rajput	2	4	0	61	105	26.25	–	1	1
R.J. Shastri	3	6	0	81	157	26.16	–	1	1
Kapil Dev	3	6	0	78	128	21.33	–	1	1
C. Sharma	3	5	2	38	57	19.00	–	–	–
M. Azharuddin	3	6	0	43	112	18.66	–	–	4
S. Viswanath	3	5	0	20	31	6.20	–	–	11
Maninder Singh	2	3	1	3	3	1.50	–	–	2

Also batted: R.M.H. Binny (1 match) 19 (1ct); G. Sharma (1 match); 10*, 1; L. Shivaramakrishnan (1 match) 18, 21 (1ct).

Bowling	O	M	R	W	Avge	Best	5wI	10wM
C. Sharma	109	12	383	14	27.35	5-118	1	–
Kapil Dev	129.4	30	372	11	33.81	3-74	–	–
Maninder Singh	86.3	27	212	6	35.33	4-31	–	–
R.J. Shastri	122.3	31	270	6	45.00	3-74	–	–

Also bowled: M. Amarnath 15-2-31-1; R.M.H. Binny 12-0-49-2; G. Sharma 15-6-35-0; L. Shivaramakrishnan 38-5-117-0.

Statistical Highlights of the Tests

1st Test, SCC Ground, Colombo. Ahangama took a wicket with his fourth ball in Test cricket. Madugalle (403 minutes) and Ranatunga (327 minutes) scored their first Test hundreds. Only a defiant innings of 408 minutes by Vengsarkar ensured India a draw. For the first time, Sri Lanka dismissed the opposition twice, thanks to De Mel and Rumesh Ratnayake returning career-best figures, the latter being then the Sri Lanka record. Amal Silva created another national record with his nine dismissals in the match.

2nd Test, P.S. Stadium, Colombo. A public holiday was decreed to celebrate Sri Lanka's first Test victory, in their 14th match. Weerasinghe, at 17 years 189 days, became the youngest Sri Lankan Test cricketer. Rumesh Ratnayake (9-125) returned the best match figures for his country, while Amal Silva was the first wicket-keeper to score a hundred and have 9 dismissals in the same match. This gave him a total of 17ct/1st for the two games. Sharma took 5 wickets for the first time. Gavaskar was out stumped for only the second time in his 188-innings Test career.

3rd Test, Kandy. Sri Lanka won a series for the first time. Set 377 to win, they were 34-3 when Mendis joined Dias. They put on a record 216 for the fourth wicket, both batsmen scoring hundreds and passing 1,000 Test runs. Amal Silva collected 4 more dismissals to give him 22, a record for a three-match series. Three more wickets for Ratnayake made him the first Sri Lankan bowler to take 20 wickets in a series. Amarnath recorded his 9th Test hundred, off only 207 balls. Kapil Dev passed Bishen Bedi (266 wickets) in his 71st Test when he had Silva caught behind.

One-Day Internationals

25 August at Singhalese Sports Club Ground, Colombo. INDIA won by 2 wickets. Toss: India. Sri Lanka 241-6 (45 overs) (R.L. Dias 80, A. Ranatunga 64). India 242-8 (44.3 overs) (D.B. Vengsarkar 89, R.J. Shastri 67). Award: R.L. Dias (80).

21 September at P. Savaranamuttu Stadium, Colombo. SRI LANKA won by 14 runs. Toss: India. Sri Lanka 171-5 (28 overs) (R S. Madugalle 50★). India 157-4 (28 overs) (D.B. Vengsarkar 50). Award: R.S. Madugalle (50★).

22 September at P.S. Stadium, Colombo. Toss: Sri Lanka. ABANDONED (rain). India 194-6 (40 overs) (D.B. Vengsarkar 55). Sri Lanka 32-4 (9.2 overs). Award: D.B. Vengsarkar (55).

Indian Tour of Sri Lanka

First-Class Matches: Played 5; Won 0, Lost 1, Drawn 4
All Matches: Played 8; Won 1, Lost 2, Drawn 4, Abandoned 1

First-Class Averages

Batting and Fielding	M	I	NO	HS	R	Avge	100	50	Ct/St
M. Amarnath	2	4	1	116*	216	72.00	1	1	–
D.B. Vengsarkar	4	7	1	133	310	51.66	1	2	4
S.M. Gavaskar	5	9	2	52	243	34.71	–	2	4
M. Azharuddin	5	9	1	66	265	33.12	–	2	5
Kapil Dev	4	7	0	78	186	26.57	–	2	2
K. Srikkanth	5	9	0	64	233	25.88	–	1	1
L.S. Rajput	4	7	0	61	174	24.85	–	1	3
R.J. Shastri	4	7	0	81	168	24.00	–	1	1
L. Shivaramakrishnan	3	4	0	21	61	15.25	–	–	4
C. Sharma	5	7	2	38	72	14.40	–	–	2
S. Viswanath	5	7	0	38	92	13.14	–	–	15/1
G. Sharma	3	4	2	12	25	12.50	–	–	1
Maninder Singh	3	4	2	3	3	1.50	–	–	3

Also batted: R.M.H. Binny (1 match) 19 (1ct); R.S. Ghai (2 matches) 1, 1.

Bowling	O	M	R	W	Avge	Best	5wI	10wM
C. Sharma	140	15	483	17	28.41	5-118	1	–
Kapil Dev	147.5	34	411	13	31.61	3-74	–	–
Maninder Singh	134.3	39	329	8	41.12	4-31	–	–
R.J. Shastri	153.3	45	317	7	45.28	3-74	–	–

Also bowled: M. Amarnath 15-2-31-1; M. Azharuddin 4-0-24-0; R.M.H. Binny 12-0-49-2; S.M. Gavaskar 6-2-19-0; R.S. Ghai 34-7-101-1; L.S. Rajput 5-1-19-0; G. Sharma 76-20-161-4; L. Shivaramakrishnan 89-15-238-4; K. Srikkanth 4-0-30-0; D.B. Vengsarkar 7-0-31-1.

Pakistan v Sri Lanka

Sri Lanka were soon brought back to earth after the heady excitement of their victory over India. Within four weeks, in mid-October, they began a three-Test series in Pakistan which was to end in a conclusive defeat 2–0.

Even in the drawn first Test when they made 479, Sri Lanka could take little comfort, for Pakistan passed their score with only two wickets down, Qasim Omar and the captain, Javed Miandad, making 200 apiece. This was on one of the flattest of all Faisalabad pitches, despite promises by the authorities of something livelier. Whether by intent or because of the early date in the season, the remaining two pitches at Sialkot and Karachi did give the bowler a chance. This factor and the return to the Pakistan side after two years' absence of Imran Khan turned the series decisively in their favour.

At Sialkot, Imran, Waseem Akram, and Mohsin Kamal moved the ball about on a lively pitch and soon had Sri Lanka out for 157. Only Wettimuny played with any certainty. Pakistan's reply was founded on a patient opening stand of 88 by the experienced Mudassar Nazar and Mohsin Khan. Subsequently the batsmen fared little better than had Sri Lanka's as Ravi Ratnayeke (eight wickets) and the rather sharper Ramesh Ratnayake (two wickets) bowled their way through the strong Pakistan batting, limiting the lead to 102.

Sri Lanka's second innings suffered an early setback when Imran trapped Wettimuny for nought, but Amal Silva and Madugalle made 98 for the second wicket and the deficit had almost vanished when, as often before, Mudassar, at his gentle medium pace, took two vital wickets and cleared the way. Imran finished off the innings, taking 5 for 40 in all, and Pakistan made the 99 runs needed, losing only two wickets.

This match stimulated interest in the series among a public too accustomed to predictable draws on slow true pitches, but the Sri Lankans came under severe criticism for their behaviour during the second innings, this provoked by admittedly unconvincing umpiring decisions.

Like its predecessor, the third Test lasted only 3½ days, following a similar course, though this time an unusually generous covering of grass was taken off the Karachi pitch and the leg-spinner Abdul Qadir took 5 for 44 in Sri Lanka's first innings of 162. Pakistan soon lost four wickets to the medium pace of De Mel, but the middle batting repaired the innings, Miandad, Rameez Raja, and Imran each passing 50. The lead was 133 and, despite a brilliant innings of 105 by the young Aravinda De Silva, batting at number three with a skill and confidence approached by no one else, Pakistan again needed under 100 to win. Mudassar and Mohsin rushed them to victory by 10 wickets in 17 overs.

Aravinda, who had also made 122 in the high-scoring first Test, was Sri Lanka's player of the series; Miandad, whose lowest score was 40, was Pakistan's. Pakistan won all four one-day matches.

Pakistan v Sri Lanka 1985-86 1st Test
Match Drawn
Played at Iqbal Stadium, Faisalabad, 16, 17, 18, 19, 20, 21 October
Toss: Sri Lanka. Umpires: Mahboob Shah and Khizer Hayat
Debuts: nil

Sri Lanka
S. Wettimuny	lbw b Qadir	52
S.A.R. Silva†	c Shoaib b Imran	17
R.S. Madugalle	b Mudassar	5
R.L. Dias	c Ashraf b Jalaluddin	48
L.R.D. Mendis*	lbw b Imran	15
A. Ranatunga	c Shoaib b Qadir	79
P.A. De Silva	c Ashraf b Imran	122
J.R. Ratnayeke	run out	34
A.L.F. De Mel	c Ashraf b Wasim Akram	17
R.J. Ratnayake	lbw b Qadir	56
R.G.C.E. Wijesuriya	not out	7
Extras	(B4, LB11, W2, NB10)	27
		479

Pakistan
Mudassar Nazar	lbw b Ratnayake	78
Shoaib Mohammad	c Silva b Ratnayake	33
Qasim Omar	b Ratnayeke	206
Javed Miandad*	not out	203
Zaheer Abbas	did not bat	
Salim Malik	"	
Imran Khan	"	
Ashraf Ali†	"	
Abdul Qadir	"	
Wasim Akram	"	
Jalaluddin	"	
Extras	(B6, LB17, W1, NB11)	35
	(3 wkts)	555

Pakistan	O	M	R	W
Imran Khan	49	15	112	3
Wasim Akram	42.3	12	98	1
Jalaluddin	39	12	89	1
Mudassar Nazar	13.3	3	29	1
Abdul Qadir	54.3	17	132	3
Shoaib	2	1	4	0

Sri Lanka	O	M	R	W
De Mel	27	3	106	0
Ratnayake	32	4	93	2
Ratnayeke	29.5	3	117	1
Wijesuriya	44	13	102	0
Ranatunga	18	1	74	0
Madugalle	7	1	18	0
De Silva	5	0	22	0

Fall of Wickets
Wkt	SL 1st	P 1st
1st	23	86
2nd	40	158
3rd	125	555
4th	129	–
5th	165	–
6th	286	–
7th	352	–
8th	391	–
9th	443	–
10th	479	–

Pakistan v Sri Lanka 1985-86 2nd Test
Pakistan won by 8 wickets
Played at Jinnah Park, Sialkot, 27, 28, 29, 31 October
Toss: Pakistan. Umpires: Javed Akhtar and Mian Aslam
Debuts: Pakistan – Salim Yousuf

Sri Lanka
S. Wettimuny	c Yousuf b Imran	45	lbw b Imran		0
S.A.R. Silva†	c Omar b Mudassar	12	c Wasim b Mudassar		35
R.S. Madugalle	c Yousuf b Kamal	0	c Miandad b Kamal		65
R.L. Dias	c Omar b Kamal	21	lbw b Mudassar		7
L.R.D. Mendis*	c Mudassar b Kamal	20	c Yousuf b Wasim Akram		3
A. Ranatunga	not out	25	c Malik b Imran		28
P.A. De Silva	hit wicket b Imran	2	c Yousuf b Wasim Akram		8
J.R. Ratnayeke	c Yousuf b Imran	0	not out		17
A.L.F. De Mel	lbw b Wasim Akram	1	b Imran		0
R.J. Ratnayake	b Imran	1	c sub (Ramiz Raja) b Imran		2
R.G.C.E. Wijesuriya	lbw b Wasim Akram	8	lbw b Imran		0
Extras	(B6, LB2, W3, NB11)	22	(B9, LB10, NB16)		35
		157			**200**

Pakistan
Mudassar Nazar	c Silva b Ratnayeke	78	not out		24
Mohsin Khan	lbw b Ratnayeke	50	run out		44
Qasim Omar	c Wijesuriya b Ratnayeke	1	c Ranatunga b De Mel		3
Javed Miandad*	lbw b Ratnayeke	40			
Zaheer Abbas	b Ratnayeke	4			
Salim Malik	lbw b Ratnayeke	22			
Imran Khan	c sub (A.P. Gurusinha) b Ratnayeke	6			
Salim Yousuf†	lbw b Ratnayeke	23	(4) not out		13
Abdul Qadir	c Silva b Ratnayeke	10			
Wasim Akram	c Silva b Ratnayeke	4			
Mohsin Kamal	not out	4			
Extras	(B5, LB3, W1, NB8)	17	(B4, LB4, NB8)		16
		259	(2 wkts)		**100**

Pakistan	O	M	R	W	O	M	R	W
Imran Khan	19	3	55	4	18.3	5	40	5
Wasim Akram	14.2	4	38	2	19	4	74	2
Mohsin Kamal	17	3	50	3	12	2	38	1
Mudassar Nazar	6	1	6	1	11.5	1	28	2
Abdul Qadir					1.1	0	1	0

Sri Lanka	O	M	R	W	O	M	R	W
De Mel	15	3	63	0	10	1	43	1
Ratnayake	18	2	77	2	6	0	24	0
Ratnayeke	23.2	5	83	8	7.4	1	25	0
Ranatunga	3	0	18	0				
Wijesuriya	4	1	10	0				

Fall of Wickets
Wkt	SL 1st	P 1st	SL 2nd	P 2nd
1st	41	88	0	76
2nd	41	93	98	82
3rd	81	181	111	–
4th	99	185	121	–
5th	101	209	147	–
6th	101	216	163	–
7th	110	216	188	–
8th	130	245	188	–
9th	131	252	200	–
10th	157	259	200	–

In Sri Lanka's first innings R.L. Dias (5) retired hurt at 49 and resumed at 170.

Pakistan v Sri Lanka 1985-86 3rd Test
Pakistan won by 10 wickets
Played at National Stadium, Karachi, 7, 8, 9, 11 November
Toss: Sri Lanka. Umpires: Khizer Hayat and Mahboob Shah
Debuts: Sri Lanka – A.P. Gurusinha

Sri Lanka

S. Wettimuny	b Wasim Akram	17	c Yousuf b Imran	10
J.R. Ratnayeke	b Qadir	36	c Yousuf b Imran	3
R.S. Madugalle	lbw b Wasim Akram	0	(8) b Tausif	5
R.L. Dias	c Yousuf b Imran	7	c Malik b Qadir	4
L.R.D. Mendis*	c Miandad b Qadir	15	(7) b Imran	2
A. Ranatunga	c Miandad b Tausif	12	(5) c Yousuf b Wasim Akram	25
P.A. De Silva	c & b Qadir	13	(3) c Yousuf b Tausif	105
A.P. Gurusinha†	lbw b Imran	17	(6) c Yousuf b Tausif	12
A.L.F. De Mel	st Yousuf b Qadir	3	lbw b Tausif	18
R.J. Ratnayake	not out	21	c Omar b Tausif	22
R.G.C.E. Wijesuriya	lbw b Qadir	2	not out	2
Extras	(B5, LB10, W1, NB3)	19	(B5, LB11, NB6)	22
		162		**230**

Pakistan

Mudassar Nazar	c Gurusinha b De Mel	16	not out	57
Mohsin Khan	c Gurusinha b De Mel	13	not out	36
Qasim Omar	c Ranatunga b De Mel	8		
Javed Miandad*	lbw b De Mel	63		
Ramiz Raja	c & b De Mel	52		
Salim Malik	b De Mel	4		
Imran Khan	c Ratnayake b Ratnayeke	63		
Salim Yousuf†	lbw b Ratnayeke	27		
Abdul Qadir	c Wettimuny b Wijesuriya	19		
Tausif Ahmed	b Ratnayeke	1		
Wasim Akram	not out	5		
Extras	(B13, LB8, W2, NB1)	24	(B1, LB3, NB1)	5
		295	(0 wkts)	**98**

Pakistan	O	M	R	W	O	M	R	W
Imran Khan	20	9	36	2	14.1	5	28	3
Wasim Akram	14	7	17	2	14	4	24	1
Tausif Ahmed	22	10	50	1	23.2	8	54	5
Abdul Qadir	20.5	5	44	5	25.5	4	102	1
Mudassar Nazar					3	0	6	0

Sri Lanka	O	M	R	W	O	M	R	W
De Mel	22	1	109	6	3	0	28	0
Ratnayake	15	2	48	2	4	0	33	0
Ratnayeke	15	4	48	1	6	1	24	0
Wijesuriya	22	5	68	1	3.4	1	9	0
Ranatunga	1	0	1	0				

Fall of Wickets

Wkt	SL 1st	P 1st	SL 2nd	P 2nd
1st	27	27	14	–
2nd	28	43	15	–
3rd	60	60	57	–
4th	89	68	104	–
5th	90	153	132	–
6th	106	228	139	–
7th	122	259	157	–
8th	125	288	191	–
9th	151	290	221	–
10th	162	295	230	–

Test Match Averages: Pakistan v Sri Lanka 1985-86

Pakistan

Batting and Fielding	M	I	NO	HS	R	Avge	100	50	Ct/St
Javed Miandad	3	3	1	203*	306	153.00	1	1	3
Mudassar Nazar	3	5	2	78	253	84.33	–	3	1
Qasim Omar	3	4	0	206	218	54.50	1	–	3
Mohsin Khan	2	4	1	50	143	47.66	–	1	–
Salim Yousuf	2	3	1	27	63	31.50	–	–	11/1

Also batted: Abdul Qadir (3 matches) 10, 19 (1ct); Imran Khan (3 matches) 6, 63; Mohsin Kamal (1 match) 4*; Ramiz Raja (1 match) 52; Salim Malik (3 matches) 22, 4 (2ct); Shoaib Mohammad (1 match) 33 (2ct); Tausif Ahmed (1 match) 1; Wasim Akram (3 matches) 4, 5* (1ct); Zaheer Abbas (2 matches) 4. Anil Dalpat (3ct) and Jalaluddin played in one match but did not bat.

Bowling	O	M	R	W	Avge	Best	5wI	10wM
Imran Khan	120.4	37	271	17	15.94	5-40	1	–
Tausif Ahmed	45.2	18	104	6	17.33	5-54	1	–
Abdul Qadir	102.2	26	279	9	31.00	5-44	1	–
Wasim Akram	103.5	31	251	8	31.27	2-17	–	–

Also bowled: Jalaluddin 39-12-89-1; Mohsin Kamal 29-5-88-4; Mudassar Nazar 34.2-5-69-4; Shoaib Mohammad 2-1-4-0.

Sri Lanka

Batting and Fielding	M	I	NO	HS	R	Avge	100	50	Ct/St
P.A. De Silva	3	5	0	122	250	50.00	2	–	–
A. Ranatunga	3	5	1	79	169	42.25	–	–	2
R.J. Ratnayake	3	5	1	56	102	25.50	–	1	1
S. Wettimuny	3	5	0	52	124	24.80	–	1	1
J.R. Ratnayeke	3	5	1	36	90	22.50	–	–	–
S.A.R. Silva	2	3	0	35	64	21.33	–	–	4
R.L. Dias	3	5	0	48	87	17.40	–	–	–
R.S. Madugalle	3	5	0	65	75	15.00	–	1	–
L.R.D. Mendis	3	5	0	20	55	11.00	–	–	–
A.L.F. De Mel	3	5	0	18	39	7.80	–	–	1
R.G.C.E. Wijesuriya	3	5	2	8	19	6.33	–	–	1

Also batted: A.P. Gurusinha (1 match) 17, 12 (2ct).

Bowling	O	M	R	W	Avge	Best	5wI	10wM
J.R. Ratnayeke	81.5	14	297	10	29.70	8-83	1	–
R.J. Ratnayake	75	8	275	6	45.83	2-48	–	–
A.L.F. De Mel	77	8	350	7	50.00	6-109	1	–

Also bowled: P.A. De Silva 5-0-22-0; R.G.C.E. Wijesuriya 73.4-20-189-1; R.S. Madugalle 7-1-18-0; A. Ranatunga 22-1-93-0.

Statistical Highlights of the Tests

1st Test, Faisalabad. Javed Miandad and the Pakistan selectors insisted on an old pitch being used, which resulted in 1,034 runs being scored for the loss of only 13 wickets. Even Imran Khan, returning after two years of injury, could get no life or lift. Aravinda De Silva, 93* at close of play on his 20th birthday, duly completed his maiden Test hundred the next morning – in great style with a 6 off Imran. In all, he batted for 510 minutes, hitting 3 sixes and 17 fours. Miandad (203 not out) made his third double hundred (14th Test hundred) and shared in a 3rd-wicket partnership of 397 with Qasim Omar (206), who fell 5 short of his personal best. It was the 8th highest stand for any Test wicket and the 2nd highest for the third.

2nd Test, Sialkot. This was the first Test at this venue, the 59th Test venue in history. Ravi Ratnayeke returned the best innings analysis (8-83) for his country. Zaheer Abbas, instrumental in having the Test played at Sialkot, announced his retirement from Test cricket. Javed Miandad said he wished to resign the captaincy with effect from the end of the series, and Imran Khan was appointed his successor.

3rd Test, Karachi. Zaheer Abbas withdrew from the match after all, leaving 78 Tests, 5,062 runs (avg 44.79) beside his name in the records. Abdul Qadir took 5 wickets for the 9th time but Pakistan did not find batting that much easier on a very difficult pitch. Javed Miandad broke his right thumb, so Imran took over the captaincy earlier than planned, before he, too, was injured, and replaced by Mudassar. In Sri Lanka's second innings, only the youthful Aravinda De Silva managed to survive, with 105 in 265 minutes. This time it was Tausif Ahmed who returned his best figures (5-54). Mudassar and Mohsin Khan saw their country safely home before lunch on the fourth day.

One-Day Internationals

14 October at Shahi Bagh Stadium, Peshawar. PAKISTAN won by 8 wickets. Toss: Pakistan. Sri Lanka 145 (39.2 overs). Pakistan 147-2 (32.5 overs) (Shoaib Mohammad 72*). Award: Mudassar Nazar (8-0-32-2 and 40).

23 October at Municipal Stadium, Gujiranwala. PAKISTAN won by 15 runs. Toss: Sri Lanka. Pakistan 224-5 (40 overs) (Salim Malik 72*, Zaheer Abbas 61). Sri Lanka 209-7 (40 overs) (P.A. De Silva 86). Award: P.A. De Silva (86).

25 October at Gadaffi Stadium, Lahore. PAKISTAN won by 5 wickets. Toss: Pakistan. Sri Lanka 228-7 (38 overs) (R.S. Madugalle 73). Pakistan 231-5 (36.3 overs) (Javed Miandad 91*, Ramiz Raja 56). Award: Javed Miandad (91*).

3 November at Niaz Stadium, Hyderabad. PAKISTAN won by 89 runs. Toss: Sri Lanka. Pakistan 216-7 (39 overs) (Javed Miandad 56, Ramiz Raja 45). Sri Lanka 127 (37.2 overs). Award: Javed Miandad (56).

Cornhill Insurance

Cornhill Insurance
Test our appeal

Cornhill Insurance Test Series

Cornhill Insurance Group
32 Cornhill, London EC3V 3LJ

You'll find our competitive range of insurances equally appealing for your car, house, life and business. Ask your broker about Cornhill Insurance today.

Australia v New Zealand

This three-match series belonged to Richard Hadlee, whose magnificent fast bowling enabled New Zealand to win their first Test in Australia, then to record their first series victory in seven attempts against Australia. At the age of 34, when bowlers of his ilk (there have not been many) usually are on a pension, Hadlee finished with the remarkable figures of 33 for 401 off 169.3 overs, conceding a fraction more than 12 runs a wicket and taking a wicket every five overs (or 31 balls).

New Zealand trounced Australia by an innings and 41 runs in Brisbane, lost by 4 wickets in Sydney and won by 6 wickets in Perth. New Zealand had won only two of their previous 15 tests against Australia – by 5 wickets in Christchurch in 1974 and in Auckland in 1982. This was only New Zealand's third series in Australia, having lost 0–2 in each of the three-Test series in 1973-74 and 1980-81.

Allan Border, the Australian captain, said his players seemed to have 'a mental block' about Hadlee, who enjoyed the better of the pitch and atmospheric conditions in Brisbane, then had to toil on unsatisfactory, slow, low pitches in Sydney and Perth. His 15-wicket haul in Brisbane was the eighth-best bowling performance in Test history, and his 9 for 52 in the first innings had been bettered by only two Englishmen – Jim Laker, who took 10 for 53 and 9 for 37 against Australia at Old Trafford in 1956, and George Lohmann, who took 9 for 28 against South Africa at Johannesburg in 1895-96.

At the end of the series, in which he won two Man of the Match awards and, of course, was adjudged the Player of the Series, Hadlee said his success in Australia had been partly due to a technique change suggested by New Zealand's assistant team manager Glenn Turner. 'For years I have had the umpire standing a foot behind the stumps,' he said. 'Early in this tour, Turner said he wanted me to bowl closer to the line of the stumps. After some experimenting with a rubbish bin at the nets, we worked out that the best place for the umpire was six feet back, and after that it became just a matter of line and length.'

The Australians maintained their newly won reputation for being gracious losers, according to Hadlee, who said: 'The camaraderie between the Australian and England teams (in 1985) was great, and the same spirit existed in this series. At some stage or other, every Australian player came up and said, 'well bowled', and Allan Border was exceptional in this regard, even when batting out in the middle. When I first came into Test cricket to play against the Australians (1973-74), it was 'kill, kill, kill, knock his effing head off', and that type of thing. It was all aggro, verbal abuse, the chipping away and calling you all sorts of names to upset your concentration. It was a technique, I suppose. A part of gamesmanship. It was probably an unfair tactic. That was the way I thought Australian cricket, Australian sport, was played. That was their hard approach. It probably rubbed off on one or two New Zealanders in the end and probably hardened us up a little bit.'

Australia v New Zealand 1985-86 1st Test

New Zealand won by an innings and 41 runs
Played at Woolloongabba, Brisbane, 8, 9, 10, 11, 12 November
Toss: New Zealand. Umpires: A.R. Crafter and R.A. French
Debuts: New Zealand – V.R. Brown

Australia

K.C. Wessels	lbw b Hadlee	70	(2) c Brown b Chatfield		3
A.M.J. Hilditch	c Chatfield b Hadlee	0	(1) c Chatfield b Hadlee		12
D.C. Boon	c Coney b Hadlee	31	c Smith b Chatfield		1
A.R. Border*	c Edgar b Hadlee	1	not out		152
G.M. Ritchie	c M. Crowe b Hadlee	8	c Coney b Sneddon		20
W.B. Phillips†	b Hadlee	34	b Hadlee		2
G.R.J. Matthews	b Hadlee	2	c Coney b Hadlee		115
G.F. Lawson	c Hadlee b Brown	8	(9) c Brown b Chatfield		7
C.J. McDermott	c Coney b Hadlee	9	(8) c & b Hadlee		5
D.R. Gilbert	not out	0	c Chatfield b Hadlee		10
R.G. Holland	c Brown b Hadlee	0	b Hadlee		0
Extras	(B9, LB5, NB2)	16	(LB3, NB3)		6
		179			**333**

New Zealand

B.A. Edgar	c Phillips b Gilbert	17
J.G. Wright	lbw b Matthews	46
J.F. Reid	c Border b Gilbert	108
M.D. Crowe	b Matthews	188
J.V. Coney*	c Phillips b Lawson	22
J.J. Crowe	c Holland b Matthews	35
V.R. Brown	not out	36
R.J. Hadlee	c Phillips b McDermott	54
I.D.S. Smith†	not out	2
E.J. Chatfield	did not bat	
M.C. Snedden	"	
Extras	(B2, LB11, NB32)	45
	(7 wkts dec)	**553**

New Zealand	O	M	R	W	O	M	R	W
Hadlee	23.4	4	52	9	28.5	9	71	6
Chatfield	18	6	29	0	32	9	75	3
Snedden	11	1	45	0	19	3	66	1
M. Crowe	5	0	14	0	9	2	19	0
Brown	12	5	17	1	25	5	96	0
Coney	7	5	8	0	3	1	3	0

Australia	O	M	R	W
Lawson	36.5	8	96	1
McDermott	31	3	119	1
Gilbert	39	9	102	2
Matthews	31	5	110	3
Holland	22	3	106	0
Border	0.1	0	0	0
Wessels	1	0	7	0

Fall of Wickets

Wkt	A 1st	NZ 1st	A 2nd
1st	1	36	14
2nd	70	85	16
3rd	72	309	16
4th	82	362	47
5th	148	427	67
6th	150	471	264
7th	159	549	272
8th	175	–	291
9th	179	–	333
10th	179	–	333

Australia v New Zealand 1985-86 2nd Test
Australia won by 4 wickets
Played at Sydney Cricket Ground, 22, 23, 24, 25, 26 November
Toss: Australia. Umpires: B.E. Martin and M.W. Johnson
Debuts: Australia – R.B. Kerr

New Zealand

J.G. Wright	c O'Donnell b Wright	38	c & b Matthews	43
B.A. Edgar	c Border b Holland	50	c & b Holland	52
J.F. Reid	c Kerr b Holland	7	b Matthews	19
M.D. Crowe	run out	8	b Holland	0
J.V. Coney*	c Border b Holland	8	b Holland	7
J.J. Crowe	b Holland	13	c & b Holland	6
V.R. Brown	lbw b Holland	0	b Bright	15
I.D.S. Smith†	c Hookes b Bright	28	c & b Bright	12
R.J. Hadlee	lbw b Holland	5	lbw b Gilbert	26
J.G. Bracewell	not out	83	not out	2
S.L. Boock	lbw b Gilbert	37	c Boon b Bright	3
Extras	(B6, LB8, NB2)	16	(B1, LB4, NB3)	8
		293		**193**

Australia

W.B. Phillips†	b Bracewell	31	c Bracewell b Boock	63
R.B. Kerr	lbw b Hadlee	7	c Wright b Bracewell	7
D.C. Boon	lbw b Hadlee	0	c Reid b Bracewell	81
A.R. Border*	b Bracewell	20	st Smith b Bracewell	11
B.M. Ritchie	c J. Crowe b Hadlee	89	c M. Crowe b Hadlee	13
D.W. Hookes	run out	0	not out	38
G.R.J. Matthews	c Smith b Hadlee	50	lbw b Hadlee	32
S.P. O'Donnell	not out	20	not out	2
R.J. Bright	lbw b Boock	1		
D.R. Gilbert	c Smith b Hadlee	0		
R.G. Holland	st Smith b Boock	0		
Extras	(B5, LB2, NB2)	9	(B3, LB9, NB1)	13
		227	(6 wkts)	**260**

Australia	O	M	R	W	O	M	R	W
Gilbert	20.3	6	41	1	9	2	22	1
O'Donnell	6	2	13	0	5	4	4	0
Bright	34	12	87	2	17.5	3	39	3
Matthews	17	3	32	0	30	11	55	2
Holland	47	19	106	6	41	16	68	4

New Zealand	O	M	R	W	O	M	R	W
Hadlee	24	2	65	5	27.1	10	58	2
M. Crowe	5	2	15	0	2	1	7	0
Bracewell	25	9	51	2	30	7	91	3
Boock	29.5	14	53	2	22	4	49	1
Brown	13	3	35	0	7	0	28	0
Coney	1	0	1	0	9	1	15	0

Fall of Wickets

Wkt	NZ 1st	A 1st	NZ 2nd	A 2nd
1st	79	19	100	27
2nd	92	22	106	132
3rd	109	48	107	144
4th	112	71	119	163
5th	128	71	131	192
6th	128	186	137	258
7th	161	224	162	–
8th	166	225	163	–
9th	169	226	190	–
10th	293	227	193	–

Australia v New Zealand 1985-86 3rd Test
New Zealand won by 6 wickets
Played at WACA Ground, Perth, 30 November, 1, 2, 3, 4 December
Toss: New Zealand. Umpires: R.C. Isherwood and P.J. McConnell
Debuts: nil

Australia

W.B. Phillips†	c Smith b Chatfield	37	c Smith b Chatfield	10
R.B. Kerr	c Smith b Chatfield	17	b Hadlee	0
D.C. Boon	c Bracewell b Hadlee	12	b Hadlee	50
A.R. Border*	c Smith b Hadlee	12	b Hadlee	83
G.M. Ritchie	lbw b Coney	6	c M. Crowe b Coney	44
D.W. Hookes	c Bracewell b Coney	14	b Bracewell	7
G.R.J. Matthews	b Hadlee	34	lbw b Hadlee	14
G.F. Lawson	c J. Crowe b Hadlee	11	c J. Crowe b Hadlee	21
C.J. McDermott	b Chatfield	36	lbw b Bracewell	11
D.R. Gilbert	not out	12	b Hadlee	3
R.G. Holland	c M. Crowe b Hadlee	4	not out	0
Extras	(LB6, NB2)	8	(B2, LB5, NB9)	16
		203		**259**

New Zealand

J.G. Wright	c Phillips b Lawson	20	(2) b Gilbert	35
B.A. Edgar	c Hookes b McDermott	74	(1) c Border b Matthews	16
J.F. Reid	b Gilbert	7	c Phillips b Gilbert	28
M.D. Crowe	lbw b McDermott	71	not out	42
J.V. Coney*	c Phillips b Lawson	19	b Gilbert	16
J.J. Crowe	lbw b Holland	17	not out	2
R.J. Hadlee	c Hookes b Holland	26		
I.D.S. Smith†	c Matthews b Lawson	12		
J.G. Bracewell	not out	28		
B.L. Cairns	c Ritchie b Holland	0		
E.J. Chatfield	c Phillips b Lawson	3		
Extras	(B1, LB7, NB14)	22	(B7, LB7, NB11)	25
		299	(4 wkts)	**164**

New Zealand	O	M	R	W	O	M	R	W
Hadlee	26.5	6	65	5	39	11	90	6
Cairns	14	1	50	0	26	6	59	0
Chatfield	16	6	33	3	30	9	47	1
Coney	21	11	43	2	8	5	9	1
Bracewell	6	3	6	0	28.5	8	47	2

Australia	O	M	R	W	O	M	R	W
Lawson	47	12	79	4	21	7	35	0
McDermott	33	9	66	2	13	1	27	0
Gilbert	31	9	75	1	23	5	48	3
Holland	40	12	63	3	8	1	27	0
Matthews	5	3	6	0	9	3	13	1
Hookes	1	0	2	0				

Fall of Wickets

Wkt	A 1st	NZ 1st	A 2nd	NZ 2nd
1st	38	43	3	47
2nd	63	55	28	77
3rd	78	184	109	121
4th	85	191	195	149
5th	85	215	207	–
6th	114	253	214	–
7th	131	256	234	–
8th	159	273	251	–
9th	190	276	255	–
10th	203	299	259	–

Test Match Averages: Australia v New Zealand 1985-86

Australia

Batting and Fielding	M	I	NO	HS	R	Avge	100	50	Ct/St
A.R. Border	3	6	1	152*	279	55.80	1	1	4
G.R.J. Matthews	3	6	0	115	247	41.16	1	1	2
G.M. Ritchie	3	6	0	89	180	30.00	–	1	1
W.B. Phillips	3	6	0	63	177	29.50	–	1	7
D.C. Boon	3	6	0	81	175	29.16	–	2	1
D.W. Hookes	2	4	1	38*	59	19.66	–	–	3
C.J. McDermott	2	4	0	36	61	15.25	–	–	–
G.F. Lawson	2	4	0	21	47	11.75	–	–	–
D.R. Gilbert	3	5	2	12*	25	8.33	–	–	–
R.B. Kerr	2	4	0	17	31	7.75	–	–	1
R.G. Holland	3	5	1	4	4	1.00	–	–	3

Also batted: R.J. Bright (1 match) 1 (1ct); A.M.J. Hilditch (1 match) 0, 12;
S.P. O'Donnell (1 match) 20*, 2* (1ct); K.C. Wessels (1 match) 70, 3.

Bowling	O	M	R	W	Avge	Best	5wI	10wM
R.J. Bright	51.5	15	126	5	25.20	3-39	–	–
R.G. Holland	158	51	370	13	28.46	6-106	1	1
D.R. Gilbert	122.3	31	288	8	36.00	3-48	–	–
G.R.J. Matthews	92	25	216	6	36.00	3-110	–	–
G.F. Lawson	104.5	27	210	5	42.00	4-79	–	–

Also bowled: A.R. Border 0.1-0-0-0; D.W. Hookes 1-0-2-0;
C.J. McDermott 77-13-212-3; S.P. O'Donnell 11-6-17-0; K.C. Wessels 1-0-7-0.

New Zealand

Batting and Fielding	M	I	NO	HS	R	Avge	100	50	Ct/St
M.D. Crowe	3	5	1	188	309	77.25	1	1	4
B.A. Edgar	3	5	0	74	209	41.80	–	3	1
J.G. Wright	3	5	0	46	182	36.40	–	–	1
J.F. Reid	3	5	0	108	169	33.80	1	–	1
R.J. Hadlee	3	4	0	54	111	27.75	–	1	2
V.R. Brown	2	3	1	36*	51	25.50	–	–	3
J.J. Crowe	3	5	1	35	73	18.25	–	–	3
I.D.S. Smith	3	4	1	28	54	18.00	–	–	7/3
J.V. Coney	3	5	0	22	72	14.40	–	–	4

Also batted: S.L. Boock (1 match) 37, 3; J.G. Bracewell (2 matches) 83*, 2*, 28* (3ct);
B.L. Cairns (1 match) 0; E.J. Chatfield (2 matches) 3. M.C. Snedden played in one match but did not bat.

Bowling	O	M	R	W	Avge	Best	5wI	10wM
R.J. Hadlee	169.3	42	401	33	12.15	9-52	5	2
E.J. Chatfield	96	30	184	7	26.82	3-33	–	–
J.G. Bracewell	89.5	27	195	7	27.85	3-91	–	–

Also bowled: S.L. Boock 51.5-18-102-3; V.R. Brown 57-13-176-1; B.L. Cairns
40-7-109-0; J.V. Coney 49-23-79-3; M.D. Crowe 21-5-55-0; M.C. Snedden 30-4-111-1.

Statistical Highlights of the Tests

1st Test, Brisbane. For the third successive time Australia lost a Test by an innings. Hadlee (9-52) took 5 wickets in a Test innings for the 20th time. It was the fourth best analysis in Test history, the best of his first-class career, and the best in any Test at Brisbane. His 2nd innings 6-71 gave him the best match figures (15-123) for any Brisbane Test, the 5th time he had taken 10 wickets in a Test. New Zealand's total of 553-7 dec was their best in any Test. Martin Crowe's 188 was the highest for New Zealand against Australia in any Test. With Reid (108), he put on 224, a record 3rd-wicket partnership for New Zealand against any country. Allan Border (152*) recorded his 15th Test hundred and became the fourth highest scorer for Australia (5,485), passing Ian Chappell (5,345) and Doug Walters (5,357). Greg Matthews (115) scored his first hundred and with Border put on 197, a record 6th-wicket stand for Australia against New Zealand. Coney took his 50th Test catch. Hilditch was dropped from the Test side, having got out to the hook in his fifth consecutive Test innings.

2nd Test, Sydney. Bracewell and Boock scored 124 off 208 balls, only the 11th last-wicket partnership of 100 in all Tests. Holland took 6-106 and 4-68, to give him 10 wickets in a Sydney Test for the second time, but his duck gave him a world record of five in a row! Hadlee again took 5 wickets in the innings (22nd time). Wright and Edgar put on 100 for the first wicket, the first three-figure opening stand for New Zealand since February 1974, the 58th Test played since then. There were four caught and bowled dismissals in the New Zealand second innings, equalling the record set at Lord's in 1890 in England's first innings. Ritchie passed 1,000 Test runs when he reached 13.

3rd Test, Perth. McDermott scored 36, his highest in Tests. Crowe, batting with a runner, passed 1,000 Test runs. Hadlee (5-65 and 6-90) took his series tally to 33, a New Zealand record in any series, beating Bruce Taylor's 27 against West Indies in 1971-72. It was the 24th time he had taken 5 wickets in an innings, the 6th 10 wickets in a match. He finished the series with 299 wickets, sixth in the world ranking. Border ended the series with 279 runs, Martin Crowe with 309, both records for matches between the two countries in Australia.

New Zealand Tour of Australia 1985-86

First-Class Matches: Played 6; Won 2, Lost 1, Drawn 3
All Matches: Played 18; Won 8, Lost 4, Drawn 5, No Result 1

First-Class Averages

Batting and Fielding	M	I	NO	HS	R	Avge	100	50	Ct/St
M.D. Crowe	4	7	2	242*	562	112.40	2	1	4
B.A. Edgar	6	10	–	122	389	38.90	1	3	3
J.J. Crowe	6	11	4	79*	252	36.00	–	1	8
J.V. Coney	6	11	2	89	303	33.66	–	1	10
J.G. Wright	6	11	–	46	331	30.09	–	–	4
J.F. Reid	5	9	–	108	241	26.77	1	–	4
R.J. Hadlee	5	6	–	54	151	25.16	–	1	3
V.R. Brown	5	8	3	36*	121	24.20	–	–	6
I.D.S. Smith	5	7	3	28	93	23.25	–	–	8/2

Also batted: (4 matches) S.L. Boock 0, 37, 3 (1ct); B.L. Cairns 25, 4, 0 (3ct); (3 matches) E.J. Chatfield 0, 3 (3 ct); M.C. Snedden 26; (2 matches) J.G. Bracewell 83*, 2*, 28* (3ct); (1 match) T.J. Franklin 13 (1ct); E.E. McSweeney 26* (1ct/1st).

Bowling	O	M	R	W	Avge	Best	5wI	10wM
R.J. Hadlee	241.3	65	537	37	14.51	9-52	5	2
J.G. Bracewell	89.5	27	195	7	27.85	3-91	–	–
E.J. Chatfield	139	44	252	8	31.50	3-33	–	–
S.L. Boock	202.5	49	560	17	32.94	4-83	–	–
V.R. Brown	189	29	624	14	44.57	4-75	–	–
M.C. Snedden	107	13	364	6	60.66	4-88	–	–
B.L. Cairns	145.5	32	389	6	64.83	2-46	–	–

Also bowled: J.V. Coney 66-26-132-3; M.D. Crowe 21-5-55-0.

Australia v India

India outplayed Australia in all three Tests of this disappointing series, yet it was drawn 0–0, leaving Indian captain Kapil Dev to reflect on his captaincy record of 20 Tests without a win. India were desperately unlucky not to have won at least the second Test, at Melbourne, where bad weather, which plagued the series, intervened when victory virtually was a formality.

India's dominance was best illustrated by their consistent batting deeds, which produced scores of 520 on a perfect Adelaide pitch, 445 and 59 for 2 on an unsatisfactory Melbourne pitch, and 600 for 4 declared on a Sydney pitch that did not afford the Australian spinners the ascendancy they had enjoyed in recent seasons. For all their misfortune and the Australians' inadequacies, the Indians were guilty of some unimaginative cricket at crucial times, and this contributed to their failure to win a series in Australia for the first time.

Kapil Dev's team still produced some memorable individual performances, prompted by the captain himself, who had an eight-wicket haul in Australia's first innings at Adelaide. Then Sunil Gavaskar's unbeaten 166 — his 31st Test century — lifted his Test aggregate to 9,006. He failed twice at Melbourne, but made amends with an 8½-hour 172 at Sydney, where Kris Srikkanth scored his maiden Test century off only 97 balls in 2½ hours after having been dropped at 2 — as had Gavaskar. Mohinder Amarnath's consistency also was rewarded with a Sydney century (138), the highest of his 10 Test hundreds.

India's bowling in the second and third Tests was dominated by left-arm orthodox spinner Ravi Shastri and off-spinner Shivlal Yadav, who shared 28 wickets at an exceptionally economical rate.

It was a difficult period for the selectors, who were trying to avoid Australia's fifth consecutive series loss without the services of the 16 players who had defected to South Africa, plus the retired Kepler Wessels and fast bowler Geoff Lawson, whose form had suffered because of groin and back injuries.

Three new players emerged — Western Australia's 6ft 8in left-arm opening bowler Bruce Reid, 22, West Australian batsman Geoff Marsh, 27, and New South Wales all-rounder Steve Waugh, 22. With 11 wickets, the thin Reid was easily Australia's most successful bowler against India and showed immense potential. Marsh made a convincing 92 in a double-century opening stand with David Boon at Sydney.

Relishing his new opening role, Boon made impressive centuries at both Adelaide and Sydney, Greg Ritchie and Greg Matthews scored hundreds at Adelaide and Melbourne, respectively, and Allan Border reserved his traditional batting heroics for his second innngs at Melbourne (163 in nearly seven hours) and his first innings at Sydney (71 in four hours).

There was considerable acrimony between the teams, and Kapil Dev was scathing in his criticism of the umpiring standards after the rain-inspired draw at Melbourne.

Australia v India 1985-86 1st Test
Match Drawn
Played at Adelaide Oval, 13, 14, 15, 16, 17 December
Toss: Australia. Umpires: A.R. Crafter and S.G. Randell
Debuts: Australia – M.G. Hughes, G.R. Marsh and B.A. Reid

Australia

W.B. Phillips†	c Yadav b Kapil Dev	11		
D.C. Boon	c Vengsarkar b Kapil Dev	123	(1) not out	11
G.R. Marsh	c Sharma b Binny	5	(2) not out	2
A.R. Border*	b Kapil Dev	49		
G.M. Ritchie	c Kirmani b Kapil Dev	128		
D.W. Hookes	b Yadav	34		
G.R.J. Matthews	lbw b Kapil Dev	18		
R.J. Bright	not out	5		
C.J. McDermott	lbw b Kapil Dev	0		
B.A. Reid	c Gavaskar b Kapil Dev	2		
M.G. Hughes	c Vengsarkar b Kapil Dev	0		
Extras	(LB4, NB2)	6	(LB3, NB1)	4
		381	(0 wkt)	**17**

India

S.M. Gavaskar	not out	166‡
K. Srikkanth	c Ritchie b McDermott	51
C. Sharma	c Phillips b Reid	54
D.B. Vengsarkar	c Phillips b Hughes	7
M. Azharuddin	c Phillips b Reid	17
M. Amarnath	c Marsh b McDermott	37
R.J. Shastri	b Reid	42
Kapil Dev*	lbw b Bright	38
R.M.H. Binny	c Phillips b McDermott	38
S.M.H. Kirmani†	c Boon b Reid	7
N.S. Yadav	c Hughes b Hookes	41
Extras	(B2, LB7, W1, NB12)	22
		520

India	O	M	R	W	O	M	R	W
Kapil Dev	38	6	108	8	3	1	3	0
Binny	24	7	56	1				
Sharma	19	3	70	0	2	0	9	0
Yadav	27	6	66	1	2	1	2	0
Shastri	38	11	70	0	1	1	0	0
Amarnath	3	0	9	0				

Australia	O	M	R	W	O	M	R	W
McDermott	48	14	131	3				
Hughes	38	6	123	1				
Reid	53	22	113	4				
Bright	44	15	80	1				
Matthews	17	2	60	0				
Hookes	2	0	4	1				

Fall of Wickets

Wkt	A 1st	I 1st	A 2nd
1st	19	95	–
2nd	33	131	–
3rd	124	171	–
4th	241	187	–
5th	318	247	–
6th	374	273	–
7th	375	333	–
8th	375	409	–
9th	381	426	–
10th	381	520	–

‡ Retired hurt 39 at 97-1 and resumed at 247-5.

Australia v India 1985-86 2nd Test
Match Drawn
Played at Melbourne Cricket Ground, 26, 27, 28, 29, 30 December
Toss: India. Umpires: R.A. French and R.C. Isherwood
Debuts: Australia – S.R. Waugh

Australia

W.B. Phillips†	b Yadav	7	(7) c Srikkanth b Yadav	13
D.C. Boon	lbw b Shastri	14	c & b Kapil Dev	19
G.R. Marsh	c Shivarama b Yadav	30	(1) c Shivarama b Shastri	19
A.R. Border*	c & b Shivarama	11	(3) st Kirmani b Yadav	163
D.W. Hookes	b Shastri	42	(4) c Srikkanth b Shastri	0
S.R. Waugh	c Kapil Dev b Shivarama	13	(5) b Shastri	5
G.R.J. Matthews	not out	100	(6) c Azharuddin b Shivarama	16
R.J. Bright	b Shastri	28	lbw b Kapil Dev	20
C.J. McDermott	c Kapil Dev b Shastri	1	c & b Shastri	2
B.A. Reid	c Srikkanth b Kapil Dev	1	c Shivarama b Yadav	13
D.R. Gilbert	c Kirmani b Yadav	4	not out	10
Extras	(B5, LB6)	11	(B11, LB16, NB1)	28
		262		**308**

India

S.M. Gavaskar	b Gilbert	6	b Reid	8
K. Srikkanth	lbw b Gilbert	86	c Bright b Reid	38
M. Amarnath	c Phillips b Reid	45	not out	3
D.B. Vengsarkar	c & b Matthews	75	not out	1
M. Azharuddin	b Matthews	37		
R.J. Shastri	c Phillips b Waugh	49		
Kapil Dev*	c Hookes b Reid	55		
R.M.H. Binny	c Matthews b Reid	0		
S.M.H. Kirmani†	c Phillips b Waugh	35		
L. Shivaramakrishnan	c Phillips b Reid	15		
N.S. Yadav	not out	6		
Extras	(B4, LB15, NB17)	36	(B4, LB1, NB4)	9
		445	(2 wkts)	**59**

India	O	M	R	W	O	M	R	W
Kapil Dev	23	6	38	1	22	7	53	2
Binny	3	0	11	0				
Shastri	37	13	87	4	47	13	92	4
Yadav	27.5	10	64	3	38.5	15	84	3
Shivarama	13	2	51	2	13	1	43	1
Amarnath					3	0	9	0

Australia	O	M	R	W	O	M	R	W
McDermott	15	5	52	0	6	1	17	0
Gilbert	22	1	81	2	4	0	9	0
Reid	38.2	11	100	4	8	2	23	2
Bright	31	8	76	0	7	4	5	0
Matthews	31	7	81	2				
Waugh	11	5	36	2				

Fall of Wickets

Wkt	A 1st	I 1st	A 2nd	I 2nd
1st	22	15	32	39
2nd	26	116	54	57
3rd	41	172	54	–
4th	90	246	84	–
5th	109	291	126	–
6th	127	370	161	–
7th	193	372	202	–
8th	195	420	205	–
9th	216	425	231	–
10th	262	445	308	–

Australia v India 1985-86 3rd Test
Match Drawn
Played at Sydney Cricket Ground, 2, 3, 4, 5, 6 January
Toss: India. Umpires: P.J. McConnell and S.G. Randell
Debuts: nil

India

S.M. Gavaskar	b Holland	172
K. Srikkanth	b Reid	116
M. Amarnath	c Bright b Gilbert	138
Kapil Dev*	b Gilbert	42
D.B. Vengsarkar	not out	37
M. Azharuddin	not out	59
R.J. Shastri	did not bat	
C. Sharma	"	
L. Shivaramakrishnan	"	
N.S. Yadav	"	
S.M.H. Kirmani†	"	
Extras	(B5, LB9, NB22)	36
	(4 wkts dec)	**600**

Australia

D.C. Boon	b Kapil Dev	131	(2) run out		25
G.R. Marsh	c Gavaskar b Shastri	92	(1) c Azharuddin b Yadav		28
A.R. Border*	c Sharma b Shastri	71	(7) c Shivarama b Yadav		4
G.M. Ritchie	c Kapil Dev b Yadav	14	(3) not out		17
W.B. Phillips†	c Srikkanth b Yadav	14	c Srikkanth b Shastri		22
G.R.J. Matthews	c Amarnath b Yadav	40	c Kapil Dev b Yadav		17
S.R. Waugh	c Shivarama b Yadav	8	(4) lbw b Shastri		0
R.J. Bright	c Kirmani b Shastri	3	not out		0
D.R. Gilbert	c Azharuddin b Yadav	1			
B.A. Reid	st Kirmani b Yadav	4			
R.G. Holland	not out	1			
Extras	(LB14, NB3)	17	(B3, LB2, NB1)		6
		396	(6 wkts)		**119**

Australia	O	M	R	W	O	M	R	W
Gilbert	37	3	135	2				
Reid	34	8	89	1				
Bright	41	7	121	0				
Holland	21	6	113	1				
Matthews	29	2	95	0				
Waugh	7	0	33	0				

India	O	M	R	W	O	M	R	W
Kapil Dev	25	8	65	1	7	3	11	0
Shastri	57	21	101	4	25	12	36	2
Yadav	62.3	20	99	5	33	22	19	3
Shivarama	22	2	79	0	9	0	37	0
Sharma	13	2	38	0	3	0	11	0

Fall of Wickets

Wkt	I 1st	A 1st	A 2nd
1st	191	217	57
2nd	415	258	57
3rd	485	277	60
4th	510	302	87
5th	–	369	111
6th	–	387	115
7th	–	388	–
8th	–	390	–
9th	–	395	–
10th	–	396	–

Test Match Averages: Australia v India 1985-86

Australia

Batting and Fielding	M	I	NO	HS	R	Avge	100	50	Ct/St
G.M. Ritchie	2	3	1	128	159	79.50	1	–	1
D.C. Boon	3	6	1	131	323	64.60	2	–	1
A.R. Border	3	5	0	163	298	59.60	1	1	–
G.R.J. Matthews	3	5	1	100*	191	47.75	1	–	2
G.R. Marsh	3	6	1	92	176	35.20	–	1	1
D.W. Hookes	2	3	0	42	76	25.33	–	–	1
R.J. Bright	3	5	2	28	56	18.66	–	–	2
W.B. Phillips	3	5	0	22	67	13.40	–	–	8
D.R. Gilbert	2	3	1	10*	15	7.50	–	–	–
S.R. Waugh	2	4	0	13	26	6.50	–	–	–
B.A. Reid	3	4	0	13	20	5.00	–	–	–
C.J. McDermott	2	3	0	2	3	1.00	–	–	–

Also batted: R.G. Holland (1 match) 1*; M.G. Hughes (1 match) 0 (1ct).

Bowling	O	M	R	W	Avge	Best	5wI	10wM
B.A. Reid	133.2	43	325	11	29.54	4-100	–	–

Also bowled: R.J. Bright 123-34-282-1; D.R. Gilbert 63-4-225-4; R.G. Holland 21-6-113-1; D.W. Hookes 2-0-4-1; M.G. Hughes 38-6-123-1; C.J. McDermott 69-20-200-3; G.R.J. Matthews 77-11-236-2; S.R. Waugh 18-5-69-2.

India

Batting and Fielding	M	I	NO	HS	R	Avge	100	50	Ct/St
S.M. Gavaskar	3	4	1	172	352	117.33	2	–	2
M. Amarnath	3	4	1	138	223	74.33	1	–	1
K. Srikkanth	3	4	0	116	291	72.75	1	2	5
D.B. Vengsarkar	3	4	2	75	120	60.00	–	1	2
M. Azharuddin	3	3	1	59*	113	56.50	–	1	3
R.J. Shastri	3	2	0	49	91	45.50	–	–	1
Kapil Dev	3	3	0	55	135	45.00	–	1	5
S.M.H. Kirmani	3	2	0	35	42	21.00	–	–	3/2
R.M.H. Binny	2	2	0	38	38	19.00	–	–	–

Also batted: Chetan Sharma (2 matches) 54 (2ct); L. Shivaramakrishnan (2 matches) 15 (6ct); N.S. Yadav (3 matches) 41, 6* (1ct).

Bowling	O	M	R	W	Avge	Best	5wI	10wM
N.S. Yadav	191.1	74	334	15	22.26	5-99	1	–
Kapil Dev	118	31	276	12	23.00	8-106	1	–
R.J. Shastri	205	71	386	14	27.57	4-87	–	–

Also bowled: M. Amarnath 6-0-18-0; R.M.H. Binny 27-7-67-1; C. Sharma 37-5-128-0; L. Shivaramakrishnan 57-5-210-3.

Statistical Highlights of the Tests

1st Test, Adelaide. Boon scored his first Test hundred in his 19th innings, and Ritchie his third, being his first in Australia. Kapil Dev took 8-106, the best analysis for India against Australia in Australia. In the process he took his 50th wicket against Australia. The last five wickets fell in 39 balls for 7 runs. India's total of 520 was their highest against Australia in either country. Gavaskar (166*) had an eventful match on the way to his 31st Test hundred. He retired hurt at his overnight score of 39* and was unable to bat on the third day. He resumed on the fourth day at the fall of the fifth wicket. At 7 he passed 1,000 runs against Australia, and at 160 became the first player to score 9,000 Test runs. It was his 192nd Test innings. Yadav (41) became Hookes' first Test wicket, but not until he and Gavaskar had added 94 for the 10th wicket, a record for India against Australia.

2nd Test, Melbourne. Matthews, who made 100 not out, was aided by Bright (28 off 76 balls) in a stand of 66 for the 7th wicket, a record for Australia against India, and last man Gilbert (4 in 19 balls), who came out when Matthews was still only 59. Kapil Dev (55) passed 3,000 Test runs, the 8th Indian batsman to do so. Shivarama was Phillips' 50th Test dismissal – all caught. In the second innings Border recorded his 16th Test hundred, giving him over 1,000 runs in Tests during 1985. Again Gilbert provided admirable support (10* off 65 balls), helping Border add a record 77 for the 10th wicket.

3rd Test, Sydney. India's 600-4 dec was their second highest in all Tests, and their best outside India. For only the fourth time in Test history the first three batsmen scored hundreds. Gavaskar's 172 was his highest against Australia, ending only three short of the best-ever by India against Australia. Amarnath's 138 was his 10th Test hundred and his best score. He ended the series with 3,680 runs from 54 Tests, the fourth in the ranks of Indian batsmen. Together with Gavaskar he added a record 224 for the 2nd wicket. Srikkanth's 116, his first Test hundred, came off just 117 balls, and he needed a runner after scoring only 10; 22 runs came from one Holland over (4, 0, 6, 4, 4, 4). The 1st wicket partnership of 191 was one short of the record against Australia and was the 21st hundred partnership involving Gavaskar. Boon (131) and Marsh (92) registered 217, the 7th 200 opening stand for Australia, the 1st since 1966 and the first 100 opening partnership for 36 tests. Yadav, with 5-99 and 3-19, recorded his best for both innings and match in his 26th Test. Border (71) passed 1,000 runs against India. Kapil Dev ended the series with 281 wickets, eighth in world ranking.

A disappointing feature of the summer was the large number of no-balls bowled, particularly by Australia. There were 139 in the 6 Tests, 73 against New Zealand and 66 in the India series. The outstanding culprit was Gilbert with 58.

OVERSEAS CRICKET 1985-86/AUSTRALIA v INDIA 65

Indian Tour of Australia 1985-86

First-Class Matches: Played 6; Won 1, Lost 0, Drawn 4, No Play Possible 1
All Matches: Played 21; Won 8, Lost 7, Drawn 4, No Play Possible 2

First-Class Averages

Batting and Fielding	M	I	NO	HS	R	Avge	100	50	Ct/St
S.M. Gavaskar	4	5	1	172	360	90.00	2	–	3
C. Sharma	3	3	1	67	148	74.00	–	2	6
M. Amarnath	5	7	2	138	297	59.40	1	–	1
M. Azharuddin	5	6	1	77	245	49.00	–	2	5
K. Srikkanth	5	7	0	116	342	48.85	1	2	5
Kapil Dev	4	5	0	88	223	44.60	–	2	6
D.B. Vengsarkar	5	7	2	75	187	37.40	–	1	2
N.S. Yadav	5	4	2	41	67	33.50	–	–	1
R.J. Shastri	4	3	0	49	92	30.66	–	–	1
R.M.H. Binny	3	3	0	44	82	27.33	–	–	–
S.M.H. Kirmani	4	4	0	35	69	17.25	–	–	8/2

Also batted: R.S. Ghai (1 match) 0★ (1ct); A. Malhotra (1 match) 67, 12 (1ct); K.S. Moore (1 match) 35★ (1ct/1st); L. Shivaramakrishnan (4 matches) 4, 15 (8ct).
R.R. Kulkarni played in one match but did not bat.

Bowling	O	M	R	W	Avge	Best	5wI	10wM
Kapil Dev	153	42	356	18	19.77	8-106	1	–
N.S. Yadav	245.1	85	478	19	25.15	5-99	1	–
R.J. Shastri	258	85	495	14	35.35	4-87	–	–
L. Shivaramakrishnan	120.4	12	427	11	38.81	3-75	–	–
C. Sharma	72	9	257	5	51.40	4-55	–	–

Also bowled: M. Amarnath 16-4-37-0; R.M.H. Binny 39-14-91-2; R.S. Ghai 13-3-40-1; R.R. Kulkarni 11-1-27-0.

New Zealand v Australia

In just one and a half sessions on the fourth day of the final Test of a long, trying summer, all Australia's good work of the previous two matches was destroyed at Eden Park. Australia's pitiful collapse to the controlled, demanding off-spin of John Bracewell allowed New Zealand to win the Test, and, for the second time in five months, a series over their closest international cricket rivals.

Batting a second time, with a first innings advantage of 56, Australia capitulated in spectacular manner on a pitch which necessitated concentration and sound technique, to be dismissed for just 103. New Zealand got the 160 for victory, admirably displaying those two qualities with fighting half-centuries from John Wright and Ken Rutherford.

Bracewell's 6 for 32, off 22 overs, represented his best return of a chequered test career, while David Boon batted through the innings, the first Australian to do so since Ian Redpath on the same ground 12 years earlier.

New Zealand have now beaten every Test nation at home in the last seven years, but for Australia the tragedy was that until that fourth-day disaster they had shown that they were starting to find their feet again after managing just two wins in the previous 14 Tests.

They had performed reasonably well in a rain-affected first Test at Wellington. Boon and Geoff Marsh had provided a solid, composed start and, after Richard Hadlee had removed Allan Border to claim his 300th Test wicket, Greg Ritchie and Greg Matthews stabilized a difficult situation with a record-breaking fifth-wicket stand of 213.

Three significant contributions rescued New Zealand from trouble, after they were at one stage five down and 98 runs shy of the follow-on mark. Ken Rutherford exorcized West Indian fast bowlers from his mind with an innings of real quality; Jeremy Coney completed a fine century — his third in Tests — one ball before the game ended prematurely on the fourth morning; and Hadlee carved a thunderous 72, setting a seventh-wicket record against Australia in tandem with his captain.

Border, with centuries in each innings, and a mature 74 by Stephen Waugh ensured safety at Christchurch, where rain again intervened. Coney continued his impressive form before he fell, two runs short of a second consecutive century, foolishly hooking.

But the real highlight was a marvellous 137 by Martin Crowe, punctuated as it was by a trip to hospital to have stitches inserted in his chin, courtesy of a Bruce Reid bouncer. With a bevy of splendid strokes, Crowe showed his true, glorious potential.

The outstanding bowling performance of the match, not surprisingly, came from Hadlee, his 25th haul of five or more wickets in Tests.

Australia managed to salvage something from the tour by winning the last two of the four 'pyjama' games to level that series, inspired perhaps by Border's threat to resign the captaincy after the first one-day international loss at Dunedin. But it was small compensation for that disastrous day a fortnight earlier at Eden Park.

New Zealand v Australia 1985-86 1st Test
Match Drawn
Played at Basin Reserve, Wellington, 21, 22, 23, 24, 25 (np) February
Toss: New Zealand. Umpires: F.R. Goodall and S.J. Woodward
Debuts: New Zealand – S.R. Gillespie; Australia – S.P. Davis, T.J. Zoehrer

Australia

D.C. Boon	c Smith b Troup	70
G.R. Marsh	c Coney b Chatfield	43
W.B. Phillips	b Gillespie	32
A.R. Border*	lbw b Hadlee	13
G.M. Ritchie	b Troup	92
G.R.J. Matthews	c Rutherford b Coney	130
S.R. Waugh	c Smith b Coney	11
T.J. Zoehrer†	c sub (J.G.Bracewell) b Coney	18
C.J. McDermott	b Hadlee	2
B.A. Reid	not out	0
S.P. Davis	c & b Hadlee	0
Extras	(B2, LB9, W4, NB9)	24
		435

New Zealand

T.J. Franklin	c Border b McDermott	0
B.A. Edgar	c Waugh b Matthews	38
J.F. Reid	c Phillips b Reid	32
S.R. Gillespie	c Border b Reid	28
M.D. Crowe	b Matthews	19
K.R. Rutherford	c sub (R.J. Bright) b Reid	65
J.V. Coney*	not out	101
R.J. Hadlee	not out	72
I.D.S. Smith	did not bat	
G.B. Troup	"	
E.J. Chatfield	"	
Extras	(B2, LB6, W1, NB15)	24
	(6 wkts)	**379**

New Zealand

	O	M	R	W
Hadlee	37.1	5	116	3
Chatfield	36	10	96	1
Troup	28	6	86	2
Gillespie	27	2	79	1
Coney	18	7	47	3

Australia

	O	M	R	W
McDermott	25.3	5	80	1
Davis	25	4	70	0
Reid	31	6	104	3
Matthews	37	10	107	2
Border	4	3	1	0
Waugh	4	1	9	0

Fall of Wickets

	A	NZ
Wkt	1st	1st
1st	104	0
2nd	143	57
3rd	166	94
4th	166	115
5th	379	138
6th	414	247
7th	418	–
8th	435	–
9th	435	–
10th	435	–

New Zealand v Australia 1985-86 2nd Test
Match Drawn
Played at Lancaster Park, Christchurch, 28 February, 1, 2, 3, 4 March
Toss: New Zealand. Umpires: B.L. Aldridge and F.R. Goodall
Debuts: nil

Australia

G.R. Marsh	b Hadlee	28	(2) lbw b Bracewell		15
D.C. Boon	c Coney b Hadlee	26	(1) c Coney b Troup		6
W.B. Phillips	c Smith b Chatfield	1	b Hadlee		25
A.R. Border*	b Chatfield	140	not out		114
G.M. Ritchie	lbw b Hadlee	4	c Smith b Bracewell		11
G.R.J. Matthews	c Smith b Hadlee	6	c sub (J. Crowe) b Hadlee		3
S.R. Waugh	lbw b Hadlee	74	c Smith b Bracewell		1
T.J. Zoehrer†	c Coney b Hadlee	30	c Rutherford b Bracewell		13
R.J. Bright	c Smith b Bracewell	21	not out		21
D.R. Gilbert	b Hadlee	15			
B.A. Reid	not out	1			
Extras	(B1, LB9, NB8)	18	(LB6, W1, NB3)		10
		364	(7 wkts dec)		**219**

New Zealand

J.G. Wright	c Zoehrer b Gilbert	10	(2) not out		4
B.A. Edgar	lbw b Reid	8	(1) c & b Matthews		9
J.F. Reid	c Zoehrer b Waugh	2	not out		0
M.D. Crowe	c Waugh b Reid	137			
K.R. Rutherford	lbw b Gilbert	0			
J.V. Coney*	c Reid b Waugh	98			
R.J. Hadlee	c Zoehrer b Reid	0			
I.D.S. Smith	b Waugh	22			
J.G. Bracewell	c Marsh b Reid	20			
G.B. Troup	lbw b Waugh	10			
E.J. Chatfield	not out	2			
Extras	(B6, LB8, NB16)	30	(NB3)		3
		339	(1 wkt)		**16**

New Zealand	O	M	R	W	O	M	R	W
Hadlee	44.4	8	116	7	25	4	47	2
Troup	34	4	104	0	15	0	50	1
Chatfield	36	13	56	2	17	6	29	0
Bracewell	27	9	46	1	33	12	77	4
Coney	9	0	28	0	3	1	10	0
Crowe	2	1	4	0				
Reid					1	1	0	0

Australia	O	M	R	W	O	M	R	W
Gilbert	26	4	106	2	7	4	9	0
Reid	34.3	8	90	4	4	0	7	0
Waugh	23	6	56	4				
Bright	18	6	51	0				
Matthews	6	1	22	0	3	3	0	1

Fall of Wickets

Wkt	A 1st	NZ 1st	A 2nd	NZ 2nd
1st	57	17	15	13
2nd	58	29	32	–
3rd	58	29	76	–
4th	64	48	120	–
5th	74	124	129	–
6th	251	190	130	–
7th	319	263	167	–
8th	334	311	–	–
9th	358	331	–	–
10th	364	338	–	–

New Zealand v Australia 1985-86 3rd Test
New Zealand won by 8 wickets
Played at Eden Park, Auckland, 13, 14, 15, 16, 17 March
Toss: Australia. Umpires: R.L. McHarg and S.J. Woodward
Debuts: New Zealand – G.K. Robertson

Australia

D.C. Boon	c Coney b Hadlee	16	(2) not out		58
G.R. Marsh	c Coney b Hadlee	118	(1) lbw b Hadlee		0
W.B. Phillips	c Smith b Bracewell	62	c Bracewell b Chatfield		15
A.R. Border*	c Smith b Chatfield	17	(5) b Bracewell		6
T.J. Zoehrer†	c Coney b Robertson	9	(4) lbw b Chatfield		1
G.M. Ritchie	c Smith b Chatfield	56	lbw b Chatfield		1
G.R.J. Matthews	b Bracewell	5	st Smith b Bracewell		4
S.R. Waugh	c Reid b Bracewell	1	b Bracewell		0
R.J. Bright	c Smith b Hadlee	5	b Bracewell		0
C.J. McDermott	lbw b Bracewell	9	b Bracewell		6
B.A. Reid	not out	0	c Hadlee b Bracewell		8
Extras	(B2, LB11, NB3)	16	(LB4)		4
		314			**103**

New Zealand

J.G. Wright	c Zoehrer b McDermott	56	c Boon b Matthews		59
B.A. Edgar	lbw b Matthews	24	b Reid		1
K.R. Rutherford	b Matthews	0	not out		50
M.D. Crowe	lbw b Matthews	0	not out		23
J.F. Reid	c Phillips b Bright	16			
J.V. Coney*	c Border b McDermott	93			
R.J. Hadlee	b Reid	33			
I.D.S. Smith†	b Waugh	3			
J.G. Bracewell	c Boon b Bright	4			
G.K. Robertson	st Zoehrer b Matthews	12			
E.J. Chatfield	not out	1			
Extras	(B7, LB8, NB1)	16	(B18, LB4, NB5)		27
		258	(2 wkts)		**160**

New Zealand

	O	M	R	W	O	M	R	W
Hadlee	31	12	60	3	20	6	48	1
Robertson	24	6	91	1				
Chatfield	29	10	54	2	18	9	19	3
Crowe	3	2	4	0				
Bracewell	43.3	19	74	4	22	8	32	6
Coney	5	0	18	0				

Australia

	O	M	R	W	O	M	R	W
McDermott	17	2	47	2	14	3	29	0
Reid	19	2	63	1	12.4	2	30	1
Matthews	34	15	61	4	31	18	46	1
Bright	22	4	58	2	22	11	29	0
Waugh	5	1	4	1	4	1	4	0

Fall of Wickets

Wkt	A 1st	NZ 1st	A 2nd	NZ 2nd
1st	25	73	0	6
2nd	193	73	28	106
3rd	225	73	35	–
4th	225	103	59	–
5th	278	107	62	–
6th	293	170	71	–
7th	294	184	71	–
8th	301	203	71	–
9th	309	250	85	–
10th	314	258	103	–

Test Match Averages: New Zealand v Australia 1985-86

New Zealand

Batting and Fielding	M	I	NO	HS	R	Avge	100	50	Ct/St
J.V. Coney	3	3	1	101*	292	146.00	1	2	7
M.D. Crowe	3	4	1	137	179	59.66	1	–	–
R.J. Hadlee	3	3	1	72*	105	52.50	–	1	2
J.G. Wright	2	4	1	59	129	43.00	–	2	–
K.R. Rutherford	3	4	1	65	115	38.33	–	2	2
J.F. Reid	3	4	1	32	50	16.66	–	–	1
B.A. Edgar	3	5	0	38	80	16.00	–	–	–

Also batted: J.G. Bracewell (2 matches) 20, 4 (1ct); E.J. Chatfield (3 matches) 2*, 1*; T.J. Franklin (1 match) 0; S.R. Gillespie (1 match) 28; G.K. Robertson (1 match) 12; I.D.S. Smith (3 matches) 22, 3 (11ct/1st); G.B. Troup (2 matches) 10.

Bowling	O	M	R	W	Avge	Best	5wI	10wM
J.G. Bracewell	125.3	48	229	15	15.26	6-32	1	1
R.J. Hadlee	157.5	35	387	16	24.18	7-116	1	–
E.J. Chatfield	136	48	254	8	31.75	3-19	–	–

Also bowled: J.V. Coney 35-8-103-3; M.D. Crowe 5-3-8-0; S.R. Gillespie 27-7-79-1; J.F. Reid 1-1-0-0; G.K. Robertson 24-6-91-1; G.B. Troup 77-10-240-3.

Australia

Batting and Fielding	M	I	NO	HS	R	Avge	100	50	Ct/St
A.R. Border	3	5	1	140	290	72.50	2	–	3
D.C. Boon	3	5	1	70	176	44.00	–	2	2
G.R. Marsh	3	5	0	118	204	40.80	1	–	1
G.M. Ritchie	3	5	0	92	164	32.80	–	2	–
G.R.J. Matthews	3	5	0	130	148	29.60	1	–	1
W.B. Phillips	3	5	0	62	135	27.00	–	1	2
S.R. Waugh	3	5	0	74	87	17.40	–	1	2
R.J. Bright	2	4	1	21*	47	15.66	–	–	–
T.M. Zoehrer	3	5	0	30	71	14.20	–	–	4/1
B.A. Reid	3	4	3	8	9	9.00	–	–	1
C.J. McDermott	2	3	0	9	17	5.66	–	–	–

Also batted: S.P. Davis (1 match) 0; D.R. Gilbert (1 match) 15.

Bowling	O	M	R	W	Avge	Best	5wI	10wM
S.R. Waugh	36	9	83	5	16.60	4-56	–	–
G.R.J. Matthews	111	47	236	8	29.50	4-61	–	–
B.A. Reid	101.1	18	294	9	32.66	4-90	–	–

Also bowled: A.R. Border 4-3-1-0; R.J. Bright 62-22-138-2; S.P. Davis 25-4-70-0; D.R. Gilbert 33-8-115-2; C.J. McDermott 56.3-10-156-3.

Statistical Highlights of the Tests

1st Test, Wellington. Hadlee took his 300th Test wicket when he dismissed Allan Border, becoming the 6th bowler to achieve the feat. Matthews (130) made his 3rd Test hundred, and highest score, in 306 minutes, and with Ritchie put on 213 for a new 5th-wicket record against New Zealand. Coney, in his first match as captain in New Zealand, reached his 3rd hundred, in 191 balls. He shared in two record partnerships against Australia, for the 6th wicket (109) with Rutherford and the 7th (132 unbroken) with Hadlee. Cousins Bruce Reid (Australia) and John Reid (New Zealand) played in the match.

2nd Test, Christchurch. Border became only the 2nd Australian batsman to score hundreds in both innings twice passing 6,000 runs in his 1st innings, the 4th Australian to do so and 14th in the world. In the 2nd, he passed Harvey (6,149) leaving only Greg Chappell and Don Bradman ahead of him. Hadlee became the most capped New Zealand player (62 Tests), and passed Trueman (307) and Gibbs (309) to end with 311 wickets. He took 5 wickets for the 25th time, to equal Botham's record. The dismissal of Phillips in the 2nd innings gave him his 100th wicket against Australia.

3rd Test, Auckland. New Zealand secured their 5th victory over Australia in 21 Tests to retain the Trans-Tasman Trophy won in Perth in December. It was the first time Australia had been beaten twice by the same side in the same season. Marsh brought up his maiden hundred off 224 balls and put on 168 with Phillips for a new 2nd-wicket record against New Zealand. Zoehrer was the first batsman to be 'night-watchman' in both innings of a Test. Australia lost 5 second-innings wickets for 12 runs before lunch on the fourth day, helping Bracewell to 5- and 10-wicket hauls and his 50th wicket in Tests. Only Boon managed to resist, becoming the 10th Australian to carry his bat, the first since Redpath in 1973-74, also at Auckland. 103 is the lowest score for Australia against New Zealand. In the second innings Rutherford was given out caught behind, but recalled to the crease by Border when Zoehrer indicated that he had taken the ball off a half-volley.

One-Day Internationals (Rothmans Cup)

10 March at Carisbrook, Dunedin. NEW ZEALAND won by 30 runs. Toss: Australia. New Zealand 186-6 (50 overs). Australia 156 (47 overs) (R.J. Hadlee 9-5-15-4). Awards: N.D. Crowe (47, 10-4-23-2, and 2ct) and R.J. Hadlee (21* and 9-5-15-4).

22 March at Lancaster Park, Christchurch. NEW ZEALAND won by 53 runs. Toss: Australia. New Zealand 258-7 (49† overs) (B.A. Edgar 74, J.V. Coney 64, K.R. Rutherford 64). Australia 205 (45.4 overs). Award: J.V. Coney (64).

26 March at Basin Reserve, Wellington. AUSTRALIA won by 3 wickets. Toss: New Zealand. New Zealand 229-9 (50 overs) (K.R. Rutherford 79). Australia 232-7 (49.3 overs) (S.R. Waugh 71, G.R. Marsh 53, W.B. Phillips 53). Awards: W.B. Phillips (53 and 1ct/1st) and S.R. Waugh (71 and 7-0-31-1).

31 March at Eden Park, Auckland. AUSTRALIA won by 44 runs. Toss: Australia. Australia 231 (44.5 oveers) (G.R.J. Matthews 54, G.M. Ritchie 53). New Zealand 187-9 (45 overs). Award: G.R.J. Matthews (54, 9-1-33-3, and 3ct).

† Australia were fined $500 for not bowling 50 overs.

Australian Tour of New Zealand 1985-86

First-Class Matches: Played 5; Won 1, Lost 1, Drawn 3
All Matches: Played 11; Won 5, Lost 3, Drawn 3

First-Class Averages

Batting and Fielding	M	I	NO	HS	R	Avge	100	50	Ct/St
A.R. Border	4	6	1	140	367	73.40	2	1	3
D.C. Boon	4	7	1	109	302	50.33	1	2	2
G.R. Marsh	5	8	1	118	349	49.85	2	–	3
G.M. Ritchie	5	8	1	92	292	41.71	–	3	1
G.R.J. Matthews	5	8	1	130	223	31.85	1	1	5
W.B. Phillips	5	9	0	62	251	27.88	–	1	2
B.A. Reid	5	6	4	28*	54	27.00	–	–	1
T.J. Zoehrer	5	8	0	71	172	21.50	–	1	7/2
S.R. Waugh	5	8	0	74	124	15.50	–	1	4
R.J. Bright	4	7	1	21*	82	13.66	–	–	1
C.J. McDermott	3	5	0	19	40	8.00	–	–	1
S.P. Davis	3	3	2	2*	3	3.00	–	–	1

Also batted: D.R. Gilbert (2 matches) 0, 15.

Bowling	O	M	R	W	Avge	Best	5wI	10wM
S.R. Waugh	53	12	151	7	21.57	4-56	–	–
B.A. Reid	132.4	24	372	13	28.61	4-25	–	–
G.R.J. Matthews	153	52	388	12	32.33	4-61	–	–
R.J. Bright	115.2	32	305	9	33.88	5-42	1	–
C.J. McDermott	79.3	15	240	6	40.00	3-61	–	–

Also bowled: A.R. Border 4-3-1-0; S.P. Davis 71-13-214-3; D.R. Gilbert 51-11-184-3; W.B. Phillips 2-0-6-0.

Sri Lanka v Pakistan

Controversies marred Pakistan's three-Test tour of Sri Lanka, which saw the home team record its second Test victory and draw the series one-all.

Trouble began from the outset of the series. The first Test, in Kandy, which Pakistan won quite convincingly by an innings on the fourth day, saw the walk-out staged by Arjuna Ranatunga. 'Sledging' is now part of the game, but Ranatunga could not put up with it (it disturbed his concentration, he said) when Pakistani fielders showed their dissent after a bat and pad catch offered by him was disallowed by the umpire.

The second Test, at the Colombo Cricket Club grounds, will go down in history for providing the first instance of a batsman going after the spectators instead of what he is supposed to do — going after the bowlers. Javed Miandad tarnished his good name as a world-class batsman, when he charged at the spectators with bat raised after being dismissed in the second innings. Miandad's excuse for such an action was that a stone was thrown at him (it did not hit him) and that spectators used abusive language. Whatever the cause, Miandad's boorish action was condemned by all and sundry.

Prior to this incident there was the case of the ball going out of shape and the Pakistan captain, accompanied by their manager 'armed' with a copy of *Wisden Cricketers' Almanack*, coming onto the field to tell the umpires about the condition of the replacement ball. These actions were quite unnecessary, and in the view of many were an attempt to prolong inevitable defeat inside three days.

Pakistan also wanted to call off the tour in protest at spectator abuse and poor umpiring — problems which are not unknown in their own country, as Sri Lanka captain Duleep Mendis was quick to point out. Imran Khan, the captain, blamed bad umpiring for spoiling the relationship between the two teams and with the spectators.

The final Test, at the P. Saravanamuttu Stadium, was played in a calm atmosphere and saw Pakistan miss a glorious opportunity of winning the series, being let down by some atrocious fielding.

Ranatunga, missed four times before reaching 30 and six times in all, made a career best 135, and Asanka Gurusinghe, missed twice after 70, hit a maiden century in his third Test. They put together the highest partnership for Sri Lanka in Test cricket — 240 for the fourth wicket — and were the most successful batsmen for the home side in the series.

Sri Lanka's search for a successor to leg-spinner D.S. De Silva was still left unsolved. The majority of the wickets in the series was shared again by the fast-medium bowlers, who accounted for 36 of the 40 wickets.

Pakistan's best bat was Ramiz Raja, who scored the only century for them in the series. Imran took the most number of wickets in the series, 15, the first of which carried him past the 250 mark. Both countries benefited a lot by infusing young blood.

Sri Lanka v Pakistan 1985-86 1st Test
Pakistan won by an innings and 20 runs
Played at Asgiriya Stadium, Kandy, 23, 24, 25, 27 February
Toss: Sri Lanka. Umpires: A.C. Felsinger and S. Ponnadurai
Debuts: Sri Lanka – K.P.J. Warnaweera; Pakistan – Zulqarnain

Sri Lanka

S. Wettimuny	lbw b Imran	0	c Ramiz b Wasim Akram	8
S.A.R. Silva†	c Zulqarnain b Wasim	3	absent hurt	–
P.A. De Silva	c Zulqarnain b Imran	11	b Tausif	5
R.L. Dias	b Tausif	11	b Tausif	26
L.R.D. Mendis*	c Mudassar b Imran	6	c Mudassar b Tausif	4
A. Ranatunga	b Tausif	18	st Zulqarnain b Tausif	33
J.R. Ratnayeke	b Qadir	4	(2) b Imran	7
A.L.F. De Mel	b Tausif	23	(7) b Tausif	0
R.J. Ratnayake	c Malik b Qadir	4	(8) st Zulqarnain b Tausif	4
E.A.R. De Silva	not out	10	(9) not out	4
K.P.J. Warnaweera	c Imran b Qadir	3	(10) b Imran	0
Extras	(LB7, W2, NB7)	16	(LB3, W6, NB1)	10
		109		**101**

Pakistan

Mudassar Nazar	c Mendis b Ratnayake	81
Mohsin Khan	lbw b De Mel	1
Qasim Omar	lbw b Ratnayake	11
Javed Miandad	lbw b E.A.R. De Silva	4
Ramiz Raja	lbw b Warnaweera	3
Salim Malik	c P.A. De Silva b De Mel	54
Imran Khan*	c sub (R.S. Mahanama) b Ranatunga	7
Abdul Qadir	b Ratnayake	11
Zulqarnain†	b De Mel	5
Tausif Ahmed	not out	23
Wasim Akram	run out	19
Extras	(B4, W7)	11
		230

Pakistan	O	M	R	W	O	M	R	W
Imran Khan	9	0	20	3	16	5	29	2
Wasim Akram	8	3	21	1	5	3	5	1
Tausif Ahmed	13	4	32	3	15	7	45	6
Abdul Qadir	12.4	3	29	3	7	1	19	0

Sri Lanka	O	M	R	W	O	M	R	W
De Mel	17.2	5	50	3				
Ratnayeke	10	1	26	0				
Ratnayake	23	2	57	3				
Warnaweera	7.3	2	26	1				
E.A.R. De Silva	17	7	37	1				
Ranatunga	15.3	6	30	1				

Fall of Wickets

Wkt	SL 1st	P 1st	SL 2nd
1st	0	1	14
2nd	14	28	19
3rd	25	49	31
4th	37	52	43
5th	44	154	74
6th	59	167	74
7th	69	173	80
8th	78	181	100
9th	100	191	101
10th	109	230	–

Sri Lanka v Pakistan 1985-86 2nd Test
Sri Lanka won by 8 wickets
Played at Colombo Cricket Club, Colombo, 14, 15, 16, 18 March
Toss: Sri Lanka. Umpires: K.T. Francis and D.C.C. Perera
Debuts: Sri Lanka – S.D. Anurasiri, A.K. Kuruppuarachchi, R.S. Mahanama

Pakistan

Mudassar Nazar	c de Alwis b Kuruppuarachchi	3	lbw b Kuruppuarachchi	1
Mohsin Khan	lbw b Kuruppuarachchi	35	c de Alwis b De Mel	2
Qasim Omar	lbw b De Mel	3	c de Alwis b Ratnayeke	52
Javed Miandad	c de Alwis b De Mel	0	(5) lbw b Ratnayeke	36
Ramiz Raja	lbw b De Mel	32	(4) c de Alwis b Ratnayeke	21
Salim Malik	c Mahanama b Kuruppuarachchi	42	c Wettimuny b Ratnayeke	30
Imran Khan*	c Mendis b Ratnayeke	8	c de Silva b De Mel	0
Tausif Ahmed	b Ratnayeke	0	(9) lbw b Ratnayeke	1
Wasim Akram	c De Mel b Kuruppuarachchi	0	(8) c Ranatunga b De Mel	0
Zulqarnain†	c De Silva b Kuruppuarachchi	1	lbw b Kuruppuarachchi	5
Mohsin Kamal	not out	1	not out	13
Extras	(LB4, W2, NB1)	7	(B1, LB6, NB4)	11
		132		**172**

Sri Lanka

S. Wettimuny	c Zulqarnain b Mudassar	37	c Malik b Imran	7
R.S. Mahanama	run out	10	c Zulqarnain b Imran	8
A.P. Gurusinha	c Imran b Wasim Akram	23	not out	9
P.A. De Silva	c sub (Shoaib Mohammad) b Kamal	37	not out	1
A. Ranatunga	c Omar b Wasim Akram	77		
L.R.D. Mendis*	c Mohsin Khan b Imran	5		
J.R. Ratnayeke	c Imran b Wasim Akram	38		
R.G. de Alwis†	c Miandad b Kamal	10		
A.L.F. De Mel	c Zulqarnain b Imran	11		
S.D. Anurasiri	c Ramiz b Wasim Akram	4		
A.K. Kuruppuarachchi	not out	0		
Extras	(B7, LB3, W4, NB7)	21	(B2, LB2, W1, NB2)	7
		273	(2 wkts)	**32**

Sri Lanka	O	M	R	W	O	M	R	W
De Mel	16	6	39	3	16	1	79	3
Kuruppuarachchi	14.5	2	44	5	10.3	1	41	2
Ratnayeke	17.4	8	29	2	17	3	37	5
Ranatunga	1	0	12	0				
Anurasiri	2	1	4	0	2	0	8	0

Pakistan	O	M	R	W	O	M	R	W
Imran Khan	27	5	78	2	7	2	18	2
Wasim Akram	27.3	9	55	4	6	1	10	0
Mohsin Kamal	15	0	52	2				
Mudassar Nazar	14	2	36	1				
Tausif Ahmed	11	2	40	0				
Salim Malik	1	0	2	0				

Fall of Wickets

Wkt	P 1st	SL 1st	P 2nd	SL 2nd
1st	3	40	6	19
2nd	12	69	6	31
3rd	12	82	72	–
4th	72	130	93	–
5th	78	147	131	–
6th	124	227	136	–
7th	124	248	136	–
8th	130	265	145	–
9th	131	272	154	–
10th	132	273	172	–

Sri Lanka v Pakistan 1985-86 3rd Test
Match Drawn
Played at Saravanamuttu Stadium, Colombo, 22, 23, 24, 26, 27 March
Toss: Sri Lanka. Umpires: D.P. Buuultjens and H.C. Felsinger
Debuts: Sri Lanka – K.N. Amalean; Pakistan – Zakir Khan

Sri Lanka

S. Wettimuny	c Ramiz b Wasim Akram	0	c Ramiz b Wasim Akram	14
R.S. Mahanama	c Zulqarnain b Qadir	41	b Imran	4
A.P. Gurusinha	c Zulqarnain b Imran	39	not out	116
A. Ranatunga	c Imran b Zakir	53	(5) not out	135
P.A. De Silva	c Mohsin b Zakir	16	(4) c Miandad b Imran	25
L.R.D. Mendis*	c Zulqarnain b Imran	58		
J.R. Ratnayeke	c Miandad b Zakir	7		
R.G. de Alwis†	b Imran	18		
A.L.F. De Mel	not out	14		
S.D. Anurasiri	b Imran	8		
K.N. Amalean	lbw b Qadir	2		
Extras	(B7, LB9, W6, NB3)	25	(B19, LB7, W1, NB2)	29
		281	(3 wkts)	**323**

Pakistan

Mudassar Nazar	c de Alwis b De Mel	8
Mohsin Khan	lbw b Amalean	12
Qasim Omar	c de Alwis b Ratnayeke	19
Javed Miandad	lbw b Amalean	23
Ramiz Raja	lbw b Ratnayeke	122
Salim Malik	c sub (S.M.S. Kaluperuma) b Ratnayeke	29
Imran Khan*	c de Alwis b Ranatunga	33
Abdul Qadir	b Amalean	20
Zulqarnain†	c de Alwis b Ratnayeke	13
Wasim Akram	run out	11
Zakir Khan	not out	0
Extras	(B10, LB7, W1, NB10)	28
		318

Pakistan	O	M	R	W	O	M	R	W
Imran Khan	32	11	69	4	25	4	56	2
Wasim Akram	22	8	41	1	29	11	72	1
Zakir Khan	24	6	80	3	21	4	70	0
Mudassar Nazar	7	2	19	0	10	2	29	0
Abdul Qadir	23.5	3	56	2	22	5	70	0
Salim Malik					1	1	0	0

Sri Lanka	O	M	R	W	O	M	R	W
De Mel	27	3	90	1				
Amalean	18.2	1	59	3				
Ratnayeke	30	4	116	4				
Anurasiri	15	11	9	0				
Ranatunga	11	5	26	1				

Fall of Wickets

Wkt	SL 1st	P 1st	SL 2nd
1st	12	24	18
2nd	79	32	18
3rd	109	49	83
4th	149	87	–
5th	202	158	–
6th	218	234	–
7th	251	278	–
8th	260	305	–
9th	272	318	–
10th	281	318	–

Test Match Averages: Sri Lanka v Pakistan 1985-86

Sri Lanka

Batting and Fielding	M	I	NO	HS	R	Avge	100	50	Ct/St
A.P. Gurusinha	2	4	2	116*	187	93.50	1	–	–
A. Ranatunga	3	5	1	135*	316	79.00	1	2	1
P.A. De Silva	3	6	1	37	95	19.00	–	–	4
L.R.D. Mendis	3	4	0	58	73	18.25	–	1	2
A.L.F. De Mel	3	4	1	23	48	16.00	–	–	1
R.S. Mahanama	2	4	0	41	63	15.75	–	–	1
J.R. Ratnayeke	3	4	0	38	56	14.00	–	–	–
S. Wettimuny	3	6	0	37	66	11.00	–	–	1

Also batted: K. Amalean (1 match) 2; S.D. Anurasiri (2 matches) 4, 8; R.G. de Alwis (2 matches) 10, 18 (9ct); E.A.R. De Silva (1 match) 10*, 4* (1ct); R.L. Dias (1 match) 11, 26; A.K. Kuruppuarachchi (1 match) 0*; R.J. Ratnayake (1 match) 4, 4; S.A.R. Silva (1 match) 3; K.P.J. Warnaweera (1 match) 3, 0.

Bowling	O	M	R	W	Avge	Best	5wI	10wM
A.K. Kuruppuarachchi	25.2	3	85	7	12.14	5-44	1	–
J.R. Ratnayeke	74.4	14	208	11	18.90	5-37	1	–
A.L.F. De Mel	76.2	15	259	10	25.90	3-39	–	–

Also bowled: K. Amalean 18.2-1-59-3; S.D. Anurasiri 19-12-21-0; E.A.R. De Silva 17-7-37-1; K.P.J. Warnaweera 7.3-2-26-1; A. Ranatunga 27.3-11-68-2; R.J. Ratnayake 23-2-57-3.

Pakistan

Batting and Fielding	M	I	NO	HS	R	Avge	100	50	Ct/St
Ramiz Raja	3	4	0	122	178	44.50	1	–	4
Salim Malik	3	4	0	54	155	38.75	–	1	2
Mudassar Nazar	3	4	0	81	93	23.25	–	1	2
Qasim Omar	3	4	0	52	85	21.25	–	1	1
Javed Miandad	3	4	0	36	63	15.75	–	–	3
Mohsin Khan	3	4	0	35	50	12.50	–	–	2
Imran Khan	3	4	0	33	48	12.00	–	–	4
Tausif Ahmed	2	3	1	23*	24	12.00	–	–	–
Wasim Akram	3	4	0	19	30	7.50	–	–	–
Zulqarnain	3	4	0	13	24	6.00	–	–	8/2

Also batted: Abdul Qadir (2 matches) 11, 20; Mohsin Kamal (1 match) 1*, 13*; Zakir Khan (1 match) 0*.

Bowling	O	M	R	W	Avge	Best	5wI	10wM
Tausif Ahmed	39	13	117	9	13.00	6-45	1	–
Imran Khan	116	27	270	15	18.00	4-69	–	–
Wasim Akram	97.3	35	204	8	25.50	4-55	–	–
Abdul Qadir	65.3	12	174	5	34.80	3-29	–	–

Also bowled: Mohsin Kamal 15-0-52-2; Mudassar Nazar 31-6-84-1; Salim Malik 2-1-2-0; Zakir Khan 45-10-150-3.

Statistical Highlights of the Tests

1st Test, Kandy. Imran Khan dismissed Wettimuny for his 250th Test wicket (55th Test). De Mel became the first Sri Lankan bowler to take 50 Test wickets (10th Test). Tausif improved on his figures at Karachi, returning his best for both innings and match. On the last afternoon, Pakistan disapproved of some of the umpiring decisions, and the batsmen left the field for 30 minutes. Madugalle missed the match, having played in all Sri Lanka's previous 18 Tests.

2nd Test, Colombo CC Ground. Pakistan were dismissed for 132, their lowest total against Sri Lanka, the main architect being debutant Kuruppuarachchi, with 5 wickets. Ranatunga became the fourth Sri Lankan batsman to pass 1,000 Test runs when he reached 74. Mudassar took his 50th Test wicket in his 57th match. Sri Lanka's second Test win came on the fourth day.

3rd Test, P.S. Stadium, Colombo. Ramiz Raja scored his maiden Test hundred off 242 balls, with 17 fours. Gurusinha and Ranatunga batted throughout the fifth day in an unbroken stand of 240, the highest for any Sri Lanka wicket. Gurusinha (116) took 437 minutes and Ranatunga (135) hit 4 sixes and 14 fours, becoming the highest run-scorer for his country. Pakistan dropped no fewer than five catches offered by him before he reached 30!

One-Day Internationals

2 March at Asgiriya Stadium, Kandy. PAKISTAN won by 8 wickets. Toss: Pakistan. Sri Lanka 124-6 (23 overs). Pakistan 125-2 (21.3 overs) (Mohsin Khan 59). Award: Mohsin Khan (59).

8 March at Tyronne Fernando Stadium, Moratuwa. MATCH ABANDONED. Toss: Sri Lanka. Pakistan 125-8 (38 overs).

9 March at Ketterama Stadium, Colombo. MATCH ABANDONED without a ball bowled.

11 March at Singhalese Sports Club, Colombo. PAKISTAN won by 8 wickets. Toss: Pakistan. Sri Lanka 160-8 (38 overs) (A. Ranatunga 74*; Wasim Akram 9-1-28-4). Pakistan (target 101 in 24 overs) 103-2 (23 overs). Award: A. Ranatunga (74*).

Pakistan Tour of Sri Lanka 1985-86

First-Class Matches: Played 5; Won 1, Lost 1, Drawn 3
All Matches: Played 9; Won 3, Lost 1, Drawn 3, No Result 1, No Play 1

First-Class Averages

Batting and Fielding	M	I	NO	HS	R	Avge	100	50	Ct/St
Ramiz Raja	5	7	2	122	323	64.60	1	2	4
Salim Malik	5	6	0	106	278	46.33	1	1	3
Mohsin Khan	4	6	1	101*	163	32.60	1	–	4
Qasim Omar	5	7	0	62	165	23.57	–	2	1
Javed Miandad	4	6	0	43	119	19.83	–	–	3
Mudassar Nazar	4	6	0	81	114	19.00	–	1	2
Tausif Ahmed	3	4	2	23*	38	19.00	–	–	–
Imran Khan	4	5	0	38	86	17.20	–	–	6
Wasim Akram	5	5	0	19	34	6.80	–	–	1
Zulqarnain	5	5	1	13	24	6.00	–	–	9/2

Also batted: Mohsin Kamal (3 matches) 1*, 13* (1ct); Zakir Khan (3 matches) 0*, 3, 0*; Abdul Qadir (2 matches) 11, 20; Rizwan-uz-Zaman (1 match) 18; Salim Yousuf (1 match) 1 (1ct); Shoaib Mohammad (1 match) 8.

Bowling	O	M	R	W	Avge	Best	5wI	10wM
Tausif Ahmed	62	20	151	10	15.10	6-45	1	–
Imran Khan	135	34	301	17	17.70	4-69	–	–
Wasim Akram	143.3	56	291	12	24.25	4-55	–	–
Abdul Qadir	65.3	12	174	5	34.80	3-29	–	–
Zakir Khan	94	24	275	7	39.28	3-80	–	–

Also bowled: Mohsin Kamal 51-4-215-3; Mudassar Nazar 43-8-135-1; Qasim Omar 1-0-5-0; Rizwan-uz-Zaman 7-2-5-0; Salim Malik 3-1-3-0; Zulqarnain 1-0-3-0.

Benson & Hedges World Series Cup

After losing 1–2 to New Zealand and scrambling three draws against India, the last thing the Test-weary Australians seemingly wanted to do was climb on the hectic World Series Cup merry-go-round. Allan Border, their captain, mirrored the feelings of many players when, on the last night of the series against India, he said of the one-day competition: 'It's a different game. It probably shouldn't be called cricket.'

Five weeks later, Border led the Australians on a victory lap of honour of the Melbourne Cricket ground, watched by a cheering crowd of nearly 75,000. The Australians suddenly were $97,500 richer — and none of them complained too much about the rigors of the 'pyjama game'.

Australia won the World Series Cup for the third time by beating India in the first two of the scheduled three finals. They won by 11 runs at Sydney in a day-night match shortened from 50 to 44 overs each because of rain, and they enjoyed a comfortable 7-wicket margin at Melbourne.

It was heady stuff after all the gloom and doom of the twin Test series, and prompted Border to say: 'This side shows more fight than in the past. This team has the character to fight its way out of trouble.' Indian captain Kapil Dev said: 'Australia is getting combined again.'

The extent of Australia's enforced rebuilding programme was evident in the composition of half their side, which contained virtually unknown international names of a few months earlier — Geoff Marsh, Dean Jones, Steve Waugh, Tim Zoehrer, Bruce Reid, and Simon Davis.

Marsh, Reid, and Davis figured prominently among the leading batsmen and bowlers of the 17-game competition. The 10 opening partnerships of new combination Boon and Marsh realized 34, 18, 9, 152, 50, 0, 98, 146, 69, and 31, and played a big part in Australia's leading the table after each of the three teams had completed their 10 preliminary matches.

The late inclusion of Jones and Dirk Wellham lifted the Australians' fielding, which already was well served by Border, Waugh, and Greg Matthews. Waugh also prospered with the bat, and pace bowlers Reid and Davis showed admirable control. Zoehrer put in two polished performances with the gloves after Wayne Phillips had been ruled out of the finals because of a damaged finger. The injury signalled the beginning of the end of Phillips's generally unhappy term as Australia's wicket-keeper.

Marsh made the only hundred of the competition (125 against India in the eighth match). Reid took a hat-trick against New Zealand in the 13th match. Australia's 70 against New Zealand in the 12th match equalled their lowest limited-overs score (against England in 1977). And both Hadlee and Kapil Dev completed the 100 wickets – 1,000 runs double in one-day internationals.

The statistics whirred by, the crowds flocked in, the TV ratings climbed... and the Australians were finally winners for a change. It mightn't be cricket, but it's here to stay.

OVERSEAS CRICKET 1985-86/BENSON & HEDGES WORLD SERIES

Qualifying Rounds

9 January at Melbourne Cricket Ground (floodlit). AUSTRALIA v NEW ZEALAND. Toss: Australia. New Zealand 161-7 (29 overs) (M.D. Crowe 71). Rain curtailed play.

11 January at Woolloongabba, Brisbane. INDIA beat NEW ZEALAND by 5 wickets. Toss: India. New Zealand 259-9 (50 overs) (M.D. Crowe 76, B.A. Edgar 75). India 263-5 (48 overs) (M. Amarnath 61, Kapil Dev 54*, K. Srikkanth 50). Award: Kapil Dev (54*, 10-0-28-1).

12 January at Woolloongabba, Brisbane. AUSTRALIA beat INDIA by 4 wickets. Toss: Australia. India 161 (43 overs). Australia 164-6 (45.2 overs). Award: G.R.J. Matthews (46* and 2 catches).

14 January at Sydney Cricket Ground (floodlit). AUSTRALIA beat NEW ZEALAND by 4 wickets. Toss: Australia. New Zealand 152 (49.2 overs) (J.V. Coney 58; D.R. Gilbert 10-0-46-5). Australia 153-6 (45.1 overs) (G.M. Ritchie 68). Award: D.R. Gilbert.

16 January at Melbourne Cricket Ground (floodlit). INDIA beat AUSTRALIA by 8 wickets. Toss: India. Australia 161 (44.2 overs) (S.R. Waugh 73*). India 162-2 (40.2 overs) (S.M. Gavaskar 59, M. Amarnath 58*). Award: S.R. Waugh (73*).

18 January at WACA Ground, Perth. NEW ZEALAND beat INDIA by 3 wickets. Toss: New Zealand. India 113 (44.2 overs). New Zealand 115-7 (40.1 overs) (S.M. Gavaskar 3 catches). Award: M.D. Crowe (33, 4-0-20-1 and 2 catches).

19 January at WACA Ground, Perth. AUSTRALIA beat NEW ZEALAND by 4 wickets. Toss: Australia. New Zealand 159-6 (50 overs) (J.J. Crowe 63). Australia 161-6 (45.1 overs) (A.R. Border 58, M.D. Crowe 3 catches). Award: A.R. Border (58 and 1 catch).

21 January at Sydney Cricket Ground (floodlit). AUSTRALIA beat INDIA by 100 runs. Toss: India. Australia 292-6 (50 overs) (G.R. Marsh 125, D.C. Boon 83, A.R. Border 52). India 192-4 (50 overs) (S.M. Gavaskar 92*). Award: G.R. Marsh (125).

23 January at Melbourne Cricket Ground (floodlit). NEW ZEALAND beat INDIA by 5 wickets. Toss: New Zealand. India 238-8 (50 overs) M. Amarnath 74, Kapil Dev 47, D.B. Vengsarkar 43, E.J. Chatfield 10-2-28-4). New Zealand 239-5 (49.5 overs) (M.D. Crowe 67). Award: M.D. Crowe 67 and 5-0-13-0).

25 January at Adelaide Oval. INDIA beat NEW ZEALAND by 5 wickets. Toss: India. New Zealand 172 (49.2 overs) (R.J. Hadlee 71). India 174-5 (46 overs) (M. Azharuddin 69*, S.R. Gillespie 10-3-30-4). Award: M. Azharuddin (69*).

26 January at Adelaide Oval. AUSTRALIA beat INDIA by 36 runs. Toss: India. Australia 262-8 (50 overs) (S.R. Waugh 81). India 226 (45.3 overs) (S.M. Gavaskar 77, R.J. Shastri 55; B.A. Reid 10-0-53-5). Award: B.A. Reid.

27 January at Adelaide Oval. NEW ZEALAND beat AUSTRALIA by 206 runs. Toss: New Zealand. New Zealand 276-7 (50 overs) (B.A. Edgar 61, J.G. Wright 61, A.R. Border 3 catches). Australia 70 (26.3 overs). Award: R.J. Hadlee (24 and 5-1-14-3).

29 January at Sydney Cricket Ground (floodlit). AUSTRALIA beat NEW ZEALAND by 99 runs. Toss: Australia. Australia 239-7 (50 overs) (D.C. Boon 64, D.M. Jones 53). New Zealand 140 (42.4 overs) B.A. Reid hat-trick. Award: D.C. Boon (64).

31 January at Melbourne Cricket Ground (floodlit). INDIA beat AUSTRALIA by 6 wickets. Toss: Australia. Australia 235 (50 overs) (D.C. Boon 76, G.R. Marsh 74, Kapil Dev 9-0-30-4). India 238-4 (48.5 overs) (D.B. Vengsarkar 77*, S.M. Gavaskar 72). Award: D.B. Vengsarkar (77*).

2 February at Launceston. INDIA beat NEW ZEALAND by 22 runs. Toss: New Zealand. India 202-9 (48 overs). New Zealand 168-9 (45 overs) (New Zealand target 190 in 45 overs due to mid-innings rain). Award: Chetan Sharma (38* and 9-1-35-1).

Qualifying Table	P	W	NR	L	Points
AUSTRALIA	10	6	1	3	13
INDIA	10	5	–	5	10
New Zealand	10	3	1	6	7

Final Round Results

5 February at Sydney Cricket Ground (floodlit). AUSTRALIA beat INDIA by 11 runs. Toss: India. Australia 170-8 (44 overs) (D.C. Boon 50). India 159 (43.4 overs).

9 February at Melbourne Cricket Ground. AUSTRALIA beat INDIA by 7 wickets. Toss: Australia. India 187 (50 overs) (M. Amarnath **handled ball** 15). Australia 188-3 (47.2 overs) (A.R. Border 65*).

Player of the Finals award: G.R.J. Matthews.

Leading Averages (Qual: 8 innings or 10 wkts)

Batting and Fielding	M	I	NO	HS	R	Avge	100	50	Ct
S.M. Gavaskar	10	10	1	92*	385	42.77	–	4	5
D.B. Vengsarkar	8	8	1	77*	283	40.42	–	1	4
D.C. Boon	12	11	0	83	418	38.00	–	4	2
S.R. Waugh	12	10	3	81	266	38.00	–	2	2
J.V. Coney	10	10	2	58	278	34.75	–	1	7
G.R. Marsh	10	10	0	125	344	34.40	1	1	4
M.D. Crowe	10	10	0	76	330	33.30	–	3	7
C. Sharma	12	8	4	38*	124	31.00	–	–	2
M. Amarnath	11	11	1	74	309	30.90	–	3	4
R.J. Hadlee	10	10	3	71	199	28.42	–	1	–

Bowling	O	M	R	W	Avge	Best	5wI
S.P. Davis	102.1	20	299	18	16.61	3-10	–
E.J. Chatfield	84.2	19	261	14	18.64	4-28	–
R.J. Hadlee	82.1	16	282	15	18.80	3-14	–
Kapil Dev	113	17	391	20	19.55	4-30	–
S.R. Gillespie	68.1	8	265	13	20.38	4-30	–
B.A. Reid	109	7	428	17	25.17	5-53	1
R.M.H. Binny	77	8	316	12	26.33	3-26	–
C. Sharma	98.2	1	490	17	28.82	3-26	–
D.R. Gilbert	78	2	376	13	28.92	5-46	1
R.J. Shastri	116	6	404	12	33.66	2-31	–

Pakistan v West Indies (1-day)

West Indies' short tour of Pakistan in which they played five one-day international matches in 10 days in November and December 1985 could be rated a success both in the crowds which the matches attracted and in the closeness of the result. West Indies won the last match to take the series 3–2.

A less satisfactory feature was the crowd behaviour during the deciding match, in Karachi, where riots and the like are not new. The match had to be reduced from the scheduled 40 overs to 38 a side when the indiscipline included the throwing of bottles and stones at players on the field.

The series began unpromisingly for Pakistan in Gujiranwala where Viv Richards, the West Indian captain, gave one of his most devastating displays, 80 not out off 39 balls in 31 minutes. However, two days later on a faster pitch in Lahore, Pakistan bowled West Indies out, Abdul Qadir taking 4 for 17, and won comfortably.

On a bare pitch in Peshawar, West Indies prevailed in the third match, Holding and Marshall taking most of the wickets, but Pakistan came back in the fourth in Rawalpindi with some good batting by Shoaib Mohammad and Miandad.

Apart from Mohsin Khan, the Pakistan batsmen made little show against Marshall and Holding in the final match.

One-Day Internationals

27 November at Municipal Stadium, Gujiranwala. WEST INDIES won by 8 wickets. Toss: West Indies. Pakistan 218-5 (40 overs) (Mudassar Nazar 77). West Indies 224-2 (35.3 overs) (I.V.A. Richards 80*, A.L. Logie 78*). Award: I.V.A. Richards (80* and 2-0-16-0).

29 November at Gadaffi Stadium, Lahore. PAKISTAN won by 6 wickets. Toss: Pakistan. West Indies 173 (36.2 overs) (I.V.A. Richards 53; Abdul Qadir 5.2-0-17-4). Pakistan 175-4 (38.3 overs). Award: Abdul Qadir (5.2-0-17-4).

2 December at Shahi Bagh Stadium, Peshawar. WEST INDIES won by 40 runs. Toss: West Indies. West Indies 201-5 (40 overs) (I.V.A. Richards 66, D.L. Haynes 60). Pakistan 161 (39.3 overs) (M.A. Holding 7.3-0-17-4). Award: I.V.A. Richards (66).

4 December at Rawalpindi Cricket Club Ground. PAKISTAN won by 5 wickets. Toss: West Indies. West Indies 199-8 (40 overs) (R.B. Richardson 92*). Pakistan 203-5 (39.1 overs) (Javed Miandad 67*, Shoaib Mohammad 53). Award: Shoaib Mohammad (53 and 8-0-30-1).

6 December at National Stadium, Karachi. WEST INDIES won by 8 wickets. Toss: Pakistan. Pakistan 127-7 (38 overs) (Mohsin Khan 54). West Indies 128-2 (34.1 overs). Award: M.D. Marshall (8-1-25-2).

Sri Lanka v England 'B'

Careful consideration will have to be given to the future structure of England 'B' tours if they are to achieve their dual objective of bridging the gap between county and Test cricket and giving the selectors the chance to assess the performances of promising candidates against international class opposition.

Although the tour as a whole was wrecked by political problems, an extended tour of Sri Lanka provided a stiff test as well as highlighting the shortcomings. Realistically, the exercise should have paralleled a major tour as far as possible, with five day Tests and a full squad of players. The latter deficiency was emphasized by the woefully unbalanced attack (only the single spinner) and the early return through illness of the vice-captain, Barnett.

Although all the first class matches were drawn and England lost the one day series, there were individual successes, most notably the emergence of a high class wicket-keeper-batsman in Rhodes. His keeping was impeccable and he batted with skill and flair. Of the main batsmen, Smith and Slack were consistent scorers, while Athey's marathon in the final Test was a fine effort.

The bowling was more disappointing, although the seamers mostly had to toil in unfavourable conditions. Agnew and Pringle were steady, and Lawrence impressed with his courage and willingness to learn. The lone spinner, Cook, bowled well until the third Test and then faded.

Sadly, the standard of fielding was poor, particularly when compared with the Sri Lankans. Indeed, the quality of Sri Lankan cricket in general was a revelation, particularly the host of high class young batsmen. Three teenagers, Gurusinha, Mahanama, and Tillekaratne, scored centuries against the tourists, and the first two have since played full Tests.

Unofficial Tests (4-day)

21-24 January at Sinhalese SC, Colombo. MATCH DRAWN. Toss: England 'B'. England 'B' 363 (W.N. Slack 96, S.J. Rhodes 77*, C.L. Smith 62) and 121-5 dec (S.J. Rhodes 57). Sri Lanka 245 (A.P. Gurusinha 111; N.G.B. Cook 44.4-20-69-6) and 111-4.

26-29 January at Colombo CC, Colombo. MATCH DRAWN. Toss: England 'B'. Sri Lanka 428-8 dec (S. Wettimuny 138, S.M.S. Kaluperuma 70, R.S. Mahanama 58, A. Ranatunga 52) and 127-3. England 'B' 365 (C.L. Smith 76, M.D. Moxon 52, K.J. Barnett 51 ret hurt, W.N. Slack 50).

6-9 February at Asgiriya Stadium, Kandy. MATCH DRAWN. Toss: Sri Lanka. Sri Lanka 271 (P.A. de Silva 81, A.P. Gurusinha 67) and 180-9 dec. (S.N. Ranasinghe 68). England 'B' 160 (C.D.U.S. Weerasinghe 30.3-12-49-5, K.P.T. Warnaweera 35-16-72-5) and 221-5 (W.N. Slack 67).

16-19 February at Colombo CC, Colombo. MATCH DRAWN. Toss: Sri Lanka. England 'B' 369-8 dec. (D.W. Randall 92, W.N. Slack 85, C.L. Smith 51) and 167-3 (D.W. Randall 60*). Sri Lanka 390-6 dec. (M.A.R. Samarasekera 110, R.S. Mahanama 67, R.S. Madugalle 57, T.L. Fernando 56).

22-25 February at Galle Stadium, Galle. MATCH DRAWN. Toss: Sri Lanka. Sri Lanka 231 (D. Wickremasinghe 87; N.G. Cowans 20-6-50-6) and 272 (H.P. Tillekaratne 105*, S. Warnakulasuriya 50). England 'B' 335-6 dec. (C.W.J. Athey 184, C.L. Smith 70*).

England 'B' tour of Sri Lanka 1985-86
First-Class Matches: Played 7; Won 0, Lost 0, Drawn 7
All Matches: Played 12, Won 2, Lost 3, Drawn 7
First-Class Averages

Batting and Fielding	M	I	NO	HS	R	Avge	100	50	Ct/St
C.L. Smith	6	9	1	116	419	52.37	1	4	1
S.J. Rhodes	7	10	4	77*	292	48.66	–	2	9/3
C.W.J. Athey	7	11	1	184	451	45.10	1	1	13
W.N. Slack	6	10	0	96	431	43.10	–	4	–
D.W. Randall	5	8	1	92	212	30.28	–	2	5
K.J. Barnett	4	6	2	51*	112	28.00	–	1	1
M.C.J. Nicholas	6	8	1	49	172	24.57	–	–	5
M.D. Moxon	4	5	0	52	110	22.00	–	1	5
D.R. Pringle	5	8	3	38*	105	21.00	–	–	2
D.V. Lawrence	5	5	1	27	63	15.75	–	–	1
N.G.B. Cook	7	7	2	39	68	13.60	–	–	4
T.M. Tremlett	5	5	1	21	27	6.75	–	–	3
J.P. Agnew	6	4	0	9	10	2.50	–	–	–

Also batted: N.G. Cowans (3 matches) 2*, 0*; N. Gifford (1 match) 4* (3ct).

Bowling	O	M	R	W	Avge	Best	5wI	10wM
N. Gifford	53	14	128	7	18.28	4-81	–	–
D.R. Pringle	129.5	38	273	12	22.75	4-23	–	–
J.P. Agnew	185.3	37	458	17	26.94	3-57	–	–
N.G.B. Cook	340.5	126	739	24	30.79	6-69	1	1
N.G. Cowans	83	23	229	7	32.71	6-50	1	–
D.V. Lawrence	145	22	525	7	75.00	3-50	–	–

Also bowled: C.W.J. Athey 12-2-51-2; K.J. Barnett 11 2 52 2; M.D. Moxon 5-1-15-0; M.C.J. Nicholas 18-5-45-1; D.W. Randall 0.4-0-7-1; W.N. Slack 8-0-15-0; C.L. Smith 23.5-6-72-1; T.M. Tremlett 123-35-302-3.

One-day Internationals

1 February at Tyronne Fernando Stadium, Moratuwa. SRI LANKA won by 4 wickets. Toss: Sri Lanka. England 'B' 162-8 (45 overs) (C.P. Ramanayake 9-1-36-4). Sri Lanka 163-6 (41.3 overs) (D.S.B.P. Kuruppu 80). Award: D.S.B.P. Kuruppu (80).

2 February at Kettarama Stadium, Colombo. SRI LANKA won by 4 wickets. Toss: Sri Lanka. England 'B' 178-9 (45 overs) (C.W.J. Athey 70). Sri Lanka 182-6 (41.2 overs). Award: R.S. Mahanama (39* and 2ct).

4 February at Asgiriya Stadium, Kandy. ENGLAND 'B' won by 4 runs. Toss: Sri Lanka. England 'B' 194-9 (45 overs) (M.C.J. Nicholas 50). Sri Lanka 190 (45 overs) (S.A.R. Silva 53). Award: M.C.J. Nicholas (50).

11 February at P.S. Stadium, Colombo. SRI LANKA won by 8 runs. Toss: England 'B'. Sri Lanka 185-8 (44 overs) (R.S. Mahanama 111*). England 'B' 177-9 (44 overs) (C.L. Smith 67; S.K. Ranasinghe 9-1-43-4). Award: R.S. Mahanama (111*).

13 February at Nondescripts CC, Colombo. Toss: England 'B'. ENGLAND 'B' won by 7 wickets. Toss: England 'B'. Sri Lanka 204-5 (45 overs) (M.A.R. Samarasekera 68, H.P. Tillakeratne 59*). England 'B' 207-3 (43.2 overs) (W.N. Slack 122*, C.L. Smith 60*). Award: W.N. Slack (122*).

South Africa v Unofficial Australians

South Africa, with an ageing but still richly talented group of players, defeated a rebel team of Australians, led by Kim Hughes, in a series of three internationals and six one-day matches. In the 'Tests', as they were called in South Africa, Clive Rice's Springboks won 1–0, careering to a 188-run victory over five days at Johannesburg after they had had the better of drawn four-day matches at Durban (rain affected) and Cape Town. They also won the one-day series 4–2 after going two down.

This was the fifth rebel tour organized by the South African Cricket Union, who were fighting a cause of self-preservation because of their continued exclusion from the International Cricket Conference and their inability to be granted even a hearing at the annual July meetings of the ICC in London. The 16 Australians were banned by the Australian Cricket Board from playing Test cricket for three years (until 1988-89), although they will be eligible to resume their first-class careers in Australia in 1987-88. Their two-season contracts with the SACU were worth $A200,000 each.

The Australians' first tour, given increased credibility because of Hughes' high profile, spread over 12 weeks — without a hitch and in the manner of a normal cricket tour. Attendances at the three internationals, particularly Durban and Johannesburg, were nowhere near as big as the SACU had forecast, but the six one-day games attracted capacity and near-capacity crowds, culminating in a record 30,000 at Johannesburg's Wanderers Stadium for the fifth game.

While the apartheid policies of South Africa's National Party Government remain abhorrent to most of the world, it seems South African cricket cannot do any more to eliminate racial barriers than it has over the past decade. The impression is that sporting boycotts affect sportsmen much more than they influence politicians.

Unofficial Tests

26, 27, 28, 29 December at Kingsmead, Durban. MATCH DRAWN. Toss: South African XI. South African XI 393 (R.G. Pollock 108, H.R. Fotheringham 70, S.J. Cook 52; R.M. Hogg 32-13-88-5, C.G. Rackemann 42.1-6-115-5) and 203-7 dec (H.R. Fotheringham 100★). Australian XI 359 (M.D. Taylor 109, G. Shipperd 59, T.G. Hogan 53) and 32-2.

1, 2, 3, 4 January at Newlands, Cape Town. MATCH DRAWN. Toss: South African XI. South African XI 430 (S.J. Cook 91, R.G. Pollock 79, P.N. Kirsten 72) and 202-5 dec (S.J. Cook 70). Australian XI 304 (J. Dyson 95, K.J. Hughes 53, G.N. Yallop 51) and 224-4 (K.J. Hughes 97★).

16, 17, 18, 20, 21 January at Wanderers, Johannesburg. SOUTH AFRICAN XI won by 188 runs. Toss: Australian XI. South African XI 211 (K.A. McKenzie 72; C.G. Rackemann 26.4-3-84-8) and 305 (K.A. McKenzie 110, R.G. Pollock 65★, C.E.B. Rice 50). Australian XI 267 (S.B. Smith 116) and 61.

Other Overseas Results

Three-Nations Tournament 1985 Sharjah (UAE)

15 Nov. WEST INDIES beat PAKISTAN by 7 wickets. Toss: Pakistan. Pakistan 196-4 (44 overs)(Mohsin Khan 86). West Indies 199-3 (44.1 overs)(R.B. Richardson 99*, I.V.A. Richards 51). Award: R.B. Richardson (99*).

17 Nov. PAKISTAN beat INDIA by 48 runs. Toss: India. Pakistan 203-4 (45 overs) (Mudassar Nazar 67, Rameez Raja 66). India 155 (40.4 overs) (S.M. Gavaskar 63). Award: Mudassar Nazar (67 and 9-0-43-2).

22 Nov. WEST INDIES beat INDIA by 8 wickets. Toss: India. India 180-4 (45 overs) (S.M. Gavaskar 76). West Indies 186-2 (41.3 overs) (D.L. Haynes 72*, R.B. Richardson 72). Award: R.B. Richardson (72).

Player of the Series: R.B. Richardson.

Asia Cup (Sri Lanka)

30 Mar. PAKISTAN beat SRI LANKA by 81 runs. Pakistan 197 (45 overs). Sri Lanka 116 (33.5 overs). Award: Abdul Qadir (7.5-1-24-3).

31 Mar. PAKISTAN beat BANGLADESH by 7 wickets. Bangladesh 94 (35.3 overs) (Wasim Akram 9-2-19-4). Pakistan 98-3 (32.1 overs) (Mudassar Nazar 47*). Award: Wasim Akram.

2 Apr. SRI LANKA beat BANGLADESH by 7 wickets. Bangladesh 131-8 (45 overs) (M. Abedin 40). Sri Lanka 132-3 (31.3 overs) (A.P. Gurusinghe 44*, A. Ranatunga 41*). Award: A. Ranatunga (9-1-17-2 and 41*).

Final: 6 Apr. SRI LANKA beat PAKISTAN by 5 wickets. Pakistan 191-9 (45 overs) (Javed Miandad 67; K. Amalean 9-1-46-4). Sri Lanka 195-5 (42.2 overs) (A. Ranatunga 57, P.A. De Silva 52). Award: A. Ranatunga (9-1-27-0 and 57).

Sri Lanka won the Asia Cup

Triangular Tournament (Sri Lanka)

5 Apr. NEW ZEALAND beat SRI LANKA by 6 wickets. Sri Lanka 137-9 (43 overs). New Zealand 140-4 (36.3 overs). Award: W. Watson (9-2-15-3).

6 Apr. The Asia Cup Final (see above) formed the 2nd match of the Triangular Tournament.

7 Apr. PAKISTAN beat NEW ZEALAND by 4 wickets. New Zealand 214-8 (42 overs) (M.D. Crowe 75, J.J. Crowe 42, J.G. Wright 42; Mohsin Kamal 8-0-47-4). Pakistan 217-6 (40.4 overs) (Javed Miandad 68). Award: Javed Miandad.

Pakistan won the tournament on run-rate.

Australasian Cup Sharjah (UAE)

10 Apr. INDIA beat NEW ZEALAND by 3 wickets. Toss: India, New Zealand 132-8 (44 overs). India 134-7 (41.4 overs). Award: E.J. Chatfield (9-5-14-3).

11 Apr. PAKISTAN beat AUSTRALIA by 8 wickets. Toss: Australia. Australia 202-7 (50 overs) (G.M. Ritchie 60*, D.C. Boon 44). Pakistan 206-2 (49.1 overs) (Mudassar Nazar 95, Mansoor Elahi 56*, Mohsin Khan 46). Award: Mudassar Nazar.

13 Apr. INDIA beat SRI LANKA by 3 wickets. Toss: India. Sri Lanka 205-9 (50 overs) (A.P. Gurusinghe 68). India 206-7 (49.1 overs) (S.M. Gavaskar 71, K. Srikkanth 59). Award: S.M. Gavaskar.

15 Apr. PAKISTAN beat NEW ZEALAND by 10 wickets. Toss: Pakistan. New Zealand 64 (35.5 overs) (Abdul Qadir 10-4-9-4). Pakistan 66-0 (22.4 overs). Award: Abdul Qadir.

18 Apr. PAKISTAN beat INDIA by 1 wicket. Toss: Pakistan. India 245-7 (50 overs) (S.M. Gavaskar 92, K. Srikkanth 75, D.B. Vengsarkar 50). Pakistan 248-9 (50 overs) (Javed Miandad 116*). Award: Javed Miandad.

Cricket in Australia

New South Wales, with a new look team, won the Sheffield Shield for the third time in four seasons and the 39th time in 83 seasons. Led by Dirk Wellham, New South Wales retained the title of Australia's premier state by drawing the five-day final with Queensland at Sydney, in a match described as the best in Australia since the previous Shield final a year earlier.

For Queensland, the eternal bridesmaids, it was their third consecutive final, following their losses to Western Australia (by four wickets) at Perth in 1983-84 and to New South Wales (by one wicket) at Sydney in 1984-85. New South Wales again stole the decisive advantage of having the final played at Sydney instead of Brisbane by leading Queensland on the first innings by 101 runs in their last (drawn) preliminary match in Sydney two weeks before the final. Having finished two points — 54 to 56 — behind New South Wales in the table, Queensland not only forfeited the home-ground advantage; they had to defeat New South Wales outright to win the Shield for the first time (at their 54th attempt). In another gripping finish, New South Wales hung on for the draw they needed, and at 258 for 8 were only 18 runs short of converting a first innings deficit of 142 into victory.

Requiring 276, New South Wales started the last day at 21 for 0, were 109 for 2 at lunch, and 190 for 6 at tea. In the end, spin bowlers Murray Bennett and Bob Holland became unlikely batting heroes by surviving the last 10 overs to deny Queensland victory. Left-arm fast bowler Michael Whitney used a dressing-room telephone to broadcast the tense finale to the three New South Welshmen — Greg Matthews, Steve Waugh, and Dave Gilbert — who were in New Zealand with the Australian team.

They were among the eight players New South Wales were without from the previous season's final. The others were John Dyson, Steve Smith, and Steve Rixon, who had gone to South Africa with Kim Hughes's rebel team of Australians, Pakistan captain Imran Khan, and Peter Clifford, whose form had slipped. Geoff Lawson's back injury kept him out for most of the season, forcing him to miss the final for the second year in a row. Queensland had to replace five players from the side in the 1984-85 final — Allan Border and Greg Ritchie (in New Zealand) and rebel South African tourists Carl Rackemann, John Maguire, and Trevor Hohns. New Zealand tourist Craig McDermott, like Lawson, could not play in the previous final because of injury.

Border's international commitments restricted him to only four Shield matches for Queensland, yet he topped the competition's batting averages — 568 at 94.66 — and won the Benson & Hedges Sheffield Shield Cricketer of the Year award. With 18 points (awarded by umpires on a match-by-match basis), Border finished ahead of Victorian pace bowler Simon Davis and West Australian opening batsman Mike Veletta (17), and Tasmanian opening bowler Roger Brown (15). Border won $2,000 and a gold tray and goblets.

In Border's absence, Kepler Wessels led Queensland in the Shield final, which became his last appearance in Australia before he returned to South Africa to take up a sports administrator's position with the University of Port Elizabeth and to continue his first-class career with Eastern Province. Wessels also was expected to play for Hughes's rebel team in the major matches of their second tour of South Africa.

Wessels announced his retirement from Test cricket after Australia's first Test of the summer (against New Zealand) because of a contractual dispute with the Australian Cricket Board. And he could not contain his bitterness at the presentation ceremony immediately after the Shield final when he said: 'I would like to thank Mr (Fred) Bennett (the ACB chairman) and the Australian Cricket Board for forcing me out of Australian cricket and giving me the chance to play the whole season with the nicest blokes I have ever met.' Wessels's courageous contributions of 166 and 29 in the Shield final boosted his Shield aggregate for the season to 890 at 52.35. Only New South Wales opener Mark Taylor (919 at 54.05) scored more Shield runs. In the first-class aggregates, Wessels was one of only three players to score more than 1,000 runs.

The Shield final also saw the last first-class appearance of Queensland's former Test fast bowler Jeff Thomson, who retired to concentrate on landscape gardening and fishing. There was much sympathy for Thomson — 'good old Thommo' — because of Queensland's failure to win the Shield, but, typically, he put up a brave performance in the final and finished as the leading Shield wicket-taker for the season.

New South Wales' success was built round the consistency of opening batsmen Taylor and Steve Small, the late run-spurt by Mark O'Neill (Norm's son), the 53 wickets shared by spinners Bennett and Holland, the successful comeback from injury of Whitney, and the polished wicket-keeping of Greg Dyer, who made a fine, unbeaten 88 in the final and who was chosen for the Australian team's tour of India.

Victoria, who have not won the Shield since 1979-80, emerged as a potential force in the immediate future by climbing from fifth to third position in the six-team competition. Western Australia were rebuilding, South Australia lacked bowling support for young medium-pacer Andrew Zesers and Gladstone Small, of Warwickshire and England, and Tasmania suffered from inexperience.

Western Australia defeated Victoria by 19 runs in the McDonald's Cup final replay, after the first attempt had been ruined by rain (with Western Australia 129 for 2 off 26.2 of their 50 overs).

In a bid to boost the spectator appeal of the Shield competition, a new points system will be introduced next season. Six points will be awarded for an outright win, irrespective of a first innings lead or deficit. If an outright result is not achieved, only two points will be given for a first innings lead, but a team that leads on the first innings and then loses outright will not get any points. And no points will be awarded for drawn or abandoned matches.

New South Wales v Queensland 1985-86 Sheffield Shield Final
Match Drawn
Played at Sydney Cricket Ground, 14, 15, 16, 17, 18 March
Toss: Queensland

Queensland

Batsman	Dismissal	Runs	2nd Innings	Runs
B.A. Courtice	c Dyer b Bower	8	(2) st Dyer b Bennett	22
R.B. Kerr	c M. Taylor b Whitney	64	(1) st Dyer b Bennett	34
K.C. Wessels*	c Dyer b Whitney	166	c Small b P. Taylor	29
C.B. Smart	c M. Taylor b Whitney	0	(5) b P. Taylor	2
T.J. Barsby	c Dyer b Whitney	0	(7) c M. Taylor b P. Taylor	10
G.S. Trimble	b Waugh	112	(4) run out	0
A.B. Henschell	not out	44	(6) not out	20
R.B. Phillips†	c M. Taylor b P. Taylor	5	c Bower b P. Taylor	6
H. Frei	c Small b Whitney	1	not out	1
J.R. Thomson	c Dyer b Whitney	0		
D. Tazelaar	not out	3		
Extras	(B6, LB8, W1, NB18)	33	(LB2, W3, NB4)	9
	(9 wkts dec)	**436**	(7 wkts dec)	**133**

New South Wales

Batsman	Dismissal	Runs	2nd Innings	Runs
S. Small	c Courtice b Frei	39	c Kerr b Wessels	50
M. Taylor	c Phillips b Tazelaar	41	c Phillips b Frei	30
M.J. Bennett	c Phillips b Tazelaar	11	(9) not out	2
D.M. Wellham*	lbw b Henschell	7	(3) run out	80
R.J. Bower	c Tazelaar b Frei	3	(4) c Phillips b Tazelaar	12
M.D. O'Neill	b Henschell	20	(5) c Phillips b Henschell	1
M. Waugh	c Phillips b Thomson	41	(6) c Smart b Wessels	24
G.C. Dyer†	not out	88	(7) run out	0
P. Taylor	c Smart b Thomson	0	(8) lbw b Tazelaar	42
R.G. Holland	lbw b Thomson	5	not out	0
M.J. Whitney	c Smart b Tazelaar	0		
Extras	(B4, LB4, W1, NB30)	39	(B3, LB3, W2, NB9)	17
		294	(8 wkts)	**258**

NSW	O	M	R	W	O	M	R	W
Whitney	34	7	65	6	10	4	14	0
Waugh	27	4	71	1	5	0	25	0
Bower	7	1	28	1				
Holland	39	9	92	0	5	0	25	0
Bennett	27	5	65	0	13	0	36	2
P. Taylor	25	3	78	1	13	1	31	4
O'Neill	6	1	23	0				

Queensland	O	M	R	W	O	M	R	W
Thomson	29	3	91	3	19	5	41	0
Frei	37	7	87	2	26	8	71	1
Tazelaar	22	4	48	3	20	6	57	2
Henschell	19	2	48	2	29	13	45	1
Trimble	2	0	12	0	2	0	12	0
Wessels					16	5	26	2

Fall of Wickets

Wkt	QLD 1st	NSW 1st	QLD 2nd	NSW 2nd
1st	34	53	62	64
2nd	141	95	71	97
3rd	148	112	71	115
4th	148	116	85	116
5th	327	124	106	182
6th	412	149	122	184
7th	425	248	131	254
8th	426	251	–	254
9th	427	264	–	–
10th	–	294	–	–

Sheffield Shield 1985-86

Final Table	P	W	D	L	1st Innings points	Total points
NEW SOUTH WALES	10	4	5	1	24	56
QUEENSLAND	10	4	6	0	22*	54
Victoria	10	2	7	1	32	48
Western Australia	10	2	7	1	26*	42
South Australia	10	2	4	4	12	28
Tasmania	10	0	3	7	4	4

8 points win, 4 points 1st innings lead, *Including 2 points for match in which 1st innings was not completed.

Leading First-Class Averages

Batting (Qual. 8 innings)	State	M	I	NO	HS	R	Avge	100	50	Ct
M.D. O'Neill	NSW	6	9	2	178*	588	84.00	3	–	4
A.R. Border	Q	11	19	2	194	1247	73.35	6	3	9
G.M. Wood	WA	10	15	3	133	741	61.75	3	5	5
P.A. Hibbert	VIC	10	16	3	148	695	53.46	3	2	7
G.R.J. Matthews	NSW	11	19	2	184	890	52.35	4	1	5
R.W. Gartrell	WA	4	8	2	104	313	52.16	1	1	1
G.R. Marsh	WA	8	14	3	138	563	51.18	2	2	3
D.C. Boon	TAS	9	17	1	196	818	51.12	3	3	3
M. Taylor	NSW	12	20	1	118	937	49.31	2	5	15
K.C. Wessels	Q	13	22	1	167	1030	49.04	3	4	13
G.A. Bishop	SA	11	21	1	224*	965	48.25	3	2	11
D.W. Hookes	SA	12	22	1	243	1001	47.66	3	3	19
M.R.J. Veletta	WA	10	16	1	130	715	47.66	2	6	10

Bowling (Qual. 20 wkts)	State	O	M	R	W	Avge	Best	5wI	10wM
M.J. Whitney	NSW	195.3	43	483	22	21.95	6-65	1	–
S.P. Davis	VIC	243.1	74	550	25	22.00	6-19	3	–
C.D. Matthews	WA	283.2	62	757	31	24.41	5-23	2	–
G.F. Lawson	NSW	248.5	65	513	21	24.42	4-79	–	–
K.H. Macleay	WA	378.4	100	913	35	26.08	6-93	1	–
G.S. Trimble	Q	263.2	59	759	29	26.17	5-50	1	–
M.J. Bennett	NSW	446.1	144	877	32	27.40	4-38	–	–
D.R. Gilbert	NSW	290.3	62	794	28	28.35	4-16	–	–
B.A. Reid	WA	367.1	101	875	30	29.16	6-54	1	–
M.G. Hughes	VIC	390	77	1125	37	30.40	5-53	2	–
G.C. Small	SA	415.4	74	1244	39	31.89	7-42	2	–
G.R.J. Matthews	NSW	274.4	82	639	20	31.95	5-22	1	–
R.G. Holland	NSW	661.4	214	1555	48	32.39	8-33	4	1

McDonald's Cup

Semi-Finals

15 February at Sydney. VICTORIA beat NEW SOUTH WALES by 4 wickets. Toss: New South Wales. New South Wales 191-9 (50 overs) (P.S. Clifford 73). Victoria 194-6 (48.1 overs) (P.W. Young 97*). Award: P.W. Young (97* and 1 ct).

16 February at Brisbane. WESTERN AUSTRALIA beat QUEENSLAND by 7 wickets. Toss: Queensland. Queensland 212 (48.4 overs) (R.B. Kerr 74, T.J. Barsby 55*). Western Australia 214-3 (44 overs) (M.R.J. Veletta 105*). Award: M.R.J. Veletta (105* and 1 ct).

Final

10 March at Melbourne. WESTERN AUSTRALIA beat VICTORIA by 19 runs. Toss: Victoria. Western Australia 167 (38 overs) (W. Andrews 71; D. Hickey 8-2-26-5). Victoria 148 (36.5 overs). Award: D. Hickey (8-2-26-5). Note: The final scheduled for 9 March was abandoned owing to rain. The match 10 March was restricted to 38 overs per side.

Cricket in South Africa

Two features dominated the 1985-86 South African cricket season: one was Transvaal's fall from the pedestal of undisputed provincial champions, and the other was the emergence of young players of potential on a scale that the country has not witnessed since the early 1970s.

Transvaal lost both their Castle Currie Cup crown — the only domestic first-class competition — and the Benson & Hedges night series title to Western Province. Although they retained the limited-overs Nissan Shield trophy, they lost the invincible image they had enjoyed for the previous three seasons.

Clive Rice's side had very much the same playing staff as in the previous seasons, and their top-order batsmen showed little, if any, sign of falling from grace. Rice and Graeme Pollock both struggled to recover from injury and regain form in the last two months of the season, but they still had plenty of batting strength in Jimmy Cook, Henry Fotheringham, Kevin McKenzie, and Alan Kourie, while the young all-rounder Brian McMillan made a spectacular batting debut just when Transvaal needed him.

The one problem that Transvaal could not solve was the inability of the feared West Indian fast bowler Sylvester Clarke to find his best form, largely as the result of persisting injuries. He broke down again when Rice needed him in the second innings of the Currie Cup final at Newlands.

At that stage, Western Province, needing a meagre 143 to win, collapsed in a dismal heap to 49 for 8 with almost the full 20 overs still to be bowled in the final hour. Had Clarke been fit, the new champions would have had little chance of surviving, but captain Adrian Kuiper and wicket-keeper Richie Ryall managed to keep the rest of the attack at bay and a draw was enough to take the honours. Their success was well deserved, however, as they had outplayed Transvaal for the first three days.

The big factors in their success were a new-found stability and consistency in their top-order batting, coupled with the ability of their two main strike bowlers, Garth Le Roux and Stephen Jefferies, to come through a season without major injury.

The return of Kenny McEwan was no coincidence. With his Essex experience behind him, he was the outstanding batsman in the competition, and the confidence he brought to Western Province gradually rubbed off on the other leading players. Le Roux finished as the leading wicket-taker in the competition.

Another factor was the appointment of the former England and Surrey seamer Robin Jackman as the Western Province manager-coach. He struck up a very good relationship with Kuiper and his side, and there was certainly a big improvement in both Western Province's tactical approach to each match and in the direction and organization of practices.

In the final of the Benson & Hedges night series, they played Northern

Transvaal, and it took a brilliant innings from McEwan to prevent the Pretoria side from winning a major trophy.

An oddity of the season was that Eastern Province B side managed to tie two of their six matches — something that had never happened even once before in the entire history of South African first-class cricket.

As far as the emergence of young talent was concerned, this was the best season for more than a decade, when the likes of Kepler Wessels, Allan Lamb, and Peter Kirsten first began to make their mark as players of international calibre. Probably the best prospect was Transvaal's Brian McMillan, who, in three Currie Cup matches at the end of the season, had scores of 85, 53no, 80, 43, 4, and 34. His talent has now been recognized by Warwickshire, and his progress in England will be followed with a great deal of South African interest.

Roy Pienaar, long recognized as a stroke player of exceptional talent, finally made his mark as an opening batsman for Northern Transvaal, and he was the one player to stand up to the Transvaal seam battery with some success in the Currie Cup semi-final.

Western Province's teenage prodigy Daryll Cullinan was slightly disappointing by the high standards that have been set for him, too often getting himself out when well set in the 30s and 40s. But he finally made his way to a maiden Currie Cup half-century in the Newlands final. He was more effective in limited-overs cricket.

The other young batsman to reach first-class maturity was Eastern Province's Mark Rushmere, who made a maiden Currie Cup century against Natal and generally impressed with his ability to handle the pressure that is so often his lot, playing for one of the weaker A section sides.

It was on the bowling side, however, that there was cause for even more optimism. This is one department where the South African game has been weak following the retirement of Vintcent van der Bijl and Mike Procter, the ageing of Clive Rice, and the loss of pace of Garth Le Roux.

Perhaps the most exciting prospect is the Free State schoolboy Alan Donald, who has the ability to generate tremendous pace. At the moment, however, he lacks the accuracy and variations of some of the other young bowlers, such as his provincial team-mate Corrie van Zyl, Transvaal's Hugh Page, and Western Province's big left-hander, Brett Matthews.

Matthews, who looks more like a rugby union lock forward than a pace merchant, turned out to be something of a sensation, first for SA Universities against the touring Australians and later in the Currie Cup final. In this latter match he dismissed Graeme Pollock, Clive Rice, and Kevin McKenzie in six balls in the second innings, and this 23-year-old chartered accountant is certainly a name to note for the future.

Transvaal v Western Province 1985-86 Currie Cup Final
Match drawn. (Western Province won the Currie Cup by virtue of winning the League.)
Played at Newlands, Cape Town, 7, 8, 9, 10 March
Umpires: D.H. Bezuidenhout and O.R. Schoof

Western Province
A.G. Elgar	c Jennings b Radford	65	b Radford	5
L. Seeff	c Fotheringham b Clarke	44	c Kourie b Page	9
P.N. Kirsten	c Jennings b Radford	66	c Jennings b Radford	1
K.S. McEwan	c Jennings b Page	28	b Clarke	1
D.J. Cullinan	b Page	56	c Jennings b Page	12
A.P. Kuiper*	c McKenzie b Radford	48	not out	20
G.J. Turner	not out	26	c Jennings b Page	1
G.S. Le Roux	not out	6	c McKenzie b Kourie	3
S.T. Jefferies	did not bat		c McKenzie b Clarke	1
R.J. Ryall†	″		not out	17
B.A. Matthews	″		did not bat	
Extras	(B4, LB15, W5, NB5)	29	(B4, LB3, NB3)	10
	(6 wkts dec)	368	(8 wkts)	80

Transvaal
S.J. Cook	c Ryall b Matthews	23	c Ryall b Jefferies	102
H.R. Fotheringham	c Seeff b Kuiper	59	lbw b Le Roux	0
B.M. McMillan	c Kuiper b Jefferies	4	c Ryall b Le Roux	34
R.G. Pollock	c Matthews b Le Roux	32	c Ryall b Matthews	26
C.E.B. Rice*	b Matthews	1	c Ryall b Matthews	0
K.A. McKenzie	c Ryall b Jefferies	7	c Seef b Matthews	0
A.J. Kourie	lbw b Le Roux	46	c Seeff b Le Roux	82
R.V. Jennings†	lbw b Jefferies	1	c Kuiper b Jefferies	6
H.A. Page	c Ryall b Jefferies	16	c Cullinan b Jefferies	7
N.V. Radford	b Jefferies	10	(11) not out	13
S.T. Clarke	not out	0	(10) b Jefferies	15
Extras	(LB6, W3, NB4)	13	(B3, LB3, W4, NB3)	13
		212		298

Transvaal	O	M	R	W	O	M	R	W
Clarke	24	7	74	1	13	7	16	2
Radford	25	2	96	3	14	4	15	2
Kourie	21	6	56	0	11	5	21	1
Page	18	3	74	2	11	6	18	3
McMillan	12	3	39	0				

W. Province	O	M	R	W	O	M	R	W
Le Roux	19	3	72	2	24	3	67	3
Jefferies	19.2	5	50	5	33	4	90	4
Kuiper	12	1	30	1	7	1	20	0
Matthews	22	8	47	2	26	6	66	3
Kirsten					17	2	42	0

Fall of Wickets
Wkt	WP 1st	T 1st	T 2nd	WP 2nd
1st	123	41	1	5
2nd	123	54	82	7
3rd	192	117	142	8
4th	233	122	142	26
5th	298	126	142	29
6th	356	144	222	31
7th	–	155	236	48
8th	–	194	252	49
9th	–	212	270	–
10th	–	212	298	–

Currie Cup Final Table

	P	W	L	D	1st Innings points Batting	1st Innings points Bowling	Total points
WESTERN PROVINCE	6	4	0	2	26	25	91
Transvaal	6	2	0	4	20	27	67
Northern Transvaal	6	1	1	4	20	27	57
Natal	6	1	1	4	19	23	52
Eastern Province	6	1	2	3	10	19	39
Border	6	1	2	3	12	14	36
Orange Free State	6	0	4	2	14	22	36

Currie Cup Semi-Final

14, 15, 16, 17 February at Wanderers, Johannesburg. TRANSVAAL beat NORTHERN TRANSVAAL by 277 runs. Transvaal 319 (B.M. McMillan 80, M.S. Venter 63) and 320-9 dec (K.A. McKenzie 84, H.R. Fotheringham 64, B.M. McMillan 53, S.J. Cook 51, I.F.N. Weideman 4-60). Northern Transvaal 218 (R.F. Pienaar 74, N.V. Radford 5-57) and 144 (K.D. Verdoorn 55, R.C. Ontong 50, S.T. Clarke 6-19).

Western Province, as leaders, qualified automatically for the final.

Leading First-Class Averages

Batting (Qual. 8 inngs)

	Province	M	I	NO	HS	R	Avge	100	50
C.R. Norris	Trans B	6	11	4	126*	477	68.14	3	–
K.S. McEwan	WProv	7	11	2	142	510	56.66	2	2
B.M. McMillan	Trans/TB	5	9	1	129	419	52.37	1	3
M.W. Rushmere	EProv	8	15	4	128	570	51.81	1	1
R.G. Pollock	Trans	9	15	2	113	671	51.61	2	5
R.M. Bentley	Natal	6	9	1	134*	410	51.25	1	2
H.R. Fotheringham	Trans	11	20	2	114*	841	46.72	3	4
A.L. Wilmot	Border	7	12	2	108*	448	44.80	1	2
S.J. Cook	Trans	11	20	1	124	840	44.21	2	5
K.A. McKenzie	Trans	9	14	2	110	511	42.58	1	2
M.S. Venter	Trans/TB	7	12	1	225*	459	41.72	1	1
S.F.A.F. Bacchus	Border	7	12	0	134	494	41.16	1	2

Bowling (Qual. 25 wkts)

	Province	O	R	W	Avge	Best	5wI	10wM
B.A. Matthews	WProv/B	303.4	625	42	14.88	5-32	1	–
G.R. Dilley	Natal	206.4	486	30	16.20	7-63	1	–
E.O. Simons	WProv	190	474	28	16.92	5-52	1	–
H.A. Page	Trans	280.1	751	42	17.88	5-31	1	–
N.V. Radford	Trans	213.5	627	35	17.91	5-52	2	–
G.S. Le Roux	WProv	334.3	884	49	18.04	5-54	1	–
P. Anker	Boland	308.2	562	31	18.12	5-34	2	1
O. Henry	Boland	344	757	38	19.92	7-82	4	–
C.J.P.G. van Zyl	OFS	277	624	31	20.12	5-54	1	–
S.T. Jefferies	WProv	293.4	810	35	23.14	5-30	2	–
C.D. Mitchley	NTrans	238.5	695	30	23.16	5-26	2	–
J.C. van Duyker	NTrans	231.4	643	26	24.73	4-29	–	–

Nissan Shield Final

22 February at Wanderers, Johannesburg. TRANSVAAL beat WESTERN PROVINCE by 7 wickets. Western Province 230-6 (55 overs) (K.S. McEwan 66, A.P. Kuiper 47*, P.N. Kirsten 44). Transvaal 234-3 (54 overs) (H.R. Fotheringham 71, C.E.B. Rice 59*).

Cricket in the West Indies

For the first time in three seasons, the Shell Shield was contested with the leading West Indies players at home and available. In order to ensure that the Shield was restored to its rightful place as the premier domestic first-class competition, the West Indies Board stipulated that Test selection would be conditional on participation. Windward Islands fast bowler Winston Davis was the only Test player who opted to take up a contract in Australia instead.

As was to be expected, the Test players dominated the Shield, regained by Barbados for the 12th time in its 20 seasons. Captained for the first time by Joel Garner, Barbados defeated the 1985 champions, Trinidad & Tobago, by an innings in the opening match and never surrendered the lead after that, clinching the Shield with victory over Jamaica in Bridgetown in the crucial match.

Barbados triumphed because they got more from their Test players than did the other teams. Their bowling was spearheaded by Garner and Malcolm Marshall. The first three in their order — Desmond Haynes, Gordon Greenidge and Carlisle Best — were the major influences in the batting.

The other teams lacked Barbados' all-round consistency. Trinidad & Tobago eventually finished second, mainly on the strength of their spinners, their captain, Ranjie Nanan, surpassing Andy Roberts' overall Shield record with 30 wickets for a tally, after 13 seasons, of 185. The main Leeward Islands batsmen, captain Vivian Richards and Richie Richardson, were short of form, while Jamaica, who mounted a strong early challenge, had batting as weak as its fast bowling was strong.

The four Jamaican fast bowlers took 78 wickets in the five matches between them, and only 3 went to a spinner. Courtney Walsh had 29, Patrick Patterson, the sensation of the season, 22, captain Michael Holding 15, and Aaron Daley 12. Yet only the Test player Jeffrey Dujon averaged more than 30 for them.

For Trinidad & Tobago, the Test batsmen Larry Gomes and Gus Logie were disappointing. And while the Harper brothers, Roger and Mark, were outstanding for Guyana, neither they nor the Windward Islands were consistent enough to have any realistic chance at the Shield.

Roger Harper led Guyana for the first time and was the season's leading all-rounder with 262 runs and 22 wickets. His elder brother, Mark, at last converted the potential that had been evident since he was a teenager into productive return with 398 runs at an average of 132.67, when called in for the last three matches of the season.

Batsmen generally faltered on pitches of uneven bounce which brought criticism from several captains, as they did from the captain and manager of the England team later. There were only six totals of over 300 — as against nine of under 150 — including a record low for the Shield, 41 by Guyana on the opening day, when Patterson destroyed them with 7 for 24 on the fast and unpredictable Sabina Park pitch.

The only young player to use the opportunity to advance his credentials was Winston Benjamin, the 21-year-old Leeward Islands fast bowler from Antigua, who did well enough to gain his place on the West Indies team for its tour of Pakistan later in the year.

In the repeat of the 1984 final between the same teams at the same venue, St. John's, Antigua, Jamaica defeated the Leewards Islands by six wickets to clinch the Geddes Grant/Harrison Line Trophy in the 50-overs competition.

Shell Shield

Final Table	P	W	L	D	1st innings points in draw	Total points
BARBADOS	5	3	0	2	2	64
Trinidad & Tobago	5	3	2	0	0	48
Leeward Islands	5	1	1	2	1	32†
Jamaica	5	2	3	0	0	32
Windward Islands	5	1	3*	0	0	25†
Guyana	5	1	2	2	0	24

* Points include 5 for 1st innings lead in match lost. † Points include 4 for abandoned match. (16 points for win, 4 points for draw, 4 points for 1st innings lead in draw.)

Leading First Class Averages

Batting	Team	M	I	NO	HS	R	Avge	100	50
M.A. Harper	Guyana	4	7	2	149*	434	86.80	2	1
D.L. Haynes	Barbados	10	18	3	131	914	60.93	3	5
R.M. Otto	Leeward Is	5	8	1	165	396	56.57	1	3
I.V.A. Richards	Leeward Is	9	11	1	132	518	51.80	2	2
C.A. Best	Barbados	9	15	1	179	640	45.71	2	2
L.L. Lawrence	Leeward Is	4	6	0	113	269	44.83	1	1
C.G. Greenidge	Barbados	9	14	1	90	578	44.46	–	5
T. Mohamed	Guyana	5	9	1	200*	332	41.50	1	1
R.A. Harper	Guyana	8	14	3	72	433	39.36	–	4
R.B. Richardson	Leeward Is	10	17	2	160	575	38.33	2	2
A. Rajah	T & T	5	9	1	69	297	37.12	–	3
A.F.D. Jackman	Guyana	6	11	0	120	391	35.54	1	2
P.J.L. Dujon	Jamaica	11	14	1	75	407	31.30	–	4
H.A. Gomes	T & T	10	15	1	168*	434	31.00	1	1

Qualification: 6 innings; 250 runs.

Bowling	Team	O	R	W	Avge	Best	5wI	10wM
J. Garner	Barbados	332.1	866	57	15.19	6-28	3	–
R. Nanan	T & T	253.3	508	33	15.39	5-52	3	–
M.D. Marshall	Barbados	296.3	835	50	16.70	6-85	1	1
C.A. Walsh	Jamaica	216	680	39	17.43	8-92	2	1
C.G. Butts	Guyana	274	593	34	17.44	6-57	3	–
R.A. Harper	Guyana	247.5	552	30	18.40	4-29	–	–
B.P. Patterson	Jamaica	246.5	813	41	19.82	7-24	1	–
A.H. Gray	T & T	158.3	478	24	19.91	5-50	2	–
W.K.M. Benjamin	Leeward Is	158	400	20	20.00	5-47	1	–
M.A. Holding	Jamaica	193.1	680	33	20.60	4-38	–	–

Qualification: 20 wickets.

Cricket in New Zealand

Despite being the popular pick for bottom place, Otago showed what a solid team performance can achieve by winning the Shell Trophy title by 14 points. Captained by former New Zealand wicket-keeper Warren Lees, Otago made sure of claiming the trophy in the final round of the competition with a first innings win over the most disappointing team of the series, Canterbury.

For once, Canterbury had performed admirably, reaching 401 for 8 in their first innings at Carisbrook. However, showing the sort of consistency that had been their cornerstone all summer, Otago rattled up 403 for 5, with the first six batsmen all making significant contributions.

It was the third time Lees has led Otago to the three-day championship, and his enterprising captaincy, allied to a fine team spirit, was a key factor. Otago claimed five outright victories in the eight rounds, and suffered just one loss. Five times they achieved first innings advantage.

In Ken Rutherford and Stu McCullum, Otago had the most successful opening pair of the competition. Rutherford's 639 runs at 53.25 put him back in the New Zealand team, while the stocky, left-handed McCullum (584 at 48.67) was fourth in the national averages. Richard Hoskin, Derek Walker, John Lindsay, and Brian McKechnie all made notable contributions. The bowling was based on solid toil from the 36-year-old medium-pacer John Cushen and the English professional Neil Mallender, while Lees chalked up the most dismissals, 24, among the provincial wicket-keepers.

Auckland produced New Zealand's two brightest medium-fast bowling hopes, Brian Barrett and Willie Watson, heavy scoring from the long-legged opener Trevor Franklin, and the outstanding innings of the summer, Dipak Patel's 174 at Lancaster Park. It was, opined long-time Canterbury cricket watchers, the finest, most technically proficient innings on the ground in many years.

Wellington, solid without really threatening to overhaul Otago, who led from the start, leant heavily on the all-round skills of Evan Gray and the consistently demanding bowling of Paul Allott. Northern Districts were workmanlike, lacked penetration with the ball, but threw up a player with a bright future in Grant Bradburn.

A new-ball attack comprising Derek Stirling and Gary Robertson should have given Central Districts a sharp edge. But their greatest problem was bowling teams out. Scott Briasco and John Smith had good seasons with the bat, but the absence of Martin Crowe left a gaping hole that was never satisfactorily plugged.

Having won the Shell Cup one-day series under John Wright, Canterbury should have been a strong title contender for the more important three-day contest. Instead, they had a disastrous series. The charitably minded suggested the departure of Wright and Richard Hadlee was too much to overcome. In truth, bad captaincy, poor team spirit, and a lack of discipline and determination in the middle earned Canterbury the ranking they deserved.

Shell Trophy

Final Table	P	W	L	D	1st Innings points	Penalty points	Total points
OTAGO	8	4	1	3	20	–	70
Auckland	8	4	2	2	20	–	68
Wellington	8	3	0	5	16	–	56
Northern Districts	8	3	3	2	12	1	47
Central Districts	8	1	4	3	12	2	24
Canterbury	8	0	5	3	8	–	8

(12 points for win, 4 points for 1st innings lead)

Leading First-Class Averages

Batting	Team	M	I	NO	HS	R	Avge	100	50
M.D. Crowe	C. Districts	4	6	1	137	318	63.60	1	1
P.N. Webb	Auckland	8	13	5	115	441	55.12	1	2
D.J. Boyle	Canterbury	3	6	1	149	267	53.40	1	–
K.R. Rutherford	Otago	11	17	2	126	753	50.20	3	4
E.J. Gray	Wellington	8	13	2	128*	545	49.54	2	3
S.J. McCullum	Otago	8	13	1	134	584	48.66	1	3
G.K. Robertson	C. Districts	10	11	4	99*	303	43.28	–	3
T.D. Ritchie	Wellington	8	13	3	60	420	42.00	–	2
R.N. Hoskin	Otago	8	12	2	111	401	40.10	1	2
C.J. Smith	C. Districts	9	17	0	103	674	39.64	2	3
M.J. Greatbatch	Auckland	7	12	4	119*	316	39.50	1	1
T.J. Franklin	Auckland	9	16	1	176	592	39.46	1	5
D.J. White	N. Districts	9	17	2	209	578	38.53	1	2
R.T. Hart	C. Districts	6	11	1	207	379	37.90	1	1
D.J. Walker	Otago	8	11	2	106	341	37.88	1	1
R.H. Vance	Wellington	8	13	0	114	488	37.53	1	3
P.J. Kelly	Auckland	8	9	1	93	292	36.50	–	2
D.N. Patel	Auckland	8	14	1	174	469	36.07	1	1
A H Jones	Wellington	7	11	3	99	286	35.75	–	2
C.M. Kuggeleijn	N. Districts	9	14	2	74	424	35.33	–	3

Qualification: 6 innings.

Bowling	Team	O	R	W	Avge	5wI	10wM
P.J.W. Allott	Wellington	230.4	460	30	15.33	3	–
J.G. Bracewell	Auckland	178.3	358	22	16.27	1	1
E.J. Gray	Wellington	330.2	748	34	22.00	2	1
J.A.J. Cushen	Otago	350.1	711	31	22.93	2	–
G.B. Troup	Auckland	286.5	695	30	23.16	2	–
V.R. Brown	Canterbury	210.1	487	20	24.35	1	–
N.A. Mallender	Otago	227.1	597	24	24.87	–	–
D.N. Patel	Auckland	355.1	756	29	26.06	1	–
S.W. Duff	C. Districts	218.2	604	21	28.76	1	1
S.J. Scott	N. Districts	271.1	721	24	30.04	–	–
G.K. Robertson	C. Districts	269.4	967	32	30.21	1	–
S.M. Carrington	N. Districts	259.5	792	25	31.68	–	–
J.K. Lindsay	Otago	187.3	647	20	32.35	–	–
D.A. Stirling	C. Districts	217	866	26	33.30	1	–
P.J. Visser	C. Districts	298.3	903	26	34.73	1	–

Qualification: 20 wickets.

Cricket in India

The Indian domestic season of 1985-86 saw the runs flow. In the 11 longer-duration matches for the Duleep Trophy, Irani Trophy, and Ranji Trophy (knock-out), there were as many as 24 centuries.

Bombay and West Zone dominated the domestic tournaments except for the Ranji Trophy, which was claimed by Delhi. Surprisingly, their final was not against Bombay, who had succumbed to Kapil Dev-led Haryana in the semi-finals. But the message of the season was the decline of the South as a force in Indian cricket.

In limited-overs cricket, West Zone won the Deodhar Trophy, while Bombay triumphed narrowly over Delhi in the Wills Trophy. The same pattern prevailed in the Duleep Trophy, which West Zone won, leaving Bombay to beat the Rest of India combination in the one-match Irani Trophy on the basis of first innings lead.

The South produced an entirely unexpected qualifier for the knock-out stage of the Ranji Trophy in Andhra. Normally, or traditionally, it has been two of three teams, Karnataka, Tamil Nadu, and Hyderabad. But Andhra, despite lacking big names, produced the sort of team effort so rarely encountered to head the zone table before being beaten by Rajasthan in the quarter-finals.

With the increase in Tests, limited-overs internationals, and foreign tours, there is much more for cricketers to play for and aspire to these days. The Duleep Trophy and Irani Trophy tournaments, which took place before the Indian team travelled to Australia, helped the borderline cases. The Ranji Trophy knock-out stage helped those challenging for places to Sharjah and England with the Indian team.

Despite the domination by batsmen, some bowlers also had their moments. In the West v North Duleep Trophy clash, which produced a feast of batsmanship — Lalchand Rajput (221), Vengsarkar (110), Mohinder Amarnath (136), and Ashok Malhotra (116) — two left-arm spinners were not overwhelmed. Maninder Singh took 5 for 145 for North while Shastri had 8 for 145 as West went through on first innings lead.

Similarly, in the Duleep Trophy final between West and South, in which Gavaskar (119) and Vengsarkar (147) made authoritative centuries, off-spinner Shivlal Yadav more than held his own with 6 for 110. That performance impressed opponents as well as the national selectors.

Maninder Singh, who missed the trip to Australia, did not waste his time for the rest of the season. He was the bowler instrumental in Delhi's regaining the Ranji Trophy with a match haul of 11 wickets for 90 runs in the final against Haryana (including 8 for 54 in the second innings). He was then picked for the tours to Sharjah and England.

But the most significant bowling performance of the season came as usual from Kapil Dev, against Bombay. Seven wickets at vital stages in the game completed Bombay's rout, and every Bombay batsman was left dreading when the Indian and Haryana captain (and the country's leading bowler) would decide to come on again.

Delhi v Haryana 1985-86 Ranji Trophy Final
Delhi won by an innings and 41 runs
Played at Delhi, 28, 29, 30, 31 March, 1 April
Umpires: S. Banerjee and V.K. Ramaswamy

Haryana

Ashwini Kumar	c Shashikant b Azad	74	c Shashikant b Maninder	12
Deepak Sharma	c Lamba b Madan Lal	26	b Maninder	36
Aman Kumar	c Prabhakar b Maninder	32	c Madan Lal b Prabhakar	7
A. Malhotra	c Bhaskar Pillai b Azad	34	b Maninder	98
R. Chadda	c Ajay Sharma b Maninder	17	st Shashikant b Maninder	2
R. Jolly	c Shukla b Maninder	9	lbw b Maninder	16
Kapil Dev*	c Prabhakar b Azad	2	b Maninder	25
Salim Ahmed†	run out	55	lbw b Maninder	1
Chetan Sharma	c Shashikant b Prabhakar	18	c Azad b Maninder	0
S. Talwar	run out	0	not out	0
Sharanjit Singh	not out	4	did not bat	
Extras	(LB5, NB12)	17	(B4, LB2, NB6)	12
		288		**209**

Delhi

R. Lamba	c Sharanjit b C. Sharma	25
S.C. Khanna†	lbw b Chetan Sharma	5
M. Prabhakar	run out	115
Kirti Azad	c Aman Kumar b Talwar	107
M. Amarnath	c D. Sharma b Talwar	194
K. Bhaskar Pillai	c Ahmed b Kapil Dev	2
Madan Lal*	b Talwar	14
Ajay Sharma	c D. Sharma b Jolly	110
R.C. Shukla	lbw b Talwar	15
Maninder Singh	not out	14
Shashikant	b D. Sharma	7
Extras	(B5, LB7, W5, NB15)	32
		638

Delhi	O	M	R	W	O	M	R	W
Madan Lal	14	1	55	1	7	1	13	0
Prabhakar	14.5	1	54	2	10	2	25	1
Maninder Singh	41	15	66	3	33.1	17	54	8
Azad	32	9	90	3	22	2	83	0
Shukla	6	1	15	0	6	0	20	0
Ajay Sharma	2	1	3	0	1	0	8	0

Haryana	O	M	R	W
Chetan Sharma	25	3	101	2
Kapil Dev	38	8	148	1
Talwar	58	4	194	4
Sharanjit Singh	20.3	6	58	0
Deepak Sharma	31.2	3	90	1
Jolly	9	1	23	1
Malhotra	4	0	12	0

Fall of Wickets

Wkt	H 1st	D 1st	H 2nd
1st	68	9	28
2nd	123	47	40
3rd	150	230	46
4th	180	299	52
5th	203	311	106
6th	205	363	140
7th	207	565	204
8th	268	604	204
9th	268	629	209
10th	288	638	209

Leading First-Class Averages

Batting (Qualification: 500 runs)	I	NO	HS	R	Avge	100
K. Azad (Delhi)	11	1	215	858	85.80	4
M.D. Gunjal (Maharashtra)	8	0	176	677	84.62	3
M. Prabhakar (Delhi)	10	3	119	502	71.71	3
C.S. Pandit (Bombay)	11	3	130*	570	71.25	2
R. Lamba (Delhi)	11	1	231	691	69.10	3
K. Bhaskar Pillai (Delhi)	13	5	140	544	68.00	3
K.V.S.D. Kamaraju (Andhra)	11	1	110*	552	55.20	2
D. Meher Baba (Andhra)	11	0	134	557	50.63	1
A. Malhotra (Haryana)	12	1	116	549	49.90	1
L.S. Rajput (Bombay)	16	2	221	670	47.85	1
R. Chadda (Haryana)	13	0	159	581	44.69	2

Bowling (Qualification: 25 wickets)	O	M	R	W	Avge
Asim Khan (Maharashtra)	193.4	48	454	26	17.46
Maninder Singh (Delhi)	325.5	102	691	39	17.71
P. Sunderam (Rajasthan)	137	25	486	26	18.69
Avinash Kumar (Bihar)	214.1	48	578	28	20.64
S. Talwar (Haryana)	417.2	57	1147	46	24.93
K.D. Mokashi (Bombay)	336	63	987	26	37.96

Irani Trophy
24, 25, 26, 27, 28 October at Nagpur. MATCH DRAWN. Toss: Bombay. Bombay 472 (C.S. Pandit 123, R.J. Shastri 112, R.R. Kulkarni 97, L.S. Rajput 50; R.S. Ghai 6-130) and 400 (S.S. Hattangadi 85, D.B. Vengsarkar 83, S.M. Patil 78, R.J. Shastri 68). Rest of India 312 (M. Azharuddin 100*, Kapil Dev 70, A. Malhotra 52; R.J. Shastri 4-68) and 342-7 (K. Bhaskar Pillai 103*, M. Prabhakar 74; K.D. Mokashi 4-101).

Duleep Trophy
Final: 17, 18, 19, 20 October at Bangalore. WEST ZONE beat SOUTH ZONE by 9 wickets. Toss: South Zone. South Zone 305 (R.M.H. Binny 115, R.D. Khanbilkar 98; A. Patel 4-86) and 236 (K. Srikkanth 120; A. Patel 4-95). West Zone 453 (D.B. Vengsarkar 147, S.M. Gavaskar 119, S.M. Patil 65, R.J. Shastri 55*; N.S. Yadav 6-109) and 89-1.

Cricket in Pakistan

A record number of 102 matches was played in the 1985-86 Pakistan season, which lasted nearly nine months. Once again the leading cricketers were missing from the domestic tournaments because of their engagements in Test matches at home and abroad. However, there were some brilliant performances by youngsters.

Karachi dominated the first-class matches, whereas the leading team of the country, United Bank, were the biggest disappointment. Karachi Whites won the BCCP Patron's Trophy by virtue of their first innings lead against Lahore City Whites in a match marred by rain. In a tournament contested between the City and Zonal teams, Masood Anwar of Rawalpindi and Ali Zia of Lahore City Whites scored double centuries. Test player Rizwan-uz-Zaman scored 670 runs in four matches, including two centuries. His team-mate from Karachi Whites, Iqbal Sikander, finished with 29 wickets, with an average of 9.48.

The Quaid-e-Azam Trophy, Pakistan's premier domestic competition was also won by Karachi, after a lapse of 15 years. Karachi won 7 of their 11 matches, mainly through some fine performances by their spinners, Iqbal Qasim, Ijaz Faqih, and Iqbal Sikander. Their leading batsmen were Rizwan-uz-Zaman, Zafar Ahmed, and Moin-ul-Atiq.

In all, 12 teams participated in the tournament, which was contested by a few sub-standard teams such as Zones A, B, C, and D, comprising players from remote parts of the country. Prominent teams such as PIA, National Bank, and Muslim Commercial Bank failed to qualify for the tournament. Karachi thus availed themselves of the opportunity to enlist players of those teams, making them stronger than the other contestants.

The last of the season's first-class tournaments, the PACO Cup Pentangular, was won by the host team PACO. Shahid Mahboob led the team to the championship by gaining 59 points from four games. Lahore finished second.

It was a season dominated by the bowlers. No less than 13 of them took 50 wickets or more. Nine batsmen passed the 1,000 runs mark, Ijaz Ahmed of PACO scoring most runs, but Rizwan-uz-Zaman of Karachi topping the averages and scoring five hundreds. The highest wicket-taker was Test cricketer Ijaz Faqih of Karachi, whose 107 wickets surpassed Abdul Qadir's record haul of 103 in 1982-83. Anil Dalpat was the leading wicket-keeper, finishing with 67 victims.

The Wills Cup limited-overs tournament was won by PIA. Led by Zaheer Abbas, they defeated United Bank in a closely contested final. The highlight of the season, however, was a 2-0 win for Pakistan in the Test series against Sri Lanka, and later a five-match one-day series against the West Indies which the visitors won 3-2.

Leading First-Class Averages

Batting (Team)	M	I	NO	HS	R	Avge	100
Rizwan-uz-Zaman (Karachi)	8	15	2	175	1198	92.15	5
Moin-ul-Atiq (Karachi)	12	17	5	203*	972	81.00	4
Nasir Valika (United Bank)	12	21	8	100*	865	66.53	1
Asif Mujtaba (Karachi)	16	22	6	131*	869	54.31	1
Arshad Pervez (Sargodha/Habib Bank)	14	24	3	119	1113	53.00	3
Shahid Saeed (Railways)	14	27	2	136	1210	48.40	3
Zafar Ahmed (Karachi)	15	23	5	117*	864	48.00	3
Ijaz Ahmed (Gujranwala/PACO†)	18	33	1	182	1476	46.12	5
Ali Zia (Lahore City/United Bank)	17	26	2	229*	1091	45.45	3
Masood Anwar (Rawalpindi/ADBP)	14	22	2	202*	903	45.15	2
Saadat Ali (Lahore City/United Bank)	17	29	1	140	1210	43.21	2
Shahid Anwar (Lahore City/Lahore)	18	33	3	163*	1279	42.63	3
Tariq Javed (Rawalpindi/Zone D)	11	19	2	154*	718	42.23	2
Shakir Javed (Faisalabad/Zone C)	9	18	2	164	673	42.06	2
Aamer Malik (Lahore Cty/Lahore/ADBP)	14	24	1	122	938	40.78	4
Mansoor Rana (Lahore City/Lahore/ADBP)	19	31	3	140	1124	40.14	2
Umar Rasheed (PACO†)	14	25	4	112	841	40.04	1
Ashraf Ali (Lahore City/United Bank)	16	24	7	72*	677	39.82	–
Tariq Alam (HBFC†)	9	16	3	107	514	39.53	2
Farooq Shera (Bahawalpur/Zone B)	11	21	3	135	709	39.38	3
Aamer Sohail (Lahore City/Lahore)	14	22	3	101	727	38.26	1
Shafiq Ahmed (Lahore City/United Bank)	18	28	0	124	1028	36.71	2
Sajid Ali (Karachi)	14	23	1	157*	786	35.72	2
Manzoor Elahi (Multan/ADBP)	13	21	0	129	740	35.23	2

Qualification: 8 innings, average 35.00.

Bowling	O	R	W	Avge	Best	5wI
Sikander Bakht (United Bank)	189.5	581	14	14.17	6-54	4
Mohammad Nazir (Railways)	783.2	1269	88	14.42	6-41	9
Iqbal Sikander (Karachi)	342.5	1038	65	15.96	6-29	5
Ijaz Fakih (Karachi)	743	1719	107	16.06	6-20	11
Iqbal Qasim (Karachi)	453.3	1024	62	16.51	7-39	3
Sajjad Akbar (Lahore City/Lahore)	687.1	1626	96	16.93	7-40	6
Mohammad Riaz (Lahore City/Zone D)	402	1049	61	17.19	8-66	7
Sajid Hussain (Rawalpindi/Zone D)	264.4	745	42	17.73	7-65	3
Ali Ahmed (HBFC†)	241	723	39	18.53	7-70	2
Saleem Jaffer (Karachi/United Bank)	452	1539	80	19.23	6-20	6
Nadeem Ghauri (Railways)	727.5	1678	87	19.28	7-38	8
Shahid Aziz (United Bank)	209.4	650	33	19.69	6-44	4
Raja Afaq (Rawalpindi/ADBP)	373.2	955	48	19.89	5-80	3
Akram Raza (Lahore City/Lahore)	494.2	1179	58	20.32	7-82	4
Qasim Shera (Bahawalpur/Zone B)	203.1	762	37	20.59	6-50	4
Ali Zia (Lahore City/United Bank)	335.2	902	41	22.00	8-60	1
Kasim Mehdi (HBFC†)	289.1	758	34	22.29	6-13	4
Abdur Raqeeb (Habib Bank)	386.1	1071	47	22.78	6-23	4
Ghaffar Kazmi (Lahore City/ADBP)	512.5	1490	65	22.92	7-55	4
Mohammad Altaf (Bahawalpur/Zone B)	397.1	1217	53	22.96	6-63	3
Shakeel Shah (Lahore/Zone B)	191.3	715	30	23.83	6-51	2
Masood Anwar (PACO†)	535.4	1328	55	24.14	6-55	3

Qualification: 20 wickets, average 25.00.

† Teams: HBFC – House Building Finance Corporation; PACO – Pakistan Automobile Corporation.

Cricket in Sri Lanka

Singhalese SC and Nondescript CC, the two clubs which contribute almost 90 percent of players to the Sri Lanka Test team, finished as joint champions when the first-ever final of the Lakspray Trophy championships ended in a no-result. The three-day contest was reduced to a farce when intermittent rain allowed barely eight hours' play, with not a ball being bowled on the final day.

NCC, captained by Ravi Ratnayeke in the absence of Ranjan Madugalle (broken thumb by courtesy of England B fast bowler Jonathan Agnew), were greatly in debt to the batting of Test leg-spinner Asoka De Silva for their final total of 234. Reduced to 81 for 6 by lunch on the first day by medium-pacers Mahinda Halangoda and Nishantha Ranatunga — younger brother of Arjuna — NCC were rescued by a plucky innings of 76 by De Silva. He slammed three sixes and six fours, two of the sixes coming in a 20-run assault on the youngest Wettimuny brother, leg-spinner Nimal, in one over. The tail wagged incessantly, with the last four wickets contributing 153 runs.

SSC replied boldly, making 56 without loss through Sidath Wettimuny, the captain, and the eldest of the Ranatunga brothers, Dhammika. But the rain had the final say.

Both SSC and NCC qualified for the final by virtue of heading the respective groups in the final round, in which eight teams competed. The top four teams of each group in the preliminary round qualified for the final round. NCC, Moors SC, Burgher RC, and Colombo Colts CC came through from Group A, and SSC, Tamil Union, Bloomfield, and Panadura SC from Group B. Altogether 18 clubs participated, the same as last season.

SSC went through the season unbeaten, while NCC suffered one loss, against Moors SC in the final round. Last year's champions, Colombo CC, went through a lean period, winning only three of their eight preliminary round games, and failing to qualify.

The new system provided fewer opportunities for players, only six batsmen topping 500 runs and only one bowler (Lakshman Aloysius of Tamil Union) taking 50 wickets.

Arjuna Ranatunga (SSC) scored runs not only against the touring England B and Pakistan teams, but also in the domestic competition, where he topped the batting with an average of over 100. He scored most hundreds — three — which included the season's highest, 194 against Nomads. That game also produced the highest total of the season — 586 for 8 declared off 98 overs — all scored on the first day's play, and the fastest century — off 64 balls by Sri Lanka captain Duleep Mendis. Priyalal Rodrigo (Moors SC), who made his international mark against England B, had the highest aggregate — 588.

Spinners dominated the bowling averages with four occupying the top six positions. Medium-pacers Ravi Ratnayeke and Arjuna Ranatunga were the two exceptions. Ajith Ekanayake (Kurunegala YCC), a right-arm leg-spin bowler, returned the best figures for the season with 8 for 16 against Galle CC, who were put out for the lowest total — 49.

Lakspray Trophy Final

7, 8, 9 March at Moors SC Grounds, Colombo. NO RESULT. Umpires: A.C.U. Wickremasinghe and B.C. Cooray. Nondescript CC 234 (E.A.R. de Silva 76; M. Halangoda 4-97, N. Ranatunga 4-56). Singhalese SC 56-0.

Nondescript CC and Singhalese SC share the trophy.

Leading Lakspray Trophy Averages

Batting (Qual: 250 runs)	M	I	NO	HS	R	Avge	100	50
A. Ranatunga (SSC)	5	5	0	194	503	100.60	3	0
D. Ranatunga (SSC)	8	8	2	184*	454	75.67	1	2
S.K. Ranasinghe (Bloomfield)	6	7	2	123	373	74.60	1	3
L.R.D. Mendis (SSC)	7	8	0	104	567	70.87	1	4
S. Jeganathan (NCC)	7	7	2	121	340	68.00	1	2
M.A.C.P. Rodrigo (Moors SC)	9	12	2	103	588	58.80	2	2

Bowling (Qual: 15 wkts)	O	M	R	W	Avge	5wI	10wM
J.R. Ratnayeke (NCC)	164.4	41	350	38	9.21	2	0
A. Ranatunga (SSC)	40.4	20	168	17	9.88	1	1
A. Ekanayake (Kurunegala YCC)	121.4	29	306	27	11.33	2	0
R.G.C.E. Wijesuriya (CCC)	172.2	61	325	28	11.60	4	0
E.A.R. de Silva (NCC)	163.4	59	253	21	12.04	1	0
S. Himbutugoda (Police)	109.4	30	219	17	12.88	1	0

Tours to England
1986

India in England

India's success in winning a series in England, two-nil with the third match a closely fought draw, was not unheralded. Many weeks before Kapil Dev and his team arrived in England, the Indian selectors took a step which should have been a warning that this side would be better equipped for English conditions than its predecessors. They left out Sivaramakrishnan, the brilliant young leg-spinner who took six wickets in each of the first three innings in which he bowled against England in 1984-85 and who later made a considerable impact in Australia.

To the distant observer, this omission meant two things — that modern Indian cricket had realism and that it had resources. The selection took into account the fact that Sivaramakrishnan took only five wickets in the last three and a half Tests in India, when Mike Gatting and others had come out on top. It recognized that several much-vaunted and talented Indian leg-spinners of the past, such as Gupte in 1959, had not reproduced their home form on English pitches. It suggested that India had other bowlers who might be more effective and less vulnerable (Maninder Singh), and it gave the overall impression of a businesslike down-to-earth appraisal of what was needed in England.

Though much praise had been given at the time to the feat of David Gower's side in coming from behind to beat India two-one, time had dulled many people's memory of what a remarkable achievement it really was against a side better equipped on paper. There may also have been a tendency to forget that India's World Cup victory in England in 1983 had been shown not to be a flash in the pan by their subsequent success in the Benson and Hedges World Championship of Cricket in Australia. And if they had played on pitches favourable to their medium pace bowlers and spinners in England in June 1983, why should they not do so again in June 1986?

It was a fair guess, too, that England would have been badly unsettled by their recent mauling in West Indies and, even without the suspension of Botham, might have had problems of team selection which they had been spared while Australia were being comfortably beaten in 1985.

Thus there was a very good case for making India favourites, a position confirmed when they had the better of the Texaco series, winning one match easily and losing the other only narrowly. It was already clear that in the ensuing Test series India were likely to have much greater depth of batting and more accurate bowling.

The opening partnership of Gavaskar and Srikkanth never quite repeated its most specacular achievements of the past, but usually gave a start which the experience of Mohinder Amarnath and the placid mastry of Vengsarkar developed. Kapil Dev and the other batsmen carried on in their various ways and with the confidence of a side in form. A batsman as technically competent and as obdurate as the excellent wicket-keeper More is a depressing discovery low in the order for bowlers just when they think they have worked through the stiffest opposition. English crowds may not have seen the best of Azharuddin, but he still made useful runs.

The batsman who had the most influence on the series was undoubtedly Vengsarkar, who made very few mistakes on pitches which were usually giving the bowler a little help. At Lord's, his 126 not out gave India a first innings lead of 49, when they had looked for much of the third day as if they would finish a similar number behind. It brought India's requirement in the last innings down from a difficult one to one fairly easily attainable. His 61 and 102 not out in a low-scoring match gave India a massive advantage at Headingley. His technical excellence and calm approach to batting were a model to all.

As a whole, the Indian batsmen were well suited to the slow pitches and handled the pace and spin which England put against them with an assurance and efficiency not always shown by their predecessors in the days of uncovered pitches.

Kapil Dev captained the side with an amiable wisdom born of much experience of English conditions and English cricket. He did much to win the first Test with an inspired piece of bowling on the fourth morning, but the extra strength in fast medium bowling required for a tour of England was provided by the adaptability of the hard-working Sharma. Roger Binny at his medium pace was another who advertised the virtue of bowling at the stumps on a full length, and the spin of Maninder Singh and Shastri was never taken lightly by the England batsmen. Maninder's agility in the field was an asset, and India's fielding throughout was of the highest order. In the past, English crowds have not often seen the sort of fielding, with lightning reflexes near the wicket, which Indian sides are wont to display when they are on top at home. This was reminiscent of it.

The tour may have come just at the right time for Indian cricket, when it had the right blend of talented youth and talented experience. It certainly underlined the self-confidence and expertise of present-day Indian cricket. This was almost certainly the strongest Indian side, both in morale and talent, to tour England and it will be interesting to see how well its standards are maintained in the Test arena of the later 1980s.

First Test, Lords, 5, 6, 7, 9, 10 June.
India won by 5 wickets.

India won a well deserved victory, their first at Lord's and only their second in a Test in England, mainly on the strength of their better bowling.

They put England in on the first morning of a match played in cold and usually threatening weather, and though Gooch struggled through to a hundred reached in 5¼ hours, the Indian bowlers nearly always had the conrolling hand. Sharma's ability to make the odd ball dart back off the pitch helped him to take 4 for 48, and England finished the first day at 245 for 5. Except during a fifth-wicket stand of 147 between Gooch and Pringle, the batsmen never looked at ease against medium-paced bowlers who moved the ball off the pitch, sometimes quite sharply, and against spinners who could turn the ball slowly.

On a shortened second day, India replied to England's 294 with a painstaking 83 for 1, but next day, when the atmosphere was drier and the pitch slightly quicker, they too lost wickets, and but for a cultured innings of 126 not out by Vengsarkar would have finished well behind instead of with a first innings lead of 47.

In the uncertain weather and in the expectation that the pitch would become easier, the popular estimate had so far been of a draw. But on the Monday morning the match was won and lost by an outstanding piece of bowling by Kapil Dev, whose opening spell from the Pavilion end epitomized the greater accuracy of the Indian bowlers. They bowled at the stumps, which was a major requirement for success on a pitch always capable of producing the unexpected. By contrast, Dilley, though he took six wickets, and Ellison were too often wide of the target.

England started the day 8 for 0, but in six overs Kapil Dev removed Robinson, Gooch, and Gower. They were then 35 for 3, and, despite a dogged stand of 73 between Gatting and Lamb, relieved by some well executed attacking strokes, England never promised subsequently to escape defeat. Runs had to be squeezed out against the continued accuracy of the Indian bowling, and when the innings ended at the close of the fourth day, India needed only 134 to win.

The weather forecast did not promise them an easy passage next day, but the start was delayed for only 20 minutes. India were then made to work hard, and at 78 for 4 still had plenty to do. But they had longer batting than England, who by then had both Dilley and Emburey out of the attack through injury, and Kapil Dev, coming in at 110 and establishing himself carefully, finished the match with three fours and a six off Edmonds.

INDIA IN ENGLAND 1986

ENGLAND v INDIA   FIRST TEST   LORD'S   June 5/6 1986   ENGLAND 1st INNS

No	Batsman	How out	Bowler	Runs	Wkt	Total	6	4	Mins	Balls
1	GOOCH	B	SHARMA	114	5	245	1	12	355	280
2	ROBINSON	c AZHARUDDIN	MANINDER	35	1	66	-	5	94	70
3	GOWER *	c MORE	SHARMA	18	2	92	-	2	41	38
4	GATTING	B	SHARMA	0	3	92	-	-	2	2
5	LAMB	c SRIKKANTH	SHARMA	6	4	98	-	1	8	8
6	PRINGLE	B	BINNY	63	7	269	-	7	277	244
7	EMBUREY	c AMARNATH	KAPIL DEV	7	6	264	-	-	55	42
8	DOWNTON †	LBW	SHARMA	5	8	271	-	-	38	33
9	ELLISON	c KAPIL DEV	BINNY	12	9	287	-	2	46	34
10	DILLEY	c MORE	BINNY	4	10	294	-	1	37	20
11	EDMONDS	NOT	OUT	7	-	-	-	1	9	8
	Extras	B - LB 15 W 1 NB 7		23						
				294						

Bowler	O	M	R	W	NB	W
KAPIL DEV	31	8	67	1		
BINNY	18.2	4	55	3	1	
SHARMA	32	10	64	5	5	
MANINDER	30	15	45	1		
AMARNATH	7	1	18	-	3	
SHASTRI	10	3	30	-		

Wkt	Partnership between		Runs	Balls
1	Gooch	Robinson	66	144
2	— . —	Gower	26	80
3	— . —	Gatting	0	2
4	— . .	Lamb	6	14
5	— . —	Pringle	147	341
6	Pringle	Emburey	19	90
7	— . —	Downton	5	28
8	Downton	Ellison	2	30
9	Ellison	Dilley	16	38
10	Dilley	Edmonds	7	12

INDIA won the toss + elected to field   Test debut: MORE
Lunch: 81-1 (31 overs) Gooch 24* Gower 13* (1 run = 1000 v India)
Tea: 156-4 (65 overs) Gooch 63* Pringle 19*
New Ball: 220-4 (88.3 overs)
Gooch 100 in 255 balls 1/6 10/4   6th Test 100/2nd v India/2nd at Lord's
Close: 245.5 (96 overs) Pringle 51* Emburey 0*
2nd day: Rain/B&SP until 11.30   7 overs deducted   Shastri unable to bowl
Lunch: 271-8 (120 overs) Ellison 0*
Sharma 5w/2   9th Indian 5w at Lord's

Inns Time: 489 minutes   128.2 overs + 9nb
12th Men: J.G. THOMAS and C.S. PANDIT
Umpires: K.E. PALMER and D.R. SHEPHERD

Hrs	Balls	Runs
1	93	42
2	98	39
3	97	23
4	108	52
5	97	55
6	92	34
7	99	22
8	84	22
9		
10		
11		
12		
13		

Runs	Balls	Last 50
50	109	-
100	256	147
150	385	129
200	485	100
250	593	98
300		
350		
400		
450		
500		
550		
600		
650		

INDIA IN ENGLAND 1986

ENGLAND v INDIA   FIRST TEST   LORD'S   June 6/7 1986   INDIA 1st INNS

No	Batsman	How out	Bowler	Runs	Wkt	Total	6	4	Mins	Balls
1	GAVASKAR	c EMBUREY	DILLEY	34	2	90	-	2	198	133
2	SRIKKANTH	c GATTING	DILLEY	20	1	31	-	4	37	36
3	AMARNATH	c PRINGLE	EDMONDS	69	3	161	-	10	250	241
4	VENGSARKAR	NOT	OUT	126	-	-	-	16	326	213
5	AZHARUDDIN	C + B	DILLEY	33	4	232	-	6	80	76
6	SHASTRI	c EDMONDS	DILLEY	1	5	238	-	-	10	8
7	BINNY	LBW	PRINGLE	9	6	252	-	2	24	19
8	KAPIL DEV *	c LAMB	ELLISON	1	7	253	-	-	4	3
9	SHARMA	B	PRINGLE	2	8	264	-	-	12	12
10	MORE †	LBW	PRINGLE	25	9	303	-	4	29	31
11	MANINDER SINGH	c LAMB	EMBUREY	6	10	341	-	1	66	59
	Extras	B - LB 5 W 1 NB 9		15						
				341						

Bowler	O	M	R	W	NB	W
DILLEY	34	7	146	4	7	
ELLISON	29	11	63	1	1	1
EMBUREY	27	13	28	1		
EDMONDS	22	7	41	1	1	
PRINGLE	25	7	58	3		

Wkt	Partnership between		Runs	Balls
1	Gavaskar	Srikkanth	31	55
2	— · · —	Amarnath	59	265
3	Amarnath	Vengsarkar	71	153
4	Vengsarkar	Azharuddin	71	142
5	— · —	Shastri	6	12
6	— · —	Binny	14	34
7	— · —	Kapil Dev	1	4
8	— · —	Sharma	11	19
9	— · —	More	39	43
10	— · —	Maninder	38	106

England 294   Start: 2.29   47 overs left June 6
Tea: 41-1 (18 overs) Gavaskar 14* Amarnath 5*   253 behind
BLSP: 4.20   45-1 (23.1 overs) Gavaskar 16* Amarnath 6*
Resume: 5.20 - play scheduled until 7.00
Close: 83-1 (51 overs) Gavaskar 30* Amarnath 27*   213 behind
2nd day: Lunch: 169.3 (85 overs) Vengsarkar 31* Azharuddin 4*   125 behind
New Ball: 182.3 (92.3 overs)
Tea: 267-8 (113 overs) Vengsarkar 81* More 3*   27 behind

Inns Time: 528 minutes   137 overs + 9 nb

Hrs	Balls	Runs
1	86	33
2	94	20
3	106	27
4	93	62
5	111	20
6	107	46
7	76	42
8	80	57
9		
10		
11		
12		
13		

Runs	Balls	Last 50
50	153	-
100	340	187
150	435	95
200	574	139
250	660	86
300	725	65
350		
400		
450		
500		
550		
600		
650		

INDIA IN ENGLAND 1986

ENGLAND v INDIA   FIRST TEST   LORD'S   June 7/9 1986   ENGLAND 2nd INNS

No	Batsman	How out	Bowler	Runs	Wkt	Total	6	4	Mins	Balls
1	GOOCH	LBW	KAPIL DEV	8	2	23	-	-	49	35
2	ROBINSON	c AMARNATH	KAPIL DEV	11	1	18	-	-	39	28
3	GOWER *	LBW	KAPIL DEV	8	3	35	-	2	28	19
4	GATTING	B	SHARMA	40	5	113	-	6	121	83
5	LAMB	c MORE	SHASTRI	39	4	108	-	7	89	83
6	PRINGLE	c MORE	KAPIL DEV	6	6	121	-	-	28	19
7	DOWNTON †	c SHASTRI	MANINDER	29	7	164	-	4	125	109
8	ELLISON	c MORE	BINNY	19	8	170	-	1	120	104
9	EMBUREY	c + B	MANINDER	1	9	170	-	-	22	10
10	DILLEY	NOT	OUT	2	-	-	-	-	57	57
11	EDMONDS	c BINNY	MANINDER	7	10	180	-	-	46	37
	Extras	B - LB 6 W 1 NB 3		10						
				180						

Bowler	O	M	R	W	NB	W
KAPIL DEV	22	7	52	4		
SHARMA	17	4	48	1	2	
BINNY	15	3	44	1	2	1
SHASTRI	20	8	21	1		
MANINDER	20.4	12	9	3		
AMARNATH	2	2	-	-		

Wkt	Partnership between		Runs	Balls
1	Gooch	Robinson	18	58
2	— . —	Gower	5	10
3	Gower	Gatting	12	26
4	Gatting	Lamb	73	141
5	— . —	Pringle	5	16
6	Pringle	Downton	8	27
7	Downton	Ellison	43	187
8	Ellison	Emburey	6	17
9	Emburey	Dilley	0	16
10	Dilley	Edmonds	10	86

India 1st inns lead 47   2 overs left June 7   Start: 5.45
Close: 8-0 (4 overs) Gooch 5* Robinson 3*   39 behind
4th Day. Lunch: 89-3 (32 overs) Gatting 31* Lamb 29*   42 ahead
Tea: 151-6 (65 overs) Downton 24* Ellison 8*   104 ahead

Inns Time: 371 minutes   96.4 overs + 4 nb

Hrs	Balls	Runs
1	82	31
2	86	55
3	93	28
4	103	35
5	101	15
6	97	15
7		
8		
9		
10		
11		
12		
13		

Runs	Balls	Last 50
50	128	-
100	218	90
150	368	150
200		
250		
300		
350		
400		
450		
500		
550		
600		
650		

INDIA IN ENGLAND 1986

ENGLAND v INDIA   FIRST TEST   LORD'S   June 10 1986   INDIA 2nd INNS

No	Batsman	How out	Bowler	Runs	Wkt	Total	6	4	Mins	Balls
1	GAVASKAR	c DOWNTON	DILLEY	22	2	31	-	4	63	58
2	SRIKKANTH	c GOOCH	DILLEY	0	1	10	-	-	20	10
3	AMARNATH	LBW	PRINGLE	8	3	76	-	1	93	50
4	VENGSARKAR	B	EDMONDS	33	4	78	-	2	60	56
5	AZHARUDDIN	RUN	OUT	14	5	110	-	2	40	30
6	SHASTRI	NOT	OUT	20	-	-	-	3	50	44
7	KAPIL DEV*	NOT	OUT	23	-	-	1	4	18	10
8	BINNY									
9	SHARMA	DID NOT BAT								
10	MORE †									
11	MANINDER SINGH									
	Extras	B 1 LB 9 W 1 NB 5		16						

136 - 5

Bowler	O	M	R	W	NB	W
DILLEY	10	3	28	2	5	
ELLISON	6	-	17	-		
PRINGLE	15	5	30	1		
EDMONDS	11	2	51	1	1	

Wkt	Partnership between		Runs	Balls
1	Gavaskar	Srikkanth	10	31
2	— · —	Amarnath	21	57
3	Amarnath	Vengsarkar	45	79
4	Vengsarkar	Azharuddin	2	15
5	Azharuddin	Shastri	32	56
6	Shastri	Kapil Dev	26*	54
7				
8				
9				
10				

India need 134 to win on last day (96 overs)
Start delayed until 11.20 - 5 overs deducted
Lunch: 72-2 (23 overs) Amarnath 7* Vengsarkar 28*
                62 to win
NB: Embury injured 12.33 Dilley injured 12.45
12th men: P. Bent + R. Pook
• Embury/Downton/Edmonds

India won by 5 wickets   Man of the Match: Kapil Dev
Kapil Dev's 1st Test win (21st time as captain)
India's 1st win at Lord's

India won £6,000   Attendance: 57,509
Inns Time: 177 minutes   42 overs + 6 nb

Hrs	Balls	Runs
1	89	30
2	69	46
3	88	42
4		
5		
6		
7		
8		
9		
10		
11		
12		
13		

Runs	Balls	Last 50
50	110	—
100	221	111
150		
200		
250		
300		
350		
400		
450		
500		
550		
600		
650		

Second Test, Headingley, 19, 20, 21, 23 June.
India won by 279 runs.

India won their second Test victory in the series — and with it the series — in even more convincing fashion than their first at Lord's a fortnight earlier. Their superiority had the same root causes, their vastly more accurate bowling, their greater depth of batting, and the technical excellence of the batting of Dilip Vengsarkar, who made 61 and 102 not out, this in a match in which the next highest score was 35.

England had made five changes from the side that played at Lord's, including one forced on them by a shoulder injury to Gower. In a low-scoring match India admittedly had the best of the conditions, not least on the first day when, under a clear sky, they reached 128 before their third wicket fell. The ball had already begun to move off the pitch for the faster bowlers — it also turned slowly throughout. When in the late afternoon the weather clouded over, the swinging ball accentuated the movement of the pitch. At one stage, 4 wickets fell for 10 runs before Madan Lal and More, coming together at 213 for 8, steadied the ship.

Even so, India's 235 for 8 seemed to represent a promising first day's work by the England bowlers, if the sunny conditions of previous days returned. The second day, however, was overcast, and though India's last 2 wickets were able to add another 37 runs, thus re-emphasizing the batting ability in their lower order, the outcome of the match was soon determined when England batted.

Kapil Dev and Madan Lal moved the ball about on a full length in a way that confounded England's early batsmen. Binny followed, also making the batsmen play almost all the time, and took five wickets with his medium pace. The fielding was of a high standard, and desperation was soon evident in the England response. Some batsmen were unlucky to receive the almost unplayable ball, others played injudicious strokes, and in just 45.1 overs England were bowled out for 102.

India scarcely found batting any easier that evening and finished at 70 for 5. But in the sunshine on Saturday, batting was made to look much less complicated by Vengsarkar's patience and judgement of the right ball to hit, and by the support given him by the later batsmen. Even at the start of the day, India, 240 ahead, had been almost certainly safe. By the time the innings ended, England needed 408 and were in a hopeless position.

The pitch by then was not likely to lift any batting side's confidence. Occasionally the ball would scarcely leave the ground after pitching, sometimes turning like a medium-paced off-break or leg-break. This time Kapil Dev did not have to do the job with the faster bowlers and himself. The spin of Maninder and Shastri was equally effective, so much so that they finished the day having in only 12.1 overs removed Athey, Smith, and the nightwatchman Lever for 14 runs. England were 90 for 6.

Gatting battled away on the fourth morning throughout the 77 minutes play needed by India to wrap up the series, and was undefeated after nearly 2½ hours in all. But the relative certainty with which he was playing at the end was only achieved through the experience gained from many narrow escapes, especially against Maninder.

INDIA IN ENGLAND 1986

ENGLAND v INDIA SECOND TEST HEADINGLEY June 19/20 1986 INDIA 1st INNS

No	Batsman	How out	Bowler	Runs	Wkt	Total	6	4	Mins	Balls
1	GAVASKAR	c FRENCH	PRINGLE	35	2	75	-	4	96	71
2	SRIKKANTH	c EMBUREY	PRINGLE	31	1	64	-	5	79	62
3	SHASTRI	c PRINGLE	DILLEY	32	3	128	1	2	80	66
4	VENGSARKAR	c FRENCH	LEVER	61	5	203	1	6	187	153
5	AZHARRUDIN	LBW	GOOCH	15	4	163	-	2	55	43
6	PANDIT	c EMBUREY	PRINGLE	23	7	211	-	2	87	67
7	KAPIL DEV *	LBW	LEVER	0	6	203	-	-	1	1
8	BINNY	c SLACK	EMBUREY	6	8	213	-	1	33	27
9	MADAN LAL	c GOOCH	DILLEY	20	9	267	-	2	89	62
10	MORE †	NOT	OUT	36	-	-	-	6	82	72
11	MANINDER SINGH	c GOOCH	DILLEY	3	10	272	-	-	7	10
	Extras	B - LB 5	W - NB 5	10						
				272						

Bowler	O	M	R	W	NB	W
DILLEY	24.2	7	54	3	7	
LEVER	30	4	102	2		
PRINGLE	27	6	47	3		
EMBUREY	17	4	45	1	1	
GOOCH	6	-	19	1		

Wkt	Partnership between		Runs	Balls
1	Gavaskar	Srikkanth	64	122
2	---	Shastri	11	24
3	Shastri	Vengsarkar	53	112
4	Vengsarkar	Azharuddin	35	86
5	---	Pandit	40	103
6	Pandit	Kapil Dev	0	1
7	---	Binny	8	29
8	Binny	Madan Lal	2	22
9	Madan Lal	More	54	121
10	More	Maninder	5	14

India won the toss and elected to bat
Test debuts: B.N. FRENCH, C.S. PANDIT, J. BIRKENSHAW
Lunch: 92-2 (31 overs) Shastri 20* Vengsarkar 3*
Tea: 174-4 (63 overs) Vengsarkar 47* Pandit 9*
Close: 235-8 (93 overs) Madan Lal 12* More 11*
New Ball: 239-8 (93.2 overs)

Inns Time: 410 minutes 104.2 overs + 8 nb
12th Men: R.M. ELLISON and R.M. LAMBA
Umpires: J. BIRKENSHAW and D.J. CONSTANT

Hrs	Balls	Runs		Runs	Balls	Last 50
1	93	49		50	94	-
2	96	43		100	215	121
3	95	38		150	314	99
4	96	44		200	435	121
5	86	31		250	583	148
6	99	30		300		
7				350		
8				400		
9				450		
10				500		
11				550		
12				600		
13				650		

INDIA IN ENGLAND 1986

ENGLAND v INDIA SECOND TEST HEADINGLEY June 20 1986 ENGLAND 1st INNS

No	Batsman	How out	Bowler	Runs	Wkt	Total	6	4	Mins	Balls
1	GOOCH	c BINNY	KAPIL DEV	8	2	14	-	2	26	22
2	SLACK	B	MADAN LAL	0	1	4	-	-	4	2
3	SMITH	B	MADAN LAL	6	3	14	-	1	25	18
4	LAMB	c PANDIT	BINNY	10	5	41	-	2	35	21
5	GATTING *	c MORE	BINNY	13	4	38	-	1	23	22
6	ATHEY	c MORE	MADAN LAL	32	10	102	-	4	134	72
7	PRINGLE	c SRIKKANTH	BINNY	8	6	63	-	-	42	35
8	EMBUREY	c KAPIL DEV	BINNY	0	7	63	-	-	1	1
9	FRENCH †	B	BINNY	8	8	71	-	1	6	10
10	DILLEY	B	SHASTRI	10	9	100	-	-	61	60
11	LEVER	NOT	OUT	0	-	-	-	-	9	12
	Extras	B 1 LB 2 W - NB 4		7						
				102						

Bowler	O	M	R	W	NB	W
KAPIL DEV	18	7	36	1		
MADAN LAL	11¹	3	18	3		
BINNY	13	1	40	5	4	
SHASTRI	3	1	5	1		

Wkt	Partnership between		Runs	Balls
1	Gooch	Slack	4	8
2	— . —	Smith	10	32
3	Smith	Lamb	0	4
4	Lamb	Gatting	24	37
5	— . —	Athey	3	10
6	Athey	Pringle	22	69
7	— . —	Emburey	0	1
8	— . —	French	8	10
9	— . —	Dilley	29	94
10	— . —	Lever	2	16

India 272
Start: 11.59   76 overs remain June 20
Lunch: 41-4 (15 overs) Lamb 10* Athey 2* 231 behind
Binny 5w/l

Inns Time: 192 minutes   45.1 overs + 4 nb

Hrs	Balls	Runs		Runs	Balls	Last 50
1	84	39		50	128	—
2	81	32		100	254	126
3	94	29		150		
4				200		
5				250		
6				300		
7				350		
8				400		
9				450		
10				500		
11				550		
12				600		
13				650		

118 INDIA IN ENGLAND 1986

ENGLAND v INDIA   SECOND TEST   HEADINGLEY   June 20/21 1986   INDIA 2nd INNS

No	Batsman	How out	Bowler	Runs	Wkt	Total	6	4	Mins	Balls
1	GAVASKAR	c FRENCH	LEVER	1	1	9	-	-	22	19
2	SRIKKANTH	B	DILLEY	8	2	9	-	1	29	18
3	SHASTRI	LBW	LEVER	3	3	29	-	-	23	13
4	VENGSARKAR	NOT	OUT	102	-	-	-	10	282	216
5	AZHARUDDIN	LBW	LEVER	2	4	35	-	-	13	9
6	PANDIT	B	PRINGLE	17	5	70	-	3	56	42
7	MORE †	c SLACK	PRINGLE	16	6	102	-	1	39	27
8	KAPIL DEV *	c GATTING	LEVER	31	7	137	1	4	31	23
9	MADAN LAL	RUN	OUT	22	8	173	-	4	54	48
10	BINNY	LBW	PRINGLE	26	9	233	1	3	53	35
11	MANINDER SINGH	c GATTING	PRINGLE	1	10	237	-	-	9	9
	Extras	B 4 LB 4 W - NB -		8						
				237						

Bowler	O	M	R	W	NB	W
DILLEY	17	2	71	1		
LEVER	23	5	64	4		
PRINGLE	22.3	6	73	4		
EMBUREY	7	3	9	-		
GOOCH	7	2	12	-		

Wkt	Partnership between		Runs	Balls
1	Gavaskar	Srikkanth	9	33
2	Srikkanth	Shastri	0	7
3	Shastri	Vengsarkar	20	27
4	Vengsarkar	Azharuddin	6	17
5	- . -	Pandit	35	90
6	- . -	More	32	59
7	- . -	Kapil Dev	35	41
8	- . -	Madan Lal	36	92
9	- . -	Binny	60	80
10	- . -	Maninder	4	13

India 1st inns lead 170
30 overs left June 20
Close: 70-5 (30 overs) Vengsarkar 33* More 0* 240 ahead
3rd Day: Lunch: 171-7 (60 overs) Vengsarkar 66* Madan Lal 21* 341 ahead
Vengsarkar 100 in 213 balls 10/4 /11th 100
12th man: D.W. Randall
• Pringle/French

Inns Time: 313 minutes   76.3 overs

Hrs	Balls	Runs	Runs	Balls	Last 50
1	81	31	50	110	-
2	93	37	100	228	118
3	90	53	150	298	70
4	84	47	200	412	114
5	96	59	250		
6			300		
7			350		
8			400		
9			450		
10			500		
11			550		
12			600		
13			650		

INDIA IN ENGLAND 1986

ENGLAND v INDIA SECOND TEST HEADINGLEY June 21/23 1986 ENGLAND 2nd INNS

No	Batsman	How out	Bowler	Runs	Wkt	Total	6	4	Mins	Balls
1	GOOCH	c SRIKKANTH	KAPIL DEV	5	1	12	–	1	19	19
2	SLACK	c GAVASKAR	BINNY	19	2	46	–	2	62	51
3	SMITH	c MORE	SHASTRI	28	4	77	–	4	105	69
4	LAMB	c MORE	BINNY	10	3	63	–	1	27	26
5	GATTING *	NOT	OUT	31	–	–	–	4	145	124
6	ATHEY	c MORE	MANINDER	8	5	90	–	–	27	35
7	LEVER	c MORE	MANINDER	0	6	90	–	–	4	1
8	PRINGLE	LBW	MANINDER	8	7	101	–	–	28	20
9	EMBUREY	c AZHARRUDIN	KAPIL DEV	1	8	104	–	–	10	11
10	FRENCH †	c VENGSARKAR	MANINDER	5	9	109	–	1	17	16
11	DILLEY	RUN	OUT	2	10	128	–	–	16	11
Extras		B – LB 9 W – NB 2		11						
				128						

Bowler	O	M	R	W	NB	W
KAPIL DEV	19.2	7	24	2		
MADAN LAL	9.4	2	30	–		
MANINDER	16.3	6	26	4	1	
BINNY	8	1	18	2	1	
SHASTRI	10	3	21	1		

Wkt	Partnership between		Runs	Balls
1	Gooch	Slack	12	30
2	Slack	Smith	34	63
3	Smith	Lamb	17	63
4	– . –	Gatting	14	50
5	Gatting	Athey	13	58
6	– . –	Lever	0	7
7	– . –	Pringle	11	49
8	– . –	Emburey	3	22
9	– . –	French	5	30
10	– . –	Dilley	19	34

England need 408 to win Start: 3.00 41 overs remain June 21
Tea: 31-1 (11 overs) Slack 13* Smith 9* 377 to win
Close: 90-6 (41.1 overs) Gatting 10* 318 to win
Kapil Dev injured back 54.2 overs – over completed by Madan Lal
. Madan Lal

India won by 279 runs Man of the Match: D.B. Vengsarkar
(before lunch 4th day)
India's 1st win at Headingley
India's 2nd series win in England

India won £6,000   Attendance: 33,850
Total Time: 236 minutes   63.3 overs + 2nb

Hrs	Balls	Runs
1	90	46
2	82	24
3	112	27
4		
5		
6		
7		
8		
9		
10		
11		
12		
13		

Runs	Balls	Last 50
50	106	–
100	285	179
150		
200		
250		
300		
350		
400		
450		
500		
550		
600		
650		

Third Test, Edgbaston, 3, 4, 5, 7, 8 July.
Match Drawn.

The third Test may have been played after the series was decided, but was in no way an anticlimax, for the result was in doubt until rain interrupted play after tea on the last day. Played on a pitch that never allowed the batsman to relax, it was settled in one sense in the first day and a half, for without Mike Gatting's 183 not out England would certainly have lost.

Gatting came in at 61 for 3 — England had been 0 for 2 — and was soon faced with a score of 88 for 4. But after reaching 30 he took charge with a fine show of strokes and swept past 100 in 139 balls. He then settled in on a careful course for a second 100 as if determined to stay and squeeze every possible run out of his later partners. Gatting's innings was the more remarkable when one notes that no one else in his side reached 50, and the next highest score in the match was Amarnath's 79.

When England were all out soon after lunch on the second day, 390 seemed a healthy score, for batting had not been without its problems. The ball occasionally deviated at different heights for the faster bowlers and turned for the spinners.

But English hopes of a first-innings lead were thwarted by a dashing response by the Indian batsmen, whose contribution right down the order illustrated the unusual depth of their batting. When the innings ended on the third evening, it was the fifth instance in Test history of a tie on first innings. By a strange coincidence two of the other cases occurred in matches starting on the same day in February 1973 — between New Zealand and Pakistan in Auckland and West Indies and Australia in Kingston.

Speculation was rife over the week-end as to the outcome, and did not die down after Monday's play, when England, after promising better, declined against the lively Sharma to 231 for 9. Four runs were added on the last morning.

The 236 which India needed was not an excessive target for a strong batting side on this pitch and against this opposition. Yet in the history of Test cricket in England, it was a figure that had rarely been exceeded to win a match.

What India seemed to need to simplify their task was a vigorous opening stand between Gavaskar and Srikkanth, and this was duly provided. It ended at 58, but at 101 for 1 a third Indian victory in the series seemed imminent. By then, however, Edmonds was turning the ball a lot, and to the wicket of Srikkanth he quickly added those of Amarnath and the formidable Vengsarkar to catches at the wicket and Shastri to one at slip. In between, Gavaskar was caught at the wicket off Foster. Suddenly India were 105 for 5 and England could scent victory.

Soon after tea, however, 50 minutes was lost through bad light and rain. India had already decided that a prudent halt to adventure was needed, and Azharuddin and More played out the remaining overs safely.

INDIA IN ENGLAND 1986

ENGLAND v INDIA THIRD TEST EDGBASTON July 3/4 1986 ENGLAND 1st INNS

No	Batsman	How out	Bowler	Runs	Wkt	Total	6	4	Mins	Balls
1	GOOCH	c MORE	KAPIL DEV	0	1	0	-	-	2	4
2	BENSON	B	MANINDER	21	3	61	-	2	98	66
3	ATHEY	c MORE	KAPIL DEV	0	2	0	-	-	6	3
4	GOWER	LBW	SHARMA	49	4	88	-	6	53	81
5	GATTING*	NOT	OUT	183	-	-	2	20	383	294
6	PRINGLE	c AMARNATH	SHASTRI	44	5	184	1	5	106	95
7	EMBUREY	c SHASTRI	MANINDER	38	6	278	-	6	92	69
8	FOSTER	B	BINNY	17	7	327	-	3	52	32
9	EDMONDS	B	SHARMA	18	8	367	-	2	50	30
10	FRENCH†	B	SHARMA	8	9	384	-	1	34	23
11	RADFORD	c GAVASKAR	SHARMA	0	10	390	-	-	15	10
	Extras	B - LB 7	W - NB 5	12						

390

Bowler	O	M	R	W	NB	W
KAPIL DEV	31	6	89	2		
BINNY	17	1	53	1	4	
SHARMA	29.3	2	130	4	2	
MANINDER	25	3	66	2	2	
SHASTRI	14	1	45	1		

Wkt	Partnership between		Runs	Balls
1	Gooch	Benson	0	4
2	Benson	Athey	0	9
3	— · —	Gower	61	124
4	Gower	Gatting	27	42
5	Gatting	Pringle	96	174
6	— · —	Emburey	94	141
7	— · —	Foster	49	74
8	— · —	Edmonds	40	68
9	— · —	French	17	47
10	— · —	Radford	6	24

England won the toss and elected to bat
Test debuts: M.R.BENSON, N.V.RADFORD
Gower 27 = 5808 (past Compton)
Lunch: 87-3 (28 overs) Gower 48* Gatting 14*
Tea: 196-5 (61 overs) Gatting 76* Emburey 0*
Gatting 100 in 139 balls 2/6, 12/4 / HSTC in Eng / 5th 100
New Ball: 293-6 (86.3 overs)
Close: 315-6 (90 overs) Gatting 141* Foster 13*
2nd Day: Lunch: 389-9 (116 overs) Gatting 182* Radford 0*

Inns Time: 486 minutes   116.3 overs + 8 nb
12th men: G.R.DILLEY and C.S.PANDIT
Umpires: H.D.BIRD and B.J.MEYER

Hrs	Balls	Runs
1	83	27
2	85	60
3	95	50
4	100	55
5	94	58
6	82	60
7	79	46
8	80	33
9		
10		
11		
12		
13		

Runs	Balls	Last 50
50	130	-
100	205	75
150	285	80
200	377	92
250	457	80
300	528	71
350	607	79
400		
450		
500		
550		
600		
650		

INDIA IN ENGLAND 1986

ENGLAND v INDIA   THIRD TEST   EDGBASTON   July 4/5 1986   INDIA 1st INNS

No	Batsman	How out	Bowler	Runs	Wkt	Total	6	4	Mins	Balls
1	GAVASKAR	B	PRINGLE	29	2	58	-	6	57	36
2	SRIKKANTH	c PRINGLE	RADFORD	23	1	53	-	3	40	34
3	AMARNATH	B	EDMONDS	79	4	228	-	9	260	237
4	VENGSARKAR	c GOOCH	RADFORD	38	3	139	-	4	104	101
5	AZHARRUDIN	c FRENCH	FOSTER	64	5	266	-	6	209	134
6	SHASTRI	c GOOCH	FOSTER	18	6	275	-	2	79	57
7	KAPIL DEV *	c FRENCH	FOSTER	26	7	302	-	5	40	21
8	MORE †	c FRENCH	EMBUREY	48	10	390	-	4	167	119
9	BINNY	c GOWER	EMBUREY	40	8	370	-	4	106	87
10	SHARMA	c GOWER	PRINGLE	9	9	385	-	2	14	10
11	MANINDER SINGH	NOT	OUT	0	-	-	-	-	12	9
	Extras	B 1 LB 9 W 1 NB 5		16						
				390						

Bowler	O	M	R	W	NB	W
RADFORD	35	3	131	2	5	
FOSTER	41	9	93	3		
PRINGLE	21	2	61	2		1
EDMONDS	24	7	55	1	1	
EMBUREY	18.5	7	40	2		

Wkt	Partnership between		Runs	Balls
1	Gavaskar	Srikkanth	53	61
2	—.—	Amarnath	5	24
3	Amarnath	Vengsarkar	81	197
4	—.—	Azharddin	89	218
5	Azharddin	Shastri	38	98
6	Shastri	Kapil Dev	9	11
7	Kapil Dev	More	27	37
8	More	Binny	68	162
9	—.—	Sharma	15	21
10	—.—	Maninder	5	16

England 390   Start: 1.54   61 overs remain July 4
Gavaskar 115 Tests ⓡ
Tea: 90-2 (28 overs) Amarnath 17* Vengsarkar 15*
Close: 182-3 (62 overs) Amarnath 59* Azharuddin 20*
                                             208 behind
New Ball: 239-4 (87 overs)
BLSP: 12.40 240-4 (87.2 overs) Lunch: 12.55 – 1.35 Rain
Resume: 2.25 16 overs deducted RSP: 2.54 258-4 (94 overs)
Resume: 3.02 3 overs deducted
Tea: 306-7 (108 overs) More 14* Binny 0*   84 behind
(4.10)

5th time Test history: Scores level on 1st innings

Inns Time: 554 minutes   139.5 overs + 6 nb

Hrs	Balls	Runs		Runs	Balls	Last 50
1	87	58		50	51	—
2	114	39		100	205	154
3	108	55		150	305	100
4	81	39		200	437	132
5	100	34		250	544	107
6	85	35		300	638	94
7	72	46		350	757	119
8	93	35		400		
9	87	44		450		
10				500		
11				550		
12				600		
13				650		

INDIA IN ENGLAND 1986

ENGLAND v INDIA   THIRD TEST   EDGBASTON   July 5/7/8 1986   ENGLAND 2nd INNS

No	Batsman	How out	Bowler	Runs	Wkt	Total	6	4	Mins	Balls
1	GOOCH	LBW	SHARMA	40	1	49	-	5	50	43
2	BENSON	B	SHASTRI	30	2	102	-	2	139	96
3	ATHEY	c MORE	SHARMA	38	4	163	-	2	171	114
4	GOWER	c GAVASKAR #	SHARMA	26	3	152	1	1	68	52
5	GATTING *	LBW	SHARMA	26	5	190	-	3	51	44
6	PRINGLE	c MORE	MANINDER	7	6	190	-	1	35	31
7	EMBUREY	NOT	OUT	27	-	-	-	2	119	110
8	FOSTER	RUN	OUT	0	7	190	-	-	4	4
9	EDMONDS	c BINNY	MANINDER	10	8	217	-	1	54	40
10	FRENCH †	c MORE	SHARMA	1	9	229	-	-	32	31
11	RADFORD	c AZHARRUDIN	SHARMA	1	10	235	-	-	16	14
Extras		B 10 LB 6 W 2 NB 11		29						

Total: 235

Bowler	O	M	R	W	NB	W
KAPIL DEV	7	1	38	-		
BINNY	16	1	41	-	5	
SHARMA	24	4	58	6	9	2
AMARNATH	2	1	2	-		
MANINDER	22	5	41	2		
SHASTRI	23	8	39	1	1	

Wkt	Partnership between		Runs	Balls
1	Gooch	Benson	49	65
2	Benson	Athey	53	130
3	Athey	Gower	50	102
4	—.—	Gatting	11	26
5	Gatting	Pringle	27	51
6	Pringle	Emburey	0	7
7	Emburey	Foster	0	10
8	—.—	Edmonds	27	91
9	—.—	French	12	68
10	—.—	Radford	6	29

Scores level on 1st innings - 390
Start due 6.50   BLSP   No further play July 5
4th Day: Lunch: 88-1 (26 overs) Benson 25* Athey 11*
Gavaskar's 100th Test catch   7th player - 1st Indian
Tea: 171-4 (54 overs) Gatting 10* Pringle 4*
• More
Close: 231-9 (90 overs) Emburey 24* Radford 1*
Sharma: 10-188   BB India v Eng in England

Inns Time: 383 minutes   94 overs + 15 nb

Hrs	Balls	Runs
1	75	51
2	92	37
3	88	36
4	85	47
5	92	26
6	114	32
7		
8		
9		
10		
11		
12		
13		

Runs	Balls	Last 50
50	66	-
100	188	122
150	292	104
200	431	139
250		
300		
350		
400		
450		
500		
550		
600		
650		

INDIA IN ENGLAND 1986

ENGLAND v INDIA   THIRD TEST   EDGBASTON   July 8 1986   INDIA 2nd INNS

No	Batsman	How out	Bowler	Runs	Wkt	Total	6	4	Mins	Balls
1	GAVASKAR	c FRENCH	FOSTER	54	4	104	-	6	159	135
2	SRIKKANTH	c PRINGLE	EDMONDS	23	1	58	-	4	81	50
3	AMARNATH	c FRENCH	EDMONDS	16	2	101	-	2	55	47
4	VENGSARKAR	c FRENCH	EDMONDS	0	3	101	-	-	5	3
5	AZHARRUDIN	NOT	OUT	29	-	-	-	2	146	106
6	SHASTRI	c EMBUREY	EDMONDS	0	5	105	-	-	5	6
7	MORE †	NOT	OUT	31	-	-	-	2	125	125
8	KAPIL DEV *									
9	BINNY	DID NOT BAT								
10	SHARMA									
11	MANINDER SINGH									
	Extras	B 1 LB 15 W 1 NB 4		21						
				174-5						

Bowler	O	M	R	W	NB	W
FOSTER	22	9	48	1	1	1
RADFORD	3	-	17	-		
PRINGLE	16	5	33	-		
EDMONDS	28	11	31	4	3	
EMBUREY	7	1	19	-		
GATTING	2	-	10	-		

Wkt	Partnership between		Runs	Balls
1	Gavaskar	Srikkanth	58	120
2	— . —	Amarnath	43	96
3	— . —	Vengsarkar	0	9
4	— . . —	Azharuddin	3	21
5	Azharuddin	Shastri	1	8
6	— . . —	More	69*	218
7				
8				
9				
10				

India need 236 to win   Start: 11.24   Min 84 overs July 8
Lunch: 65-1 (24 overs) Gavaskar 37* Amarnath 0*   171 to win
Tea: 126-5 (55 overs) Azharuddin 5* More 9*   110 to win
29 overs (min) remain   BLSP: 4.20   131-5 (60.4 overs) 105 to win
Resume: 5.09   17 overs remain + 4 balls Pringle's over
Match Drawn   Man of the Match: M.W.Gatting
Men of the Series: M.W.Gatting / D.B.Vengsarkar

Attendance: 42,750   Series Attendance: 134,109
Inns Time: 293 minutes   78 overs + 4 nb

Hrs	Balls	Runs
1	90	51
2	96	45
3	86	10
4	100	26
5		
6		
7		
8		
9		
10		
11		
12		
13		

Runs	Balls	Last 50
50	88	-
100	198	110
150	413	215
200		
250		
300		
350		
400		
450		
500		
550		
600		
650		

Test Match Averages: England v India 1986

England

Batting and Fielding	M	I	NO	HS	R	Avge	100	50	Ct/St
M.W. Gatting	3	6	2	183*	293	73.25	1	–	3
G.A. Gooch	3	6	0	114	175	29.16	1	–	5
D.I. Gower	2	4	0	49	101	25.25	–	–	2
D.R. Pringle	3	6	0	63	136	22.66	–	1	4
C.W.J. Athey	2	4	0	38	78	19.50	–	–	–
A.J. Lamb	2	4	0	39	65	16.25	–	–	2
J.E. Emburey	3	6	1	38	74	14.80	–	–	4
P.H. Edmonds	2	4	1	18	42	14.00	–	–	1
G.R. Dilley	2	4	1	10	18	6.00	–	–	1
B.N. French	2	4	0	8	22	5.50	–	–	9/–

Also batted: M.A. Benson (1 match) 21, 30; P.R. Downton (1match) 5, 29 (1ct);
R.M. Ellison (1 match) 12, 19; N.A. Foster (1 match) 17, 0; J.K. Lever (1 match)
0*, 0; N.V. Radford (1 match) 0, 1; R.T. Robinson (1 match) 35, 11; W.N. Slack (1 match)
0, 19 (1ct); C.L. Smith (1 match) 6, 28.

Bowling	O	M	R	W	Avge	Best	5wI	10wM
D.R. Pringle	126.3	31	302	13	23.33	4-73	–	–
P.H. Edmonds	85	27	178	7	25.42	4-31	–	–
J.K. Lever	53	9	166	6	27.66	4-64	–	–
G.R. Dilley	85.2	19	299	10	29.90	4-146	–	–

Also bowled: R.M. Ellison 35-11-80-1; J.E. Emburey 76.5-28-141-4; N.A. Foster
63-18-141-4; M.W. Gatting 2-0-10-0; G.A. Gooch 13-2-31-1; N.V. Radford 38-3-148-2.

India

Batting and Fielding	M	I	NO	HS	R	Avge	100	50	Ct/St
D.B. Vengsarkar	3	6	2	126*	360	90.00	2	1	1
K.S. More	3	5	2	48	156	52.00	–	–	16/–
M. Amarnath	2	4	0	79	172	43.00	–	2	3
M. Azharuddin	3	6	1	64	157	31.40	–	1	3
S.M. Gavaskar	3	6	0	54	175	29.16	–	1	3
R.M.H. Binny	3	4	0	40	81	20.25	–	–	3
Kapil Dev	3	5	1	31	81	20.25	–	–	2
K. Srikkanth	3	6	0	31	105	17.50	–	–	3
R.J. Shastri	3	6	1	32	74	14.80	–	–	2
Maninder Singh	3	4	1	6	10	3.33	–	–	1

Also batted: C. Sharma (2 matches) 2, 9; Madan Lal (1 match) 20, 22; C.S. Pandit
(1 match) 23, 17 (1ct).

Bowling	O	M	R	W	Avge	Best	5wI	10wM
Maninder Singh	114.1	4	187	12	15.58	4-26	–	–
C. Sharma	102.3	20	300	16	18.75	6-58	2	1
R.M.H. Binny	87.2	11	251	12	20.91	5-40	1	–
Kapil Dev	128.2	36	306	10	30.60	4-52	–	–
R.J. Shastri	80	24	161	5	32.20	1-5	–	–

Also bowled: M. Amarnath 11-4-20-0; Madan Lal 20.5-5-48-3.

Statistical Highlights of the Tests

1st Test, Lord's. India won their second Test in England, their first at Lord's. Kapil Dev won his first Test in 21 as captain. Vengsarkar became the first overseas player to score three Test hundreds at Lord's. (Five England players have done this.) It was his 10th hundred in his 83rd Test. He had been on 95 when India's 9th wicket fell but Maninder lasted 60 balls to add 38 and see Vengsarkar past 100. Sharma took 5 wickets for the first time in Tests. Gooch scored his 6th hundred in his 54th Test and Pringle made his highest score. After the defeat the selectors announced that Gatting would captain England in the remaining two Tests in the series.

2nd Test, Headingley. Gatting was the 10th Middlesex captain to captain England. India had won the series by lunch on the fourth day. It was their second series win in England. The last had been 1971, which had been their last anywhere in the world. Gavaskar played his 114th Test, equalling Colin Cowdrey's record. Athey, recalled to the Test side, made the highest score for England in the match – 32. Binny took 5 wickets for the first time. Kapil Dev (23) passed 1,000 runs against England in the second innings. Shastri was given out lbw although there were three fielders behind square leg, unnoticed by either umpire. Madan Lal was called up to join the Indian party from Ashton-under-Lyne. 17 wickets fell on the second day. Vengsarkar scored another hundred, this time being on 99 at the fall of the 9th wicket. Once again he was supported by Maninder. Vengsarkar had now been top scorer in all four Indian innings in the series to date, with 126 not out, 33, 61, and 102 not out.

3rd Test, Edgbaston. Gavaskar played in a record 115th Test, his 99th consecutive match, and his first innings was a record 200th. In the second innings he completed his 72nd score of fifty or more. He also caught Gower to give him his 100th Test catch, only the seventh player in the world, and the first Indian. For only the fifth time in Test history the first innings scores were level. Gatting scored his 5th Test hundred. Sharma returned his best analysis and, with 10-188 in the match, achieved the best bowling for India against England in England. England used 19 players in the series. Only once before (South Africa v England in 1895-96) had more – 20 – been used.

THE MAGAZINE THE PLAYERS READ TOO

A probe into the past, present and future

The best in words and pictures

MONTHLY THROUGHOUT THE YEAR

Take out a subscription from:
WISDEN CRICKET MONTHLY
UNIT 8, GROVE ASH, BLETCHLEY,
MILTON KEYNES MK2 2BW.
TEL: 0908 71981

Texaco Trophy

England and India each won one of the two 55-over Texaco Trophy matches played over the last week-end in May. The Texaco Trophy went to India on the faster scoring rate — with justification, for theirs was easily the more convincing of the two victories.

They won at the Oval by nine wickets with 7.4 overs to spare after bowling England out for 162. Srikkanth's wicket was lost to the first ball of their innings, but there were few moments thereafter when the partnership between Gavaskar and Azharuddin seemed likely to be broken. One of the few occurred with the score only 8, when Gavaskar gave a straightforward return catch to Dilley. The bowler missed it in his followthrough, and nothing happened subsequently to suggest that the result would have been much different if he had held it.

India, in fact, with their accurate medium pace and spin bowling, looked far better equipped for the limited-over game on a slow pitch which allowed some movement in the England innings and even took a little spin.

Though the result was different at Old Trafford two days later, the overall impression remained that India were not unworthy of their current standing as world champions at the limited-over game. England, batting second, probably had slightly the better of another slow pitch, but they were made to work very hard almost to the end before they won by 5 wickets with 7 balls to spare. India had set them a stiff task through a dashing innings by Srikkanth and a sensible and robust sixth-wicket stand of 104 between Shastri and Kapil Dev.

A third-wicket partnership of 115 between Gower and Lamb, which ended unluckily when Lamb was run out by the bowler's deflection, laid the foundation to England's reply, but Gatting and Pringle still had to fight hard against tight bowling and athletic fielding to keep England in sight of victory.

Ian Botham returns. With his first ball in the Oval Test he had the New Zealand opening batsman Bruce Edgar caught at second slip. In his second over, he had Jeff Crowe lbw, which gave him his 356th Test wicket, one more than the previous record of Dennis Lillee.

Patrick Patterson, whose 7 for 73 in the first Test on a rough pitch in Jamaica started the decline of England on their winter tour. During the English season subsequently he had only moderate success for Lancashire, taking 48 wickets at 27.27 a piece.

ABOVE: Mike Gatting in Kingston, Jamaica, on 18 February 1986, the worst day of his eventful year. Hit in the face by a bouncer from Malcolm Marshall during the first one-day international, he had to return home for an operation on his nose.

BELOW: Second Test, Port of Spain, Trinidad. The only England wicket out of 80 in the first four Tests not taken by the West Indian fast bowlers. Wilf Slack, having started for an ambitious single, is sent back by Graham Gooch and returns just too late.

Dilip Vengsarkar on the way to becoming the first overseas player to make three Test hundreds at Lord's. His 126 not out gave India a first-innings lead of 47, from which they went on to win the first Test by 5 wickets.

ABOVE: Chetan Sharma, India's fast-medium bowler and chief wicket-taker, 16 at 18.75 each.

RIGHT: David Gower on the balcony at Lord's with Graham Gooch (left) during his last Test as captain. He was relieved of the job at the end of the match.

Martin Crowe, during his fine innings of 106 for New Zealand in the drawn first Test at Lord's.

Bob Taylor on his unexpected return to the first-class scene – one of the three wicket-keepers used by England at Lord's before Bruce French recovered from an injury received while batting and took his proper place.

LEFT: Richard Hadlee, from round the wicket, ends a useful innings of 28 by Greg Thomas during the first innings of the second Test, at Trent Bridge, which New Zealand won by 8 wickets.

BELOW: Ian Botham driving during his spectacular 59 not out in the third Test at The Oval.

ABOVE: Essex, Britannic Assurance Champions, 1986. *Standing*: P.J. Pritchard, J.H. Childs, C. Gladwin, A.W. Lilley, I.L. Pont, D.R. Pringle, N.A. Foster, T.D. Topley, A.R. Border. *Seated*: D.E. East, B.R. Hardie. S. Turner, G.A. Gooch (captain), K.W.R. Fletcher, J.K. Lever, D.L. Acfield, K.R. Pont.

RIGHT: Neil Foster of Essex, the only English bowler to take 100 wickets in the 1986 season.

ABOVE: Hampshire, John Player Special League Champions, 1986. *Back row*: I. Chivers, T.C. Middleton, A. Aymes, C.A. Connor, M. O'Connor, R.J. Scott.
Middle row: C.L. Smith, K.J. Shine, P.J. Bakker, J.R. Ayling, S.J.W. Andrew, K.D. James, R.A. Smith, P. Sainsbury (coach).
Front row: C.F. Goldie, N.G. Cowley, D.R. Turner, M.C.J. Nicholas (captain), V.P. Terry, T.M. Tremlett, R.J. Parks, R.J. Maru.
Insets: M.D. Marshall, C.G. Greenidge.

LEFT: Tim Tremlett, Hampshire's all-rounder, who had much to do with their John Player success.

LEFT: Mike Gatting holds the Benson & Hedges Cup aloft after Middlesex beat Kent by 2 runs in the rain.

BELOW: Clive Radley, top scorer for Middlesex as in other finals, played a fine innings of 54 before being run out in the Benson & Hedges final at Lord's.

ABOVE: Sussex celebrate after beating Lancashire by 7 wickets in the NatWest final.

BELOW: NatWest Trophy final – the great moment of Sussex's day. Dermot Reeve (second from right), later to be named Man of the Match, is congratulated after having Clive Lloyd lbw. The former West Indies captain walks sadly away after being out fourth ball in what was expected to be his last innings at Lord's.

Phillip De Freitas, the 20-year-old Leicestershire all-rounder who burst on the scene during the 1986 season and was chosen for the winter tour.

ABOVE: James Boiling won *The Daily Telegraph* under-19 award for bowling.

LEFT: Mark Crawley, winner of *The Daily Telegraph* under-19 award for batting.

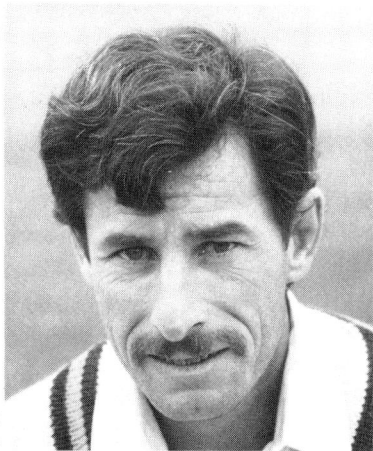

1 ◀

2 ▶

3 ▶

4 ▶

The Daily Telegraph Cricketers of the Year (see pages 19-20):
1 Joel Garner (West Indies)
2 Richard Hadlee (New Zealand)
3 Allan Border (Australia)
4 Ken McEwan (South Africa)
5 James Whitaker (England)
6 Sunil Gavaskar (India)
7 Rizwan-uz-Zaman (Pakistan)
8 Arjuna Ranatunga (Sri Lanka)

ABOVE: Denis Compton and the sweep. Read E.W. Swanton on Compton's first-class debut 50 years ago (page 21).

LEFT: Jim Laker takes the 19th wicket, Old Trafford, 1956, the victim the Australian wicket-keeper Len Maddocks. Laker's obituary is on page 242.

England v India 1st Texaco Trophy International
India won by 9 wickets
Played at Kennington Oval, London, 24 May
Toss: India. Umpires: D.R. Shepherd and A.G.T. Whitehead
Man of the Match: M. Azharuddin (Adjudicator: R.G.D. Willis)

England		Runs	Mins	Balls	6s	4s
G.A. Gooch	c Azharuddin b Sharma	30	84	52	1	1
G. Fowler	run out (Maninder/Pandit)	20	95	77	–	1
M.W. Gatting	c Kapil Dev b Shastri	27	58	58	–	1
D.I. Gower*	c Kapil Dev b Shastri	0	1	1	–	–
A.J. Lamb	c Kapil Dev b Maninder	0	8	7	–	–
D.R. Pringle	c Azharuddin b Sharma	28	85	66	–	1
P.R. Downton†	c Azharuddin b Binny	4	19	17	–	–
R.M. Ellison	c and b Binny	10	15	15	–	–
J.E. Emburey	run out (Pandit)	20	32	22	–	2
G.R. Dilley	c Pandit b Sharma	6	11	12	–	–
L.B. Taylor	not out	1	6	6	–	–
Extras	(B 1, LB 10, W 3, NB 2)	16				
	(55 overs; 216 minutes)	162				

India		Runs	Mins	Balls	6s	4s
K. Srikkanth	c Downton b Dilley	0	1	1	–	–
S.M. Gavaskar	not out	65	186	132	–	5
M. Azharuddin	not out	83	184	154	–	8
D.B. Vengsarkar	did not bat					
S.M. Patil	"					
R.J. Shastri	"					
Kapil Dev*	"					
C.S. Pandit†	"					
C.J. Sharma	"					
R.M.H. Binny	"					
Maninder Singh	"					
Extras	(LB 9, W 4, NB 2)	15				
	(47.2 overs; 186 minutes)	163-1				

India	O	M	R	W
Kapil Dev	11	1	32	0
Binny	11	2	38	2
Sharma	11	2	25	3
Maninder	11	1	31	1
Shastri	11	0	25	2

England	O	M	R	W
Dilley	11	0	53	1
Taylor	7	1	30	0
Pringle	8.2	4	20	0
Ellison	10	1	36	0
Emburey	11	2	15	0

Fall of Wickets

Wkt	E	I
1st	54	0
2nd	67	–
3rd	67	–
4th	70	–
5th	102	–
6th	115	–
7th	131	–
8th	138	–
9th	151	–
10th	162	–

England v India 2nd Texaco Trophy International
England won by 5 wickets
Played at Old Trafford, Manchester, 26 May
Toss: England. Umpires: H.D. Bird and D.J. Constant
Man of the Match: D.I. Gower (Adjudicator: F.C. Hayes)

India		Runs	Mins	Balls	6s	4s
K. Srikkanth	c Fowler b Emburey	67	108	93	–	5
S.M. Gavaskar	c Gooch b Ellison	4	6	6	–	1
M. Azharuddin	c Gower b Edmonds	7	55	39	–	–
D.B. Vengsarkar	b Emburey	29	51	46	–	2
S.M. Patil	b Dilley	12	28	27	–	1
R.J. Shastri	not out	62	102	72	–	4
Kapil Dev*	c Downton b Dilley	51	70	45	–	5
C. Sharma	not out	8	10	6	–	–
C.S. Pandit†	did not bat					
R.M.H. Binny	"					
Maninder Singh	"					
Extras	(B 5, LB 4, W 2, NB 3)	14				
	(55 overs; 222 minutes)	**254-6**				

England		Runs	Mins	Balls	6s	4s
G.A. Gooch	lbw b Kapil Dev	10	27	17	–	1
G. Fowler	c and b Binny	10	40	33	–	1
D.I. Gower*	b Binny	81	138	94	–	4
A.J. Lamb	run out (Sharma)	45	103	71	–	3
M.W. Gatting	run out (Pandit)	39	84	53	–	2
D.R. Pringle	not out	49	72	52	–	3
P.R. Downton†	not out	4	8	4	–	–
R.M. Ellison	did not bat					
P.H. Edmonds	"					
J.E. Emburey	"					
G.R. Dilley	"					
Extras	(LB 13, W 5)	18				
	(53.5 overs; 237 minutes)	**256-5**				

England	O	M	R	W
Dilley	11	2	46	2
Ellison	11	0	55	1
Pringle	11	0	49	0
Edmonds	11	1	49	1
Emburey	11	1	46	2

India	O	M	R	W
Kapil Dev	10	0	41	1
Binny	10	1	47	2
Sharma	9.5	0	49	0
Shastri	11	0	37	0
Maninder	11	0	55	0
Azharuddin	2	0	14	0

Fall of Wickets

Wkt	I	E
1st	4	18
2nd	49	27
3rd	109	142
4th	117	157
5th	130	242
6th	234	–
7th	–	–
8th	–	–
9th	–	–
10th	–	–

India won the Texaco Trophy on faster run-rate in the series.
Men of the Series Awards: D.I. Gower & R.J. Shastri

Indian Tour of England 1986

First-Class Matches: Played 11; Won 3, Lost 0, Drawn 8
All Matches: Played 19; Won 7, Lost 2, Drawn 9, No Result 1

First-Class Averages

Batting and Fielding	M	I	NO	HS	R	Avge	100	50	Ct/St
D.B. Vengsarkar	8	11	3	126*	536	67.00	2	3	3
Kapil Dev	6	9	4	115*	273	54.60	1	1	5
M. Azharuddin	10	14	3	142	596	54.18	2	3	12
M. Amarnath	9	13	3	101	473	47.30	1	2	7
R. Lamba	5	7	0	116	301	43.00	1	2	1
C.S. Pandit	6	8	2	91	252	42.00	–	3	10/–
K.S. More	7	8	2	52	228	38.00	–	1	22/1
S.M. Gavaskar	8	12	1	136*	372	33.81	1	1	5
R.J. Shastri	8	10	2	70*	220	27.50	–	2	4
C. Sharma	9	5	2	39	79	26.33	–	–	2
K. Srikkanth	9	14	0	90	344	24.57	–	1	5
S.M. Patil	6	8	0	57	188	23.50	–	2	4
R.M.H. Binny	8	9	1	64	182	22.75	–	1	6
M. Prabhakar	6	6	1	33	77	15.40	–	–	1
Maninder Singh	8	5	2	6*	16	5.33	–	–	3

Also batted: N.S. Yadav (7 matches) 13*, 9* (3ct); Madan Lal (1 match) 20, 22.

Bowling	O	M	R	W	Avge	Best	5wI	10wM
Kapil Dev	186.2	50	461	20	23.05	5-35	1	–
C. Sharma	221.3	34	736	31	23.74	6-58	2	1
Maninder Singh	257.1	71	612	21	29.14	4-26	–	–
N.S. Yadav	188.4	39	534	15	35.60	6-30	1	–
M. Prabhakar	119	25	353	9	39.22	3-42	–	–
R.M.H. Binny	182.2	29	637	16	39.81	5-40	1	–
R.J. Shastri	217	57	494	12	41.16	3-44	–	–

Also bowled: M. Amarnath 43.2-12-68-4; M. Azharuddin 20-1-68-0; R. Lamba 16-4-49-1; Madan Lal 20.5-5-48-3; C.S. Pandit 2.1-0-14-0; S.M. Patil 38-6-122-2; K. Srikkanth 20-0-91-3.

New Zealand in England

New Zealand came to England in June 1986 with their confidence higher than it had ever been before at the start of a tour of this country — and justifiably so. They had just won two three-match Test series home and away against Australia. They had in Richard Hadlee almost certainly the world's finest fast-medium bowler, and indeed all-rounder, and Hadlee, already having played for much of the season with Nottinghamshire, was known to be fit and in great form. New Zealand had at last won a Test match in England at Headingley on their previous visit in 1983, and moreover had won it without Hadlee's taking a wicket, thus scotching any idea that they were a one-man band. They could, in fact, consider that they were thoroughly well equipped all round for the task ahead; and when they arrived, they could not have helped having their confidence boosted by finding that an England team, shattered by their experience at the hands of the West Indian fast bowlers, were in the process of losing to India.

In the event, New Zealand did win 1–0, even if they were a little lucky that rain ruined the final Test when a revived England were well on top. But until then, Jeremy Coney's side had had much the better of an amicably conducted series. Coney's generous act in allowing England a probably unprecedented licence in replacing their injured wicket-keeper Bruce French during the first Test at Lord's helped towards the harmonious progress of the series, which was in marked contrast with that between India and Australia as reported a few weeks later from India. The fullness of Hadlee's length, and that of his colleagues, compared with that of most contemporary fast bowlers, made the series also a pleasant one for the spectator.

New Zealand came with a seasoned opening pair in John Wright and Bruce Edgar and, of course, an equally experienced pair of bowlers in Hadlee and Chatfield. One of the most impressive tributes to the all-round strength of the team was the way in which, after Chatfield had dropped out for a time with an injury in the middle of the tour, two young fast-medium bowlers, Watson and Stirling, rose to the occasion in support of Hadlee, bowling remarkably few loose balls to batsmen looking for something to ease a passage which was being made very difficult for them by Hadlee at the other end.

When at last the England batsmen found their stride and a good batting pitch at The Oval, Gower and Gatting, followed by Botham, launched an assault that the younger bowlers would probably not have been able to contain. But the weather was on their side and England's effort, refreshing though it was, had come too late.

Until then, New Zealand's bowling had been strengthened by the fact that their spinners, Bracewell and Gray, had posed more problems than are usually expected from visiting spinners unaccustomed to English conditions. Each took 37 wickets on the tour at under 30 apiece, good going in modern times. Bracewell bowled very straight, with excellent control and no shortage of spin. Gray's left-arm accuracy made his role at Lord's, where he bowled into the rough for a long time, especially effective.

With the subtle medium pace of Coney in support, and Martin Crowe as well when required, New Zealand had a very respectable, varied attack, which in the matches against the counties, when Hadlee was missing, was still capable of looking after itself, though not surprisingly lacking the extra penetration provided by Hadlee.

With Gray at number six, Hadlee at seven, and Bracewell capable of making a Test 100 at eight, and indeed averaging 77 in the 12 matches in which he played, the batting had far more depth than England's. It was largely through this superiority that the Trent Bridge Test was won. It did not seem to matter greatly if some of the main batsmen failed. Wright and Edgar, by their own standards, did not have a great series. Wright, however, put the memory of a 'pair' at Lord's so firmly behind him that he batted for seven hours in the last Test at the Oval for 119, an innings which, if a few hours more play had been possible, might have made all the difference between salvation and defeat for New Zealand.

Jeff Crowe played many useful innings, including the one of 66 which was mainly responsible for the win in the one-day international at Headingly. Coney has had more productive tours but was not easily dislodged. Above all, the batting had the extra class of Martin Crowe, who on almost every appearance confirmed his reputation as one of the best young batsmen in the world.

Against the counties, New Zealand, in the absence of Hadlee, had difficulty in bowling sides out twice, but usually had the better of the drawn matches. They were only once in danger of defeat, and that was excusable, for Middlesex, though not doing much in the championship, were formidable opponents to meet in the second match of the tour. Mike Gatting made 135, Middlesex mustered over 400, and on the last day the New Zealanders were facing an innings defeat. After Martin Crowe had played one of many fine innings, Gray and Smith saved the match and were not separated. Gray was revealed on the tour as a genuine all-rounder, averaging 51 with the bat while taking his 37 wickets.

Subsequent matches were not often a reliable guide to the New Zealand strength, for opponents were sometimes missing vital players and there was plenty of rain. But the tour ended with an astonishing individual performance by the youthful Rutherford in the last match of the tour at Scarborough.

Rutherford had shown occasional glimpses of his undoubted talent before arriving at Scarborough. Admittedly, the atmosphere there is not the sternest and D.B. Close's XI was not the toughest opposition, but to make 317 in 4 hours 10 minutes off 245 balls, hitting 45 fours and 8 sixes, is still an extraordinary feat. It was the second fastest 300 made in England (after C.G. Macartney's innings at Trent Bridge in 1921), the highest by a New Zealand batsman abroad, and the third highest ever by a New Zealander. It also gave notice that, though Hadlee's retirement will inevitably leave a huge gap, the New Zealand larder will not be exactly bare of talent over the next few years.

First Test, Lord's, 24, 25, 26, 28, 29 July.
Match Drawn.

Rain on the fourth afternoon spoilt a Test match that until then had been evenly balanced with perhaps a slight inclination towards New Zealand. On the last day they were the only side who could still have a realistic hope of winning, though one of Graham Gooch's best innings prevented that.

The first innings was dominated by one bowler, Richard Hadlee. Only he extracted any life from a mild pitch, and no other bowler on either side had the influence on events that he did while taking the first four wickets and gradually undermining an excellent England start. A score of 245 for 5 at the end of the first day was no springboard to better things for a side with a long tail. Edmonds, here batting at seven, had been number eleven at times in the previous series.

Next day, the innings struggled up to 307, which was temporarily made to look substantial when Dilley took the first two New Zealand wickets without either batsman scoring. But a long third-wicket stand of 210, in which Martin Crowe was always in command and Edgar, having taken 50 minutes to score his first run, emerged to find confidence and timing, lasted until after lunch on the third day, 5½ hours in all. New Zealand then declined to 342 for 9 to a combination of Edmonds's spin and some fine catching by Gatting at slip and Edmonds in the gully.

England meanwhile had been suffering casualties which had singular consequences. Willey, picked partly as a bowler, had been hit on a long-troublesome knee while batting and could not field. French, hit on the head by Hadlee, could not keep wicket and was replaced briefly by Athey; then, with permission of the New Zealand captain, by Bob Taylor who, keeping almost throughout the Crowe-Edgar partnership, showed all the old neat efficiency some years after his retirement from the first-class game; and finally by Bobby Parks of Hampshire. French reappeared for the first ball on Monday morning, which was also the last ball of the innings.

At this stage, the similarity to the Lord's Test against India in June was most marked, and there was apprehension that Hadlee might do to England's early batting on the fourth day what Kapil Dev had done then.

In fact, though Hadlee was never played easily, the main obstacle to England's progress in the second innings was the left-arm spin of Gray, bowled from over the wicket into the rough outside the right-hander's leg-stump and Gower's off-stump. At 72 for 3, only 37 ahead, England, with their long tail, seemed perilously placed. But at 110 for 3 rain ended a day's play of only 48 overs with Gooch and Gatting still there and battling hard.

On the last day, the match was not yet quite safe when Gatting lost patience with Gray towards the end of the first hour. But Gooch was not to be distracted, and, given lengthy support from Willey, he was not out until a draw had long been certain.

NEW ZEALAND IN ENGLAND 1986

ENGLAND v NEW ZEALAND   FIRST TEST   LORD'S July 24/25 1986   ENGLAND 1st INNS

No	Batsman	How out	Bowler	Runs	Wkt	Total	6	4	Mins	Balls
1	GOOCH	c SMITH	HADLEE	18	1	27	-	4	32	27
2	MOXON	LBW	HADLEE	74	3	196	-	7	246	191
3	ATHEY	c CROWE, J.J.	HADLEE	44	2	102	-	5	92	64
4	GOWER	c CROWE, M.D.	BRACEWELL	62	5	237	-	10	190	170
5	GATTING *	B	HADLEE	2	4	198	-	-	20	17
6	WILLEY	LBW	WATSON	44	7	271	-	5	136	104
7	EDMONDS	c CROWE, M.D.	HADLEE	6	6	256	-	1	47	33
8	FRENCH †	RETIRED	HURT	0	-	-	-	-	17	12
9	DILLEY	c SMITH	HADLEE	17	9	307	-	1	81	55
10	FOSTER	B	WATSON	8	8	285	-	1	21	14
11	RADFORD	NOT	OUT	12	-	-	-	1	44	36
	Extras	B 6 LB 7 W - NB 7		20						
				307						

Bowler	O	M	R	W	NB	W
HADLEE	37.5	11	80	6	9	
WATSON	30	7	70	2	1	
CROWE, M.D.	8	1	38	-		
CONEY	4	-	12	-		
BRACEWELL	26	8	65	1		
GRAY	13	9	29	-		

Wkt	Partnership between		Runs	Balls
1	Gooch	Moxon	27	50
2	Moxon	Athey	75	146
3	- . -	Gower	94	198
4	Gower	Gatting	2	35
5	- . -	Willey	39	86
6	Willey	Edmonds	19	70
7	- . -	French / Dilley	1 / 12	18 / 18
8	Dilley	Foster	14	33
9	- . -	Radford	22	69
10				

England won the toss and elected to bat
Test Debuts: M.D. MOXON, W. WATSON
Lunch: 96-1 (31 overs) Moxon 35* Athey 41* Coney inj 12.30
Tea: 195-2 (63 overs) Moxon 74* Gower 50*
New Ball: 240-5 (86.1 overs)
Close: 248-5 (93 overs) Willey 27* Edmonds 6*
2nd Day Coney still injured
French RH 0* 259-6 (99 overs) hit on head (Hadlee) 2 st.
Lunch: 295-8 (114 overs) Dilley 15* Radford 2*
Hadlee 5W/26 6th time v Eng / 3rd time 6W/Inns v Eng

Inns Time : 472 minutes   118.5 overs + 10 nb

12th Men: D.R. PRINGLE and D.A. STIRLING
Umpires: H.D. BIRD and A.G.T. WHITEHEAD

Hrs	Balls	Runs
1	92	61
2	94	34
3	102	42
4	90	58
5	97	23
6	85	30
7	79	31
8		
9		
10		
11		
12		
13		

Runs	Balls	Last 50
50	80	-
100	195	115
150	296	101
200	445	149
250	570	125
300	707	137
350		
400		
450		
500		
550		
600		
650		

NEW ZEALAND IN ENGLAND 1986

ENGLAND v NEW ZEALAND FIRST TEST LORD'S July 25/26/28 1986 NEW ZEALAND 1st INNS

No	Batsman	How out	Bowler	Runs	Wkt	Total	6	4	Mins	Balls
1	WRIGHT	B	DILLEY	0	1	2	–	–	12	10
2	EDGAR	c GATTING	GOOCH	83	3	215	–	8	357	298
3	RUTHERFORD	c GOOCH	DILLEY	0	2	5	–	–	9	9
4	CROWE, M.D.	c + b	EDMONDS	106	4	218	–	11	339	247
5	CROWE, J.J.	c GATTING	EDMONDS #	18	5	274	–	3	89	62
6	CONEY *	c GOOCH	RADFORD	51	6	292	–	6	107	83
7	GRAY	c GOWER	EDMONDS	11	7	310	–	1	30	37
8	HADLEE	B	EDMONDS	19	8	340	–	1	74	54
9	SMITH †	c EDMONDS	DILLEY	18	9	340	–	1	43	36
10	BRACEWELL	NOT	OUT	1	–	–	–	–	17	13
11	WATSON	LBW	DILLEY	1	10	342	–	–	14	10
	Extras	B 4 LB 9 W 6 NB 15		34						
				342						

® NZ v Eng

Bowler	O	M	R	W	NB	W
DILLEY	35.1	9	82	4	10	
FOSTER	25	6	56	–		3
RADFORD	25	4	71	1	6	
EDMONDS	42	10	97	4	2	
GOOCH	13	6	23	1		

Wkt	Partnership between		Runs	Balls
1	Wright	Edgar	2	16
2	Edgar	Rutherford	3	15
3	---	Crowe, M.D.	210	529
4	Crowe, M.D.	Crowe, J.J.	3	8
5	Crowe, J.J.	Coney	56	119
6	Coney	Gray	18	40
7	Gray	Hadlee	18	44
8	Hadlee	Smith	30	63
9	Smith	Bracewell	0	2
10	Bracewell	Watson	2	23

England 307 Start: 2.13 56 overs remain July 25
Athey to keep wickets / R W Taylor summoned to take over
B.S.P.: 25 5 10-2 (8.5 overs) Resume: 3.11 3 overs deducted
Tea: 30-2 (16 overs) Edgar 3* McCrowe 15* 277 behind
Close: 127-2 (53 overs) Edgar 52* McCrowe 52* 180 behind
3rd Day: R W Taylor to keep wickets until arrival R J Parks from Hampshire
B.S.P.: 11.51 163-2 (66 overs) Resume: 12.05 3 overs deducted
Parks took over (NB: Taylor no byes) at 12.50
Lunch: 193-2 (79 overs) Edgar 67* McCrowe 99* 114 behind
McCrowe 100 off 219 balls 11/4 5 fr 100
200 p/ship in 499 balls ® was 190 Congdon / Hastings (Lord's) 1973
New Ball: 233-4 (98 overs)
Tea: 272-4 (109 overs) Jerome 16* Coney 34* 35 behind
Edmonds 100th Test wicket
Close: 342-9 (140 overs) Bracewell 1* Watson 1* 35 ahead
French WK for 1 ball bowled to end innings July 28
Inns Time: 568 minutes 140.1 overs + 18 nb

Hrs	Balls	Runs
1	78	29
2	102	28
3	99	52
4	97	33
5	88	38
6	97	34
7	86	39
8	90	40
9	84	41
10		
11		
12		
13		

Runs	Balls	Last 50
50	152	–
100	249	97
150	385	136
200	511	126
250	646	135
300	743	97
350		
400		
450		
500		
550		
600		
650		

NEW ZEALAND IN ENGLAND 1986   137

ENGLAND v NEW ZEALAND   FIRST TEST   LORD'S   July 28/29 1986   ENGLAND 2nd INNS

No	Batsman	How out	Bowler	Runs	Wkt	Total	6	4	Mins	Balls
1	GOOCH	c WATSON	BRACEWELL	183	6	295	-	22	442	369
2	MOXON	LBW	HADLEE	5	1	9	-	-	19	21
3	ATHEY	B	GRAY	16	2	68	-	2	64	42
4	GOWER	B	GRAY	3	3	72	-	-	24	22
5	GATTING *	c CROWE, M.D.	GRAY	26	4	136	1	2	117	104
6	WILLEY	B	BRACEWELL	42	5	262	-	5	181	148
7	EDMONDS	NOT	OUT	9	-	-	-	2	27	23
8	FRENCH †									
9	DILLEY		DID NOT BAT							
10	FOSTER									
11	RADFORD									
	Extras	B - LB 6 W 1 NB 4		11						

295-6 dec

Bowler	O	M	R	W	NB	W
HADLEE	27	3	78	1	4	
WATSON	17	2	50	-		
GRAY	46	14	83	3		
CROWE, M.D.	4	-	13	-	1	
BRACEWELL	23+	7	57	2		1
RUTHERFORD	3	-	8	-		

Wkt	Partnership between		Runs	Balls
1	Gooch	Moxon	9	30
2	— · —	Athey	59	99
3	— · —	Gower	4	39
4	— · —	Gatting	64	203
5	— · —	Willey	126	311
6	— · —	Edmonds	33	47
7				
8				
9				
10				

NZ 1st inns lead 35   Start: 11.12   87 overs remain July 28
RSP: 12.58   72-2 (26.3 overs) Gooch 47* Gower 3*   37 ahead
Lunch taken
RSP — Resume 2.10   8 overs deducted
BLSP: 3.26   110-3 (47.5 overs) Tea taken
Gooch 64* Gatting 21*   75 ahead
No further play possible July 28
5th. Lunch: 181-4 (85 overs) Gooch 104* Willey 19*   146 ahead
Day
Gooch 100 off 234 balls 12/4 / 7th Test 100/ht v NZ/3rd at Lord's
New Ball: 186-4 (86 overs)
Gooch 150 off 337 balls 17/4
Tea: 268-5 (115 overs) Gooch 162* Edmonds 4*   233 ahead
Declaration: 4.22   260 ahead

Inns Time: 442 minutes   120.4 overs + 5 nb

Hrs	Balls	Runs
1	90	53
2	88	25
3	107	29
4	102	35
5	122	39
6	90	41
7	90	41
8		
9		
10		
11		
12		
13		

Runs	Balls	Last 50
50	87	-
100	248	161
150	417	169
200	564	147
250	661	97
300		
350		
400		
450		
500		
550		
600		
650		

138 NEW ZEALAND IN ENGLAND 1986

ENGLAND v NEW ZEALAND   FIRST TEST   LORD'S   July 29 1986   NEW ZEALAND 2nd INNS

No	Batsman	How out	Bowler	Runs	Wkt	Total	6	4	Mins	Balls
1	EDGAR	c GOWER	FOSTER	0	1	0	–	–	2	3
2	WRIGHT	c GOWER	DILLEY	0	2	8	–	–	8	3
3	RUTHERFORD	NOT	OUT	24	–	–	–	5	52	43
4	CROWE M.D.	NOT	OUT	11	–	–	–	1	46	43
5	CROWE, J.J.									
6	CONEY *									
7	GRAY		DID NOT BAT							
8	HADLEE									
9	SMITH †									
10	BRACEWELL									
11	WATSON									
	Extras	B – LB 4 W – NB 2		6						
				41-2						

Bowler	O	M	R	W	NB	W
FOSTER	3	1	13	1		
DILLEY	6	3	5	1	2	
EDMONDS	5	–	18	–		
GOWER	1	–	1	–		

Wkt	Partnership between		Runs	Balls
1	Edgar	Wright	0	3
2	Wright	Rutherford	8	6
3	Rutherford	Crowe, M.D.	33*	83
4				
5				
6				
7				
8				
9				
10				

NZ need 261 to win   25 minutes and 20 overs remain July 29

Match Drawn   Man of the Match: G.A. Gooch

Attendance: 69,184

Inns Time: 56 minutes   15 overs + 2nb

Hrs	Balls	Runs
1		.
2		
3		
4		
5		
6		
7		
8		
9		
10		
11		
12		
13		

Runs	Balls	Last 50
50		
100		
150		
200		
250		
300		
350		
400		
450		
500		
550		
600		
650		

Second Test, Trent Bridge, 7, 8, 9, 11, 12 August.
New Zealand won by 8 wickets.

England brought in two new fast bowlers in Gladstone Small and Greg Thomas, but lost what may have been an important toss. The pitch had no obviously lethal qualities, but Coney put England in and, as it proved, the best batting conditions of a match played mostly in overcast conditions fell in the second half of the New Zealand innings.

On the first day England once again struggled against Hadlee, and despite reaching 170 for 3, largely through Athey and Gower, mustered only 240 for the loss of 9 wickets, 6 to Hadlee.

Next day, still in dull weather, the England bowlers took 5 wickets for 144, but were halted by Hadlee with a mainly passive partner Gray in effective support. That evening the reply to England's 256 stood at 211 for 5, Hadlee having made 53 of the last 67 runs.

On the Saturday morning Hadlee was first missed in the slips and then caught there. This, however, merely enabled his successors to underline the depth of the New Zealand batting. On a sunny afternoon the last 4 wickets produced 171 runs, 110 of them from Bracewell, who had also made a hundred against Northants since the previous Test. This was the decisive phase of the match, not only emphasizing England's own lack of depth but producing a first innings lead of 157 for New Zealand which, if conditions deteriorated again, gave them a great chance of winning.

In the seven overs remaining on Saturday evening, they struck a considerable blow when Gooch was adjudged caught at silly point via bat and pad off Bracewell.

Hours of rain on Sunday night delayed Monday's start until 1.10, after which only 18 overs were bowled before the weather closed in again. Two more valuable wickets were taken by Hadlee and Bracewell. England, still 93 behind, clearly had a huge task to survive if there was a full day's play on the last day.

The weather on the final day was not only dry but cloudy and heavy. The ball swung, sometimes moved sharply off the pitch for Hadlee, and turned for Bracewell and Gray. The two specialist batsmen whom England had left, Gower and Gatting, each attracted a ball that turned unpredictably to find the edge. Though Embury, sweeping and dabbing in his unconventional way, made 75 out of 99, it never seemed likely that England would hold out long enough to rob New Zealand of a well deserved victory. They took 24.1 overs to make the 74 needed but, though into the last hour by then, were never pressed for time. Hadlee emerged with 10 wickets for the seventh time in a Test match, equalling a record held by Barnes, Grimmett, and Lillee. New Zealand's victory was their fourth over England in 62 Tests and only their second in England.

NEW ZEALAND IN ENGLAND 1986

ENGLAND v NEW ZEALAND   SECOND TEST   TRENT BRIDGE   August 7/8 1986   ENGLAND 1st INNS

No	Batsman	How out	Bowler	Runs	Wkt	Total	6	4	Mins	Balls
1	GOOCH	LBW	HADLEE	18	1	18	-	3	17	18
2	MOXON	B	HADLEE	9	2	43	-	1	43	28
3	ATHEY	LBW	WATSON	55	3	126	-	8	135	106
4	GOWER	LBW	GRAY	71	5	176	-	9	188	144
5	GATTING *	B	HADLEE 325	17	4	170	-	2	52	36
6	PRINGLE	c WATSON	STIRLING	21	8	205	-	3	73	64
7	EMBUREY	c SMITH	HADLEE 326	8	6	191	-	1	17	17
8	EDMONDS	c SMITH	HADLEE	0	7	191	-	-	2	2
9	THOMAS	B	HADLEE	28	9	240	-	3	75	63
10	FRENCH †	c CONEY	WATSON	21	10	256	-	2	69	48
11	SMALL	NOT	OUT	2	-	-	-	-	19	17
	Extras	B 1 LB 3 W - NB 2		6						
				256						

Bowler	O	M	R	W	NB	W
HADLEE	32	7	80	6	2	
STIRLING	17	3	62	1	2	
GRAY	13	4	30	1		
WATSON	16.5	6	51	2		
CONEY	7	1	18	-		
BRACEWELL	4	1	11	-		

Wkt	Partnership between		Runs	Balls
1	Gooch	Moxon	18	27
2	Moxon	Athey	25	37
3	Athey	Gower	83	169
4	Gower	Gatting	44	82
5	—.—	Pringle	6	40
6	Pringle	Emburey	15	30
7	—.—	Edmonds	0	2
8	—.—	Thomas	14	47
9	Thomas	French	35	78
10	French	Small	16	31

New Zealand won the toss and elected to field
Test Debut: G.C. SMALL
Lunch: 102-2 (30 overs) Athey 42* Gower 29*
RSP: 3.19   172-4 (55 overs) Gower 67* Pringle 2*   Tea taken
1 over deducted
BLSP: 5.39   240-9 (84.4 overs) French 7* Small 0*
No further play August 7
2nd Day: New Ball: 246-9 (86 overs)
Hadlee SW/27 ® / 7th time v Eng / 6w v Eng 4th time

Inns Time: 353 minutes   89.5 overs + 4 nb
12th Men: P. WILLEY and K.R. RUTHERFORD
Umpires: D.J. CONSTANT and K.E. PALMER

Hrs	Balls	Runs	Runs	Balls	Last 50
1	87	52	50	84	-
2	93	50	100	166	82
3	90	40	150	282	116
4	90	45	200	421	138
5	87	35	250	537	116
6			300		
7			350		
8			400		
9			450		
10			500		
11			550		
12			600		
13			650		

NEW ZEALAND IN ENGLAND 1986

ENGLAND v NEW ZEALAND   SECOND TEST   TRENT BRIDGE   August 8/9 1986   NEW ZEALAND 1st INNS

No	Batsman	How out	Bowler	Runs	Wkt	Total	6	4	Mins	Balls
1	WRIGHT	c ATHEY	SMALL	58	2	85	1	7	129	107
2	EDGAR	LBW	THOMAS	8	1	39	-	-	65	46
3	CROWE, J.J.	c FRENCH	SMALL	23	3	92	-	3	70	65
4	CROWE, M.D.	c EDMONDS	EMBUREY	28	5	144	-	2	82	65
5	CONEY *	RUN	OUT	24	4	142	-	3	69	52
6	GRAY	c ATHEY	EDMONDS	50	7	318	-	3	301	238
7	HADLEE	c GOOCH	THOMAS	68	6	239	-	8	167	132
8	BRACEWELL	c MOXON	EMBUREY	110	10	413	-	10	270	200
9	SMITH †	LBW	EDMONDS	2	8	326	-	-	10	14
10	STIRLING	B	SMALL	26	9	391	2	1	98	79
11	WATSON	NOT	OUT	8	-	-	-	1	30	23
	Extras	B 1 LB 4 W 2 NB 2		8						
				413						

Bowler	O	M	R	W	NB	W
SMALL	38	12	88	3	2	1
THOMAS	39	5	124	2		1
PRINGLE	20	1	58	-		
EDMONDS	28	11	52	2		
EMBUREY	42.5	17	87	2		
GOOCH	2	2	-	-		

Wkt	Partnership between		Runs	Balls
1	Wright	Edgar	39	97
2	—.—	Crowe, J.J.	46	114
3	Crowe, J.J.	Crowe, M.D.	7	9
4	Crowe, M.D.	Coney	50	107
5	—.—	Gray	2	15
6	Gray	Hadlee	95	268
7	—.—	Bracewell	79	184
8	Bracewell	Smith	8	20
9	—.—	Stirling	65	164
10	—.—	Watson	22	43

England 256   Start: 11.29   83 overs remain August 8
Lunch: 51-1 (24 overs) Wright 39* J Crowe 3*   205 behind
Tea: 142-4 (52.4 overs) M Crowe 27*   114 behind
• Small/Emburey
Close: 211-5 (89 overs) Gray 14* Hadlee 53*   45 behind
2nd Day: New Ball: 212-5 (90 overs)
Lunch: 278-6 (118 overs) Gray 34* Bracewell 29*   22 ahead
Tea: 352-8 (148 overs) Bracewell 68* Stirling 15*   96 ahead
Bracewell 100 off 194 balls 9/4 1st Test 100

Inns Time: 653 minutes   169.5 overs + 2nb

Hrs	Balls	Runs
1	90	38
2	102	25
3	88	59
4	107	34
5	97	45
6	91	24
7	78	31
8	99	43
9	84	31
10	100	44
11		
12		
13		

Runs	Balls	Last 50
50	124	-
100	246	122
150	368	122
200	479	111
250	639	160
300	761	122
350	865	104
400	1010	145
450		
500		
550		
600		
650		

142 NEW ZEALAND IN ENGLAND 1986

ENGLAND v NEW ZEALAND   SECOND TEST   TRENT BRIDGE   August 9/11/12 1986   ENGLAND 2nd INNS

No	Batsman	How out	Bowler	Runs	Wkt	Total	6	4	Mins	Balls
1	GOOCH	c CONEY	BRACEWELL	17	1	23	-	3	23	20
2	MOXON	c SMITH	HADLEE	23	2	47	-	3	59	40
3	EDMONDS	LBW	HADLEE	20	4	87	-	1	111	80
4	ATHEY	c SMITH #	BRACEWELL	6	3	63	-	-	39	34
5	GOWER	CROWE, J.J.	BRACEWELL	26	6	104	-	4	76	64
6	GATTING *	c SMITH	GRAY	4	5	98	-	1	27	24
7	PRINGLE	c GRAY	STIRLING	9	7	178	-	-	106	92
8	EMBUREY	c CROWE, M.D.	HADLEE	75	8	203	-	8	131	136
9	THOMAS	c GRAY	STIRLING	10	9	203	1	-	35	30
10	FRENCH †	NOT	OUT	12	-	-	-	2	38	30
11	SMALL	LBW	HADLEE	12	10	230	-	2	33	24
	Extras	B 4 LB 9 W 1 NB 2		16						
						230				

Bowler	O	M	R	W	NB	W
HADLEE	33.1	15	60	4	1	
STIRLING	18	5	48	2	2	
BRACEWELL	11	5	29	3		
WATSON	9	3	25	-		1
GRAY	24	9	55	1		

Wkt	Partnership between		Runs	Balls
1	Gooch	Moxon	23	35
2	Moxon	Edmonds	24	51
3	Edmonds	Athey	16	64
4	---	Gower	24	50
5	Gower	Gatting	11	55
6	---	Pringle	6	16
7	Pringle	Emburey	74	187
8	Emburey	Thomas	25	60
9	Thomas	French	0	3
10	French	Small	27	53

NZ lead 157 on 1st inns   Start 5.40   7 overs remain August 9
Close: 31-1 (7 overs) Moxon 14* Edmonds 0*   126 behind
4th Day: RSP until 1.10   22 overs deducted   (Early lunch)
BLSP: 2.25   64-3 (25.2 overs) Edmonds 13* Gower 0*   93 behind
No further play August 11
5th Day: Lunch: 134-6 (61 overs) Pringle 3* Emburey 26* 23 behind
New Ball: 203-7 (85 overs)
Hadlee 10wM/7 = ® 1st time v Eng
97 dismissals = NZ ®
Edgar injured left thumb fielding 4th ball August 12 - 3 stitches
Inns Time: 349 minutes   95.1 overs + 3nb

Hrs	Balls	Runs
1	86	47
2	88	26
3	97	31
4	126	47
5	104	46
6		
7		
8		
9		
10		
11		
12		
13		

Runs	Balls	Last 50
50	109	✓
100	260	151
150	397	137
200	513	116
250		
300		
350		
400		
450		
500		
550		
600		
650		

ENGLAND v NEW ZEALAND SECOND TEST   TRENT BRIDGE August 12 1986 NEW ZEALAND 2nd INNS

No	Batsman	How out	Bowler	Runs	Wkt	Total	6	4	Mins	Balls
1	WRIGHT	B	EMBUREY	7	2	19	-	1	44	32
2	CROWE, J.J.	LBW	SMALL	2	1	5	-	-	19	13
3	CROWE, M.D.	NOT	OUT	48	-	-	-	8	77	52
4	CONEY *	NOT	OUT	20	-	-	-	1	52	48
5	GRAY									
6	HADLEE									
7	BRACEWELL	DID NOT BAT								
8	SMITH †									
9	STIRLING									
10	WATSON									
11	EDGAR									
	Extras	B -	LB - W - NB -	0						

77-2

Bowler	O	M	R	W	NB	W
SMALL	8	3	10	1		
THOMAS	4	-	16	-		
EMBUREY	6	1	15	1		
EDMONDS	4	1	16	-		
PRINGLE	2	-	16	-		
GOWER *	-	-	4	-	1	

* no-ball

Wkt	Partnership between		Runs	Balls
1	Wright	Crowe, J.J.	5	25
2	- . -	Crowe, M.D.	14	33
3	Crowe, M.D.	Coney	58*	87
4				
5				
6				
7				
8				
9				
10				

NZ need 74 to win   Start: 4.06   54 minutes + 20 overs remain August 12
Edgar unable to bat

New Zealand won by 8 wickets   Man of the Match: R.J. Hadlee

New Zealand won £6,000   Attendance: 34,495
Inns Time: 98 minutes   24 overs + 1 no-ball

Hrs	Balls	Runs
1	79	34
2		
3		
4		
5		
6		
7		
8		
9		
10		
11		
12		
13		

Runs	Balls	Last 50
50	101	✓
100		
150		
200		
250		
300		
350		
400		
450		
500		
550		
600		
650		

Third Test, The Oval, 21, 22, 23, 25, 26 August.
Match Drawn.

Two days before the start of the third Test it was clear from every forecast that the match would be subjected to appalling weather conditions, so expectations of a finish were never high. The draw, however, had its compensations for both sides. It gave New Zealand their first win in a series in England and a thoroughly well deserved one. It gave England a badly needed boost at a time when they must have been facing the winter's series in Australia with confidence at rock bottom.

As far as the England batsmen were concerned, this was simply the result of having, for once, a pitch with a consistent bounce, though after Gatting had chosen to field, the New Zealand batsmen made heavy work of batting on the first day when they scored only 142 for 4 in 58 overs. Three of their wickets fell to Botham on his return to Test cricket, the first of them to his first ball, a short one off which Edgar was caught at second slip. Only John Wright established himself, and he, in what with better weather could have been a match-saving innings for his side, found the accurate spin of Emburey and Edmonds so inhibiting that they bowled 53 overs for 68 runs.

On the second day, New Zealand moved on to 257 for 8 in another 59 overs, by which time Wright's seven-hour innings was over. The third day was fine, and though Dilley and Botham bowled for nearly an hour before Dilley finished the New Zealand innings, England's stock was about to rise again.

They did not begin their innings particularly well, for Athey, Gooch, and Lamb were out for 63. But the exhibition of batting which followed was a joyous sight for English eyes, a stirring display of bold strokes, which gained in confidence and momentum. In 55 overs, Gower and Gatting added 219 at a run a minute and were still undefeated at the close of the third day, when England were only 6 runs behind New Zealand's 287.

The weather forecast for the Monday allowed no hope at all anywhere in the country, but play was able to start on time and it lasted for a highly significant period of 65 minutes.

Gower, resuming at 129 after one of his most handsome innings, was out almost at once, but Gatting continued in a vein hard to over-praise. He knew that there was no time to lose before the storm broke and, ignoring the proximity of his own 100, he sailed into the attack from the start. In 25 minutes with Botham he made 35 out of 41, and England's lead grew rapidly. He gave Botham time to look at the bowling, and when he was out, Botham with his massive straight driving, struck Stirling for 24 in an over. When the rain came, he had made 59 in 38 deliveries, mostly against the new ball.

In 14.5 overs that morning England had added 107 runs, but it was all in vain. No more play was possible that day and on the last day the weather allowed only six balls to be bowled.

NEW ZEALAND IN ENGLAND 1986

ENGLAND v NEW ZEALAND THIRD TEST OVAL August 21/22/23 1986   NEW ZEALAND 1st INNS

No	Batsman	How out	Bowler	Runs	Wkt	Total	6	4	Mins	Balls
1	WRIGHT	B	EDMONDS	119	8	251	-	9	428	343
2	EDGAR	c GOOCH	BOTHAM 355	1	1	17	-	-	40	21
3	CROWE, J.J.	LBW	BOTHAM (B) 356	8	2	31	-	2	13	11
4	CROWE, M.D.	LBW	DILLEY	13	3	59	-	-	60	38
5	CONEY *	c GOOCH	BOTHAM	38	4	106	1	4	57	39
6	GRAY	B	DILLEY	30	5	175	-	2	122	95
7	HADLEE	c FRENCH	EDMONDS	6	6	192	-	-	19	13
8	BRACEWELL	c ATHEY	EMBUREY	3	7	197	-	-	14	13
9	BLAIN †	c GOOCH	DILLEY	37	9	280	-	3	154	141
10	STIRLING	NOT	OUT	18	-	-	-	2	72	54
11	CHATFIELD	c FRENCH	DILLEY	5	10	287	-	-	9	10
	Extras	B 1 LB - W 1 NB 7		9						
				287						

Bowler	O	M	R	W	NB	W
DILLEY	28.2	4	92	4	8	
SMALL	18	5	36	-		1
BOTHAM	25	4	75	3		
EMBUREY	31	15	39	1		
EDMONDS	22	10	29	2		
GOOCH	4	1	15	-		

Wkt	Partnership between		Runs	Balls
1	Wright	Edgar	17	57
2	— · —	Crowe, J.J.	14	17
3	— · —	Crowe, M.D.	28	94
4	— · —	Coney	47	74
5	— · —	Gray	69	201
6	— · —	Hadlee	17	31
7	— · —	Bracewell	5	27
8	— · —	Blain	54	160
9	Blain	Stirling	29	104
10	Stirling	Chatfield	7	13

England won the toss and elected to field   50th Cornhill Test
Test Debut : T.E.BLAIN
RSP until 11.35 8 overs deducted
Lunch : 35-2 (20 overs) Wright 24* McCrowe 1*
Tea : 119-4 (47 overs) Wright 48* Gray 7*
BLSP until 4.05 1 over deducted
BLSP 4.35 142-4 (58 overs) Wright 63* Gray 15*
No further play August 21
2nd Day : Lunch : 209-7 (89 overs) Wright 93* Blain 10*   New Ball taken
Wright 100 off 289 balls 7/4 5h 100
RSP : 2.28 - 4.50, then 5.00   BLSP : 5.50 257-8 (117 overs) Blain 27* Stirling 5*
No further play August 22
Inns Time : 502 minutes   128.2 overs + 8 nb
12th men : P.WILLEY and W.WATSON
Umpires : H.D.BIRD and D.R.SHEPHERD

Hrs	Balls	Runs
1	80	31
2	93	30
3	72	45
4	112	37
5	87	32
6	102	41
7	102	34
8	103	22
9		
10		
11		
12		
13		

Runs	Balls	Last 50
50	148	-
100	233	85
150	391	158
200	505	114
250	634	129
300		
350		
400		
450		
500		
550		
600		
650		

146 NEW ZEALAND IN ENGLAND 1986

ENGLAND v NEW ZEALAND THIRD TEST OVAL August 23/25 1986 ENGLAND 1st INNS

No	Batsman	How out	Bowler	Runs	Wkt	Total	6	4	Mins	Balls
1	GOOCH	c STIRLING	HADLEE	32	2	62	-	4	86	67
2	ATHEY	LBW	HADLEE	17	1	38	-	3	44	32
3	GOWER	B	CHATFIELD	131	4	285	-	14	281	202
4	LAMB	B	CHATFIELD	0	3	62	-	-	4	5
5	GATTING *	B	CHATFIELD	121	5	326	-	13	259	198
6	BOTHAM	NOT	OUT	59	-	-	2	8	55	36
7	EMBUREY	NOT	OUT	9	-	-	-	1	29	10
8	EDMONDS									
9	FRENCH †	DID NOT BAT								
10	DILLEY									
11	SMALL									
	Extras	B - LB 9 W 5 NB 5		19						

388 - 5 dec

Bowler	O	M	R	W	NB	W
HADLEE	23.5	6	92	2	1	2
STIRLING	9	-	71	-	4	
CHATFIELD	21	7	73	3		
GRAY	21	4	74	-		
BRACEWELL	11	1	51	-		
CONEY	5	-	18	-		

Wkt	Partnership between		Runs	Balls
1	Gooch	Athey	38	63
2	— · —	Gower	24	58
3	Gower	Lamb	0	6
4	— · —	Gatting	223	350
5	Gatting	Botham	41	38
6	Botham	Emburey	62*	35
7				
8				
9				
10				

NZ 287   Start: 12.01   76 overs remain August 23
Lunch: 45-1 (14 overs) Gooch 24* Gower 1*   242 behind
Tea: 134-3 (42 overs) Gower 60* Gatting 16*   153 behind
Gower 64 past Viswanath (60 80)
Close: 281-3 (76 overs) Gower 129* Gatting 86*   6 behind
Gower 100 off 147 balls 12/4 13th 100
200 partnership in 298 balls
4th Day: New Ball: 332-5 (85.3 overs) Gatting 100 off 175 balls 10/4 6th 100
BLSP: 12.07 No further play August 25
Stirling 9th over to Botham: 4,6,4,6,0,4
Declaration August 25 at overnight score

Inns Time: 384 minutes   90.5 overs + 5 nb

Hrs	Balls	Runs
1	83	44
2	82	39
3	85	50
4	88	62
5	93	69
6	90	71
7		
8		
9		
10		
11		
12		
13		

Runs	Balls	Last 50
50	105	-
100	194	89
150	273	79
200	343	70
250	409	66
300	486	77
350	534	48
400		
450		
500		
550		
600		
650		

NEW ZEALAND IN ENGLAND 1986

ENGLAND v NEW ZEALAND THIRD TEST OVAL August 26 1986 NEW ZEALAND 2nd INNS

No	Batsman	How out	Bowler	Runs	Wkt	Total	6	4	Mins	Balls
1	WRIGHT	NOT	OUT	7	-	-	-	1	8	4
2	EDGAR	NOT	OUT	0	-	-	-	-	8	2
3	CROWE, J.J.									
4	CROWE, M.D.									
5	CONEY *		DID NOT BAT							
6	GRAY									
7	HADLEE									
8	BRACEWELL									
9	BLAIN †									
10	STIRLING									
11	CHATFIELD									
	Extras	B - LB - W - NB -		0						

7 - 0

Bowler	O	M	R	W	NB	W
BOTHAM	1	-	7	-		

Wkt	Partnership between	Runs	Balls
1	Wright Edgar	7*	6
2			
3			
4			
5			
6			
7			
8			
9			
10			

Eng lead 101 on 1st inns Start: 2.40 45 overs remain August 26
RSP: 2.43 0.3 overs Wright 4* Edgar 0*
Resume: 3.05 RSP: 3.10 7-0 (1 over) Wright 7* Edgar 0*
No further play possible
14 hours 20 minutes of scheduled 30 hours
Match Drawn Man of the Match: J.G. Wright
Men of the Series: D.I. Gower / R.J. Hadlee

Attendance: 47,434   Series Attendance: 151,113

Inns Time: 8 minutes   1 over

Hrs	Balls	Runs
1	.	
2		
3		
4		
5		
6		
7		
8		
9		
10		
11		
12		
13		

Runs	Balls	Last 50
50		
100		
150		
200		
250		
300		
350		
400		
450		
500		
550		
600		
650		

THE CLUB CRICKETER Magazine

YOU DON'T HAVE TO PLAY FOR ENGLAND TO BE .... IN OUR COVERS

Club Cricketer is *the* monthly magazine for the grass roots of our game. Full coverage of leagues, KOs, indoor, womens, university and schools cricket. Plus, all aspects of club management, from secretary to groundsman and not forgetting umpires and scorers.

Now Club Cricketer is the official journal for the N.C.A.

Regular editorial features include, letters and news, Player Profiles, Umpires Corner, Hall of Fame, Grounds for Pleasure and Tales from the Clubhouse. In addition we have regular updates on coaching, league management, sponsorship, equipment, booklist, accounts, travel and clothing. In other words — something the complete club cricket scene cannot be without.

Order your subscription now. Yearly rates for UK, Eire and BFPO are £12.00, overseas, £21.00, and special club subscription (5 copies per issue with entry into Club Cricketer's national awards scheme) is £50.00

Make your cheque/PO payable to:

**The Club Cricketer (Subscriptions),
3 Bloemfontein Avenue,
LONDON W12 7BH**

Test Match Averages: England v New Zealand 1986

England

Batting and Fielding	M	I	NO	HS	R	Avge	100	50	Ct/St
D.I. Gower	3	5	0	131	293	58.60	1	2	3
G.A. Gooch	3	5	0	183	268	53.60	1	–	6
J.E. Emburey	2	3	1	75	92	46.00	–	1	–
M.W. Gatting	3	5	0	121	170	34.00	1	–	2
B.N. French	3	3	2	21	33	33.00	–	–	3/–
M.D. Moxon	2	4	0	74	111	25.75	–	1	1
C.W.J. Athey	3	5	0	55	138	27.60	–	1	3
P.H. Edmonds	3	4	1	20	35	11.66	–	–	3

Also batted: G.R. Dilley (2 matches) 17; G.C. Small (2 matches) 2*, 12; I.T. Botham (1 match) 59*; N.A. Foster (1 match) 8; A.J. Lamb (1 match) 0; D.R. Pringle (1 match) 21, 9; N.V. Radford (1 match) 12*; J.G. Thomas (1 match) 28, 10; P. Willey (1 match) 44, 42.

Bowling	O	M	R	W	Avge	Best	5wI	10wM
G.R. Dilley	69.3	16	179	9	19.88	4-82	–	–
P.H. Edmonds	101	32	212	8	26.50	4-97	–	–

Also bowled: I.T. Botham 26-4-82-3; J.E. Emburey 79.5-33-141-4; N.A. Foster 28-7-69-1; G.A. Gooch 19-9-38-1; D.I. Gower 1-0-2-0; D.R. Pringle 22-1-74-0; N.V. Radford 25-4-71-1; G.C. Small 64-20-134-4; J.G. Thomas 43-5-140-2.

New Zealand

Batting and Fielding	M	I	NO	HS	R	Avge	100	50	Ct/St
M.D. Crowe	3	5	2	106	206	68.66	1	–	4
J.G. Bracewell	3	3	1	110	114	57.00	1	–	–
J.V. Coney	3	4	1	51	133	44.33	–	1	2
J.G. Wright	3	6	1	119	191	38.20	1	1	–
R.J. Hadlee	3	3	0	68	93	31.00	–	1	–
E.J. Gray	3	3	0	50	91	30.33	–	1	2
B.A. Edgar	3	5	1	83	92	23.00	–	1	–
J.J. Crowe	3	4	0	23	51	12.75	–	–	2

Also batted: I.D.S. Smith (2 matches) 18, 2 (7ct/0st); D.A. Stirling (2 matches) 26, 18* (1ct); W. Watson (2 matches) 1, 8* (2ct); T.E. Blain (1 match) 37; E.J. Chatfield (1 match) 5; K.R. Rutherford (1 match) 0, 24*.

Bowling	O	M	R	W	Avge	Best	5wI	10wM
R.J. Hadlee	153.5	42	390	19	20.52	6-80	2	1
J.G. Bracewell	75.4	22	213	6	35.50	3-29	–	–
E.J. Gray	117	40	271	5	54.20	3-83	–	–

Also bowled: E.J. Chatfield 21-7-73-3; J.V. Coney 16-1-48-0; M.D. Crowe 12-1-51-0; K.R. Rutherford 3-0-8-0; D.A. Stirling 44-8-181-3; W. Watson 72.5-18-196-4.

The Cricketer
INTERNATIONAL

more depth . . . more variety . . . more antiquity and more topicality than any other cricket magazine

Founded by Sir Pelham Warner in 1921.
Edited by Christopher Martin-Jenkins in 1986.

To open a subscription for 12 months, please fill in below or transfer details to a letter or postcard.

SUBSCRIPTION FORM: Only £13.85 for 12 issues (two of which are the extra large annuals) to join the regular readers of the world's largest selling cricket magazine.

PLEASE OPEN A SUBSCRIPTION (tick appropriate box)

THE CRICKETER (One-year subscriptions): Inland, Ireland, Channel Islands BFPO £13.85 ☐
Airmail £24.00 ☐ Overseas surface mail £14.85 ☐

*For subscriptions to the following countries please send; sterling as above or **Surface mail:** USA $25.04, Canada $31.22, Australia $32.65, New Zealand $39.46, Holland 67.83 guilders, Eire IR £18.26.*
Airmail: *USA $43.02, Canada $49.25, Australia $51.50, New Zealand $62.25, Holland 107 guilders.*

THE CRICKETER QUARTERLY FACTS AND FIGURES: Inland, Ireland, Channel Islands BFPO £5.90 ☐ Airmail £8.70 ☐ Overseas surface mail £5.90 ☐

*For subscriptions to the following countries please send; sterling as above or **Surface mail:** USA $10.69, Canada $13.59, Australia $14.21, New Zealand $17.18, Holland 29.53 guilders, Eire IR £8.48.*
Airmail: *USA $15.85, Canada $19.10, Australia $19.98, New Zealand $24.15, Holland 41.51 guilders (No Air Mail for Eire).*

IF THIS FORM IS USED TO RENEW AN EXISTING SUBSCRIPTION PLEASE TICK HERE ☐ AND QUOTE COMPUTER NUMBER IF KNOWN. SUBSCRIPTIONS ACCEPTED FOR ONE-YEAR PERIODS ONLY.

Name ....

Address ....

....

....

I enclose my remittance for £ ....

Payable to THE CRICKETER LTD, Beech Hanger, Ashurst, Tunbridge Wells, Kent TN3 9ST.

T

NEW ZEALAND IN ENGLAND 1986

Statistical Highlights of the Tests

1st Test, Lord's. Edmonds took his 100th wicket in his 39th Test when he dismissed Jeff Crowe. He is the second Middlesex bowler to achieve this feat. Hadlee took five wickets for the 26th time, once again coming level with Botham's record. Martin Crowe's 5th Test hundred formed the basis of a record 210 for the 3rd wicket against England with Edgar. Gooch's 7th hundred was his third at Lord's and the highest score for England against New Zealand at that ground. Wright got his first Test 'pair'. One of the more unusual features of this match was that England used four wicket-keepers and three substitute fielders!

2nd Test, Trent Bridge. New Zealand recorded their second Test win in England, whereas England lost their eighth match in the last 10, during which they failed to achieve first innings lead. Gower passed 6,000 runs in his 85th Test, the 6th England player and 16th in the world. Hadlee took five wickets for the 27th time, to head the table alone. He also took 10 in the match for the 7th time, only the fourth bowler to do this, his 10-140 being the best bowling for New Zealand in a Test in England. During the match he passed Willis (325) and ended with 332, third in the world ranking. Smith created a new national record for wicket-keepers, passing the late Ken Wadsworth's haul of 92ct/4st. Bracewell scored his maiden Test hundred, assisted by Stirling for 98 minutes and Watson for half-an-hour. Five other players – Athey, Embury, Gray, Stirling, and Watson – all made their highest Test scores. Only 18 overs were possible on the fourth day. Gower bowled the last ball of the match and was no-balled for throwing.

3rd Test, Kennington Oval. This was the 50th Test sponsored by Cornhill Insurance, who presented commemorative medallions to the players and officials. New Zealand took the series after the match was drawn, almost 16 hours' play being lost to rain and bad light. Botham took the wicket of Edgar with his first ball on his Test recall. This enabled him to equal Lillie (355) at the head of the table. Eleven balls later Jeff Crowe became number 356, and the world record was Botham's alone. Wright scored his 5th hundred in his 49th Test and it was the highest score for New Zealand against England at The Oval. Gower, in his turn, scored his 13th hundred in his 86th Test. The hundred took only 147 balls, curiously being his first first-class hundred of the season. Gatting's 6th hundred came up in 175 balls, and together they put on a record 4th-wicket stand against New Zealand of 223. Botham's 59 not out came off 34 balls, his fifty off just 32. All but 12 of the runs came off the second new ball. Stirling suffered 4,6,4,6,0,4 to find his way into the record books with 24 hit off one over. Rain stopped play five balls later at 12.07 on the fourth day and only one over was possible on the fifth day.

Texaco Trophy

The second Texaco Trophy series of the season closely followed the pattern of the first. England, having lost the first match, won the second at Old Trafford, but lost the two-match series on overall scoring rate.

New Zealand's win at Headingley by 47 runs was helped by wayward England running between wickets, for though the relaid pitch was not entirely consistent, their score of 217 for 8, reached after a long struggle from 54 for 4, scarcely seemed enough. New Zealand owed much to Jeff Crowe's 66, but England seemed to have acquitted themselves reasonably well in the field.

After an opening stand of 38, however, England's innings was undermined by the accuracy of Hadlee, Bracewell, and Coney, by agile fielding, and by three run-outs in ech of which one partner was left stranded by a failure in communication.

At Old Trafford two days later, however, it was England's performance in the field that provoked criticism, not least from the crowd at the end of New Zealand's innings. England had conceded 126 runs in the last 10 overs, 71 in the last 4, and 26 in the last over bowled by Gooch, hitherto the most economical bowler. The criticism ignored three things: one was that England had injuries to six players, which interfered with their throwing and mobility in the field; another was that a high-class player in Martin Crowe at his best was well established to attack in the final overs with one of the great modern strikers of the ball in Richard Hadlee; a third was that this, for once, was a superb batting pitch.

To their great credit, Gooch and Athey played from the start as if recognizing that the scoring of 285 was within England's scope, and when Gooch was out at 193 in the 35th over they were well in advance of the required rate. New batsmen coming in naturally found slightly more difficulty in maintaining the pace, but Athey, having passed 100 out of 198 in 138 minutes off 116 balls, stayed sensibly in control and finished the match with three fours off Bracewell in the 54th over.

England v New Zealand 1st Texaco Trophy International
New Zealand won by 47 runs
Played at Headingley, Leeds, 16 July
Toss: New Zealand. Umpires: J. Birkenshaw and B.J. Meyer
Man of the Match: J.J. Crowe (Adjudicator: D.B. Close)

New Zealand		Runs	Mins	Balls	6s	4s
B.A. Edgar	lbw b Foster	0	16	11	–	–
J.G. Wright	c Richards b Ellison	21	83	55	–	2
K.R. Rutherford	b Ellison	11	38	32	–	–
M.D. Crowe	b Ellison	9	16	16	–	2
J.V. Coney*	run out (Gatting)	27	61	54	–	3
J.J. Crowe	c and b Foster	66	97	94	–	7
R.J. Hadlee	lbw b Dilley	11	20	15	–	1
E.J. Gray	not out	30	57	34	–	2
I.D.S. Smith†	run out (Lamb/Richards)	4	16	9	–	–
J.G. Bracewell	not out	10	16	13	–	–
E.J. Chatfield	did not bat					
Extras	(LB 18, W 7, NB 3)	28				
	(55 overs; 216 minutes)	**217-8**				

England		Runs	Mins	Balls	6s	4s
G.A. Gooch	b Hadlee	18	45	37	–	4
M.R. Benson	c Chatfield b Bracewell	24	67	58	–	3
D.I. Gower	b Coney	18	52	38	–	1
A.J. Lamb	run out (Bracewell/Gray)	33	40	45	–	5
M.W. Gatting*	b Gray	19	43	27	1	1
D.R. Pringle	c Rutherford b Gray	28	58	42	–	2
C.J. Richards†	run out (J. Crowe/Bracewell)	8	9	11	–	1
J.E. Emburey	lbw b Bracewell	0	1	2	–	–
R.M. Ellison	run out (Rutherford/Bracewell)	12	16	12	1	–
N.A. Foster	b Hadlee	5	15	11	–	–
G.R. Dilley	not out	2	10	8	–	–
Extras	(LB 1, W 2)	3				
	(48.2 overs; 183 minutes)	**170**				

England	O	M	R	W
Dilley	11	1	37	1
Foster	9	1	27	2
Pringle	9	0	42	0
Ellison	11	1	43	3
Emburey	11	0	30	0
Gooch	4	0	20	0

New Zealand	O	M	R	W
Hadlee	9.2	0	29	2
Chatfield	8	2	24	0
Bracewell	11	2	27	2
Crowe, M.D.	4	0	15	0
Gray	11	1	55	2
Coney	5	0	19	1

Fall of Wickets

Wkt	NZ	E
1st	9	38
2nd	36	48
3rd	48	83
4th	54	103
5th	112	131
6th	138	143
7th	165	144
8th	187	162
9th	–	165
10th	–	170

England v New Zealand 2nd Texaco Trophy International
England won by 6 wickets
Played at Old Trafford, Manchester, 18 July
Toss: England. Umpires: K.E. Palmer and N.T. Plews
Man of the Match: C.W.J. Athey (Adjudicator: D. Lloyd)

New Zealand		Runs	Mins	Balls	6s	4s
J.G. Wright	c Pringle b Emburey	39	100	71	–	3
B.A. Edgar	lbw b Dilley	5	12	10	–	–
K.R. Rutherford	b Edmonds	63	118	111	–	5
M.D. Crowe	not out	93	106	74	2	11
J.V. Coney*	run out (Gatting/Richards)	1	5	5	–	–
J.J. Crowe	b Pringle	48	60	55	–	4
R.J. Hadlee	not out	18	10	6	1	2
E.J. Gray	did not bat					
I.D.S. Smith†	"					
J.G. Bracewell	"					
W. Watson	"					
Extras	(LB 2, W 14, NB 1)	17				
	(55 overs; 208 minutes)	**284-5**				

England		Runs	Mins	Balls	6s	4s
G.A. Gooch	c and b Coney	91	130	102	–	9
C.W.J. Athey	not out	142	205	172	–	14
D.I. Gower	c Wright b Coney	9	25	18	–	1
A.J. Lamb	b Bracewell	28	37	27	–	3
M.W. Gatting*	b Crowe	7	4	4	–	1
D.R. Pringle	not out	0	4	–	–	–
C.J. Richards†	did not bat					
J.E. Emburey	"					
N.A. Foster	"					
P.H. Edmonds	"					
G.R. Dilley	"					
Extras	(LB 5, W 3, NB 1)	9				
	(53.4 overs; 205 minutes)	**286-4**				

England	O	M	R	W
Dilley	9	0	55	1
Foster	7	0	40	0
Pringle	10	2	63	1
Gooch	7	0	48	0
Edmonds	11	1	42	1
Emburey	11	1	34	1

New Zealand	O	M	R	W
Hadlee	11	1	34	0
Watson	11	1	46	0
Crowe, M.D.	6	0	36	1
Bracewell	10.4	0	67	1
Gray	4	0	39	0
Coney	11	0	59	2

Fall of Wickets

Wkt	NZ	E
1st	16	193
2nd	89	219
3rd	133	265
4th	136	274
5th	249	–
6th	–	–
7th	–	–
8th	–	–
9th	–	–
10th	–	–

New Zealand won the Texaco Trophy on faster run-rate in the series.
Men of the Series Awards: C.W.J. Athey and M.D. Crowe.

New Zealand Tour of England 1986

First-Class Matches: Played 15; Won 4, Lost 0, Drawn 11
All Matches: Played 18; Won 6, Lost 1, Drawn 11

First-Class Averages

Batting and Fielding	M	I	NO	HS	R	Avge	100	50	Ct/St
J.G. Bracewell	12	11	6	110	386	77.20	2	–	2
M.D. Crowe	12	18	6	106	787	65.58	2	6	10
J.V. Coney	13	17	5	140*	688	57.33	1	4	7
K.R. Rutherford	12	19	3	317	848	53.00	2	3	7
E.J. Gray	13	13	4	108	467	51.88	1	4	9
B.A. Edgar	12	19	5	110*	590	42.14	1	4	5
J.G. Wright	12	19	1	119	668	37.11	1	5	4
J.J. Crowe	13	19	2	159	624	36.70	1	4	11
I.D.S. Smith	9	9	3	48	215	35.83	–	–	20/4
R.J. Hadlee	3	3	0	68	93	31.00	–	1	–
D.A. Stirling	11	7	3	26	116	29.00	–	–	4
T.E. Blain	9	9	2	37	172	24.57	–	–	16/1
T.J. Franklin	7	10	0	96	227	22.70	–	1	5
W. Watson	12	6	3	10	30	10.00	–	–	3
B.J. Barrett	8	4	3	5*	8	8.00	–	–	1

Also batted: E.J. Chatfield (7 matches) 0*, 5 (3ct).

Bowling	O	M	R	W	Avge	Best	5wI	10wM
Hadlee	153.5	42	390	19	20.52	6-80	2	1
Coney	75	23	194	7	27.71	2-14	–	–
Bracewell	411	122	1042	37	28.16	6-55	2	1
Gray	438.2	144	1087	37	29.37	7-61	3	–
Chatfield	191.4	47	457	13	35.15	3-73	–	–
Stirling	255	36	1025	28	36.60	5-98	1	–
Watson	308.1	60	963	26	37.03	4-31	–	–
Barrett	157.5	18	610	15	40.66	3-32	–	–

Also bowled: M.D. Crowe 49.5-8-190-2; Edgar 1-0-2-0; Franklin 1-0-5-0; Rutherford 5-0-25-0; Smith 2-0-8-0; Wright 4-1-13-0.

COUNTY CRICKET
SWEATERS
White Cable Sweaters

ALL WOOL Also Courtelle

Trimmed in Club Colours

TO ORDER

Also Club Ties and Scarves

Available through your local stockists
Manufactured in tradtional styling by

LUKE EYRES LTD.

149B Histon Road
Cambridge CB4 3DE
England

Tel: 0223 64711

English season 1986

Britannic Assurance Championship

Essex came from behind to win the Britannic Assurance Championship with something to spare. It was the third time in four years that they had been champions and the fourth since they won for the first time in their history in 1979.

The issue was settled soon after the start of their penultimate match at Trent Bridge on September 10, when Essex earned the three bowling points which were all they needed to put them out of reach of Nottinghamshire, the only side by then left with a mathematical chance of catching them.

They had been led for part of the last month by Gloucestershire, who suffered yet another of the disappointments which have marked their history since they were last recorded as champions from a much smaller field in 1877. In modern times, the mind goes back to 1947 when they lost the toss and a vital match with Middlesex at Cheltenham; to 1977 when they led on the morning of the last day of the season, only to finish third when Hampshire made light of scoring 270 to win; to 1985 when, having finished bottom the year before, they rose from the ashes to deliver a stiff challenge only to fade into third place. Since the War they have four times finished second and five times third.

This year, perhaps, they relied more than before on their two fast bowlers, Courtney Walsh and David Lawrence, but until the beginning of August there seemed no reason why the same recipe should not carry them through their remaining seven matches, given similar pitches. After their first match at Cheltenham, they led Essex by 54 points. Admittedly they had played two matches more, but it is usually best to have the points in the bag. Many a side has lost its chance of the championship not on the field but sitting in the dressing-room praying in vain for the rain to stop.

To record what happened subsequently it is necessary to switch to the other end of the table where, to the general surprise, Middlesex were to be found. The reigning champions had not won a championship match at the end of July, though this was clearly not a true reflection of their ability. Injuries, ill luck with the toss and weather, a few losses of form, and, of course, the loss of several players during Test matches had all combined to stop them from winning, though they had won the Benson & Hedges Cup. In early August, at full strength, they at last won a match, beating Northants, who had only lost once previously, by an innings. During a Test match they were then routed by Essex and, still with a weakened side, came to Cheltenham to play the leaders.

Gloucestershire had already suffered a minor and not unexpected reverse, for they could only draw with Notts. But now things began to go really wrong for them. They put Middlesex in, the weather over the week-end turned against them, and after a declaration by each side Middlesex won by 104 runs, with Gloucestershire taking only 2 points out of the match.

From then on Gloucestershire did not win a match; indeed they mustered only 29 points from their last 7 matches. It could not be said that Walsh and Lawrence flagged, but perhaps some of the pitches were less responsive to them, and certainly Gloucestershire did not have the variety of bowling to see them through.

By contrast, Essex began to surge forward in a way that had a wicked irony about it. After the 1984 season, Gloucestershire parted with John Childs, the left-arm spin bowler who had been with them for 10 years, and let him go to Essex. In 1985 he played in only 4 matches for Essex and took only 3 wickets for 377 runs. But in August 1986 he suddenly came into his own, bowling magnificently and somehow seeming to attract into Essex's path the sort of pitch, such as that at Folkestone, on which he could be effective. In 7 matches up to the eve of Essex's winning the championship, he took 48 wickets at 12.37 each.

Essex, second only to Middlesex in the number of players absent through Test requirements, had been a strong side for most of the season, with just the odd set-back that they quickly brushed aside. The presence of Allan Border until mid-August helped to offset Gooch's absences. Young players of the calibre of Stephenson became valuable members of the side, the batting stretched a long way down, and in Lever, Foster, and Pringle there was as strong a hand of faster bowlers as most sides possessed. With Childs's sudden emergence at the age of 35 as a top-class bowler, they had a devastating extra weapon. They finished the season as unarguably the best side and as worthy champions.

When the championship settled down in early June after a lot of rain, Lancashire were briefly on top with two victories in their first six matches. They could only double their wins in the rest of the season. Essex were in second place, and, though they slipped a little later, it is doubtful if they were ever seriously worried by any of their rivals except Gloucestershire. Notts had their moments and were always one of the better sides, but they shared Richard Hadlee with the New Zealand touring team during the second half of the season and fell too far behind to pose a serious threat. They eventually finished fourth instead of second through not taking the last Northants wicket on the last evening of the season.

Surrey were never far behind, but when they worked themselves into a challenging position by beating Lancashire on 8 August they lacked the resources to sustain the effort. Yet they still finished third, a promising position for a side with several developing players.

At the other end of the table, Somerset's domestic problems aroused so much publicity that it was remarkable they rose as high from their bottom place of 1985 as bottom but one. Yet that was still a weird position in which to find a side which, at its strongest, included Richards, Garner, and Botham. Bottom place fell to Glamorgan who, after contesting it with Middlesex for some time, slipped a long way behind. As consolation, on the last day of the season, they did record a victory over the new champions, Essex, after rain and an Essex forfeiture.

Britannic Assurance County Championship 1986 – Final Table

	P	W	L	D	1st Innings Points Batting	1st Innings Points Bowling	Total Points
1 ESSEX (4)	24	10	6	8	51	76	287
2 Gloucestershire (3)	24	9	3	12	50	65	259
3 Surrey (6)	24	8	6	10	54	66	248
4 Nottinghamshire (8)	24	7	2	15	55	80	247
5 Worcestershire (5)	24	7	5	12	58	72	242
6 Hampshire (2)	23*	7	4	12	54	69	235
7 Leicestershire (16)	24	5	7	12	55	67	202
8 Kent (9)	24	5	7	12	42	75	197
9 Northamptonshire (10)	24	5	3	16	53	60	193
10 Yorkshire (11)	24	4	5	15	62	59	193†
11 Derbyshire (13)	24	5	5	14	42	70	188‡
12 Middlesex (1)	24	4	9	11	47	65	176
13 Warwickshire (15)	24	4	5	15	61	51	176
14 Sussex (7)	23*	4	7	12	46	56	166
15 Lancashire (14)	23*	4	5	14	41	51	156
16 Somerset (17)	23*	3	7	13	52	52	152
17 Glamorgan (12)	24	2	7	15	39	47	118

1985 final positions are shown in brackets. * The Sussex v Somerset and Hampshire v Lancashire matches were abandoned without a ball bowled and are not included in the table. † Yorkshire total includes 8 points for the drawn match v Nottinghamshire when scores were level. ‡ Derbyshire total includes 12 points for a win in the match v Somerset which was reduced to one innings.

Points

For a win: 16 points, plus any first innings points. For winning a match reduced to a single innings because it started with less than eight hours' playing time remaining: 12 points. First innings points are awarded during the first 100 overs of each first innings:

Batting		Bowling	
150 to 199 runs	1	3 or 4 wickets	1
200 to 249 runs	2	5 or 6 wickets	2
250 to 299 runs	3	7 or 8 wickets	3
300 runs and over	4	9 or 10 wickets	4

Final Positions 1890-1986

	D	E	Gm	Gs	H	K	La	Le	M	Nh	Nt	Sm	Sy	Sx	Wa	Wo	Y
1890	—	—	—	6	—	3	2	—	7	—	5	—	1	8	—	—	3
1891	—	—	—	9	—	5	2	—	3	—	4	5	1	7	—	—	8
1892	—	—	—	7	—	7	4	—	5	—	2	3	1	9	—	—	6
1893	—	—	—	9	—	4	2	—	3	—	6	8	5	7	—	—	1
1894	—	—	—	9	—	4	4	—	3	—	7	6	1	8	—	—	2
1895	5	9	—	4	10	14	2	12	6	—	12	8	1	11	6	—	3
1896	7	5	—	10	8	9	2	13	3	—	6	11	4	14	12	—	1
1897	14	3	—	5	9	12	1	13	8	—	10	11	2	6	7	—	4
1898	9	5	—	3	12	7	6	13	2	—	8	13	4	9	9	—	1
1899	15	6	—	9	10	8	4	13	2	—	10	13	1	5	7	12	3
1900	13	10	—	7	15	3	2	14	7	—	5	11	7	3	6	12	1
1901	15	10	—	14	7	7	3	12	2	—	9	12	6	4	5	11	1
1902	10	13	—	14	15	7	5	11	12	—	3	7	4	2	6	9	1
1903	12	8	—	13	14	8	4	14	1	—	5	10	11	2	7	6	3
1904	10	14	—	9	15	3	1	7	4	—	5	12	11	6	7	13	2
1905	14	12	—	8	16	6	2	5	11	13	10	15	4	3	7	8	1
1906	16	7	—	9	8	1	4	15	11	11	5	11	3	10	6	14	2
1907	16	7	—	10	12	8	6	11	5	15	1	14	4	13	9	2	2
1908	14	11	—	10	9	2	7	13	4	15	8	16	3	5	12	6	1

ENGLISH SEASON 1986/BRITANNIC ASSURANCE CHAMPIONSHIP

	D	E	Gm	Gs	H	K	La	Le	M	Nh	Nt	Sm	Sy	Sx	Wa	Wo	Y
1909	15	14	—	16	8	1	2	13	6	7	10	11	5	4	12	8	3
1910	15	11	—	12	6	1	4	10	3	9	5	16	2	7	14	13	8
1911	14	6	—	12	11	2	4	15	3	10	8	16	5	13	1	9	7
1912	12	15	—	11	6	3	4	13	5	2	8	14	7	10	9	16	1
1913	13	15	—	9	10	1	8	14	6	4	5	16	3	7	11	12	2
1914	12	8	—	16	5	3	11	13	2	9	10	15	1	6	7	14	4
1919	9	14	—	8	7	2	5	9	13	12	3	5	4	11	15	—	1
1920	16	9	—	8	11	5	2	13	1	14	7	10	3	6	12	15	4
1921	12	15	17	7	6	4	5	11	1	13	8	10	2	9	16	14	3
1922	11	8	16	13	6	4	5	14	7	15	2	10	3	9	12	17	1
1923	10	13	16	11	7	5	3	14	8	17	2	9	4	6	12	15	1
1924	17	15	13	6	12	5	4	11	2	16	6	8	3	10	9	14	1
1925	14	7	17	10	9	5	3	12	6	11	4	15	2	13	8	16	1
1926	11	9	8	15	7	3	1	13	6	16	4	14	5	10	12	17	2
1927	5	8	15	12	13	4	1	7	9	16	2	14	6	10	11	17	3
1928	10	16	15	5	12	2	1	9	8	13	3	14	6	7	11	17	4
1929	7	12	17	4	11	8	2	9	6	13	1	15	10	4	14	16	2
1930	9	6	11	2	13	5	1	12	16	17	4	13	8	7	15	10	3
1931	7	10	15	2	12	3	6	16	11	17	5	13	8	4	9	14	1
1932	10	14	15	13	8	3	6	12	10	16	4	7	5	2	9	17	1
1933	6	4	16	10	14	3	5	17	12	13	8	11	9	2	7	15	1
1934	3	8	13	7	14	5	1	12	10	17	9	15	11	2	4	16	5
1935	2	9	13	15	16	10	4	6	3	17	5	14	11	7	8	12	1
1936	1	9	16	4	10	8	11	15	2	17	5	7	6	14	13	12	3
1937	3	6	7	4	14	12	9	16	2	17	10	13	8	5	11	15	1
1938	5	6	16	10	14	9	4	15	2	17	12	7	3	8	13	11	1
1939	9	4	13	3	15	5	6	17	2	16	12	14	8	10	11	7	1
1946	15	8	6	5	10	6	3	11	2	16	13	4	11	17	14	8	1
1947	5	11	9	2	16	4	3	14	1	17	11	11	6	9	15	7	7
1948	6	13	1	8	9	15	5	11	3	17	14	12	2	16	7	10	4
1949	15	9	8	7	16	13	11	17	1	6	11	9	5	13	4	3	1
1950	5	17	11	7	12	9	1	16	14	10	15	7	1	13	4	6	3
1951	11	8	5	12	9	16	3	15	7	13	17	14	6	10	1	4	2
1952	4	10	7	9	12	15	3	6	5	8	16	17	1	13	10	14	2
1953	6	12	10	6	14	16	3	3	5	11	8	17	1	2	9	15	12
1954	3	15	4	13	14	11	10	16	7	7	5	17	1	9	6	11	2
1955	8	14	16	12	3	13	9	6	5	7	11	17	1	4	9	15	2
1956	12	11	13	3	6	16	2	17	5	4	8	15	1	9	14	9	7
1957	4	5	9	12	13	14	6	17	7	2	15	8	1	9	11	16	3
1958	5	6	15	14	2	8	7	12	10	4	17	3	1	13	16	9	11
1959	7	9	6	2	8	13	5	16	10	11	17	12	3	15	4	14	1
1960	5	6	11	8	12	10	2	17	3	9	16	14	7	4	15	13	1
1961	7	6	14	5	1	11	13	9	3	16	17	10	15	8	12	4	2
1962	7	9	14	4	10	11	16	17	13	8	15	6	5	12	3	2	1
1963	17	12	2	8	10	13	15	16	6	7	9	3	11	4	4	14	1
1964	12	10	11	17	12	7	14	16	6	3	15	8	4	9	2	1	5
1965	9	15	3	10	12	5	13	14	6	2	17	7	8	16	11	1	4
1966	9	16	14	15	11	4	12	8	12	5	17	3	7	10	6	2	1
1967	6	15	14	17	12	2	11	3	7	9	16	8	4	13	10	5	1
1968	8	14	3	16	5	2	6	9	10	13	4	12	15	17	11	7	1
1969	16	6	1	2	5	10	15	14	11	9	8	17	3	7	4	12	13
1970	7	12	2	17	10	1	3	15	16	14	11	13	5	9	7	6	4
1971	17	10	16	8	9	4	3	5	6	14	12	7	1	11	2	15	13
1972	17	5	13	3	9	2	15	6	8	4	14	11	12	16	1	7	10
1973	16	8	11	5	1	4	12	9	13	3	17	10	2	15	7	6	14
1974	17	12	16	14	2	10	8	4	6	3	15	5	7	13	9	1	11
1975	15	7	9	16	3	5	4	1	11	8	13	12	6	17	14	10	2
1976	15	6	17	3	12	14	16	4	1	2	13	7	9	10	5	11	8
1977	7	6	14	3	11	1	16	5	1	9	17	4	14	8	10	13	12
1978	14	2	13	10	8	1	12	6	3	17	7	5	16	9	11	15	4
1979	16	1	17	10	12	5	13	6	14	11	9	8	3	4	15	2	7
1980	9	8	13	7	17	16	15	9	1	12	3	5	2	4	14	11	6
1981	12	5	14	13	7	9	16	8	4	15	1	3	6	2	17	11	10
1982	11	7	16	15	3	13	12	2	1	9	4	6	5	8	17	14	10
1983	9	1	15	12	3	7	12	4	2	6	14	10	8	11	5	16	17
1984	12	1	13	17	15	5	16	4	3	11	2	7	8	6	9	10	14
1985	13	4	12	3	2	9	14	16	1	10	7	17	6	7	15	5	11
1986	11	1	17	2	6	8	15	7	12	9	4	16	3	14	13	5	10

Derbyshire

Derbyshire ended the 1986 season much as they had finished the previous one, in obvious and increasingly urgent need of reinforcements after a summer of inconsistency occasionally illuminated by individual successes.

Barnett, a refreshingly positive captain, coped manfully with the debilitating effects of the virus which struck him down in Sri Lanka the previous winter, making more than 1,500 runs overall, and doubts about the temperament of Morris after the previous year's under-achievements were brilliantly dispelled. Morris, who made only 722 runs in 1985, ended with 1,739 in all first-class cricket, the reward for a diminished appetite for carbohydrates and flashy stroke-play.

Hill repaid those who supported his testimonial by compiling the best aggregate of his career, before announcing his retirement to take a place on the coaching staff, but elsewhere the batting was disturbingly brittle.

Though Anderson shared a record-breaking stand of 286 with Hill in the NatWest Trophy game against Cornwall, he was an increasingly tense and ineffective performer, and Roberts betrayed a reasonable start with a long sequence of poor scores and disappointingly languid displays.

With Miller compounding the expensiveness of his bowling with a modest contribution with the bat, the tailenders were often required to rescue Derbyshire, and Warner emerged as a prodigious hitter, scoring seven half-centuries in all competitions and making more than 500 runs in the Championship.

Wicket-keeping was again a source of concern. Marples could not guarantee the necessary levels of concentration and was released at the end of the season. Though Maher was not conspicuously superior with the gloves, his emergence as a dour but determined opening batsman demanded perseverance.

Jean-Jacques, a lively seamer and resourceful batsman, marked his debut by sharing a county record 10th-wicket stand of 132 against Yorkshire with Hill. Generally the bowling lacked depth. Derbyshire leaned heavily on Holding's willingness to bowl long spells, and Mortensen, who missed a month on duty with Denmark in the ICC Trophy, was a renewed force, regularly claiming his victims among the top five in the order.

Finney, so often the workhorse in the previous two seasons, was restricted by a recurring back injury, and the waywardness of Warner and the physical frailties of Newman, who contributed only 74 overs, offset the encouraging emergence of Jean-Jacques and Malcolm.

Miller's disaffection led to his leaving with a year of his contract unexpired, Essex promptly recruiting him. Morris, too, asked to be released so that he could find a county more likely to provide a stronger platform for his international aspirations. Morris was told he must stay, but Derbyshire have now spent 19 seasons outside the Championship's top six and need recruitments of quality on all fronts to hope realistically for better.

ENGLISH SEASON 1986/DERBYSHIRE

Britannic Assurance County Championship: 11th; Won 5, Lost 5, Drawn 14
All First-Class Matches: Won 5, Lost 5, Drawn 15
NatWest Bank Trophy: Lost to Surrey in 2nd round
Benson & Hedges Cup: Lost to Kent in quarter-final
John Player League: 9th; Won 7, Lost 9

Championship Averages

Batting and Fielding	M	I	NO	HS	R	Avge	100	50	Ct/St
J.E. Morris	24	38	3	191	1654	47.25	4	10	8
A. Hill	24	40	6	172*	1438	42.29	3	7	9
K.J. Barnett	24	42	3	143	1484	38.05	2	10	23
B.J.M. Maher	13	23	5	77*	626	34.77	–	5	23
P.G. Newman	3	4	2	34	62	31.00	–	–	1
R. Sharma	15	17	6	71	321	29.18	–	2	14
A.E. Warner	19	27	6	91	543	25.85	–	5	6
R.J. Finney	16	16	5	58	275	25.00	–	1	2
B. Roberts	24	36	3	124*	771	23.36	1	2	12/1
M. Jean-Jacques	9	12	3	73	208	23.11	–	1	1
C. Marples	14	23	3	57	442	22.10	–	2	30/3
I.S. Anderson	13	23	1	93	449	20.40	–	2	6
G. Miller	19	26	2	65	461	19.20	–	2	13
M.A. Holding	14	20	2	36*	295	16.38	–	–	6
D.E. Malcolm	8	6	4	29*	30	15.00	–	–	2
O.H. Mortensen	16	17	9	31*	69	8.62	–	–	1
J.G. Wright	2	3	0	7	14	4.66	–	–	1
L.J. Wood	2	2	0	5	7	3.50	–	–	–
J.P. Taylor	3	4	1	6	9	3.00	–	–	1

Also batted: A.M. Brown (1 match) 21, 9*; C.F.B.P. Rudd (1 match) 1.

Hundreds (10)

4 **J.E. Morris**: 153 v Lancs, Liverpool; 191 v Kent (Derby); 118 v Leics, Leicester; 127 v Northants, Derby.
3 **A. Hill**: 172* v Yorks, Sheffield; 130* v Sussex, Eastbourne; 119* v Hants, Derby.
2 **K.J. Barnett**: 114 v Glos, Chesterfield; 143 v Northants, Derby.
1 **B. Roberts**: 124* v Somerset, Chesterfield.

Bowling	O	M	R	W	Avge	Best	5wI	10wM
M.A. Holding	388.1	110	1045	52	20.09	7-97	4	–
O.H. Mortensen	416.2	111	1082	46	23.52	5-35	1	–
D.E. Malcolm	203.2	35	735	27	27.22	5-42	1	–
M. Jean-Jacques	159	16	599	22	27.22	8-77	1	1
R.J. Finney	301.4	59	986	28	35.21	7-54	1	–
R. Sharma	140.5	33	407	11	37.00	3-72	–	–
A.E. Warner	341.1	66	1186	28	42.35	4-38	–	–
G. Miller	604.2	180	1340	32	41.87	5-37	2	–

Also bowled: K.J. Barnett 95-24-333-5; A. Hill 9-3-22-1; B.J.M. Maher 33-2-151-3; C. Marples 4-0-48-0; J.E. Morris 44.4-5-245-1; P.G. Newman 73.1-16-198-9; B. Roberts 22-5-53-2; C.F.B.P. Rudd 28.3-7-90-0; J.P. Taylor 72-10-254-6; L.J. Wood 39-8-95-2.

Essex

Essex, who had waited until 1979 for their first County Championship success, won the title for the third time in four years last season. It was indeed a triumph for Gooch in his first season as captain. Owing to duties for England, Gooch played in only 13 Championship matches, but, at all times, he had an invaluable deputy and adviser in his predecessor Fletcher and, together, they brought forth the happiest of results.

Essex boasted two new names as their leading batsman and bowler in Border and Childs, and they respectively figured most prominently in the two matches to be regarded with such relevance in the county's glories.

It was against Middlesex, on a suspect Lord's wicket at the end of June, that Essex were faced with decidedly hostile bowling by Daniel and Cowans. However, the Australian captain Border batted with such skilful judgement here, to score 59 not out in the second innings, that Essex won by 5 wickets.

The Championship was virtually clinched in the last week of August when Essex gained an unlikely victory over Somerset, at Taunton. The home team had entered the final 20 overs requiring just 20 runs to win, with 5 wickets in hand and Botham still at the helm. But then the left-arm spinner Childs had Botham caught on the boundary ropes and thereon Somerset quickly collapsed for Essex to win by 9 runs.

Prichard joined Border as the only batsmen to score 1,000 runs for Essex, and these two enjoyed many invaluable third-wicket partnerships. Prichard, 21, hit his career best score of 147 not out against Notts, at Chelmsford, and was duly awarded his county cap. Although Border had to leave the team in mid-August, with six matches still remaining, his left-handed batting played an outstanding part in Essex's Championship triumph.

Alas, Border is not now to return and, as their overseas player, the county have signed the South African fast bowler Hugh Page, who has reaped such rewards for Transvaal in the Currie Cup competition. To add further strength to their attack, Essex have also secured the services of the former Derbyshire and England off-spinner Geoff Miller.

It was, anyway, the balance of the Essex bowling attack that was such a feature last season. Foster was the only Englishman to take 100 wickets (first time in his career), Childs finished third in the national averages, and Lever and all-rounder Pringle also made solid contributions.

The success of Childs produced one of the most marked of all bowlers' changes of fortunes and improvements in form. The previous season, Childs, who had joined Essex after 10 years' service for Gloucestershire, took only 3 wickets — for 377 runs. However, in the winter he had sought some spinning tuition from England selector Fred Titmus. There were certainly most rewarding results, with excellent control of length and direction — to say nothing of his spinning skills on the advantageous wickets of Colchester in August.

ENGLISH SEASON 1986/ESSEX

Britannic Assurance County Championship: 1st; Won 10, Lost 6, Drawn 8
All First-Class Matches: Won 10, Lost 7, Drawn 9
NatWest Bank Trophy: Lost to Warwickshire in 2nd round
Benson & Hedges Cup: Lost to Nottinghamshire in quarter-final
John Player League: 2nd; Won 11, Lost 4, No Result 1

Championship Averages

Batting and Fielding	M	I	NO	HS	R	Avge	100	50	Ct/St
A.R. Border	18	29	4	150	1287	51.48	4	8	14
G.A. Gooch	13	21	0	151	778	37.04	1	5	10
P.J. Prichard	24	40	3	147*	1165	31.48	1	8	19
K.W.R. Fletcher	19	27	5	91	691	31.40	–	6	24
B.R. Hardie	21	34	4	113*	831	28.66	2	4	19
A.W. Lilley	14	24	2	87	557	25.31	–	3	5
J.P. Stephenson	13	23	1	85	551	25.04	–	3	6
I.L. Pont	2	4	3	14*	24	24.00	–	–	–
D.E. East	23	36	4	100*	712	22.25	1	2	61/19
N.A. Foster	21	27	7	53*	433	21.65	–	2	12
D.R. Pringle	15	22	2	97	370	18.50	–	1	7
N.D. Burns	2	3	0	29	54	18.00	–	–	2/2
C. Gladwin	7	13	0	73	178	13.69	–	1	4
J.K. Lever	21	25	5	38	199	9.95	–	–	1
J.H. Childs	20	21	6	30	149	9.93	–	–	4
T.D. Topley	7	9	2	23	58	8.28	–	–	7
K.R. Pont	6	11	1	31	79	7.90	–	–	1
D.L. Acfield	17	17	9	10	41	5.12	–	–	4

Also batted: S. Turner (1 match) 32, 25*.

Hundreds (9)

4 **A.R. Border:** 110 v Derbys, Derby; 150 v Glamorgan, Swansea; 138 v Surrey, Oval; 108* v Sussex, Eastbourne.
2 **B.R. Hardie:** 110 v Yorks, Chelmsford; 113* v Somerset, Taunton.
1 **D.E. East:** 100* v Glos, Colchester.
  G.A. Gooch: 151 v Worcs, Southend.
  P.J. Prichard: 147* v Notts, Chelmsford.

Bowling	O	M	R	W	Avge	Best	5wI	10wM
J.H. Childs	566.3	186	1278	85	15.03	8-58	5	3
T.D. Topley	207.1	46	651	31	21.00	5-52	2	–
N.A. Foster	715.2	154	2139	100	21.39	6-57	10	2
D.R. Pringle	336.1	85	946	41	23.07	7-46	2	–
D.L. Acfield	329.1	78	765	25	30.60	4-50	–	–
J.K. Lever	564.1	130	1812	58	31.24	6-57	3	–

Also bowled: A.R. Border 21-2-100-1; D.E. East 0.2-0-1-0; G.A. Gooch 137.4-34-329-7; B.R. Hardie 12-0-58-0; A.W. Lilley 18.3-1-104-2; I.L. Pont 32.2-2-130-3; K.R. Pont 31.5-7-85-4; J.P. Stephenson 2-0-5-0; S. Turner 21-5-72-1.

Glamorgan

Beleaguered Glamorgan suffered a traumatic season in 1986. Having made modest but perceptible improvement in 1984 and 1985, they finished comfortably bottom of the County Championship table and made no impression in the one-day competitions.

Glamorgan's problems started early, with the failure of their Pakistan Test batsman Javed Miandad to report for duty on time. The county's decision to terminate his contract was just and inevitable, but his prolific and rapid scoring was to be sorely missed.

Then Rodney Ontong, finding his form adversely affected by the cares of captaining a struggling side, resigned as skipper in July, the burden passing to Hugh Morris, the 22-year-old left-handed batsman.

Finally, Younis Ahmed decided to concentrate on his business interests, and in August asked to be released from his contract. After such a series of upheavals, Glamorgan can give themselves the cold comfort to knowing that there is nowhere to go but upwards.

There were some comforts on the playing side. Morris made great strides, his steadfast batting bringing him over 1,500 first-class runs. In addition, he made 587 runs in the John Player League and is now a most dependable performer. Mathew Maynard, still only 20, played some exhilarating innings and, though his instinct to play strokes led him too frequently into rashness, he passed 1,000 runs overall for the first time and is a player with a considerable future.

Geoff Holmes, again reliable, was the only other batsman to reach four figures. The beneficiary John Hopkins may have been too swiftly discarded after a lean start, for he returned to bat effectively and made a brilliant 142 against New Zealand at Swansea. Duncan Pauline, signed from Surrey, was given a long run, but rarely looked the part. Ontong's tally of runs was well down on previous years, but this was partly counter-balanced by the fact that more runs than expected came from John Derrick and Greg Thomas.

The bowling was undeniably weak. Ontong's late flurry of wickets took his total to 64, but he was ineffective earlier in the season. Steele's ability to take wickets finally deserted him, and he retired in August to take up the newly created post of Team Manager. The departure of Javed Miandad enabled Glamorgan to use overseas bowlers in Moseley and the young Australian Hickey. Both, however, were sadly disappointing.

Thomas, the main strike bowler, stayed fit and increased his haul of wickets. His figures, though, are not those of a potential England bowler, and will not be so until his undoubted pace and strength are complemented by control of length and line. He could claim, with justice, that pitches in Wales are not suitable for fast bowlers, and the presence of the Indian slow left-armer Ravi Shastri at Glamorgan next year seems likely to ensure that the status quo will remain.

On a brighter note, a good team performance in the county's final match brought victory over the champions Essex. Long-suffering Glamorgan supporters will be hoping that this is an omen for 1987.

ENGLISH SEASON 1986/GLAMORGAN

Britannic Assurance County Championship: 17th; Won 2, Lost 7, Drawn 15
All First-Class Matches: Won 3, Lost 7, Drawn 16
NatWest Bank Trophy: Lost to Sussex in 2nd round
Benson & Hedges Cup: Failed to qualify for quarter-final (5th in Group C)
John Player League: 12th; Won 6, Lost 9, No Result 1

Championship Averages

Batting and Fielding	M	I	NO	HS	R	Avge	100	50	Ct/St
Younis Ahmed	15	23	2	105*	845	40.23	1	4	4
H. Morris	24	42	2	128*	1512	37.80	2	11	8
J. Derrick	16	22	6	78*	496	31.00	–	4	3
M.P. Maynard	20	32	4	129	838	29.92	1	6	12
A.L. Jones	12	20	4	50	413	25.81	–	1	6
J.G. Thomas	19	25	6	70	485	25.52	–	2	6
G.C. Holmes	24	42	5	107	939	25.37	1	4	17
J.A. Hopkins	14	25	0	93	596	23.84	–	3	8
D.B. Pauline	11	19	0	97	435	22.89	–	3	3
R.C. Ontong	24	37	4	80*	744	22.54	–	6	8
T. Davies	22	28	13	41	316	21.06	–	–	25/7
J.F. Steele	11	16	4	41*	251	20.91	–	–	7
E.A. Moseley	6	8	1	19	55	7.85	–	–	–
S.J. Base	11	11	4	15*	53	7.57	–	–	3
P.D. North	4	5	2	17*	22	7.33	–	–	–
S.R. Barwick	10	8	2	9	33	5.50	–	–	3
D.J. Hickey	12	9	5	9*	19	4.75	–	–	3
P.A. Cottey	2	3	0	7	9	3.00	–	–	1

Also batted: M.L. Roberts (2 matches) 8 (2ct, 1st); M. Cann (1 match) 16* (1ct); I. Smith (1 match) 0, 0 (1ct). S.L. Watkin played in one match but did not bat.

Hundreds (5)

2 H. Morris: 128* v Kent, Maidstone; 114 v Worcs, Worcester.
1 G.C. Holmes: 107 v Worcs, Worcester.
  M.P. Maynard: 129 v Warwicks, Edgbaston.
  Younis Ahmed: 105* v Sussex, Cardiff.

Bowling	O	M	R	W	Avge	Best	5wI	10wM
R.C. Ontong	606.4	153	1774	64	27.71	8-101	2	1
S.R. Barwick	256.4	56	838	23	36.43	3-25	–	–
J.G. Thomas	397.5	60	1478	39	37.89	4-56	–	–
S.J. Base	199.5	33	727	19	38.26	4-74	–	–
E.A. Moseley	124.3	14	447	11	40.63	4-70	–	–
J. Derrick	213.2	39	705	16	44.06	3-19	–	–
D.J. Hickey	243.5	29	996	17	58.58	3-87	–	–

Also bowled: M. Cann 1-1-0-0; G.C. Holmes 107-14-427-9; J.A. Hopkins 2-0-12-0; M.P. Maynard 4-0-13-0; H. Morris 11-4-44-0; P.D. North 43.4-11-92-4; D.B. Pauline 14-0-67-2; I. Smith 24-3-111-1; J.F. Steele 134-20-534-6; S.L. Watkin 16-1-82-2; Younis Ahmed 20-4-82-0.

Gloucestershire

Gloucestershire, third in the County Championship in 1985, went one better last season, and when in early August they headed the table by 54 points it seemed that they might carry off the title for the first time. Essex, however, had two games in hand, and, though Gloucestershire once again suffered cruelly from the weather, they would surely concede that the better all-round side triumphed. It was indeed remarkable that the county did so well.

Their handicaps were considerable. Kevin Curran, their Zimbabwean all-rounder, a penetrative fast-medium bowler in 1985, suffered a stress fracture of the right shoulder and bowled only 18 gentle overs late in the season. Bill Athey, selected regularly by England, was available only intermittently. Paul Romaines broke a finger early in the campaign and struggled when he returned. And the captain, David Graveney, suffered continually with back trouble.

The team worked hard to cover these areas of weakness, none more so than the West Indian Courtney Walsh, whose steep bounce, subtle change of pace, and astonishing stamina made him the country's leading wicket-taker, with 118 in 790 overs. His 9 for 72 in Somerset's first innings at Bristol was a career best.

David Lawrence, more expensive than in 1985, still took 63 wickets in all first-class matches, and Walsh owed a good deal to his whole-hearted efforts. His hostility was constant even though his accuracy varied. Philip Bainbridge, given more opportunity owing to Curran's injury, had his successful days, notably when he took 8 for 53 in Somerset's second innings at Bristol. Lloyds' off-spin was occasionally penetrative, and Graveney, back or no back, was rarely collared.

The batting, though prolific at times, was not entirely satisfactory, the opening positions in particular giving problems. Tony Wright, despite some good innings, was not altogether convincing, and lost his place in August, and Andrew Stovold looked happier when he dropped down the order. Paul Romaines never struck form, but Keith Tomlins, signed from Middlesex, did the job capably later in the season. Lower down, Phil Bainbridge did not approach the heights of the previous summer, but still played some important innings.

Fortunately, Athey, when he appeared, was solidity itself, and Curran, though inconsistent as such furious attackers are prone to be, played some remarkable innings and was the leading scorer overall, with 1,353 runs. He made four centuries, three of them in the Championship. Lloyds, batting at number seven, scored most Championship runs. He mounted any number of rearguard actions and had his best season. Mark Alleyne, a 19-year-old from Haringey, showed high promise. Jack Russell recovered his batting form, and his wicket-keeping remained impeccable.

There remains concern over the county's poor one-day form. Early exits were made from the Benson & Hedges and NatWest competitions, and they finished last in the John Player League.

Britannic Assurance County Championship: Won 9, Lost 3, Drawn 12
All First-Class Matches: Won 9, Lost 3, Drawn 14
NatWest Bank Trophy: Lost to Leicestershire in 2nd round
Benson & Hedges Cup: Failed to qualify for quarter-final (3rd in Group C)
John Player League: 17th; Won 3, Lost 11, No Result 2

Championship Averages

Batting and Fielding	M	I	NO	HS	R	Avge	100	50	Ct/St
C.W.J. Athey	13	21	1	171*	994	49.70	1	6	17
J.W. Lloyds	24	36	9	111	1232	45.62	1	8	21
K.M. Curran	24	37	6	117*	1181	38.09	3	6	28
M.W. Alleyne	10	16	5	116*	336	30.54	1	1	4
A.W. Stovold	24	40	4	118	1072	29.77	1	7	7
K.P. Tomlins	15	27	4	75	676	29.39	–	4	1
G.E. Sainsbury	4	3	2	14*	28	28.00	–	–	–
R.C. Russell	24	31	9	71	585	26.59	–	2	51/3
P. Bainbridge	24	41	4	105	941	25.43	1	–	–
A.J. Wright	14	24	0	87	530	22.08	–	4	14
P.W. Romaines	13	24	4	67*	429	21.45	–	2	4
C.A. Walsh	23	24	6	52	221	12.27	–	1	7
D.A. Graveney	20	17	8	30*	93	10.33	–	–	19
D.V. Lawrence	22	25	5	34*	198	9.90	–	–	5
I.R. Payne	9	10	2	12	53	6.62	–	–	6

Also batted: P.H. Twizzell (1 match) 0.

Hundreds (8)

3 **K.M. Curran:** 116 v Glamorgan, Cardiff; 117* v Notts, Cheltenham; 103* v Surrey, Oval.
1 **M.W. Alleyne:** 116 v Sussex, Bristol.
  C.W.J. Athey: 171* v Northants, Northampton.
  P. Bainbridge: 105 v Notts, Cheltenham.
  J.W. Lloyds: 111 v Derbys, Gloucester.
  A.W. Stovold: 118 v Derbys, Chesterfield.

Bowling	O	M	R	W	Avge	Best	5wI	10wM
C.A. Walsh	789.5	193	2145	118	18.17	9-72	12	4
P. Bainbridge	381.1	81	1095	41	26.70	8-53	2	–
J.W. Lloyds	329.2	61	1119	34	32.91	5-111	2	–
D.A. Graveney	418	125	942	27	34.88	4-17	–	–
I.R. Payne	160.3	35	459	13	35.30	3-48	–	–
D.V. Lawrence	542.1	78	2134	59	36.16	5-84	1	–

Also bowled: C.W.J. Athey 7-1-46-0; K.M. Curran 18-3-50-0; P.W. Romaines 21.1-0-152-0; G.E. Sainsbury 109.1-25-376-8; A.W. Stovold 26-1-132-2; K.P. Tomlins 6-0-34-0; P.H. Twizzell 11.1-3-38-0; A.J. Wright 1-0-10-0.

Hampshire

Although Hampshire won seven matches, which was as many as they did in 1985, when they were runners-up, they slipped to sixth place, their tally of bonus points being 21 fewer. More than once during the campaign, Hampshire climbed as high up the table as to stand second, but could not hold their position. Indeed, they lost a lot of play to the weather in a poor summer, but then so did most of the other counties.

Hampshire's decline must have been especially disappointing as both their overseas stars, Gordon Greenidge and Malcolm Marshall, were at their peak and had outstanding seasons, topping the national batting and bowling averages, respectively. But Hampshire could not hold their own because the strike rate of their attack as a whole was not high enough. In this respect, they not only suffered from Tim Tremlett's being below par, but also from a finger injury to left-arm spinner Rajesh Maru, which kept him out of action from the middle of June to early August, causing him to miss no fewer than seven matches.

Maru, formerly Edmonds's understudy at Middlesex, was a more confident and mature bowler this season, and the extent to which his absence affected Hampshire's bowling strength can be judged from the fact that he had taken 29 wickets before his injury and claimed 19 after his return.

With 4 for 71 against Notts, Maru had a hand in Hampshire's winning their opening match, at Trent Bridge, and had 5 wickets when Hampshire scored their most notable win of the summer, against eventual champions Essex, on what was principally a pace bowler's wicket.

Greenidge or Marshall, and often both, figured prominently in each one of Hampshire's wins, and, with their high striking rate, contributed principally to their fund of bonus points. Greenidge's first-class aggregate was 2,035 runs in 34 innings, with a double-century and three centuries in his last four innings of the season. Marshall, who did not miss a single championship match all season, bowling more than 650 overs, finished with 100 wickets. Even on the deadest of pitches, he never put in less than full effort.

By their standards, Paul Terry and the Smith brothers had modest seasons, and the captain, Mark Nicholas, a distinctly poor one. Thus Hampshire were not always able to sustain the impetus provided by Greenidge, and acquired 12 batting points fewer than in 1985. Terry started encouragingly, with 74 not out and 80 in the first two matches, but did not make a hundred all season. Chris Smith only just passed the 1,000 in all first-class matches, while he had made 2,000 in 1985. His brother Robin, too, was less productive, but only marginally.

However, the younger Smith did play some vital innings that contributed to at least four Hampshire victories, such as his 50 in difficult conditions at Trent Bridge in the opening game, his robust 84 at Ilford on a Saturday dominated by seam bowlers, his century against Surrey at Basingstoke, and 73 during another triumph against Warwickshire in a match that Greenidge missed.

Hampshire, who found consolation in winning the Sunday league, suffered most, however, from lack of support in the attack for Marshall, other than whom no bowler took more than 50 wickets. Particularly disappointing was Tremlett, who in 1985 was their second-highest wicket-taker after Marshall, although his bowling in the John Player partly compensated for this.

Britannic Assurance County Championship: 6th; Won 7, Lost 4, Drawn 12, No Play 1
All First-Class Matches: Won 7, Lost 4, Drawn 14, No Play 1
NatWest Bank Trophy: Lost to Worcestershire in 2nd round
Benson & Hedges Cup: Failed to qualify for quarter-final (3rd in Group D)
John Player League: 1st; Won 12, Lost 3, No Result 1

Championship Averages

Batting and Fielding	M	I	NO	HS	R	Avge	100	50	Ct/St
C.G. Greenidge	19	32	4	222	1916	68.42	8	5	18
C.L. Smith	17	25	8	114*	964	56.70	2	7	13
R.A. Smith	23	34	6	128*	1100	39.28	2	7	19
T.M. Tremlett	19	21	11	59*	317	31.70	–	2	2
D.R. Turner	9	13	0	96	403	31.00	–	2	2
T.C. Middleton	8	14	3	68*	316	28.72	–	1	7
N.G. Cowley	17	18	6	78*	329	27.41	–	2	4
R.J. Maru	15	9	5	23	108	27.00	–	–	9
K.D. James	12	13	2	62	275	25.00	–	1	5
R.J. Parks	23	21	4	80	419	24.64	–	3	68/6
V.P. Terry	21	33	3	80	704	23.46	–	4	16
M.C.J. Nicholas	21	28	2	55	489	18.80	–	2	12
M.D. Marshall	23	23	2	51*	263	12.52	–	1	5
C.A. Connor	20	13	5	16	41	5.12	–	–	3
S.J.W. Andrew	5	5	2	7	15	5.00	–	–	2

Also batted: P.J. Bakker (1 match) 3*,3.

Hundreds (12)

8 **C.G. Greenidge:** 118 v Notts, Trent Bridge; 127* v Lancs, Old Trafford; 148 v Somerset, Bournemouth; 144* v Derbys, Portsmouth; 222 v Northants, Northampton; 103 & 180* v Derbys, Derby; 126 v Sussex, Hove.
2 **C.L. Smith:** 103* v Somerset, Bournemouth; 128* v Sussex, Southampton.
  R.A. Smith: 101 v Surey, Basingstoke; 128* v Sussex, Southampton.

Bowling	O	M	R	W	Avge	Best	5wI	10wM
M.D. Marshall	656.3	171	1508	100	15.08	6-51	5	–
R.J. Maru	438.3	132	1177	41	28.70	4-33	–	–
N.G. Cowley	345.2	69	949	33	28.75	5-17	1	–
T.M. Tremlett	424.4	103	1175	40	29.37	5-46	1	–
K.D. James	228.4	55	692	21	32.95	5-34	1	–
C.A. Connor	541.4	123	1616	49	32.97	5-60	1	–
S.J.W. Andrew	97.2	15	331	10	33.10	3-25	–	–

Also bowled: P.J. Bakker 24-5-73-1; T.C. Middleton 8-1-39-1; M.C.J. Nicholas 57-11-171-2; R.J. Parks 23-1-110-0; C.L. Smith 36-4-171-1; R.A. Smith 43.4-7-195-2; V.P. Terry 1-1-0-0; D.R. Turner 3-1-6-0.

Kent

It is perhaps not too fanciful an allegory that the excessively wet summer had a particularly damaging effect on cricket in the Garden of England. Blooms flourished fitfully and drooped, mildew set in, and, apart from a second prize in the Benson & Hedges class, Kent failed to pick up an award of any kind. In the circumstances, it is pertinent to examine both the stock and the husbandry.

The season began with much optimism, not least in the knowledge that Chris Cowdrey was to assume virtually total responsibility for team direction, both on and off the field. He had at his disposal a colourful array of home-grown talents, plus Baptiste and Alderman, two valuable hybrids from overseas. All things being equal to Cowdrey's erstwhile venturesome approach, there seemed every reason to suppose that Kent's long-promised renaissance should materialize.

Regrettably, as the summer progressed, it became exasperatingly clear that all things — that is to say all talents — were seldom equal at the same time. Furthermore, in two early matches at Canterbury, against Northants and the Indian tourists, Cowdrey revealed negative aspects of captaincy in batting on, *ad nauseam*, when declarations were called for.

Nevertheless, a decisive win against Essex, at Chelmsford — founded on excellent performances by Benson, Hinks, Alderman, and Dilley — placed Kent fifth in the championship after three matches. Three weeks elapsed before the next championship match — a virtual washout against Worcestershire — in which time they briefly topped the John Player League and progressed to the semi-finals of the Benson & Hedges.

A damp draw against Sussex at Tunbridge Wells, followed by a gambol in The Parks, and Kent had slipped to 14th position. A week of woe in the West Country, where they lost heavily to Somerset and by 4 wickets at Gloucester, virtually demolished all championship hopes.

By now, a patchwork pattern of overall performance had been established that was to continue throughout the season. The most consistent batsmen in mid-term undoubtedly were Tavaré and Taylor, whose several partnerships for the third wicket variously won matches or staved off defeat. Benson and Hinks produced bountiful innings — sometimes. Marsh grew in stature as a batsman rather than a wicket-keeper, and in mid-summer Aslett came in out of the cold at the expense of Graham Cowdrey.

Alderman and Dilley bowled exceptionally well throughout — as did the often neglected Underwood, who, while Somerset lumbered to 249 at Maidstone, bowled just 5.3 overs and took 2 for 10. The rest of the bowlers generally disappointed — not least Ellison who, having bowled 21 fruitless overs for 102 runs against Leicestershire at Canterbury, hurled the ball at the distant sight-screen in sheer frustration.

Defeat by Middlesex in the Benson & Hedges final, three days after a dismal departure from the NatWest at Trent Bridge, was perhaps the unkindest cut of all. To lose by 2 runs, in rain and gloom, seemed to confirm that Kent were truly blighted by the Summer of 86.

ENGLISH SEASON 1986/KENT

Britannic Assurance County Championship: 8th; Won 5, Lost 7, Drawn 12
All First-Class Matches: Won 5, Lost 7, Drawn 14
NatWest Bank Trophy: Lost to Nottinghamshire in 2nd round
Benson & Hedges Cup: Lost to Middlesex in final
John Player League: 6th; Won 7, Tied 1, Lost 5, No Result 3

Championship Averages

Batting and Fielding	M	I	NO	HS	R	Avge	100	50	Ct/St
M.R. Benson	20	35	2	123	1242	37.63	1	7	5
C.J. Tavare	24	40	4	105	1086	30.16	1	5	21
S.A. Marsh	24	34	6	70	829	29.60	–	6	48/3
C.S. Cowdrey	20	32	3	100	820	28.27	1	4	30
N.R. Taylor	24	40	5	88	981	28.02	–	6	10
S.G. Hinks	21	36	2	131	901	26.50	2	2	15
R.M. Ellison	19	27	6	62*	521	24.80	–	2	5
D.G. Aslett	17	23	0	63	517	22.47	–	3	17
E.A.E. Baptiste	5	6	0	80	134	22.33	–	1	1
G.R. Cowdrey	16	24	1	75	353	15.34	–	3	10
G.R. Dilley	13	20	6	30	179	12.78	–	–	6
D.L. Underwood	23	26	5	29	243	11.57	–	–	2
C.S. Dale	2	3	1	16	18	9.00	–	–	–
T.M. Alderman	19	21	8	25	102	7.84	–	–	9
A.P. Igglesden	5	5	2	8*	22	7.33	–	–	2
K.B.S. Jarvis	5	6	4	4	9	4.50	–	–	1
C. Penn	5	6	1	9	11	2.20	–	–	2

Also batted: R.P. Davis (1 match) 0* (1ct); T.R. Ward (1 match) 29, 12.

Hundreds (5)

2 S.G. Hinks: 103 v Somerset, Maidstone; 131 v Hants, Canterbury.
1 M.R. Benson: 123 v Surrey, Dartford.
  C.S. Cowdrey: 100 v Warwicks, Folkestone.
  C.J. Tavare: 105 v Northants, Canterbury.

Bowling	O	M	R	W	Avge	Best	5wI	10wM
T.M. Alderman	610	139	1882	98	19.20	8-46	9	3
E.A.E. Baptiste	137	38	327	13	25.15	4-53	–	–
G.R. Dilley	350.3	51	1156	44	26.27	6-57	3	1
C. Penn	100.5	18	369	14	26.35	5-65	1	–
D.L. Underwood	627.1	251	1368	51	26.82	7-11	1	–
A.P. Igglesden	125	25	372	11	33.81	4-46	–	–
C.S. Cowdrey	258.2	43	886	26	34.07	5-69	1	–
R.M. Ellison	350.4	79	1023	22	46.50	4-36	–	–
K.B.S. Jarvis	139.2	33	472	10	47.20	2-48	–	–

Also bowled: D.G. Aslett 35-3-187-4; M.R. Benson 7-0-55-2; G.R. Cowdrey 7-1-26-1; C.S. Dale 34-8-142-0; R.P. Davis 59.5-22-121-6; C.J. Tavare 27-6-107-2; N.R. Taylor 76.3-8-252-3.

Lancashire

For the Red Rose, the grey and windy summer of 1986 was a threshold of change. The season ended in total anticlimax with an appearance in the NatWest Trophy final at Lord's leading to a heavy defeat by Sussex and the dismissal, 24 hours later, of the club's manager Jack Bond and chief coach Peter Lever.

With the county about to finish in the bottom six of the Championship table for an 11th successive season – conversely, Lancashire have been in the top half only twice since 1972 – an accounting of some kind had to take place. The dismissal of the county captain, Clive Lloyd, for nought in the final was the shot that brought an era to a close.

The gloom was all the more apparent after the bright hopes of spring when, with Gehan Mendis joining and Pat Patterson returning from West Indies, Lancashire appeared to have the best opening partnership in England and the most hostile opening bowler.

Mendis, alas, took a month to get into his stride, Fowler was again a shooting-star, while Patterson, on slow English pitches, was often no more than ordinary. Abrahams appears doomed to spend his career seeking consistency, O'Shaughnessy struggled to stay in the first team, Lloyd was reserved mostly for one-day games, and only Fairbrother of the senior batsmen demonstrated the regular fluency and class one expects from a capped Lancashire batsman.

For much of the summer, Paul Allott strove to be both strike and stock bowler. Mike Watkinson was his chief support, also emerging as a slow-medium off-spinner of the Don Shepherd type, a promising variation. Jack Simmons played a major role in the NatWest campaign, but the left-arm David Makinson found progress harder in his second season, while Ian Folley, the left-arm spinner, had few opportunities. Andy Hayhurst had a heartening first year as an all-rounder.

Lancashire ended the autumn in uncertainty about the management and the captaincy, the chairman indicating that he did not expect appointments before the New Year. The new man needs first to discover why so many good young cricketers (Lancashire Schools and Federation still producing far more than most), fail on arrival at Old Trafford. Any investigation should begin with an examination of the character of the square.

ENGLISH SEASON 1986/LANCASHIRE 175

Britannic Assurance County Championship: 15th; Won 4, Lost 5, Drawn 14, No Play 1
All First-Class Matches: Won 5, Lost 5, Drawn 14, No Play 1
NatWest Bank Trophy: Lost to Sussex in final
Benson & Hedges Cup: Failed to qualify for quarter-final (4th in Group B)
John Player League: 13th; Won 6, Lost 9, No Result 1

Championship Averages

Batting and Fielding	M	I	NO	HS	R	Avge	100	50	Ct/St
C.H. Lloyd	6	7	0	128	328	46.85	1	2	–
N.H. Fairbrother	21	32	7	131	1158	46.32	3	7	10
G.D. Mendis	22	36	3	108	1265	38.33	2	9	–
G. Fowler	19	30	1	180	1110	38.27	1	9	7
J. Abrahams	23	37	7	189*	1134	37.80	2	6	12
D.W. Varey	6	10	2	83	271	33.87	–	2	6/1
C. Maynard	19	26	5	132*	662	31.52	1	5	29/3
P.J.W. Allott	17	19	5	65	382	27.28	–	1	9
S.J. O'Shaughnessy	10	14	3	74	291	26.45	–	2	5
J. Simmons	13	17	5	61	300	25.00	–	1	7
M.R. Chadwick	10	18	0	61	423	23.50	–	2	6
M. Watkinson	20	24	3	58*	377	17.95	–	1	14
D.J. Makinson	14	13	6	43	96	13.71	–	–	6
J. Stanworth	2	2	1	11*	13	13.00	–	–	4
A.N. Hayhurst	9	12	0	31	146	12.16	–	–	2
I. Folley	16	19	2	20*	159	9.35	–	–	7
S. Henrikson	2	2	1	6*	7	7.00	–	–	1
B.P. Patterson	17	15	5	12*	54	5.40	–	–	3
W.K. Hegg	2	2	0	4	4	2.00	–	–	2/2

Also batted: A.J. Murphy (4 matches) 1*, 0*, 1* (2ct); K.A. Hayes (1 match) 17.

Hundreds (10)

3 N.H. Fairbrother: 131 v Worcs, Old Trafford; 116* v Yorks, Old Trafford; 115* v Somerset, Old Trafford.
2 J. Abrahams: 100* v Worcs, Old Trafford; 189* v Glamorgan, Swansea.
  G.D. Mendis: 100 v Glamorgan, Swansea; 108 v Notts, Trent Bridge.
1 G. Fowler: 180 v Sussex, Hove.
  C.H. Lloyd: 128 v Warwicks, Edgbaston.
  C. Maynard: 132* v Yorks, Headingley.

Bowling	O	M	R	W	Avge	Best	5wI	10wM
J. Simmons	230.5	52	762	36	21.16	7-79	2	1
P.J.W. Allott	405.1	106	1053	43	24.48	5-32	2	–
B.P. Patterson	355.5	62	1222	40	30.55	6-46	1	1
D.J. Makinson	285.1	54	963	30	32.10	4-69	–	–
I. Folley	327	90	1009	26	38.80	4-42	–	–
M. Watkinson	454.4	69	1632	30	54.40	5-90	1	–

Also bowled: J. Abrahams 37.5-4-161-1; M.R. Chadwick 5-0-51-0; N.H. Fairbrother 22-8-48-0; G. Fowler 4-0-34-2; A.N. Hayhurst 106.1-10-418-8; S. Henriksen 17-2-61-1; A.J. Murphy 64-13-203-7; S.J. O'Shaughnessy 97-18-363-5.

Leicestershire

Leicestershire, who ended 15 years in the top 10 in the Championship by slumping to 16th in 1985, moved back to 7th last season despite a severely limiting catalogue of injuries. But they disappointed in limited-overs competitions.

With Gower on England duty for much of the summer and so drained by a year of disappointment that he missed the last few weeks of the season 'by mutual agreement', Leicestershire were rarely within two or three players of full-strength, though increased opportunities were seized eagerly by some of the younger players.

Whitaker, who was well set to become the first batsman in the country to 1,000 runs when he broke both hands against Malcolm Marshall, re-emerged with his form and confidence undimmed to score 1,526 and earn a place in the England touring party for Australia. He led the national averages until the last day of the season, when he was out for 11 in a run chase against Surrey, allowing Gordon Greenidge to overtake him.

No less emphatic was the impact of De Freitas in his first full season, and he too was rewarded with a ticket to Australia. Sustaining a testing line and length, often at high pace, and achieving movement both through the air and off the seam, the 20-year-old Dominican-born all-rounder ended with 94 victims in first-class matches and included a maiden century in his 645 runs. In his bowling, especially, the influence of coach Ken Higgs was evident, but, with Agnew and Taylor among those afflicted by fitness problems and Clift sidelined from late July by knee ligament problems, the bowling was frequently lacking in depth.

Benjamin, after a promising start, suffered injury and loss of form, Ferris again made a limited impact, and the spinners, Potter and Willey, managed only 16 Championship wickets between them. Potter, recruited from Kent, also disappointed with the bat, but Willey scored four centuries in topping 1,000 runs for the county, despite missing the early weeks of the season with knee injury and Test calls.

Boon, who missed the whole of the 1985 season after a horrific car crash, rehabilitated his career with 1,000 runs overall, and Cobb produced the concentration to reach this mark for the first time, the pair of them earning caps and compensating for the decline of Butcher and Balderstone.

Whitticase, as well as making pleasing progress behind the wicket, demonstrated a solid technique in making more than 500 runs, often in adversity.

Gower was limited to only 14 first-class innings for the county, and it was announced that he would take a year's rest from the captaincy in 1987, his testimonial year. Peter Willey will lead the side.

The conviction remained at the end of the season that, given average luck with injuries, Leicestershire had the depth of talent to challenge for honours — though the success of Whitaker and De Freitas in joining Gower in the England camp might well bring about similar depletions in 1987.

ENGLISH SEASON 1986/LEICESTERSHIRE

Britannic Assurance County Championship: 7th; Won 5, Lost 7, Drawn 12
All First-Class Matches: Won 5, Lost 7, Drawn 14
NatWest Bank Trophy: Lost to Lancashire in quarter-final
Benson & Hedges Cup: Failed to qualify for quarter-final (4th in Group A)
John Player League: 15th; Won 5, Lost 10, No Result 1

Championship Averages

Batting and Fielding	M	I	NO	HS	R	Avge	100	50	Ct/St
J.J. Whitaker	19	28	8	200*	1382	69.10	5	7	14
P. Willey	16	27	5	172*	1019	46.31	4	3	5
N.E. Briers	5	6	1	83	220	44.00	–	2	1
T.J. Boon	21	33	9	117	933	38.87	1	4	12
D.I. Gower	9	14	2	83	436	36.33	–	4	6/1
P.J. Whitticase	17	20	4	67*	554	34.62	–	5	23/1
W.K.M. Benjamin	18	18	9	57*	309	34.33	–	2	8
R.A. Cobb	23	38	3	91	982	28.05	–	7	8
P.D. Bowler	8	11	1	100*	249	24.90	1	1	2
P.A.J. De Freitas	24	28	2	106	630	24.23	1	3	6
P.B. Clift	13	14	0	49	311	22.21	–	–	12
J.C. Balderstone	14	23	1	115	410	18.63	1	–	3
L. Potter	18	27	3	81*	444	18.50	–	4	17
G.J.F. Ferris	5	6	1	17*	67	13.40	–	–	4
L. Tennant	2	2	1	12*	13	13.00	–	–	–
J.P. Agnew	17	18	5	35*	158	12.15	–	–	2
I.P. Butcher	10	16	1	39	175	11.66	–	–	8
K. Higgs	2	2	1	8	11	11.00	–	–	1
P. Gill	7	10	4	17	60	10.00	–	–	23
L.B. Taylor	15	15	6	13	48	5.33	–	–	3

Also batted: G.A.R. Harris (1 match) 6, 0*.

Hundreds (13)

5 **J.J. Whitaker:** 102* v Lancs, Old Trafford; 200* v Notts, Leicester; 100* v Yorks, Leicester; 175 v Derbys, Chesterfield; 106* v Derbys, Leicester.
4 **P. Willey:** 119 v Notts, Leicester; 172* v Hants, Leicester; 104 v Kent, Canterbury; 168* v Derbys, Leicester.
1 **J.C. Balderstone:** 115 v Sussex, Leicester.
  T.J. Boon: 117 v Yorks, Middlesbrough.
  P.D. Bowler: 100* v Hants, Bournemouth.
  P.A.J. De Freitas: 106 v Kent, Canterbury.

Bowling	O	M	R	W	Avge	Best	5wI	10wM
P.A.J. De Freitas	675.1	123	1977	89	22.21	7-44	7	1
P.B. Clift	384.2	113	901	39	23.10	4-35	–	–
J.P. Agnew	486.5	114	1397	53	26.35	5-27	1	–
G.J.F. Ferris	104	20	356	13	27.38	4-54	–	–
L.B. Taylor	280.3	77	809	27	29.96	4-106	–	–
L. Potter	112	30	318	10	31.80	3-37	–	–
W.K.M. Benjamin	438.3	83	1449	42	34.50	6-33	3	–

Also bowled: J.C. Balderstone 45-9-143-2; T.J. Boon 30.3-2-170-5; P.D. Bowler 25.4-10-57-0; N.E. Briers 13-0-60-2; I.P. Butcher 2-0-4-0; R. Cobb 10-3-41-0; G.A.R. Harris 8-1-34-0; K. Higgs 36-10-71-5; L. Tennant 8-1-35-0; J.J. Whitaker 5.2-0-47-1; P. Willey 165.5-48-372-6.

Middlesex

Middlesex did not win a first-class match in 1986 until August 5 — by which time they had lost eight, drawn seven, and, for almost seven weeks, shared with Glamorgan the last two places in the championship table. For the county who had taken the title in 1985 with eight wins and 274 points, it was a chastening experience.

Fortunes were equally bleak in the John Player League, as Middlesex floundered in the lower half of the table. Indeed, had it not been for the narrowest victory over Kent in the Benson & Hedges final, on July 12, morale at this point might well have been shattered.

Instead, the unsettled squad, variously ranged behind Mike Gatting and, mostly, Clive Radley, philosophized about their situation and hauled themselves clear of total ignominy.

Inevitably it was suggested — though not by Middlesex — that Test demands contributed significantly to the dramatic decline, yet they had lost even more players while winning the championship. The reasons, then, were more subtle — not least the indisposition of Graham Barlow, which forced him to withdraw from the side at the beginning of June.

The loss of Barlow's run-scoring potential (1,343 at 47.9 in 1985) had a detrimental side effect with regard to his established opening partner, Wilf Slack, with whom he had enjoyed a particular rapport... Barlow, the busy run-seeker, allowing Slack time to settle into his measured stride. On Barlow's withdrawal, Middlesex were seldom able to establish the essential base on which many of their 1985 successes were founded.

Another peripheral factor was Radley's unhappy habit of losing the toss — 9 times out of 11 at one stage. All of this contributed to ongoing frustration that, by the start of July, had seen them lose three successive championship matches and six in all.

A third, and perhaps more pertinent, reason for failure was the disappointing development of the younger players, who, by now, should have matured sufficiently to stand in adequately for Test and injury absentees. There were occasional exceptions, notably John Carr, who, in early June, scored 84 not out and 40 not out in the match against Worcester. Ironically, on this occasion, it was the bowlers' deficiencies — Daniel 2 for 123, Hughes 3 for 115, Fraser 0 for 72, and Tufnell 0 for 76 — that allowed Worcestershire to win by an innings and 1 run.

Perhaps the most chastening defeat came at Northampton, when, after dismissing the home side for 125 in the first innings and establishing a lead of 318, Middlesex lost by 4 wickets with 15 balls to spare. That, in fact, proved a turning point of sorts, for, in the return match at Lord's, a week later, came that first victory — by an innings and 43 runs.

The Benson boost apart, there was little else to cheer. Simon Hughes will recall his 7 for 35 against Surrey in May; Gatting, 118 off 135 balls against Northants in the NatWest and 135 against the New Zealand tourists. Downton's determined haul of runs included a century against Warwicks, at Uxbridge, and Slack, with 92 against Somerset and 100 against Derbyshire, gradually overcame the loss of his regular partner.

Britannic Assurance County Championship: 12th; Won 4, Lost 9, Drawn 11
All First-Class Matches: Won 5, Lost 9, Drawn 12
NatWest Bank Trophy: Lost to Yorkshire in 2nd round
Benson & Hedges Cup: Winners
John Player League: 10th; Won 5, Tied 1, Lost 7, No Result 3

Championship Averages

Batting and Fielding	M	I	NO	HS	R	Avge	100	50	Ct/St
M.W. Gatting	10	10	1	158	452	50.22	1	2	6
G.D. Barlow	4	5	1	107	190	47.50	1	1	1
W.N. Slack	20	30	2	106	1136	40.57	3	6	13
J.D. Carr	17	26	3	84*	782	34.00	–	5	11
P.R. Downton	21	25	3	104	669	30.40	1	4	35/5
A.J.T. Miller	22	34	4	111*	907	30.23	1	4	11
R.O. Butcher	24	34	3	171	933	30.09	1	7	14
C.T. Radley	23	31	6	113*	738	29.52	2	3	14
K.R. Brown	10	16	2	66	367	26.21	–	2	9
M.A. Roseberry	5	8	1	70*	174	24.85	–	2	1
J.F. Sykes	3	4	1	26	63	21.00	–	–	–
J.E. Emburey	11	10	1	49	163	18.11	–	–	9
N.G. Cowans	19	19	7	44*	195	16.25	–	–	4
G.D. Rose	5	6	1	52	74	14.80	–	1	–
W.W. Daniel	16	16	6	33	140	14.00	–	–	3
P.H. Edmonds	11	10	3	25	93	13.28	–	–	13
S.P. Hughes	21	24	2	47	255	11.59	–	–	3
A.R.C. Fraser	5	6	1	13	39	7.80	–	–	–
C.P. Metson	3	4	0	15	29	7.25	–	–	3
N.F. Williams	4	2	0	11	12	6.00	–	–	–
P.C.R. Tufnell	6	7	1	9	32	5.33	–	–	1

Also batted: A.G.J. Fraser (3 matches) 19*, 11*; G.K. Brown (1 match) 14, 3.

Hundreds (10)

3 W.N. Slack: 100 v Derbys, Derby; 106 v Northants, Northampton; 105* v Yorks, Headingley.
2 C.T. Radley: 103* v Derbys, Lord's; 113* v Somerset, Lords.
1 G.D. Barlow: 107 v Sussex, Lord's.
  R.O. Butcher: 171 v Surrey, Uxbridge.
  P.R. Downton: 104 v Warwicks, Uxbridge.
  M.W. Gatting: 158 v Northants, Lords.
  A.J.T. Miller: 111* v Hants, Lord's.

Bowling	O	M	R	W	Avge	Best	5wI	10wM
J.E. Emburey	251	79	505	24	21.04	5-51	1	–
W.W. Daniel	402.1	52	1387	62	22.37	4-27	–	–
N.G. Cowans	396.2	85	1265	52	24.32	5-61	–	–
S.P. Hughes	478.3	109	1522	54	28.18	7-35	1	–
P.H. Edmonds	293.4	90	623	20	31.15	4-67	–	–

Also bowled: K.R. Brown 0.4-0-10-0; R.O. Butcher 13.4-2-49-2; J.D. Carr 93.2-16-284-1; A.G.J. Fraser 36.4-12-82-5; A.R.C. Fraser 131-32-327-8; M.W. Gatting 42-18-99-5; A.J.T. Miller 1-0-5-0; G.D. Rose 64-10-277-7; W.N. Slack 17-3-75-1; J.F. Sykes 43.3-5-161-5; P.C.R. Tufnell 148-32-479-5; N.F. Williams 59.3-7-214-8.

Northamptonshire

Northamptonshire again proved to be one of the strongest of batting teams, but their bowlers had yet another frustrating time with the ball. The wicket on the County Ground continued as lifeless as ever, and it has come as best news to hear that a small committee has been formed to 'discuss improving the wicket'.

The two spinners, Cook and Harper, reaped most success, with Nick Cook the leading bowler in all matches (64 wickets) in his first season for the county after eight years with Leicestershire and nine Test matches for England. The opening bowler Griffiths, who made his debut in 1974, has not been re-engaged, but he will benefit from a well deserved testimonial this season.

There was some outstanding batting for Northants, notably by Bailey, with 1,915 runs overall, and by Lamb, who in Championship matches averaged nearly 79. Bailey who has now completed 1,000 runs in each of his first three seasons, was a particularly attractive attacking batsman, and he hit double hundreds against both Yorkshire and Glamorgan.

Lamb's success came abruptly, after being dropped from the England team for the third Test against India. He started, with his first hundred for 12 months, in playing a match-winning innings of 157 against Sussex, at Hastings, and completed his fourth hundred, with 159 against Derbyshire, in his last match of the season.

The captain, Geoff Cook, scored 1,000 runs for the 11th time in the past 12 years, and this in spite of being handicapped with a back injury. Boyd-Moss reached 1,000 runs for the county for the first time, but, after making 148 against Glamorgan, he could boast an aggregate of only 106 runs in the last 8 matches of the season.

The real batting disappointment was Larkins, who scored only 664 runs, with not a hundred to his name. He missed the start of the season with an ankle injury on the football field, and then broke his finger, at Hastings, to put paid to his surprise recall to the England team. In fact, at the time (1 July) he had an average of only 6 with the bat for the county.

Northants were blessed with the all-round powers of Harper, who had an innings of 234 against Gloucestershire in his aggregate of over 900, and took 62 wickets, and of Capel, with 853 runs and 63 wickets overall. There was also valuable batting by Wild, while in the penultimate match, at Scarborough, wicket-keeper Ripley scored a maiden hundred against his native county Yorkshire.

Two good prospects have been engaged for the coming season in N.A. Stanley, who scored 1,042 runs in 1985 for Bedford Modern School, and S. Brown, a 17-year-old left-arm fast bowler, from Bolden in the Durham Senior League.

ENGLISH SEASON 1986/NORTHAMPTONSHIRE

Britannic Assurance County Championship: 9th; Won 5, Lost 3, Drawn 16
All First-Class Matches: Won 5, Lost 3, Drawn 19
NatWest Bank Trophy: Lost to Middlesex in 1st round
Benson & Hedges Cup: Lost to Worcestershire in quarter-final
John Player League: 5th; Won 9, Lost 5, No Result 2

Championship Averages

Batting and Fielding	M	I	NO	HS	R	Avge	100	50	Ct/St
A.J. Lamb	14	20	4	160*	1261	78.81	4	8	12
R.J. Bailey	24	36	7	224*	1562	53.86	4	7	20
G. Cook	20	29	4	183	1057	42.28	3	3	16
R.A. Harper	24	29	4	234	921	36.84	1	2	32
D. Ripley	11	12	3	134*	286	31.77	1	–	12/3
R.J. Boyd-Moss	24	37	3	155	1033	30.38	2	6	7
D.J. Wild	11	16	1	85	448	29.86	–	4	2
W. Larkins	17	29	4	86	664	26.56	–	2	13
D.J. Capel	24	30	4	111	685	26.34	2	2	11
S.N.V. Waterton	13	16	4	58*	314	26.16	–	1	29/4
A.C. Storie	6	7	0	38	152	21.71	–	–	3
N.G.B. Cook	24	25	3	45	343	15.59	–	–	15
N.A. Mallender	21	19	9	37	116	11.60	–	–	4
A. Walker	17	14	9	13*	47	9.40	–	–	6
R.G. Williams	3	4	0	18	35	8.75	–	–	–
B.J. Griffiths	9	6	3	7	18	6.00	–	–	2

Also batted: A. Fordham (1 match) 5, 17; G. Smith (1 match) 3 (1ct).

Hundreds (17)

4 **R.J. Bailey:** 106 v Leics, Northampton; 200* v Yorks, Luton; 224* v Glamorgan, Swansea; 114 v Derbys, Derby.
  A.J. Lamb: 157 v Sussex, Hastings; 160* v Middlesex, Northampton; 117 v Middlesex, Lord's; 159 v Derbys, Derby.
3 **G. Cook:** 109* v Kent, Canterbury; 183 v Lancs, Northampton; 120 v Glamorgan, Northampton.
2 **R.J. Boyd-Moss:** 155 v Lancs, Northampton; 148* v Glamorgan, Northampton.
  D.J. Capel: 111 v Leics, Northampton; 103* v Somerset, Bath.
1 **R.A. Harper:** 234 v Glos, Northampton.
  D. Ripley: 134* v Yorks, Scarborough.

Bowling	O	M	R	W	Avge	Best	5wI	10wM
R.A. Harper	815.2	273	1670	62	26.93	5-84	1	–
N.G.B. Cook	807.2	264	1746	61	28.62	6-72	2	–
D.J. Capel	549.4	109	1774	52	34.11	7-86	2	–
B.J. Griffiths	208.3	40	666	19	35.05	4-59	–	–
N.A. Mallender	585	128	1636	45	36.35	5-110	1	–
A. Walker	394	72	1224	32	38.25	6-50	1	–

Also bowled: R.J. Bailey 11.5-6-12-2; R.J. Boyd-Moss 75.3-18-212-7; G. Cook 17-4-38-1; A.J. Lamb 2-2-0-0; G. Smith 23-4-94-1; D.J. Wild 87-5-329-7; R.G. Williams 36-7-111-3.

Nottinghamshire

Nottinghamshire remained one of the country's most competitive sides throughout the 1986 season, but ended up as the 'nearly' men — fourth in the Championship, third in the John Player League, semi-finalists in the Benson & Hedges Cup, and quarter-finalists in the NatWest Trophy.

In the final judgement, this must be counted not quite a success story. But it represents an admirable level of consistency for a season that began with hopes muted by the prospect of losing Hadlee for much of the time. In the event, Hadlee, in his testimonial season, persuaded New Zealand to release him for domestic duties when not required for the Tests or limited-overs internationals, and was again a major influence, topping the county's averages in both batting and bowling.

Hadlee's unfettered aggression in the middle-order built on the strength of the early batting, openers Broad and Robinson reinforcing their claim to be regarded as the Championship's most reliable opening partnership with close to 3,000 runs between them. Rice's unflagging commitment earned him 1,000 runs for the 12th time, and Johnson became, at 21, the youngest player in the county's history to achieve this mark, many of his runs coming at a pleasingly brisk rate.

Randall, 'Championship Player of the Year' in 1985, went into sudden and sharp decline, and, with Martindale's not making the expected advancement, it was Newell who responded effectively to greater opportunities at number three.

Despite Hadlee's undimmed excellence, Nottinghamshire's bowling was less reliable and there were several occasions when opponents were let off the hook — most frustratingly when Derbyshire held on for a draw after being 26 for 6 before lunch when facing a target of 364 on the final day. Saxelby, again inhibited by recurring shoulder trouble, failed to provide consistent penetration, and Cooper, another with fitness problems, was only spasmodically effective.

Rice shouldered a good deal more work, to compensate for Hadlee's occasional absences and the shortcomings of others, and Pick almost doubled his previous season's return with 50 first-class victims, including a career-best performance in the victory over Yorkshire at Worksop.

Hemmings, with 71 Championship victims at under 30 apiece, was again a source of strength. But Such, though selected for the TCCB side against New Zealand, could not sustain effective form, and it was the left-arm spin of Afford that came through successfully towards the end of the season with 29 wickets in a sequence of four matches.

French consolidated his reputation as England's most secure wicket-keeper, and Scott proved a reliable deputy. But missed catches, especially close to the bat, occasionally contributed to the problems of polishing off tailenders.

The disappointment of the failure to claim any of the four trophies for which they were genuine contenders was exacerbated by doubts about whether Hadlee and Rice would play in 1987.

Britannic Assurance County Championship: 4th; Won 7, Lost 2, Drawn 15
All First-Class Matches: Won 8, Lost 2, Drawn 16
NatWest Bank Trophy: Lost to Surrey in quarter-final
Benson & Hedges Cup: Lost to Middlesex in semi-final
John Player League: 3rd; Won 10, Lost 5, No Result 1

Championship Averages

Batting and Fielding	M	I	NO	HS	R	Avge	100	50	Ct/St
R.J. Hadlee	14	18	5	129*	720	55.38	2	3	6
R.T. Robinson	19	30	5	159*	1319	52.76	4	7	13
C.E.B. Rice	22	31	6	156*	1118	44.72	2	5	28
C.W. Scott	9	8	3	69*	220	44.00	–	1	22/1
P. Johnson	24	34	5	128	1156	39.86	3	4	24
B.C. Broad	24	40	2	122*	1476	38.84	6	6	17
C.D. Fraser-Darling	5	4	0	61	142	35.50	–	1	3
M. Newell	17	27	8	80	671	35.31	–	4	14
J.D. Birch	19	25	6	79*	636	33.47	–	4	21
K. Saxelby	9	7	4	34	99	33.00	–	–	2
B.N. French	14	14	2	58	269	22.41	–	1	30/4
D.W. Randall	13	21	0	60	392	18.66	–	1	13
E.E. Hemmings	20	21	3	54*	300	16.66	–	1	7
K.E. Cooper	16	12	5	17*	105	15.00	–	–	4
R.A. Pick	17	15	1	55	180	12.85	–	1	4
D.J.R. Martindale	2	3	0	14	27	9.00	–	–	–
J.A. Afford	14	12	7	9*	19	3.80	–	–	4
P.M. Such	4	4	0	6	9	2.25	–	–	2

Also batted: K.P. Evans (2 matches) 1 (1ct).

Hundreds (17)

6 **B.C. Broad:** 116 v Warwicks, Trent Bridge; 122 v Yorks, Worksop; 105 v Glos, Cheltenham; 116 v Sussex, Hove; 120 v Essex, Trent Bridge; 112 v Northants, Trent Bridge.
4 **R.T. Robinson:** 104 v Leics, Trent Bridge; 105 v Yorks, Worksop; 108 v Glos, Cheltenham; 159* v Kent, Trent Bridge.
3 **P. Johnson:** 128 v Essex, Chelmsford; 105* v Yorks, Worksop; 120* v Lancs, Trent Bridge.
2 **R.J. Hadlee:** 105* v Surrey, Oval; 129* v Somerset, Trent Bridge.
  C.E.B. Rice: 120 v Derbys, Derby; 156* v Middlesex, Trent Bridge.

Bowling	O	M	R	W	Avge	Best	5wI	10wM
R.J. Hadlee	393.4	108	825	57	14.47	6-31	5	1
K. Cooper	374.5	98	940	41	22.92	5-102	1	–
C.E.B. Rice	413.2	115	1111	44	25.25	4-54	–	–
E.E. Hemmings	780.3	244	2014	71	28.36	7-102	5	2
K. Saxelby	240	45	763	24	31.79	4-47	–	–
R.A. Pick	419.2	75	1455	42	34.64	6-68	1	–
J. Afford	466.4	119	1426	41	34.78	6-81	3	1
P.M. Such	132	33	382	10	38.20	3-39	–	–
C.D. Fraser-Darling	120	16	461	12	38.41	5-84	1	–

Also bowled: J.D. Birch 11-1-24-1; B.C. Broad 7-1-41-0; K.P. Evans 15-2-73-0; P. Johnson 19-1-113-0; M. Newell 2-0-19-0; D.W. Randall 3-0-17-0; R.T. Robinson 2-0-18-0.

Somerset

Somerset, bottom of the County Championship table in 1985, improved by only one place in 1986. They did not survive the early stages of the Benson & Hedges or the NatWest competitions and had only modest success in the John Player League. The reasons for their poor record are not hard to find. Their batting, despite the fact that several players returned good figures, was alarmingly inconsistent under pressure, and their bowling lacked penetration.

Ian Botham's two-month ban did little to help their cause. In addition, Brian Rose, Trevor Gard, and Jon Hardy suffered from injury, Rose missing almost half the campaign. Peter Roebuck, the new captain, was as reliable as ever with the bat, and recorded the highest score of his career when he made 221 not out against Notts at Trent Bridge. Marks was also thoroughly dependable. Nigel Felton made good progress, passing 1,000 runs in first-class cricket for the first time, and Hardy, signed from Hampshire, showed some handsome strokes and with a touch more concentration could become a fine player.

Vivian Richards, by his own exacting standards, had a moderate season. He played some dazzling innings, but despite a batting average of over 40 was not as reliable as usual when runs were important. Rose, when available, made some valuable contributions, as did Botham, but Somerset will take most comfort from the development of Richard Harden. Only 20 at the start of the season, he showed a widening range of strokes, defended solidly, and easily topped 1,000 runs.

On the bowling front, only Joel Garner had the skill to dismiss batsmen on good pitches, and even he had to work hard for his wickets, his striking rate being one victim every nine overs. Marks, the leading wicket-taker, bowled 300 more overs than Garner, but averaged 35. Colin Dredge bowled with as much heart as ever, but was also pretty costly.

Nick Taylor, a seamer signed from Surrey after starting his career with Yorkshire, met with some success in John Player matches but lacked the control to trouble batsmen when they were not subject to the presures of the limited-overs game. The slow left-armer Coombs disappointed, and the skill of the fast-medium left-armer Davis, so successful in 1984, deserted him to such an extent that his 11 first-class wickets cost 57 runs each.

The Committee's decision not to offer contracts to Richards and Garner roused a storm of protest, which was fuelled further by Botham's announcement that if the two West Indians did not play for Somerset in 1987, neither would he. A group of members sought the reinstatement of Richards and Garner and the overthrow of the present committee. A Special General Meeting was called at which the future of the three players, and of the County itself, would be decided.

ENGLISH SEASON 1986/SOMERSET

Britannic Assurance County Championship: 16th; Won 3, Lost 7, Drawn 13, No Play 1
All First-Class Matches: Won 3, Lost 7, Drawn 15, No Play 1
NatWest Bank Trophy: Lost to Lancashire in 2nd round
Benson & Hedges Cup: Failed to qualify for quarter-final (4th in Group C)
John Player League: 7th; Won 8, Lost 6, No Result 2

Championship Averages

Batting and Fielding	M	I	NO	HS	R	Avge	100	50	Ct/St
P.M. Roebuck	20	32	8	221*	1261	52.54	4	5	10
V.J. Marks	23	33	11	110	1029	46.77	1	7	8
B.C. Rose	13	22	5	129	784	46.11	2	3	3
I.T. Botham	12	19	1	139	804	44.66	2	4	8
I.V.A. Richards	18	28	1	136	1174	43.48	4	5	19
R.J. Bartlett	4	6	1	43	171	34.20	–	–	2
P.A.C. Bail	2	3	0	55	102	34.00	–	1	–
R.J. Harden	21	34	3	108	1053	33.96	2	6	12
J.J.E. Hardy	17	26	0	79	779	29.96	–	8	12
N.A. Felton	21	34	3	156*	898	28.96	2	5	8
M.R. Davis	8	7	4	21*	60	20.00	–	–	2
J. Garner	18	15	4	47	182	16.54	–	–	8
J.C.M. Atkinson	3	4	1	16*	49	16.33	–	–	–
R.V.J. Coombs	8	5	3	18	30	15.00	–	–	3
T. Gard	19	24	6	36	228	12.66	–	–	29/5
C.H. Dredge	16	20	2	40	215	11.94	–	–	7
M.D. Harman	3	5	2	15	27	9.00	–	–	1
R.J. Blitz	4	4	0	18	33	8.25	–	–	8
J.G. Wyatt	3	5	0	20	41	8.20	–	–	–
N.S. Taylor	14	16	5	24*	87	7.90	–	–	2
G.V. Palmer	3	5	0	17	29	5.80	–	–	1

Also batted: D.J. Foster (1 match) 0; N.J. Pringle (1 match) 10, 11. M.S. Turner played in one match but did not bat.

Hundreds (17)

4 **I.V.A. Richards:** 102 v Glamorgan, Taunton; 136 v Glamorgan, Cardiff; 128 v Kent, Bath; 115 v Warwicks, Weston-super-Mare.
4 **P.M. Roebuck:** 221* v Notts, Trent Bridge; 102* v Hants, Taunton; 128* v Middlesex, Lord's; 147* v Worcs, Weston-super-Mare.
2 **I.T. Botham:** 104* v Worcs, Weston-super-Mare; 139 v Lancs, Old Trafford.
  N.A. Felton: 156* v Hants, Taunton; 110 v Leics, Leicester.
  R.J. Harden: 102 v Kent, Maidstone; 108 v Sussex, Taunton.
  B.C. Rose: 107* v Kent, Bath; 129 v Middlesex, Lord's.
1 **V.J. Marks:** 110 v Sussex, Taunton.

Bowling	O	M	R	W	Avge	Best	5wI	10wM
J. Garner	419	95	1091	47	23.21	5-56	1	–
C.H. Dredge	385	87	1146	34	33.70	3-10	–	–
V.J. Marks	719.5	182	2046	57	35.89	8-100	2	1
N.S. Taylor	314.2	57	1141	28	40.75	4-40	–	–
I.T. Botham	285.1	61	961	22	43.68	6-125	1	–
R.V.J. Coombs	247.5	56	807	16	50.43	3-60	–	–
M.R. Davis	163.3	18	630	10	63.00	2-43	–	–

Also bowled: J.C.M. Atkinson 10-1-52-0; N.A. Felton 1-0-3-0; D.J. Foster 5-0-29-0; R.J. Harden 39-3-153-2; J.J.E. Hardy 1-0-5-0; M.D. Harman 67.3-12-149-1; G.V. Palmer 63-7-231-4; N.J. Pringle 10-0-48-0; I.V.A. Richards 161-32-500-9; P.M. Roebuck 24-3-120-1; B.C. Rose 11-0-57-2; M.S. Turner 15-3-55-1.

Surrey

Surrey, under their caretaker captain, Pat Pocock, and with coach Geoff Arnold assiduously stoking the boiler, were justifiably disappointed that a season in which they showed considerable all-round improvement did not, in the end, fully reward their efforts.

Having reached the semi-final of the NatWest competition, they lost agonizingly to Lancashire by 4 runs, and, after producing many fine performances in the championship, they faded from serious contention only in the last couple of weeks.

In retrospect, however, the decisive week in Surrey's championship season was that of mid-June, in which they were twice beaten in two days, by Nottinghamshire and Hampshire. On each occasion they were dismissed for fewer than a hundred — 95 in the first innings at Trent Bridge and 64 in the second at Basingstoke. The immediate effect was a slide from third to eighth in the table. Set against a summer in which the batting was generally well balanced and, occasionally, prolific, these two successive failures were particularly galling.

All the established batsmen produced excellent innings: Lynch and Jesty, having scored 152 and 99 respectively against Notts in April, within two weeks shared a century partnership against Kent in the Benson & Hedges competition. By 22 May, Clinton, with 98, had claimed his third successive championship half-century. He produced another against Leicestershire and was joined by Stewart (56) who, within a month, enjoyed a fine flurry as top-scorer at Bristol (65 not out and 52) and a magnificent 144 against Middlesex at Uxbridge. Richards, too, albeit in that fateful match at Basingstoke, was showing his mettle with an undefeated 64 and endorsed his form with a century at Uxbridge.

More significantly, perhaps, the less-seasoned batsmen and the all-rounders were living up to their potential: Falkner, a maiden century against Middlesex, and, in the same match, Medlycott, having scored 61 runs, claimed 5 wickets for 84. And so it went on: Medlycott, a career-best 6 for 63 against Kent at the Oval, and Stewart, having top-scored with 55 in the first innings, hit a splendid 166 in the second.

The front-line bowlers, meanwhile — hardworked in the 10-week absence of Thomas — had been returning some remarkable figures: Clarke, an aggregate of 8 for 75 in the championship win against Derbyshire at the Oval, and Gray, a devastating 7 for 23 in the 234-run thrashing of Kent.

Given, then, that Needham, Doughty, and newcomer Bicknell had been chipping in with worthwhile performances, the return of Thomas with scores of 49 not out and 65 in consecutive matches sustained the expectation that, in one form or another, success would crown the season.

Alas, the Benson & Hedges semi-final at The Oval proved all too prophetic. Lancashire, batting first, mustered 229 and Surrey were 225 for 9 with 7 balls to come, when Jesty, having batted magnificently and, at the end, with a runner, was brilliantly caught at deep mid-wicket.

ENGLISH SEASON 1986/SURREY

Britannic Assurance County Championship: 3rd; Won 8, Lost 6, Drawn 10
All First-Class Matches: Won 8, Lost 6, Drawn 11
NatWest Bank Trophy: Lost to Lancashire in semi-final
Benson & Hedges Cup: Failed to qualify for quarter-final (4th in Group D)
John Player League: 14th; Won 5, Tied 1, Lost 8, No Result 2

Championship Averages

Batting and Fielding	M	I	NO	HS	R	Avge	100	50	Ct/St
A.J. Stewart	24	38	3	166	1629	46.54	3	14	15
C.J. Richards	23	34	9	115	1006	40.24	2	5	39/5
N.J. Falkner	11	18	2	102	567	35.43	1	2	7
M.A. Lynch	24	38	3	152	1201	34.31	3	5	37
T.E. Jesty	19	29	1	221	955	34.10	2	4	9
G.S. Clinton	22	34	4	117	1004	33.46	1	6	10
D.J. Thomas	9	12	4	47*	222	27.75	–	–	1
M.A. Feltham	11	13	4	76	217	24.11	–	1	1
R.J. Doughty	14	18	2	61	366	22.87	–	1	10
G. Monkhouse	10	12	4	51	162	20.25	–	1	6
D.M. Ward	4	6	1	34	100	20.00	–	–	1
A.R. Butcher	15	24	0	71	477	19.87	–	3	6
A. Needham	10	16	2	52	256	18.28	–	1	5
S.T. Clarke	13	12	3	32*	156	17.33	–	–	7
K.T. Medlycott	13	14	2	61	170	14.16	–	1	8
A.H. Gray	11	14	2	28	108	9.00	–	–	4
P.I. Pocock	21	20	9	16*	93	8.45	–	–	6
M.P. Bicknell	9	10	2	9*	21	2.62	–	–	4

Also batted: G.E. Brown (1 match) 0*, 2* (4ct, 1st).

Hundreds (12)

3 M.A. Lynch: 152 v Notts, Oval; 128* v Warwicks, Oval; 119* v Kent, Dartford.
  A.J. Stewart: 144 v Middlesex, Uxbridge; 166 v Kent, Oval; 105 v Kent, Dartford.
2 T.E. Jesty: 221 v Essex, Oval; 179 v Worcs, Oval.
  C.J. Richards: 100 v Middlesex, Uxbridge; 115 v Glos, Oval.
1 G.S. Clinton: 117 v Somerset, Taunton.
  N.J. Falkner: 102 v Middlesex, Uxbridge.

Bowling	O	M	R	W	Avge	Best	5wI	10wM
S.T. Clarke	341.3	95	806	48	16.79	5-31	3	–
A.H. Gray	342.3	69	966	51	18.94	7-23	3	1
M.P. Bicknell	197	43	600	27	22.22	3-27	–	–
K.T. Medlycott	309.4	71	1077	36	29.91	6-63	3	1
M.A. Feltham	191	32	741	23	32.21	4-47	–	–
R.J. Doughty	279	46	1056	31	34.06	4-52	–	–
P.I. Pocock	394.5	107	1095	30	36.50	4-45	–	–
G. Monkhouse	233.1	69	589	14	42.07	4-37	–	–
D.J. Thomas	166.3	29	588	12	49.00	2-44	–	–

Also bowled: A.R. Butcher 68-12-249-6; G.S. Clinton 3-1-12-0; N.J. Falkner 4-1-9-1; T.E. Jesty 59-21-155-5; M.A. Lynch 23.2-2-119-2; A. Needham 67-21-163-0; C.J. Richards 5-0-34-1; A.J. Stewart 5-0-55-0.

Sussex

A chronic finger injury forced John Barclay to retire after the start of the season and abruptly hand over the captaincy to Ian Gould. But the transfer came about early enough not to create trauma, and Gould settled into a difficult job to prove a bold, inspirational captain, as reflected in Sussex's winning of the NatWest Trophy.

In the Championship, however, Sussex had a disappointing season, slipping well below last year's seventh place. Various factors contributed. They had the worst of the weather early in the season and then injuries struck to affect their batting as well as their bowling. Gould himself was laid low with a troublesome hip in August and recovered only just in time to play in the cup final at Lord's.

In addition, Sussex suffered from the imbalance of their attack, having no spinner of any class. Thus their chances of winning away from home were minimal and the only success they scored on foreign soil was against Middlesex, who themselves were in some disarray at the time.

It was a match swung by Imran Khan, who took 8 wickets for 34 to wreck Middlesex and then scored 43 while Sussex were in some distress trying to get a small score to win. However, Imran did not play frequently enough. He was consistent with the bat and took a fair crop of wickets, but the Middlesex match was the only one Sussex won when the great all-rounder was in attendance. There were many matches in which Imran's presence would have made a big difference, when pitches were hard and bouncy. Never was he more greatly missed than during the week at Eastbourne.

After the prosperous season Gehan Mendis had in 1985, Sussex were bound to miss him. They began their campaign with Allan Green and young Neil Lenham as their openers, but they were less than a third of the way through their programme when Lenham broke a finger. For a while, they experimented with Standing as Green's partner, but he could not provide the needed solidity, and ultimately the role went to Rehan Alikhan, a new signing from Surrey. A fine batsman who could exercise patience as well as play stylish strokes, Alikhan came into the side in mid-June and established himself. The uncertainty at the top of the order was minimized by Paul Parker, at number three, having a vintage season in which he scored five centuries and eight fifties.

The Wells brothers did not do themselves full justice, although the elder, Colin, achieved some measure of consistency following a splendid first century of the season against Essex at Eastbourne.

In a season in which their attack was so often depleted by injuries, Sussex were lucky that Tony Pigott stood up better than in the past, and, with the industrious Dermot Reeve, was the highest wicket-taker.

Next season, when Pakistan come to England on a full tour, Sussex will have to do without Imran for the whole summer, and, even if he has in recent years been a part-timer, they will miss him. Apart from finding a replacement from overseas, an important priority for Sussex must be the recruitment of an able spinner.

ENGLISH SEASON 1986/SUSSEX

Britannic Assurance County Championship: 14th; Won 4, Lost 7, Drawn 11, No Play 1
All First-Class Matches: Won 4, Lost 7, Drawn 13, No Play 1
NatWest Bank Trophy: Winners
Benson & Hedges Cup: Lost to Middlesex in quarter-final
John Player League: 4th; Won 10, Lost 6

Championship Averages

Batting and Fielding	M	I	NO	HS	R	Avge	100	50	Ct/St
Imran Khan	10	17	3	135*	729	52.07	2	4	1
A.C.S. Pigott	18	18	6	104*	572	47.66	1	2	4
P.W.G. Parker	23	40	5	125	1459	41.68	5	8	18
C.M. Wells	22	36	8	106	994	35.50	1	6	5
R.I. Alikhan	16	26	3	72	808	35.13	–	7	6
A.P. Wells	21	32	6	150*	842	32.38	1	2	10
I.J. Gould	18	23	5	78*	561	31.16	–	4	33
G.S. Le Roux	14	16	6	72*	298	29.80	–	1	6
A.M. Green	23	42	3	179	1106	28.35	2	3	11
D.A. Reeve	18	21	9	51	307	25.58	–	1	10
N.J. Lenham	17	28	3	77	544	21.76	–	3	6
D.K. Standing	15	22	1	65	321	15.28	–	1	9
J.R.T. Barclay	2	3	0	28	36	12.00	–	–	1
M.B. Speight	5	2	0	17	21	10.50	–	–	6
A.N. Jones	11	10	3	13	55	7.85	–	–	5
A.M. Bredin	6	6	2	8*	26	6.50	–	–	1
C.S. Mays	7	6	2	8*	19	4.75	–	–	2
A.N. Babington	5	3	1	1	1	0.50	–	–	2

Also batted: C.P. Phillipson (1 match) 6 (1ct); A.M.G. Scott (1 match) 0 (1ct).

Hundreds (12)

5 **P.W.G. Parker:** 107 v Middlesex, Lord's; 125 v Worcs, Worcester; 120 v Glos, Bristol; 100* v Derbys, Eastbourne; 111 v Notts, Hove.
2 **A.M. Green:** 179 v Glamorgan, Cardiff; 114 v Hants, Hove.
Imran Khan: 104 v Hants, Southampton; 135* v Warwicks, Edgbaston.
1 **A.C.S. Pigott:** 104* v Warwicks, Edgbaston.
A.P. Wells: 150* v Notts, Hove.
C.M. Wells: 106 v Essex, Eastbourne.

Bowling	O	M	R	W	Avge	Best	5wI	10wM
Imran Khan	294.3	62	825	33	25.00	8-34	2	–
D.A. Reeve	508.5	127	1368	51	26.82	5-32	1	–
A.C.S. Pigott	379	47	1327	48	27.64	5-50	3	–
A.N. Jones	171	26	620	21	29.52	3-36	–	–
C.M. Wells	415.2	93	1263	36	35.08	4-23	–	–
G.S. Le Roux	302.2	66	928	26	35.69	3-44	–	–

Also bowled: R.I. Alikhan 10-0-65-0; A.N. Babington 83.5-11-242-9; J.R.T. Barclay 13-2-65-0; A.M. Bredin 84-20-316-6; I.J. Gould 18.3-0-96-2; A.M. Green 170.1-25-574-7; N.J. Lenham 131-25-409-9; C.S. Mays 170.5-38-561-9; P.W.G. Parker 2-1-4-0; A.M.G. Scott 17-3-70-1; D.K. Standing 156-29-451-2; A.P. Wells 11-1-43-1.

Warwickshire

It would be easy, and more than unfair, to dismiss Warwickshire's form as an inadequate response to the complaints of those who called a Special Members' Meeting last winter. Taken at face value, Warwickshire had a year of little more than standstill. They finished in the lower half of the Britannic Assurance County Championship and John Player Special League tables, failed to reach the knock-out stage in the Benson & Hedges Cup and reserved possibly their worst display of the season for the NatWest Trophy quarter-final against Worcestershire.

Yet even those who fired their criticism at the cricket management and coaching last year would not have expected a dramatic improvement, and what they did see on the field – certainly in terms of individual development – offered some encouragement for the future.

Paul Smith made outstanding progress, scoring over 1,500 runs overall on his promotion to open, and found a new partner towards the end of the season when Andy Moles replaced the luckless Andy Lloyd.

Asif Din, always adaptable to the various demands of the number six position, had probably his most consistent year so far, and Tim Munton, a tall pace bowler from Leicestershire, hit the seam often enough to suggest he could become a more-than-useful third seamer.

Geoff Humpage again outscored every other wicket-keeper in the country – he was very close to being the first batsman anywhere to 1,000 runs – and the peerless Dennis Amiss completed his 100th first-class century 26 years after his debut. If, as Warwickshire hope, he comes back for another season, he will require only 17 runs to become the county's highest scorer of all time.

Norman Gifford, who is expected to lead the side again next season, achieved a distinction almost comparable with Amiss's hundred 100s. He became only the 33rd bowler – and 10th since the last war – to reach 2,000 first-class wickets.

Gladstone Small, the leading wicket-taker, went from strength to strength, winning an England tour place in Australia, but, again, the attack did not have the penetration to improve Warwickshire's championship position significantly.

Gordon Parsons had a moderate first season, and the main area of progress was in Smith's sometimes erratic fast bowling and the off-spin of Kevin Kerr, a South African whose Scottish birthplace gave him immediate qualification. Warwickshire used three overseas players and have further complicated this area by signing Anthony Merrick, a fast bowler from Antigua who was selected for the West Indies B side.

Anton Ferreira has retired after eight seasons, while his fellow-South African, Brian McMillan, had a mixed start in the county game. He looked the part with the bat, scoring 999 runs overall to win fifth place in the national averages. But he was not the strike bowler Warwickshire envisaged, and, later in the season, they preferred the dual option of Kallicharran and Ferreira. Nine players were released at the end of the season, leaving the decks clear for further recruitment.

ENGLISH SEASON 1986/WARWICKSHIRE

Britannic Assurance County Championship: 13th; Won 4, Lost 5, Drawn 15
All First-Class Matches: Won 5, Lost 5, Drawn 16
NatWest Bank Trophy: Lost to Worcestershire in quarter-final
Benson & Hedges Cup: Failed to qualify for quarter-final (3rd in Group A)
John Player League: 11th; Won 5, Tied 2, Lost 7, No Result 2

Championship Averages

Batting and Fielding	M	I	NO	HS	R	Avge	100	50	Ct/St
B.M. McMillan	11	19	4	136	895	59.66	3	5	10
A.I. Kallicharran	13	22	5	163*	884	52.00	4	2	12
A.J. Moles	11	18	3	102	738	49.20	2	5	5
A.M. Ferreira	10	13	5	69	354	44.25	–	3	8
D.L. Amiss	24	42	5	110	1418	38.32	4	6	10
P.A. Smith	24	42	4	119	1431	37.65	1	12	6
Asif Din	23	36	14	69*	750	34.09	–	5	11
G.W. Humpage	24	39	3	130	1216	33.77	1	6	37/8
T.A. Lloyd	15	26	0	100	791	30.42	1	6	6
D.A. Thorne	6	8	3	58	107	21.40	–	1	–
G.J. Parsons	19	23	5	58*	309	17.16	–	1	3
G.C. Small	21	23	6	45*	280	16.47	–	–	4
K.J. Kerr	13	11	4	45*	87	12.42	–	–	5
R.I.H.B. Dyer	4	8	1	28	69	9.85	–	–	4
G.J. Lord	2	4	0	17	38	9.50	–	–	2
T.A. Munton	17	13	5	19	44	5.50	–	..	–
N. Gifford	24	14	6	8	27	3.37	–	–	2

Also batted: S. Monkhouse (1 match) 0; A.R.K. Pierson (2 matches) 42*, 0*.

Hundreds (16)

4 **D.L. Amiss:** 108* v Essex, Edgbaston; 104 v Glos, Bristol; 110 v Glamorgan, Swansea; 101* v Lancs, Old Trafford.
   A.I. Kallicharran: 132* v Glos, Bristol; 163* v Glamorgan, Edgbaston; 102* v Glamorgan, Swansea; 103* v Yorks, Edgbaston.
3 **B.M. McMillan:** 134 v Yorks, Headingley; 136 v Notts, Trent Bridge; 106 v Kent, Edgbaston.
2 **A.J. Moles:** 102 v Somerset, Weston-super-Mare; 100 v Glos, Nuneaton.
1 **G.W. Humpage:** 130 v Lancs, Old Trafford.
   T.A. Lloyd: 100 v Yorks, Headingley.
   P.A. Smith: 119 v Worcs, Edgbaston.

Bowling	O	M	R	W	Avge	Best	5wI	10wM
G.C. Small	534.3	125	1573	68	23.13	5-35	2	–
N. Gifford	542.3	148	1377	58	23.74	6-27	2	–
T.A. Munton	246.4	51	803	25	32.12	4-60	–	–
K.J. Kerr	296	46	913	24	38.04	5-47	1	–
B.M. McMillan	207	34	752	17	44.23	3-47	–	–
G.J. Parsons	316.4	58	1028	23	44.69	5-75	1	–
P.A. Smith	156	18	725	13	55.76	3-36	–	–

Also bowled: Asif Din 87-8-358-4; A.M. Ferreira 125-31-391-8; A.I. Kallicharran 9-0-65-2; T.A. Lloyd 15-0-109-0; A.J. Moles 64.3-10-198-5; S. Monkhouse 10-4-34-1; A.R.K. Pierson 36-5-133-2; D.A. Thorne 53-6-174-1.

Worcestershire

It was a season of near-misses for Worcestershire: beaten semi-finalists in both the Benson & Hedges Cup and the NatWest Trophy, and fifth for a second year in succession in the Britannic Assurance County Championship, despite two more wins than in 1985.

The only blot on their consistency – and, curiously, this was a repeat of the previous year – was their inexplicable failure in the John Player Special League, a competition for which they seem ideally suited and yet one in which they have finished bottom but one for two years.

In general, though, Worcestershire were entitled to be pleased with their development, even if there is some frustration at not crossing the dividing line between potential and its fulfilment.

Only four years ago, they were possibly four or five players short of Championship-winning quality. David Smith, Steven Rhodes, and Neal Radford have bridged that gap to the point where one front-line strike bowler could put them among the honours.

The overseas market is usually the answer to this problem, but Worcestershire are unlikely to venture abroad because they are virtually pledged to support the prodigious Graeme Hick in his ambition to serve a further seven years' qualification to play Test cricket for England.

Though most counties prefer a fast bowler to a batsman for the overseas position, Hick is a justifiable exception to this rule of thumb. It was astonishing that he should score 2,004 first-class runs – the last 107 in the last innings of the season during a run-chase at six an over – in his first full campaign, and at the age of 20.

The tall powerhouse from Zimbabwe generally made his runs so quickly that Worcestershire's bowlers benefited from extra time to bowl out the opposition. Radford maintained his strike-rate of the previous season (when he was the only bowler to take 100 wickets), but missed seven Championship matches through injury and his ill-fated excursion into Test cricket.

Phil Newport, a very promising medium-fast bowler who swings the ball consistently, made the biggest strides, taking 85 first-class wickets, and Paul Pridgeon came back from two shoulder operations in 1985 to head the bowling averages.

John Inchmore, who has now retired, and Steve McEwan, a local discovery from the Birmingham League, shared the other position in the pace attack, but if there was a disappointment in the bowling, it was a combined total of only 55 Championship wickets from the spinners, Dipak Patel and Richard Illingworth.

Patel, the vice-captain, more than compensated by averaging nearly 50 at number six in the batting order. As always, this department was Worcestershire's strength, even though Phil Neale, the captain, and Damian D'Oliveira were a shade less productive than they would have liked. Tim Curtis, an opening batsman who builds an innings with old-fashioned values, was earmarked as a future England contender after scoring 1,451 runs at 50. Smith also finished with a 40-plus average despite injury troubles and some lingering effect from his rejection by the Test selectors.

Wicket-keeper Rhodes performed well at times with the bat, and was perhaps unfortunate not to win a place on the England tour after making 66 first-class dismissals.

Britannic Assurance County Championship: Won 7, Lost 5, Drawn 12
All First-Class Matches: Won 7, Lost 5, Drawn 13
NatWest Bank Trophy: Lost to Sussex in semi-final
Benson & Hedges Cup: Lost to Kent in semi-final
John Player League: 16th; Won 5, Lost 11

Championship Averages

Batting and Fielding	M	I	NO	HS	R	Avge	100	50	Ct/St
G.A. Hick	23	36	6	227*	1934	64.46	6	10	30
T.S. Curtis	23	38	9	153	1451	50.03	2	10	9
D.N. Patel	23	29	9	132*	991	49.55	3	2	5
D.M. Smith	20	28	4	165*	1041	43.37	3	5	8
P.A. Neale	24	33	7	118*	979	37.65	1	6	7
S.J. Rhodes	24	26	10	77*	506	31.62	–	3	57/8
D.B. D'Oliveira	24	39	2	146*	1055	28.51	1	3	6
P.J. Newport	22	16	4	68	281	23.41	–	1	8
R.K. Illingworth	17	14	3	39	185	16.81	–	–	9
N.V. Radford	17	12	2	30	144	14.00	–	–	13
M.J. Weston	7	11	2	30	118	13.11	–	–	2
S.M. McEwan	8	3	2	7	13	13.00	–	–	7
J.D. Inchmore	9	8	2	23*	55	9.16	–	–	3
A.P. Pridgeon	20	10	3	10*	44	6.28	–	–	9

Also batted: R.M. Ellcock (1 match) 4*; S.R. Lampitt (1 match) 11*; L.K. Smith (1 match) 2, 2 (1ct).

Hundreds (15)

6 G.A. Hick: 103 v Surrey, Worcester; 227* v Notts, Worcester; 219* v Glamorgan, Neath; 100 v Sussex, Worcester; 134 v Glos, Worcester; 107 v Glamorgan, Worcester.

3 D.N. Patel: 108 v Middlesex, Worcester; 128 v Essex, Southend; 132* v Surrey, Oval.

D.M. Smith: 102 v Warwicks, Edgbaston; 165* v Somerset, Weston-super-Mare; 100 v Glamorgan, Worcester.

2 T.S. Curtis: 122* v Yorks, Worcester; 153 v Somerset, Worcester.

1 D.B. D'Oliveira: 146* v Glos, Bristol.

P.A. Neale: 118* v Middlesex, Worcester.

Bowling	O	M	R	W	Avge	Best	5wI	10wM
A.P. Pridgeon	535	134	1396	59	23.66	6-52	1	–
N.V. Radford	584.4	122	1882	76	24.76	9-70	6	3
P.J. Newport	617.3	88	2081	83	25.07	6-48	5	1
S.M. McEwan	180.1	32	638	16	39.87	3-33	–	–
J.D. Inchmore	221.1	49	562	13	43.23	2-41	–	–
D.N. Patel	451	115	1249	28	44.60	5-88	1	–
R.K. Illingworth	551.2	188	1310	27	48.51	5-64	1	–

Also bowled: D.B. D'Oliveira 27.4-6-118-5; R.M. Ellcock 15-1-40-1; G.A. Hick 28.4-5-109-3; S.R. Lampitt 7-1-21-0; D.M. Smith 11-3-35-2; M.J. Weston 126-36-354-5.

Yorkshire

Yorkshire's summer had more silver linings than dark clouds and ended in relative peace despite the Cricket Committee's decision to end Geoffrey Boycott's playing career with the club. The season could be split neatly into two halves and two young players, Paul Jarvis and Ashley Metcalfe.

Jarvis entered his 21st year looking a right-arm fast-medium bowler of high promise, demonstrating increased control off his shorter run and a growing ability to move the ball off the seam and through the air. His increasing strength and stature also enabled him to bowl longer spells, but this, in turn, meant that he became the side's principal strike bowler. Once again too much was asked of him, and a back strain made him miss the last six weeks. Metcalfe, 22, spent a winter in Australia, where he broke a batting record for his Melbourne grade club. His increasing confidence and tight defence were evident from the start, leading to six centuries, 1,800 runs, and almost a place in the England party for Australia. A consolation was his election as Young Cricketer of the Year (with, ironically, another young Yorkshire-born batsman, James Whitaker of Leicestershire). Both Jarvis and Metcalfe won their county caps and both should become major influences in Yorkshire's future.

Martyn Moxon won his long-delayed England cap, after becoming the first Yorkshireman to score a century in each innings against a touring side (India at Scarborough), and, had he not had the misfortune to make his debut against the invincible Hadlee, might also have gone to Australia. Of the other batsmen, Boycott missed almost half the summer with a hand injury, but almost managed to score 1,000 runs for a 24th successive season. Both Kevin Sharp and Jim Love could appear highclass players on occasion, but neither was consistent.

Injuries that limited Arnie Sidebottom and Graham Stevenson to a few appearances meant that Yorkshire's brigade of younger seam bowlers, supporting Jarvis, had more opportunities than expected, and all credit is due to Simon Dennis, who showed a welcome return to form in August, Stuart Fletcher, Chris Shaw, and Peter Hartley. The last named batted so well, particularly against Warwickshire, that he deserved elevation to all-rounder status.

Phil Carrick, the vice-captain, had a disappointing time in the championship, but produced some splendid one-day returns, not least against Middlesex in the NatWest Trophy. The rapid advance of Phil Berry, the Young England off-spinner, must bring changes next year.

David Bairstow's captaincy attracted the usual quota of criticism and there is no doubt that if an outstanding challenger had emerged his three-year tenure of office might be completed. Politically the club settled down after several tempestuous years, a peace imposed by the forceful character and determination of the president, Lord Mountgarret, and the perception and wisdom of the Chairman, Brian Walsh QC. It would be premature to suggest that Yorkshire are about to become a major power again, but the proper foundations are being laid.

ENGLISH SEASON 1986/YORKSHIRE

Britannic Assurance County Championship: Won 4, Lost 5, Drawn 15
All First-Class Matches: Won 4, Lost 6, Drawn 15
NatWest Bank Trophy: Lost to Sussex in quarter-final
Benson & Hedges Cup: Failed to qualify for quarter-final (3rd in Group B)
John Player League: 8th; Won 7, Tied 1, Lost 6, No Result 2

Championship Averages

Batting and Fielding	M	I	NO	HS	R	Avge	100	50	Ct/St
G. Boycott	12	18	1	135*	890	52.35	2	7	3
A.A. Metcalfe	24	37	0	151	1582	42.75	6	5	10
P.E. Robinson	7	11	2	104*	373	41.44	1	3	5
K. Sharp	18	29	6	181	948	41.21	2	5	9
J.D. Love	21	29	5	109	831	34.62	1	4	7
P.J. Hartley	15	17	4	87*	441	33.92	–	4	7
I.G. Swallow	8	9	4	43*	141	28.20	–	–	–
D.L. Bairstow	24	33	4	88	796	27.44	–	3	41/3
M.D. Moxon	17	27	3	147	636	26.50	1	3	12
S.N. Hartley	20	28	2	78	676	26.00	–	3	5
P. Carrick	24	32	6	51	613	23.57	–	3	9
R.J. Blakey	3	5	0	46	99	19.80	–	–	4
P.W. Jarvis	15	17	7	47	183	18.30	–	–	10
S.J. Dennis	15	12	4	18*	82	10.25	–	–	3
S.D. Fletcher	14	10	3	24	67	9.57	–	–	1
C. Shaw	13	10	4	21	57	9.50	–	–	2
A. Sidebottom	10	9	2	18	65	9.28	–	–	2

Also batted: G.B. Stevenson (2 matches) 58*. P.J. Berry (1 match) 4*; D. Byas (1 match) 0 (1ct).

Hundreds (13)

6 **A.A. Metcalfe:** 108 v Worcs, Worcester; 151 v Northants, Luton; 123 v Kent, Scarborough; 108 v Notts, Sheffield; 151 v Lancs, Old Trafford; 149 v Glamorgan, Headingly.
2 **G. Boycott:** 127 v Leics, Middlesbrough; 135* v Surrey, Headingley.
  K. Sharp: 181 v Glos, Harrogate; 114* v Warwicks, Headingley.
1 **J.D. Love:** 109 v Northants, Scarborough.
  M.D. Moxon: 147 v Lancs, Old Trafford.
  P.E. Robinson: 104* v Kent, Scarborough.

Bowling	O	M	R	W	Avge	Best	5wI	10wM
P.W. Jarvis	428.4	82	1332	60	22.20	7-55	5	2
C. Shaw	281.1	60	773	29	26.65	5-38	1	–
P.J. Hartley	321.1	49	1095	41	26.70	6-68	1	–
A. Sidebottom	226.1	37	671	25	26.84	8-72	1	–
S.J. Dennis	384.3	77	1230	42	29.28	5-71	1	–
S.D. Fletcher	389	79	1172	29	40.41	5-90	1	–
P. Carrick	590.3	185	1412	31	45.54	4-111	–	–

Also bowled: D.L. Bairstow 5-3-7-0; P.J. Berry 39-13-83-1; R.J. Blakey 10.3-1-68-1; D. Byas 2-0-15-0; S.N. Hartley 45.4-8-195-4; J.D. Love 39.2-7-146-0; A.A. Metcalfe 18.1-4-75-0; M.D. Moxon 27.4-9-90-2; P.E. Robinson 11-0-115-0; K. Sharp 29-4-192-3; G.B. Stevenson 29-8-75-2; I.G. Swallow 142-36-386-5.

Oxford & Cambridge

Oxford and Cambridge may have posed little threat to the county teams but, at least, they produced excellent fare for the 142nd University Match at Lord's. Cambridge put Oxford into bat, their fast-medium Davidson took five for 58 and their opening batsman Paul Bail hit the seventh highest University Match score of 174. This was followed on the last day by a magnificent captain's innings for Oxford by Thorne (104 not out) before Cambridge won one of the most exciting of all the 100 victories in this, the oldest first-class fixture.

Cambridge bowled Oxford out for 268 inside the final hour, to be left with 106 to win in 16 overs — 6.6 runs an over. They required 11 runs off the last over and, although losing one wicket, they were blessed with a wide before a dramatic victory — by 5 wickets — from a leg-bye off the last ball of the match.

Oxford's bowling for those 16 overs was accurately shared by Thorne and Rutnagur and Cambridge soon fell behind the run rate. However, they had promoted their successful pace bowler Davidson to No. 4 in the batting order and this surprise decision proved a wise move by the Cambridge captain Price.

Davidson made brave, if ungainly, advances down the wicket to Thorne and effectively swung the bat for the top score of 26. He was still in when the last over came, from Rutnagur, and he and Browne scored 7 runs off the first 3 balls. But Davidson was run out off the next ball, to leave Cambridge still requiring four to win off the two remaining balls.

It was then that Rutnagur gave Cambridge hopes an unexpected fillip with a wide down the leg-side. Browne hit the next ball for two and the leg-bye off the final delivery finished the match.

Davidson had match figures of 9 for 150 and was Cambridge's leading bowler of the season, with 30 wickets. Fell, who scored the only University hundred before Lord's, 114 against Sussex at Hove, topped their batting averages at 26.64 and, not surprisingly, Bail's fine innings of 174 put him head of the aggregate with 428 runs.

Bail, from Millfield, batted 5¾ hours, as Cambridge asserted authority, with a total of 330 for 8 declared. He now joins a distinguished quartet of Cambridge freshmen to have scored a hundred in the University Match since the war: E.J. Craig (1961), Majid Khan (1970), P.M. Roebuck (1975), and D.R. Pringle (1979).

Thorne had a memorable match for Oxford as an all-rounder. He was top-scorer in the first innings with 61, followed it with his most accurate bowling, 2 for 42 in 32 overs, and then that fine 104 not out which almost thwarted Cambridge. The only others to have scored a hundred in this match in their year of Oxford captaincy are W.H. Game (1876), C.B. Fry (1894), R.E. Foster (1900), M. Howell (1919), E.R.T. Holmes (1927), F.G.H. Chalk (1934), M.J.K. Smith (1956), and F.S. Goldstein (1968). When Thorne bowled such a good line and length on the off-stump to that classical straight bat of Bail's, there was a high standard of cricket to watch at Lord's in the 1986 University Match.

ENGLISH SEASON 1985-86/OXFORD & CAMBRIDGE

Cambridge University v Oxford University
Cambridge University won by 5 wickets
Played at Lord's 2, 3, 4 July
Toss: Cambridge. Umpires: M.J. Kitchen and D.O. Oslear

Oxford

D.A. Hagan	c Lea b Davidson	12	c Lea b Ellison	31
A.A.G. Mee	c Brown b Ellison	41	c Bail b Davidson	0
M.J. Kilborn	c Brown b Ellison	28	c Brown b Scott	59
D.A. Thorne*	b Davidson	61	not out	104
C.D.M. Tooley	c Bail b Golding	2	b Davidson	31
R.S. Rutnagur	b Golding	5	b Golding	5
N.V. Salvi	run out	7	c Browne b Davidson	10
R.A. Rydon	c Bail b Davidson	2	c Browne b Golding	2
J.E.B. Cope†	lbw b Davidson	1	c Lea b Golding	0
T.A.J. Dawson	not out	1	c Brown b Davidson	0
M.P. Lawrence	b Davidson	0	lbw b Scott	0
Extras	(LB6, NB1)	7	(B3, LB16, W4, NB3)	26
		167		**268**

Cambridge

P.A.C. Bail	lbw b Rydon	174	c Tooley b Thorne	7
M.S. Ahluwalia	lbw b Thorne	9		
D.J. Fell	lbw b Rutnagur	22	c Lawrence b Rutnagur	20
D.W. Browne	c Cope b Rutnagur	2	(6) not out	13
D.G. Price	lbw b Thorne	0	c Tooley b Rutnagur	7
A.E. Lea	c Lawrence b Dawson	19	(2) b Rutnagur	19
A.K. Golding	b Dawson	47	not out	0
A.D. Brown†	b Dawson	4		
J.E. Davidson	not out	41	(4) run out	26
A.M.G. Scott	not out	1		
C.C. Ellison	did not bat			
Extras	(LB7, W3, NB1)	11	(B1, LB12, W1)	14
	(8 wickets declared)	**330**	(5 wkts)	**106**

Cambridge	O	M	R	W	O	M	R	W
Davidson	19.1	3	58	5	30	4	92	4
Scott	15	4	36	0	17.5	6	43	2
Ellison	10	5	19	2	11	5	21	1
Golding	22	8	39	2	30	10	51	3
Lea	13	0	9	0	10	0	42	0

Oxford	O	M	R	W	O	M	R	W
Thorne	32	11	42	2	8	0	43	1
Rydon	21	4	89	1				
Rutnagur	26	3	69	2	8	0	50	3
Dawson	28	4	92	3				
Lawrence	10	2	31	0				

Fall of Wickets

Wkt	OU 1st	CU 1st	OU 2nd	CU 2nd
1st	26	37	2	12
2nd	72	93	84	52
3rd	97	97	121	55
4th	117	100	199	68
5th	123	171	218	102
6th	163	269	229	–
7th	165	280	245	–
8th	166	289	267	–
9th	167	–	267	–
10th	167	–	268	–

Cambridge University

Results: Played 8; Won 1, Lost 1, Drawn 6

First-Class Averages

Batting	M	I	NO	HS	R	Avge
D.J. Fell†	8	15	2	114	379	29.15
C.C. Ellison†	5	3	1	51*	54	27.00
D.W. Browne†	7	13	4	61*	228	25.33
P.A.C. Bail†	8	15	0	174	379	25.26
A.K. Golding†	6	9	3	47	134	22.33
J.E. Davidson†	8	8	3	41*	103	20.60
M.S. Ahluwalia†	6	11	0	36	198	18.00
A.M.G. Scott†	7	6	5	5	17	17.00
D.G. Price†	7	13	1	60	187	15.58
T.J. Head	3	5	1	40*	62	15.50
S.R. Gorman	6	9	3	37	76	12.66
A.E. Lea†	5	8	0	19	79	9.87
A.D. Brown†	8	9	1	30	78	9.75
T.M. Lord	2	4	0	23	31	7.75

Also batted: S.D. Heath (1 match) 10; 6; J.M. Tremellem (1 match) 3, 4*.

Hundreds (2)

1 P.A.C. Bail: 174 v Oxford University, Lord's
D.J. Fell: 114 v Sussex, Hove

Bowling	O	M	R	W	Avge	Best
Ellison	127	41	325	14	23.21	5-82
Davidson	288	47	877	28	31.32	5-35
Lea	64	6	191	6	31.83	3-61
Scott	238	62	662	16	41.37	4-100
Golding	220	46	604	10	60.40	3-51

Also bowled: Bail 4-0-28-0; Browne 23-5-76-1; Gorman 49-10-184-2; Heath 7-0-39-0; Price 1.2-0-11-0; Tremellem 7-0-32-0.

Fielding

17 Brown (15 ct, 2 st); 6 Lea; 5 Bail; 4 Browne, Gorman; 3 Price, Scott; 2 Davidson, Golding; 1 Ellison, Fell, Head.

Oxford University

Results: Played 8; Won 0, Lost 5, Drawn 3

First-Class Averages

Batting	M	I	NO	HS	R	Avge
D.A. Thorne†	6	9	1	104*	334	41.75
C.D.M. Tooley†	5	8	1	60	196	28.00
D.A. Hagan†	8	14	1	88	334	25.69
N.V. Salvi†	4	7	1	36	126	21.00
M.J. Kilborn†	7	12	1	59	219	19.90
A.A.G. Mee†	8	14	1	51	183	14.07
J.D. Quinlan	5	5	1	24*	46	11.50
T.A.J. Dawson†	7	9	5	10*	32	8.00
R.A. Rydon†	5	9	1	20	64	8.00
R.S. Rutnagur†	5	7	0	24	56	8.00
T. Patel	6	8	0	18	63	7.87
D.P. Taylor	4	6	0	17	39	6.50
J.E.B. Cope†	4	5	2	8*	11	3.66
P.C. MacLarnon	4	5	1	4	9	2.25
M.P. Lawrence†	6	10	2	10*	12	1.50

Also batted: G.J. Toogood (2 matches) 1,11; M.R. Sygrove (1 match) 2, 6; S. Weale (1 match) 12, 28.

Hundreds (1)

1 D.A. Thorne: 104* v Cambridge University, Lord's

Bowling	O	M	R	W	Avge	Best
Rutnagur	136	28	439	14	31.35	3-50
Thorne	156.3	56	330	9	36.66	3-42
Dawson	195	38	649	13	49.92	3-65
Lawrence	155	28	554	7	79.14	2-28
Rydon	119	21	471	5	94.20	3-106

Also bowled: Hagan 0.1-0-4-0; Maclarnon 49-5-89-2; Patel 2-0-12-0; Quinlan 103.3-14-369-4; Sygrove 17-0-85-2; Toogood 58-16-155-4.

Fielding

6 Taylor; 5 Cope; 4 Tooley; 3 Kilborn, Mee, Thorne; 2 Dawson, Hagan, Lawrence, Quinlan, Rutnagur; 1 Patel, Rydon, Salvi.

* not out † Blue 1986

First-Class Averages

Batting
(Qual: 8 innings, avge 10; * not out)

	M	I	NO	HS	Runs	Avge	100s	50s
C.G. Greenidge	20	34	4	222	2035	67.83	8	6
J.J. Whitaker	22	32	9	200*	1526	66.34	5	8
G.A. Hick	24	37	6	227*	2004	64.64	6	11
A.J. Lamb	18	27	4	160*	1359	59.08	4	8
B.M. McMillan	12	21	4	136	999	58.76	3	6
R.J. Bailey	28	43	9	224*	1915	56.32	4	10
A.I. Kallicharran	14	23	5	163*	1005	55.83	5	2
M.W. Gatting	18	23	3	183*	1091	54.55	4	2
G. Boycott	13	20	1	135*	992	52.21	2	8
R.J. Hadlee	17	21	5	129*	813	50.81	2	4
T.S. Curtis	24	40	10	153	1498	49.93	2	10
C.H. Lloyd	7	8	1	128	347	49.57	1	2
A.R. Border	20	32	4	150	1385	49.46	4	9
A.J. Moles	11	18	3	102	738	49.20	2	5
N.H. Fairbrother	22	33	8	131	1217	48.68	3	8
Imran Khan	11	18	3	135*	730	48.66	2	4
C.L. Smith	20	30	8	114*	1061	48.22	2	7
R.T. Robinson	21	34	5	159*	1398	48.20	4	7
I.T. Botham	13	20	2	139	863	47.94	2	5
D.N. Patel	24	30	9	132*	1005	47.85	3	2
P.M. Roebuck	22	35	8	221*	1288	47.70	4	5
A.C.S. Pigott	19	18	6	104*	572	47.66	1	2
J.E. Morris	26	40	3	191	1739	47.00	4	10
A.J. Stewart	25	39	3	166	1665	46.25	3	14
A.M. Ferreira	12	15	6	69*	413	45.88	–	3
A.A. Metcalfe	26	41	1	151	1803	45.07	6	8
C.E.B. Rice	22	31	6	156*	1118	44.72	2	5
P. Willey	18	30	5	172*	1117	44.68	4	3
P.W.G. Parker	25	43	7	125	1595	44.30	6	8
V.J. Marks	25	36	12	110	1057	44.04	1	7
C.W. Scott	10	8	3	69*	220	44.00	–	1
R.J. Bartlett	6	9	2	117*	307	43.85	1	–
K.M. Curran	26	39	8	117*	1353	43.64	4	7
B.C. Rose	14	23	5	129	784	43.55	2	3
I.V.A. Richards	18	28	1	136	1174	43.48	4	5
D.M. Smith	20	28	4	165*	1041	43.37	3	5
J.W. Lloyds	26	39	9	111	1295	43.16	1	8
A. Hill	24	40	6	172*	1438	42.29	3	7
G. Cook	22	30	4	183	1084	41.69	3	3
K. Saxelby	11	8	5	34	124	41.33	–	–
R.A. Smith	25	38	8	128*	1237	41.23	2	8
C.W.J. Athey	19	31	1	171*	1233	41.10	1	7
M. Newell	19	30	9	112*	862	41.04	1	5
W.K.M. Benjamin	20	20	10	95*	404	40.40	–	3
J. Abrahams	24	38	7	189*	1251	40.35	3	6
C.J. Richards	23	34	9	115	1006	40.24	2	5
Younis Ahmed	15	23	2	105*	845	40.23	1	4
G.D. Mendis	23	37	3	108	1363	40.08	2	10
B.C. Broad	25	42	2	122	1593	39.82	6	7
B.J.M. Maher	14	24	5	126	752	39.57	1	5
D.I. Gower	14	23	2	131	830	39.52	1	6
M.R. Benson	23	39	2	128	1461	39.48	2	7

ENGLISH SEASON 1986/FIRST-CLASS AVERAGES

Batting (Contd)

	M	I	NO	HS	Runs	Avge	100s	50s
P. Johnson	26	37	5	128	1250	39.06	3	5
G. Fowler	20	32	2	180	1163	38.76	1	9
T.J. Boon	23	36	10	117	1003	38.57	1	4
G.W. Humpage	26	42	4	130	1462	38.47	3	6
K. Sharp	19	31	6	181	958	38.32	2	5
W.N. Slack	23	35	3	106	1224	38.25	3	7
G.A. Gooch	19	32	0	183	1221	38.15	3	5
C.M. Wells	24	38	9	106	1098	37.86	1	7
P.R. Downton	24	29	5	126*	906	37.75	2	5
P.A. Smith	25	44	4	119	1508	37.70	1	13
D.L. Amiss	26	45	6	110	1450	37.17	4	6
K.J. Barnett	26	45	3	143	1544	36.76	2	10
P.A. Neale	25	34	7	118*	987	36.55	1	6
D.R. Turner	10	14	1	96	472	36.30	–	3
H. Morris	26	44	2	128*	1522	36.23	2	11
R.A. Harper	25	30	4	234	933	35.88	1	2
P.E. Robinson	8	13	2	104*	392	35.63	1	3
J. Derrick	18	24	8	78*	569	35.56	–	4
N.J. Falkner	11	18	2	102	567	35.43	1	2
R.I. Alikhan	18	28	4	72	843	35.12	–	7
J.D. Love	21	29	5	109	831	34.62	1	4
T.E. Jesty	20	30	1	221	998	34.41	2	4
M.A. Lynch	25	39	3	152	1234	34.27	3	5
J.D. Birch	21	28	7	79*	718	34.19	–	4
E.A.E. Baptiste	7	8	0	113	273	34.12	1	1
J.D. Carr	17	26	3	84*	782	34.00	–	5
P.J. Hartley	15	17	4	87*	441	33.92	–	4
D.W. Varey	6	10	2	83	271	33.87	–	2
M.D. Moxon	20	33	4	147	982	33.86	3	4
D.J. Wild	14	21	3	101	608	33.77	1	4
K.W.R. Fletcher	20	28	6	91	736	33.45	–	6
M.P. Maynard	22	34	4	148	1002	33.40	2	6
C.J. Tavaré	26	42	4	123	1267	33.34	2	6
G.S. Clinton	23	35	4	117	1027	33.12	1	6
R.J. Harden	22	36	3	108	1093	33.12	2	6
A.P. Wells	23	34	7	150*	891	33.00	1	2
Asif Din	24	38	14	69*	788	32.83	–	5
P.J. Prichard	26	44	3	147*	1342	32.73	1	10
P.J. Whitticase	18	21	4	67*	554	32.58	–	5
I.J. Gould	20	24	6	78*	586	32.55	–	4
J.G. Wright	14	22	1	119	682	32.47	1	5
C. Maynard	19	26	5	132*	662	31.52	1	5
A.M. Green	25	46	3	179	1343	31.23	3	3
N.R. Taylor	26	42	5	106	1151	31.10	1	7
A.J.T. Miller	23	35	4	111*	963	31.06	1	5
R.O. Butcher	26	37	4	171	1016	30.78	1	7
S.A. Marsh	26	36	8	70	857	30.60	–	6
R.J. Boyd-Moss	27	42	3	155	1192	30.56	2	8
M.W. Alleyne	10	16	5	116*	336	30.54	1	1
N.A. Felton	23	37	3	156*	1030	30.29	3	5
D. Ripley	13	15	5	134*	301	30.10	1	–
S.J. Rhodes	25	27	10	77*	509	29.94	–	3
G.S. Le Roux	14	16	6	72*	298	29.80	–	1

Batting (Contd)	M	I	NO	HS	Runs	Avge	100s	50s
J.J.E. Hardie	19	29	0	79	863	29.75	–	8
B.R. Hardie	22	35	5	113*	883	29.43	2	4
D.J. Capel	28	36	7	111	853	29.41	2	3
C.T. Radley	25	33	6	113*	792	29.33	2	3
T.M. Tremlett	21	23	12	59*	322	29.27	–	–
R. Sharma	15	17	6	71	321	29.18	–	2
C.S. Cowdrey	21	33	3	100	873	29.10	1	5
R.J. Maru	17	10	6	23	116	29.00	–	–
K.P. Tomlins	16	29	5	75	696	29.00	–	4
D.A. Thorne	14	21	4	104*	490	28.82	1	3
A.W. Stovold	26	43	4	118	1123	28.79	1	7
D.B. D'Oliveira	25	41	3	146*	1094	28.78	1	3
R.A. Cobb	25	41	3	91	1092	28.73	–	8
T.C. Middleton	8	14	3	68*	316	28.72	–	1
J.A. Hopkins	15	26	0	142	738	28.38	1	3
G.C. Holmes	26	44	5	107	1106	28.35	1	6
T.A. Lloyd	16	28	0	100	793	28.32	1	6
S.N. Hartley	21	30	2	87	785	28.03	–	4
V.P. Terry	23	36	4	80	896	28.00	–	7
D.J. Thomas	9	12	4	47*	222	27.75	–	–
D.J. Fell	9	17	3	114	388	27.71	1	–
D.L. Bairstow	24	33	4	88	796	27.44	–	3
P. Bainbridge	26	43	4	105	1065	27.30	1	7
P.J.W. Allott	17	19	5	65	382	27.28	–	1
A.E. Warner	20	28	6	91	593	26.95	–	6
J.P. Stephenson	14	25	1	85	647	26.95	–	4
R.C. Russell	27	31	9	71	585	26.59	–	2
W. Larkins	17	29	4	86	664	26.56	–	2
P.A.C. Bail	11	20	0	174	530	26.50	1	1
S.J. O'Shaughnessy	10	14	3	74	291	26.45	–	2
M.A. Feltham	12	14	5	76	237	26.33	–	1
K.R. Brown	10	16	2	66	367	26.21	–	2
S.G. Hinks	23	38	2	131	936	26.00	2	2
N.G. Cowley	19	21	7	78*	360	25.71	–	2
D.A. Reeve	19	21	9	51	307	25.58	–	1
A.R. Butcher	16	25	0	157	634	25.36	1	3
I.G. Swallow	9	11	5	43*	152	25.33	–	–
D.W. Browne	7	13	4	61*	228	25.33	–	1
A.L. Jones	13	21	4	50	429	25.23	–	1
A.W. Lilley	15	26	2	87	604	25.16	–	3
J. Simmons	13	17	5	61	300	25.00	–	1
K.D. James	12	13	2	62	275	25.00	–	1
J.G. Thomas	22	27	6	70	523	24.90	–	2
P.D. Bowler	8	11	1	100*	249	24.90	1	1
M.A. Roseberry	5	8	1	70*	174	24.85	–	2
P.B. Clift	15	16	1	49	370	24.66	–	–
C.D.M. Tooley	6	10	1	60	221	24.55	–	1
P. Carrick	25	33	7	51	637	24.50	–	3
D.A. Hagan	9	16	1	88	364	24.26	–	2
S.N.V. Waterton	14	17	4	58*	314	24.15	–	1
R.M. Ellison	20	29	6	62*	552	24.00	–	2
J.F. Steele	12	17	5	41*	282	23.50	–	–
M.R. Chadwick	10	18	0	61	423	23.50	–	2

ENGLISH SEASON 1986/FIRST-CLASS AVERAGES

Batting (Contd)	M	I	NO	HS	Runs	Avge	100s	50s
A.K. Golding	7	11	3	47	188	23.50	–	–
D.W. Randall	14	22	1	101*	493	23.47	1	1
R.J. Parks	25	23	5	80	420	23.33	–	3
A.J. Wright	15	26	0	87	603	23.19	–	4
M. Jean-Jacques	9	12	3	73	208	23.11	–	1
R.J. Finney	17	17	5	54	277	23.08	–	1
P.A.J. De Freitas	27	30	2	106	645	23.03	1	3
R.J. Doughty	15	19	2	61	387	22.76	–	1
D.B. Pauline	12	20	0	97	455	22.75	–	3
B. Roberts	25	37	3	124*	772	22.70	1	2
R.C. Ontong	24	37	4	80*	744	22.54	–	6
D.G. Aslett	17	23	0	63	517	22.47	–	3
C. Marples	15	24	3	57	466	22.19	–	2
P.J. Newport	23	17	4	68	285	21.92	–	1
D.R. Pringle	20	32	4	97	611	21.82	–	3
N.J. Lenham	18	29	4	77	544	21.76	–	3
T. Davies	24	28	13	41	316	21.06	–	–
P.W. Romaines	15	27	4	67*	476	20.69	–	2
G. Miller	20	27	2	65	512	20.48	–	3
I.S. Anderson	13	23	1	93	449	20.40	–	2
D.E. East	25	40	4	100*	730	20.27	1	2
G. Monkhouse	10	12	4	51	162	20.25	–	1
L. Potter	20	30	3	81*	545	20.18	–	5
B.N. French	20	23	5	58	361	20.05	–	1
N.A. Foster	23	30	7	53*	458	19.91	–	2
M.J. Kilborn	7	12	1	59	219	19.90	–	1
M.C.J. Nicholas	24	32	2	55	564	18.80	–	2
J.E. Emburey	18	22	3	75	354	18.63	–	1
J.C. Balderstone	14	23	1	115	410	18.63	1	–
M. Watkinson	21	25	4	58*	389	18.52	–	1
P.W. Jarvis	15	17	7	47	183	18.30	–	–
M.S. Ahluwalia	6	11	0	36	198	18.00	–	–
D.K. Standing	17	26	3	65	412	17.91	–	1
A. Walker	19	15	10	40*	87	17.40	–	–
E.E. Hemmings	21	23	4	54*	330	17.36	–	1
R.K. Illingworth	18	15	4	39	191	17.36	–	–
S.T. Clarke	14	13	4	32*	156	17.33	–	–
K.J. Kerr	14	12	5	45*	120	17.14	–	–
A. Needham	11	17	2	52	256	17.06	–	1
G.R. Cowdrey	18	26	1	75	425	17.00	–	3
G.J. Parsons	21	24	5	58*	322	16.94	–	1
M.J. Weston	8	12	2	49	167	16.70	–	–
J. Garner	18	15	4	47	182	16.54	–	–
M.A. Holding	14	20	2	36*	295	16.38	–	–
G.C. Small	25	26	7	45*	304	16.00	–	–
N.G. Cowans	21	21	7	44*	223	15.92	–	–
M.R. Davis	9	8	4	21*	63	15.75	–	–
A.C. Storie	8	11	0	38	171	15.54	–	–
J.E. Davidson	9	10	3	41*	108	15.42	–	–
I.P. Butcher	12	19	1	58	273	15.16	–	1
K.T. Medlycott	14	15	2	61	197	15.15	–	1
D.G. Price	8	15	1	60	207	14.78	–	1
N.G.B. Cook	27	27	3	45	351	14.62	–	–

ENGLISH SEASON 1986/FIRST-CLASS AVERAGES

Batting (Contd)	M	I	NO	HS	Runs	Avge	100s	50s
P.H. Edmonds	17	19	5	31	201	14.35	–	–
A.A.G. Mee	8	14	1	51	183	14.07	–	1
W.W. Daniel	16	16	6	33	140	14.00	–	–
D.J. Makinson	15	13	6	43	96	13.71	–	–
N.V. Radford	20	16	3	30	178	13.69	–	–
J.H. Childs	22	23	7	34	214	13.37	–	–
I.R. Payne	11	12	4	30*	106	13.25	–	–
K.E. Cooper	17	13	5	19	105	13.12	–	–
C. Gladwin	8	15	0	73	195	13.00	–	1
J.P. Agnew	19	20	6	35*	181	12.92	–	–
R.A. Pick	19	17	1	55	206	12.87	–	1
S.R. Gorman	6	9	3	37	76	12.66	–	–
C.H. Dredge	17	21	3	40	227	12.61	–	–
T.D. Topley	9	11	2	45	113	12.55	–	–
M.D. Marshall	23	23	2	51*	263	12.52	–	1
S.P. Hughes	23	26	2	47	296	12.33	–	–
C.A. Walsh	23	24	6	52	221	12.27	–	1
G.R. Dilley	18	26	8	30	218	12.11	–	–
T. Gard	20	25	6	36	228	12.00	–	–
N.A. Mallender	22	20	10	37	119	11.90	–	–
K.R. Pont	7	13	1	36	142	11.83	–	–
D.L. Underwood	24	26	5	29	243	11.57	–	–
R.I.H.B. Dyer	5	10	2	28	91	11.37	–	–
A.N. Hayhurst	10	14	0	31	156	11.14	–	–
D.A. Graveney	22	18	9	30*	94	10.44	–	–
S.J. Dennis	16	12	4	18*	82	10.25	–	–

Bowling (Qual: 10 wickets in 10 innings)	O	M	R	W	Avge	Best	5wI
M.D. Marshall	656.3	171	1508	100	15.08	6-51	5
R.J. Hadlee	547.3	150	1215	76	15.98	6-31	7
J.H. Childs	640.1	212	1449	89	16.28	8-58	5
S.T. Clarke	341.3	95	806	48	16.79	5-31	3
C.A. Walsh	789.5	193	2145	118	18.17	9-72	12
A.H. Gray	342.3	69	966	51	18.94	7-23	3
T.M. Alderman	610	139	1882	98	19.20	8-46	9
M.A. Holding	388.1	110	1045	52	20.09	7-97	4
J. Simmons	230.5	52	762	36	21.16	7-79	2
P.W. Jarvis	428.4	82	1332	60	22.20	7-55	5
M.P. Bicknell	196	43	600	27	22.22	3-27	–
P.B. Clift	413.3	120	1002	45	22.26	4-35	–
J.E. Emburey	473.3	170	872	39	22.35	5-51	1
N.A. Foster	806.2	179	2349	105	22.37	6-57	10
W.W. Daniel	402.1	52	1387	62	22.37	4-27	–
P.A.J. De Freitas	743.3	139	2171	94	23.09	7-44	7
G.C. Small	636.3	157	1781	77	23.12	5-35	2
A.N. Babington	117.5	18	348	15	23.20	4-18	–
J. Garner	419	95	1091	47	23.21	5-56	1
T.D. Topley	249.4	60	744	32	23.25	5-52	2
Imran Khan	317.2	72	866	37	23.40	8-34	1
A.R. Butcher	111	28	305	13	23.46	4-25	–
O.H. Mortensen	416.2	111	1082	46	23.52	5-35	1
A.P. Pridgeon	535	134	1396	59	23.66	6-52	1

ENGLISH SEASON 1986/FIRST-CLASS AVERAGES

Bowling (Contd)	O	M	R	W	Avge	Best	5wI
N.G. Cowans	435.2	94	1380	58	23.79	5-61	1
K.E. Cooper	410.5	106	1026	43	23.86	5-102	1
N. Gifford	564.3	157	1409	59	23.88	6-27	2
D.R. Pringle	506.3	128	1348	56	24.07	7-46	2
P.J.W. Allott	405.1	106	1053	43	24.48	5-32	2
P.J. Newport	632.3	90	2146	85	25.24	6-48	5
C.E.B. Rice	413.2	115	1111	44	25.25	4-54	–
P.M. Such	231.3	69	566	22	25.72	5-36	1
G.R. Dilley	505.2	86	1634	63	25.93	6-57	3
S.P. Hughes	529.4	123	1652	63	26.22	7-35	1
D.L. Underwood	638.1	259	1371	52	26.36	7-11	1
N.G. Cowley	385.2	78	1060	40	26.50	5-17	1
P.J. Hartley	321.1	49	1095	41	26.70	6-68	1
N.V. Radford	665.4	132	2164	81	26.71	9-70	6
A. Sidebottom	226.1	37	671	25	26.84	8-72	1
D.A. Reeve	525.5	127	1411	52	27.13	5-32	1
M. Jean-Jacques	159	16	599	22	27.22	8-77	1
B.P. Patterson	391.3	70	1309	48	27.27	6-31	2
D.E. Malcolm	216.2	38	765	28	27.32	5-42	1
C. Shaw	300.1	64	848	31	27.35	5-38	1
R.A. Harper	825.2	275	1700	62	27.41	5-84	1
P. Bainbridge	414.1	89	1185	43	27.55	8-53	2
D.L. Acfield	403.1	107	912	33	27.63	5-38	1
R.C. Ontong	606.4	153	1774	64	27.71	8-101	2
J.P. Agnew	522.5	118	1528	55	27.78	5-27	1
A.C.S. Pigott	390	48	1363	49	27.81	5-50	3
R.J. Maru	497.5	147	1336	48	27.83	5-38	1
T.A. Munton	297.4	68	905	32	28.28	4-60	–
J.K. Lever	638.1	154	1990	70	28.42	6-57	3
D.J. Wild	132.3	17	429	15	28.60	4-4	–
K.T. Medlycott	356.2	86	1166	40	29.15	6-63	3
E.E. Hemmings	818.3	259	2134	73	29.23	7-102	5
P.H. Edmonds	529	162	1111	38	29.23	4-31	–
T.M. Tremlett	453.4	110	1263	43	29.37	5-46	1
A.N. Jones	171	26	620	21	29.52	3-36	–
N.G.B. Cook	870.2	290	1890	64	29.53	6-72	2
S.J.W. Andrew	141.2	33	419	14	29.92	3-25	–
L.B. Taylor	280.3	66	809	27	29.96	4-106	–
M.A. Feltham	224	48	781	26	30.03	4-47	–
S.J. Dennis	407.3	81	1318	43	30.65	5-71	1
R.A. Pick	469.1	88	1570	50	31.40	6-68	1
L. Potter	113	31	318	10	31.80	3-37	–
J.A. Afford	492.4	131	1455	45	32.33	6-81	3
D.J. Capel	633.1	131	2044	63	32.44	7-86	2
C.H. Dredge	389	83	1151	35	32.88	3-10	–
K.D. James	228.4	55	692	21	32.95	5-34	1
C.A. Connor	541.4	123	1616	49	32.97	5-60	1
J.W. Lloyds	369.2	71	1221	37	33.00	5-111	2
J.E. Davidson	326	64	998	30	33.26	5-35	2
D.A. Graveney	446	137	999	30	33.30	4-17	–
W.K.M. Benjamin	465.3	89	1541	46	33.50	6-33	3
K. Saxelby	284	54	905	27	33.51	4-47	–
C.S. Cowdrey	266.2	45	905	27	33.51	5-69	1

ENGLISH SEASON 1986/FIRST-CLASS AVERAGES

Bowling (Contd)	O	M	R	W	Avge	Best	5wI
R.J. Doughty	300	50	1104	32	34.50	4-52	–
D.J. Makinson	322.1	65	1044	30	34.80	4-69	–
B.J. Griffiths	237.3	49	741	21	35.28	4-59	–
G.S. Le Roux	302.2	66	928	26	35.69	3-27	–
V.J. Marks	744.5	189	2121	59	35.94	8-100	2
N.A. Mallender	611	138	1693	47	36.02	5-110	1
I.J. Folley	349	98	1046	29	36.06	4-42	–
D.V. Lawrence	588.1	85	2299	63	36.49	5-84	1
P.I. Pocock	394.5	107	1095	30	36.50	4-45	–
S.J. Base	222.5	39	774	21	36.85	4-74	–
R. Sharma	140.5	33	407	11	37.00	3-72	–
S.R. Barwick	292.4	61	964	26	37.07	3-25	–
C.M. Wells	458.2	103	1373	37	37.10	4-23	–
R.J. Finney	318.4	61	1057	28	37.75	7-54	1
G.J. Parsons	371.1	72	1179	31	38.03	5-24	2
I.R. Payne	215.1	58	576	15	38.40	3-48	–
J.G. Thomas	478.5	70	1746	45	38.80	4-56	–
K.J. Kerr	316	52	955	24	39.79	5-47	1
A. Walker	422	76	1314	33	39.81	6-50	1
S.M. McEwan	180.1	32	638	16	39.87	3-33	–
K.B.S. Jarvis	155.2	42	487	12	40.58	2-15	–
J. Derrick	265.2	47	897	22	40.77	3-19	–
S.D. Fletcher	414	82	1273	31	41.06	5-90	1
I.T. Botham	311.1	65	1043	25	41.72	6-125	1
D.N. Patel	453.2	115	1255	30	41.83	5-88	1
G. Monkhouse	233.1	69	589	14	42.07	4-37	–
N.S. Taylor	342.2	62	1222	29	42.13	4-40	–
G. Miller	634.2	187	1406	33	42.60	5-37	2
A.E. Warner	349.1	67	1200	28	42.85	4-38	–
A.N. Hayhurst	114.1	15	429	10	42.90	4-69	–
P. Carrick	621.3	187	1550	36	43.05	4-111	–
J.D. Inchmore	221.1	49	562	13	43.23	2-41	–
A.M.G. Scott	283	71	814	18	45.22	4-100	–
G.C. Holmes	131	21	499	11	45.36	2-22	–
D.J. Hickey	281.5	39	1102	24	45.91	5-57	1
B.M. McMillan	220	34	808	17	47.52	3-43	–
R.M. Ellison	385.4	90	1103	23	47.95	4-36	–
R.K. Illingworth	564.2	189	1361	28	48.60	5-64	1
D.J. Thomas	166.3	29	588	12	49.00	2-44	–
T.A.J. Dawson	195	38	649	13	49.92	3-65	–
M. Watkinson	504.4	86	1753	35	50.08	5-90	1
R.V.J. Coombs	256.5	58	844	16	52.75	3-60	–
A.M. Ferreira	178	47	532	10	53.20	2-61	–
D.A. Thorne	239.3	70	591	11	53.72	3-42	–
C.S. Mays	212.5	45	706	13	54.30	3-77	–
P.A. Smith	159	19	743	13	57.15	3-36	–
M.R. Davis	167.3	21	631	11	57.36	2-43	–
A.K. Golding	252	51	685	10	68.50	3-51	–

The following bowlers took 10 wickets but bowled in fewer than 10 innings:

	O	M	R	W	Avge	Best	5wI
C.C. Ellison	127	41	325	14	23.21	5-82	1
N.F. Williams	79.3	9	264	10	26.40	3-44	–
E.A.E. Baptiste	146	40	351	13	27.00	4-53	–

ENGLISH SEASON 1986/FIRST-CLASS AVERAGES

Bowling (Contd)	O	M	R	W	Avge	Best	5wI
G.J.F. Ferris	104	20	356	13	27.38	4-54	–
A.J. Murphy	91	16	288	10	28.80	3-67	–
C. Penn	117.3	24	407	14	29.07	5-65	1
A.P. Igglesden	125	25	372	11	33.81	4-46	–
A.R.C. Fraser	156	40	370	10	37.00	3-19	–
R.S. Rutnagur	164	34	528	14	37.71	3-50	–
C.D. Fraser-Darling	120	16	461	12	38.41	5-84	1
E.A. Moseley	124.3	14	447	11	40.63	4-70	–
G.E. Sainsbury	169.1	46	498	12	41.50	4-146	–

Fielding Statistics (Qualification: 20 dismissals)

83 D.E. East (64c, 19s)
81 R.J. Parks (73c, 8s)
66 S.J. Rhodes (58c, 8s)
60 R.C. Russell (56c, 4s)
51 S.A. Marsh (48c, 3s)
49 G.W. Humpage (41c, 8s)
48 P.R. Downton (43c, 5s)
48 B.N. French (44c, 4s)
44 D.L. Bairstow (41c, 3s)
44 C.J. Richards (39c, 5s)
40 T. Davies (32c, 8s)
38 M.A. Lynch
37 I.J. Gould (36c, 1s)
37 S.N.V. Waterton (32c, 5s)
36 T. Gard (30c, 6s)
35 C. Marples (31c, 4s)
32 R.A. Harper
32 C. Maynard (29c, 3s)
31 C.S. Cowdrey
30 G.A. Hick

29 K.M. Curran
28 C.E.B. Rice
25 K.W.R. Fletcher
24 K.J. Barnett
24 J.D. Birch
24 P. Gill
24 P. Johnson
24 P.J. Whitticase (23c 1s)
23 B.J.M. Maher
23 R.J. Bailey
23 C.W. Scott (22c, 1s)
22 J.W. Lloyds
21 C.W.J. Athey
21 G.A. Gooch
21 P.J. Prichard
21 R.A. Smith
21 C.J. Tavaré
20 N.G.B. Cook
20 D.A. Graveney

Benson & Hedges Cup

Middlesex won the Benson & Hedges Cup at the end of one of its most fluctuating and, latterly, thrilling finals. The margin was 2 runs after Kent needed 14 runs off the last over, 6 off the last three balls, and, through the medium of Graham Diley, 5 off the last ball.

Both sides had been knocked out of the NatWest Trophy earlier in the week, and in Middlesex's case the B & H Cup represented their last chance to maintain a record of one trophy per season under Mike Gatting's four-year captaincy.

The fluctuations began soon after Kent had won the toss and put Middlesex in on a damp, heavily overcast morning. The loss of Slack in the third over was countered by a stand of 60 between Miller and Gatting. But after Ellison had removed Gatting and Butcher with successive balls, the rest of Middlesex's innings became a struggle to reach the relative respectability of 199 for 7, a point achieved mainly by Radley and Emburey.

When Kent in reply were 20 for 3 against Daniel and Cowans, it was their batsmen who were struggling — and struggling at barely 2 runs an over. A slip catch to remember by Emburey, low at the full extent of the right arm and when the ball was almost past him, disposed of Christopher Cowdrey, and at 72 for 5 with only 20 overs left, Kent seemed out of it.

Graham Cowdrey and Baptiste then staged a remarkable recovery which seized the initiative and kept the required rate at just under 10 per over. With Ellison replacing Baptiste with no loss of momentum, Kent reached a position from which they seemed the likely winners, so well were they going.

When 19 were needed in 2 overs with 3 wickets left, including Ellison's, Gatting made a momentous decision, preferring the spin of Edmonds at the Pavilion end to the pace of Cowans. It probably won the match. With his second ball, Edmonds bowled Ellison. In the last over, bowled by Hughes, Marsh pulled the third ball for 6 but, with 6 still needed, could only score 1 run off the next 2 balls.

John Emburey received the gold award for his all-round performance, which included the 11 overs for 17 runs that had been mainly responsible for driving Kent so far behind the clock.

In the semi-finals, Kent always had the measure of Worcestershire, and Middlesex, having caused a collapse in a once prosperous Notts innings, duly made the runs needed despite the early running-out of Gatting, who still came to the final averaging 98.

In the previous rounds, Derbyshire and Essex had, like Middlesex, won all four zonal matches, but both were knocked out in the quarter-finals, by Kent and Nottinghamshire, respectively.

In the zonal matches, Scotland won their first victory in 26 B & H matches, beating Lancashire by 3 runs. They had earlier given Worcestershire a nasty shock. At the end of the first day's play in Glasgow, Worcestershire's answer to a score of 109 for 9 stood at 53 for 7, but they ultimately won by 2 wickets.

Zonal Results

Group A	P	W	L	Pts
DERBYSHIRE	4	4	–	8
NORTHAMPTONSHIRE	4	3	1	6
Warwickshire	4	2	2	4
Leicestershire	4	1	3	2
Minor Counties	4	–	4	0

Group B	P	W	L	Pts
WORCESTERSHIRE	4	3	1	6
NOTTINGHAMSHIRE	4	3	1	6
Yorkshire	4	2	2	4
Lancashire	4	1	3	2
Scotland	4	1	3	2

Group C	P	W	L	Pts
ESSEX	4	4	–	8
SUSSEX	4	3	1	6
Gloucestershire	4	2	2	4
Somerset	4	1	3	2
Glamorgan	4	–	4	0

Group D	P	W	L	Pts
MIDDLESEX	4	4	–	8
KENT	4	2	2	4
Hampshire	4	2	2	4
Surrey	4	2	2	4
Combined Universities	4	–	4	0

Note: Where two or more teams in a group have equal points, their positions are determined by the faster rate of taking wickets in all zonal matches (total balls bowled divided by wickets taken).

Final Rounds

Quarter-Finals 28, 29 May	Semi-Finals 11 June	Final 12 July
Derbyshire† (£2,250) / Kent	Kent	Kent (£9,500)
Northamptonshire† (£2,250) / Worcestershire†	Worcestershire† £4,500	
Middlesex† / Sussex (£2,250)	Middlesex†	Middlesex (£19,000)
Essex† (£2,250) / Nottinghamshire	Nottinghamshire† £4,500	Middlesex

† Home team.
Prize money in brackets.

Benson & Hedges Cup Winners

1972	Leicestershire	1977	Gloucestershire	1982	Somerset
1973	Kent	1978	Kent	1983	Middlesex
1974	Surrey	1979	Essex	1984	Lancashire
1975	Leicestershire	1980	Northamptonshire	1985	Leicestershire
1976	Kent	1981	Somerset	1986	Middlesex

Kent v Middlesex 1986 Benson & Hedges Cup Final
Middlesex won by 2 runs
Played at Lord's, 12 July
Toss: Kent. Umpires: D.J. Constant and D.R. Shepherd
Man of the Match: J.E. Emburey (Adjudicator: D.I. Gower)

Middlesex		Runs	Mins	Balls	6s	4s
W.N. Slack	b Dilley	0	9	8	–	–
A.J.T. Miller	c Marsh b Cowdrey	37	123	73	–	3
M.W. Gatting*	c Marsh b Ellison	25	71	66	–	3
R.O. Butcher	c Marsh b Ellison	0	1	1	–	–
C.T. Radley	run out (Marsh)	54	117	93	–	6
P.R. Downton†	lbw b Ellison	13	40	30	–	–
J.E. Emburey	b Baptiste	28	50	45	–	1
P.H. Edmonds	not out	15	22	13	–	–
S.P. Hughes	not out	4	8	5	–	–
N.G. Cowans	did not bat					
W.W. Daniel	"					
Extras	(LB 8, W 11, NB 4)	23				
	(55 overs; 226 minutes)	**199-7**				

Kent		Runs	Mins	Balls	6s	4s
M.R. Benson	c Downton b Cowans	1	34	23	–	–
S.G. Hinks	lbw b Cowans	13	55	35	–	1
C.J. Tavaré	c Downton b Daniel	3	13	15	–	–
N.R. Taylor	c Miller b Edmonds	19	87	78	–	1
C.S. Cowdrey*	c Emburey b Hughes	19	95	45	–	–
G.R. Cowdrey	c Radley b Hughes	58	86	70	2	3
E.A.E. Baptiste	b Edmonds	20	42	35	–	–
R.M. Ellison	b Edmonds	29	24	18	1	1
S.A. Marsh†	not out	14	13	9	1	–
G.R. Dilley	not out	4	9	3	–	–
D.L. Underwood	did not bat					
Extras	(LB 9, W 8)	17				
	(55 overs; 218 minutes)	**197-8**				

Kent	O	M	R	W
Dilley	11	2	19	1
Baptiste	11	0	61	1
Cowdrey, C.S.	11	0	48	1
Ellison	11	2	27	3
Underwood	11	4	36	0

Middlesex	O	M	R	W
Cowans	9	2	18	2
Daniel	11	1	43	1
Gatting	4	0	18	0
Hughes	9	3	34	2
Emburey	11	4	17	0
Edmonds	11	1	58	3

Fall of Wickets

Wkt	M	K
1st	6	17
2nd	66	20
3rd	66	20
4th	85	62
5th	131	72
6th	163	141
7th	183	178
8th	–	182
9th	–	–
10th	–	–

NatWest Bank Trophy

Sussex, the first champions of limited-overs cricket in England, and last winners of the competition in 1978 in its Gillette days, took the NatWest Trophy in 1986. For a county so lowly placed in the Championship and one so badly hampered by injuries, they won the title with a degree of ease that was particularly commendable as they were not drawn at home after the second round.

Only in the final against Lancashire, also former masters of the one-day game, was Sussex's supremacy at all in doubt. The match, played on a cool, dull day, had its exciting passages, but its finish, reached with 10 balls to spare, was nowhere as gripping as those of the two previous finals. In winning by 7 wickets, Sussex bettered the highest target achieved by a side batting second in the final — 243.

The occasion had emotional overtones in that it was generally accepted that this would be the great Clive Lloyd's last appearance in a Lord's final, and the whole ground stood to him as he walked out in the midst of a Lancashire collapse which followed a sound start to the innings. Perhaps overcome by the reception, Lloyd fell without scoring, to the fourth ball he faced, and soon Lancashire were reduced to 100 for 5.

That they stayed in the battle was thanks to a century stand for the sixth wicket between Neil Fairbrother and Andrew Hayhurst. The earlier collapse was wrought by Dermot Reeve who, making the ball deviate both ways off the seam, took 4 for 20 and laid instant claim to the Man of the Match award.

After losing the wicket of Alikhan at 19, Sussex encountered no problems except the growing darkness after a late tea. There was a succession of substantial partnerships. Paul Parker made 85 with great authority, and his role was then assumed by Imran Khan, who remained unbeaten with 50, having already shone with the ball during Lancashire's innings.

The rivals of the previous year's epic final made early exits. Essex, the holders, were surprisingly beaten by Warwickshire as early as in the second round. Nottinghamshire, the runners-up, scored a worthy win over Kent at this stage, but fell to Surrey at the next hurdle, and that despite Richard Hadlee's turning in an all-round performance that merited the Man of the Match award.

Lancashire were pressed hard to reach the final. Against Somerset, in the second round, they scraped through by only 3 runs, and in the semi-final, at the Oval, they only just got their nose in front, having weathered a truly great innings of 112 by Trevor Jesty, the glory of which can be assessed by the fact that the next highest contribution to a total of 225 was 19, with only four other batsmen even getting into double figures.

Except for the first round and the final, the competition was plagued by rain at every stage, and Sussex's semi-final against Worcestershire was spread over three days. Bowling first, when conditions were best suited to the purpose, they won by 5 wickets. They may have been unlucky with the draw, but they had the luck of the coin.

ENGLISH SEASON 1986/NATWEST BANK TROPHY

Gillette Cup Winners

1963	Sussex	1969	Yorkshire	1975	Lancashire
1964	Sussex	1970	Lancashire	1976	Northamptonshire
1965	Yorkshire	1971	Lancashire	1977	Middlesex
1966	Warwickshire	1972	Lancashire	1978	Sussex
1967	Kent	1973	Gloucestershire	1979	Somerset
1968	Warwickshire	1974	Kent	1980	Middlesex

NatWest Bank Trophy Winners

1981 Derbyshire 1982 Surrey 1983 Somerset 1984 Middlesex 1985 Essex 1986 Sussex

1986 Tournament

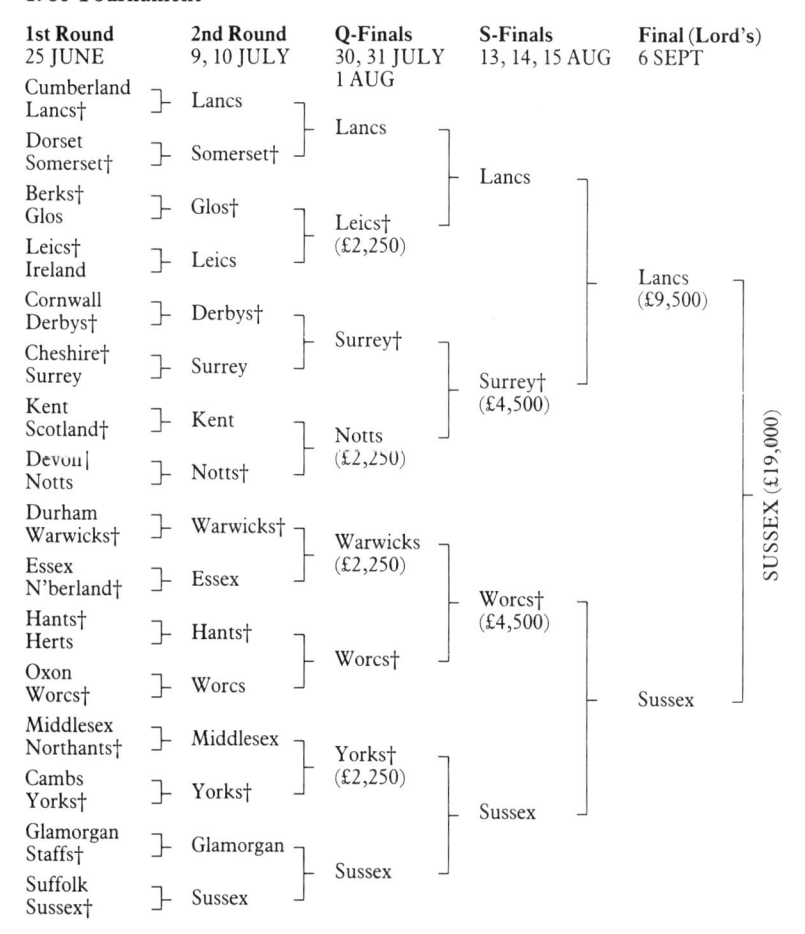

1st Round 25 JUNE	2nd Round 9, 10 JULY	Q-Finals 30, 31 JULY 1 AUG	S-Finals 13, 14, 15 AUG	Final (Lord's) 6 SEPT
Cumberland / Lancs†	Lancs	Lancs	Lancs	Lancs (£9,500)
Dorset / Somerset†	Somerset			
Berks† / Glos	Glos	Leics† (£2,250)		
Leics† / Ireland	Leics			
Cornwall / Derbys†	Derbys†	Surrey†	Surrey† (£4,500)	
Cheshire† / Surrey	Surrey			
Kent / Scotland†	Kent	Notts (£2,250)		SUSSEX (£19,000)
Devon / Notts	Notts†			
Durham / Warwicks†	Warwicks†	Warwicks (£2,250)	Worcs† (£4,500)	
Essex / N'berland†	Essex			
Hants† / Herts	Hants†	Worcs†		
Oxon / Worcs†	Worcs			Sussex
Middlesex / Northants†	Middlesex	Yorks† (£2,250)	Sussex	
Cambs / Yorks†	Yorks†			
Glamorgan / Staffs†	Glamorgan	Sussex		
Suffolk / Sussex†	Sussex			

†Home team.
Amounts in brackets show prize-money won by that county.

Lancashire v Sussex 1986 NatWest Bank Trophy Final
Sussex won by 7 wickets
Played at Lord's, 6 September
Toss: Sussex. Umpires: H.D. Bird and K.E. Palmer
Man of the Match: D.A. Reeve (Adjudicator: Sir Leonard Hutton)

Lancashire		Runs	Mins	Balls	6s	4s
G.D. Mendis	lbw b Reeve	17	71	47	–	1
G. Fowler	c Gould b C.M. Wells	24	56	44	–	3
J. Abrahams	c Pigott b Reeve	20	53	45	–	3
C.H. Lloyd*	lbw b Reeve	0	3	4	–	–
N.H. Fairbrother	b Pigott	63	153	108	–	5
S.J. O'Shaughnessy	b Reeve	4	23	23	–	–
A.N. Hayhurst	c Gould b Imran	49	87	74	–	5
C. Maynard†	c Gould b Imran	14	10	7	–	3
M. Watkinson	not out	15	19	11	1	–
J. Simmons	not out	6	13	9	–	–
P.J.W. Allott	did not bat					
Extras	(B 1, LB 17, W 6, NB 6)	30				
	(60 overs; 251 minutes)	**242-8**				

Sussex		Runs	Mins	Balls	6s	4s
R.I. Alikhan	b Allott	6	33	27	–	–
A.M. Green	st Maynard b Simmons	62	152	131	–	8
P.W.G. Parker	c Abrahams b Hayhurst	85	145	112	1	9
Imran Khan	not out	50	63	61	–	3
C.M. Wells	not out	17	35	22	1	1
A.P. Wells	did not bat					
I.J. Gould*†	"					
G.S. Le Roux	"					
D.A. Reeve	"					
A.C.S. Pigott	"					
A.N. Jones	"					
Extras	(LB 17, W 6)	23				
	(58.2 overs; 216 minutes)	**243-3**				

Sussex	O	M	R	W
Imran Khan	12	2	43	2
Le Roux	9	0	43	0
Jones	3	0	25	0
Wells, C.M.	12	3	34	1
Reeve	12	4	20	4
Pigott	12	1	59	1

Lancashire	O	M	R	W
Watkinson	11.2	0	40	0
Allott	11	3	34	1
O'Shaughnessy	6	0	52	0
Hayhurst	12	2	38	1
Simmons	12	2	31	1
Abrahams	3	0	15	0
Fairbrother	3	0	16	0

Fall of Wickets

Wkt	L	S
1st	50	19
2nd	56	156
3rd	56	190
4th	85	–
5th	100	–
6th	203	–
7th	205	–
8th	217	–
9th	–	–
10th	–	–

John Player League

The last John Player League championship was resolved on the penultimate Sunday of its 18 seasons, but by no means as perfunctorily as this suggests. In order to claim the title, Hampshire had to beat Surrey at the Oval and Notts had to lose to Kent at Canterbury.

In the event, news that Notts had been beaten by 6 wickets reached the Oval early enough to intensify an already nerve-wracking atmosphere. Hampshire, resticted to 149 for 8 — their lowest total of the season — were desperately striving to defend it as Surrey struggled to 96 for 5 at the end of the 33rd over.

All seemed well until David Thomas, dropped by Connor early on, hit an audacious 34 to put Surrey within 7 runs of victory at the start of the last over. Thomas swung, and James, on the long-on boundary, sank to his knees as he took the catch. Needham was then run out, and Gray, needing a 6 off the last ball, failed to make the necessary contact. Connor, the bowler, was visibly relieved.

So Hampshire, for the third time, took the John Player League honours, but at various times — notably in the first half of the summer — the hopes of several counties ran high. Yorkshire, for example, began with four straight wins to become the first outright leaders, on June 1.

The following Sunday, however, they allowed Gloucestershire a first victory, at Headingley, and when they lost their next match, at Lord's, Somerset rose from 'nowhere' to the top of the table with 16 points from 5 matches, morally ahead of Essex and Yorks, who had played 6.

Somerset's success was short-lived. Beaten by Notts at Bath, they slipped into 5th place, and Essex assumed the leadership with 18 points from 7 games. This was a false position, however, because, of the six sides jointly lying second with 16 points, Hampshire and Northants had played only 4 games each. Furthermore, by beating Kent and Yorkshire, respectively, they had effectively shaken out the leader board. Neither of these early front-runners was now a serious threat.

Instead, Hants and Northants became joint leaders on June 29, each with two games in hand over Notts — equal on points — and 2 points up on Essex and Kent, both ahead by one game.

For more than a month the two leaders stayed clear of the field, Hampshire inching ahead when, on July 20, Northants were beaten by Glamorgan, at Neath. Essex, meanwhile, having shaken off an excruciating 2-run defeat by Lancs at Old Trafford, returned to winning form against Somerset, Worcester, Sussex, and Leicester to find themselves joint second, with Hants, on August 11.

That was the day on which Northants were extremely grateful to take the lead by 2 points awarded for their no-result match against Somerset, at Wellingborough — the scene of Botham's record-breaking 13 sixes during an astonishing innings of 175 not out. Hampshire, less blessed by the day's rain, lost 4 valuable points at Bournemouth, where Sussex beat them on faster scoring rate.

Even worse, the following week they suffered a further set-back, by 8 wickets at Lord's, and as Essex, inspired by Hardie's undefeated 109, beat Northants at Colchester, the reigning champions moved into first place, setting the scene for a fascinating finale.

On August 24, another remarkable century — Greenidge's record-breaking 10th in Sunday League cricket — set up a Hampshire victory against Yorkshire at Bournemouth. And though Lever, with 3 for 33 on the same day, established a new John Player wicket-taking record of 341, Essex at Chelmsford were beaten by Surrey as Gray pulled him for 4 off the last ball. How that feat must have haunted Hampshire as Gray again faced that final ball at the Oval.

Final Table	P	W	L	T	NR	Pts	6s	4w
1 HAMPSHIRE (3)	16	12	3	0	1	50	37	5
2 Essex (1)	16	11	4	0	1	46	37	3
3 Nottinghamshire (12)	16	10	5	0	1	42	23	5
4 Sussex (2)	16	10	6	0	0	40	28	6
5 Northamptonshire (5)	16	9	5	0	2	40	33	2
6 Somerset (10)	16	8	6	0	2	36	61	1
7 Kent (10)	16	7	5	1	3	36	18	5
8 Yorkshire (6)	16	7	6	1	2	34	26	3
9 Derbyshire (4)	16	7	9	0	0	28	35	—
10 Warwickshire (6)	16	5	7	2	2	28	13	1
11 Middlesex (12)	16	5	7	1	3	28	10	1
12 Lancashire (14)	16	6	9	0	1	26	29	—
13 Glamorgan (14)	16	6	9	0	1	26	19	4
14 Surrey (17)	16	5	8	1	2	26	20	2
15 Leicestershire (6)	16	5	10	0	1	22	18	4
16 Worcestershire (6)	16	5	11	0	0	20	21	2
17 Gloucestershire (6)	16	3	11	0	2	16	8	—

For the first four places only, the final positions for teams finishing with equal points are decided by the most wins. 1985 final positions are shown in brackets.

Winners

1969	Lancashire	1975	Hampshire	1981	Essex
1970	Lancashire	1976	Kent	1982	Sussex
1971	Worcestershire	1977	Leicestershire	1983	Yorkshire
1972	Kent	1978	Hampshire	1984	Essex
1973	Kent	1979	Somerset	1985	Essex
1974	Leicestershire	1980	Warwickshire	1986	Hampshire

1986 Awards and Distribution of Prize Money

£19,000 and League Trophy to champions HAMPSHIRE
£9,500 to runners-up Essex
£4,250 to third-placing Nottinghamshire
£2,500 to fourth-placing Sussex
£275 to winner of each match (shared in event of 'no results' and ties)
£400 to the batsman hitting most sixes in the season: I.T. Botham (Somerset) – 23
£400 to the bowler taking four or more wickets most times in the season:
  C.E.B. Rice (Nottinghamshire) – 5
£250 to the batsman scoring the fastest 50 in a match televised on BBC2:
  (shared in 1986) C.T. Radley (Middlesex) – 49 balls v Somerset at Taunton on 11 May;
  A.P. Wells (Sussex) – 49 balls v Glamorgan at Hove on 13 July

Second XI Competition

Lancashire won the Second XI Championship in 1986 in the most convincing manner, winning 9 of their 18 matches and drawing the remainder. No other county was able to compete with a very accomplished and efficient Lancashire side.

In the matches against their closest rivals, Warwickshire, Lancashire won by 5 wickets in early May and were equally successful in early June, beating them by 10 wickets, with Hendriksen taking 5-41 and Chadwick and Hayes both scoring centuries. Only Kent and Surrey were able to amass more bowling points and Surrey and Yorkshire more batting points.

Once again, 1986 proved a prolific year for both bowler and batsman. Two double centuries were scored — Blakey 273 not out for Yorkshire v Northamptonshire and Hinks 226 for Kent v Hampshire — and well over 70 individual hundreds.

Other outstanding performances included: Tufnell's 9-79 for Middlesex against Hampshire, Barwick's 8-31 for Glamorgan, and Payne's 140 not out and 107 in the same match for Gloucestershire. Falkner all but reached a double century with 193 not out for Surrey against Sussex, and Moles scored 136 for Warwickshire and then took 5-45 against Middlesex followed by 127 not out and 48 against Gloucestershire. And opener Brown of Middlesex managed to remain on the field for the whole match against Sussex, scoring 125 not out and 79 not out.

Second XI Championship Final Table

	P	W	L	D	Batting	Bowling	Total points	Avge
1 LANCASHIRE (5)	18	9*	0	9	40	47	227	12.61
2 Warwickshire (7)	16	6	5	5	31	47	174	10.87
3 Essex (6)	13	4	3	6	35	37	136	10.46
4 Middlesex (3)	15	5	3	7	36	39	155	10.33
5 Yorkshire (12)	16	5*	1	10	43	38	157	9.81
6 Leicestershire (11)	14	4	3	7	26	40	130	9.28
7 Somerset (14)	10	3	5	2	16	23	87	8.70
8 Worcestershire (10)	12	3	5	4	19	36	103	8.58
9 Derbyshire (15)	14	3	3	8	26	38	112	8.00
10 Surrey (2)	16	2	2	12	43	48	123	7.68
11 Nottinghamshire (1)	15	3	4	8	27	37	112	7.46
12 Northamptonshire (16)	14	2	4	8	33	37	102	7.28
13 Kent (8)	15	2	3	19	27	49	108	7.20
14 Hampshire (13)	13	1	3	9	31	39	86	6.61
15 Sussex (4)	12	1	5	6	23	37	76	6.33
16 Gloucestershire (17)	13	1	3	9	25	36	77	5.92
17 Glamorgan (9)	16	1*	3	12	28	32	72	4.50

1985 final positions are shown in brackets. 16 points for win. * includes one win in 1-innings match (12pts).

Warwick Under-25 Competition

Zonal Group A	P	W	L	NR	Pts
YORKSHIRE	6	5	1	–	20
Lancashire	6	4	2	–	16
Derbyshire	6	3	3	–	12
Nottinghamshire	6	0	6	–	0

Zonal Group C	P	W	L	NR	Pts
SURREY†	6	4	2	–	16
Kent	6	4	2	–	16
Hampshire	6	3	3	–	12
Sussex	6	1	5	–	4

Zonal Group B	P	W	L	NR	Pts
MIDDLESEX*	6	4	2	–	16
Essex	6	3	1	2	16
Northamptonshire	6	3	3	–	12
Leicestershire	6	0	4	2	4

Zonal Group D	P	W	L	NR	Pts
WARWICKSHIRE	8	6	0	2	28
Glamorgan	8	5	2	1	22
Worcestershire	8	4	4	–	16
Gloucestershire	8	2	5	1	10
Somerset	8	1	7	–	4

* Qualified by virtue of most wins

† Qualified by virtue of better strike rate

Semi-Finals
SURREY beat Warwick by 118 runs
YORKSHIRE beat Middlesex by 2 runs

Final
SURREY beat Yorkshire by 6 wickets

Bain Dawes Trophy

North Zone	P	W	L	NR	Pts
NORTHAMPTONSHIRE	5	5	0	–	10
Yorkshire	5	4	1	–	8
Derbyshire	5	1	2	2	4
Nottinghamshire	5	1	3	1	3
Lancashire	5	1	3	1	3
Leicestershire	5	1	4	–	2

South-East Zone	P	W	L	NR	Pts
ESSEX	5	4	1	–	8
Kent	5	3	1	1	7
Surrey	5	3	1	1	7
Hampshire	5	1	2	2	4
Middlesex	5	1	3	1	3
Sussex	5	0	4	1	1

South-West Zone	P	W	L	NR	Pts
WORCESTERSHIRE	4	4	0	–	8
Somerset	4	3	1	–	6
Gloucestershire	4	2	2	–	4
Glamorgan	4	1	3	–	2
Warwickshire	4	0	4	–	0

Round Robin	P	W	L	NR	Pts
Northamptonshire	2	1	0	1	3
Essex	2	1	0	1	3
Worcestershire	2	0	2	0	0

Final
NORTHANTS beat Essex by 14 runs

Minor Counties

Both Minor County Competitions saw new winners emerge in 1986, so that the stranglehold achieved over the last three years by Cheshire, Durham and Herts was at last broken.

Cumberland became Minor County Champions for the first time in their history, beating Oxfordshire by two wickets with just one ball to spare in a final at Worcester which, sadly, was forced by the weather to be extended into a second day. In the knockout, Norfolk (who had a miserable time in the championship) carried all before them, eventually beating Herts in the final at St Albans by 30 runs having set a new record in the quarter-finals with 336 for 5 against Lincolnshire.

Cumberland's place at the top of the Eastern Division was won by consistently good all-round play. Oxfordshire's place at the head of the Western Division was not achieved until the very end of the season, when Dorset, their only possible rivals at this stage, had their match with Somerset II severely curtailed by rain.

Paul Atkins (Bucks) had a prolific summer with the bat to take the Wilfred Rhodes Trophy; Graham Roope, who had threatened to take that Trophy, took, instead, the Frank Edwards Trophy for bowling.

Minor Counties Championship

E. Division	P	W	L	U	T	B	NR	Pts	W. Division	P	W	L	U	T	B	NR	Pts
1 C'berland‡	9	5	1	3	0	0	0	59	1 Oxon‡	9	4	1^1	1	0	2	1	50
2 Staffs‡	9	3	0	2	0	4	0	40	2 Dorset‡	9	3	1^1	3	0	1	1	45
3 Cambs‡	9	2	1^1	3	0	3	0	35	3 Wilts‡	9	3	1	3	0	2	0	41
4 Herts‡	9	2	3^2	2	0	2	0	34	4 Somerset II	9	3	0	1	0	4	1	39
5 N'berland‡	9	2	1	3	0	2	1	33	5 Cheshire‡	9	2	2^1	3	0	2	0	34
6 Durham‡	9	1	1^1	5	0	0	2	32	6 Bucks†	9	2	1	3	0	3	0	32
7 Suffolk‡	9	2	3*	2	0	2	0	30	7 Devon‡	9	1	2*	3	1	2	0	25
8 Beds	9	1	1^1	2	1	4	0	25	8 Berks	9	1	1	2	1	3	1	23
9 Lincs	9	0	2^1	1	0	4	2	14	9 Shrops	9	0	4†	3	0	2	0	19
10 Norfolk	9	0	5^1	0	1	2	1	9	10 Cornwall	9	0	6^1	1	0	2	0	8

Points: 10 for win; in matches drawn, U = up on 1st innings (3 pts), T = tied (2), B = behind (1); NR = no result (2); 3 for 1st innings lead in match lost, the superior figure in the L column indicating the number of times 1st innings points were gained in matches lost. *Tie on 1st innings tie in match lost (2pts); †1st innings pts in 2 matches lost plus tie on 1st innings in 1 match lost. ‡ Qualified for 1987 NatWest Bank Trophy.

Leading Averages

Batting	I	NO	HS	Runs	Avge	Bowling	O	M	R	W	Avge
P.D. Atkins	11	3	160*	488	61.00	G.R.J. Roope	123	32	316	22	14.36
N.A. Riddell	14	5	101	537	59.67	R.C. Green	160.4	38	397	27	14.70
M.D. Nurton	15	3	104*	694	57.83	R.A. Bunting	154	31	453	29	15.62
N. Priestley	14	2	144	679	56.58	M.G. Stephenson	206.3	74	459	29	15.83
S. Burrow	13	4	84*	480	53.33	R.N. Busby	220.4	54	588	36	16.33
N.R. Williams	11	2	109*	472	52.44	J.E. Benjamin	140.3	20	439	26	16.88
A. Kennedy	14	2	100	624	52.00	I.E.W. Sanders	145.3	29	411	24	17.13
M.G. Stephenson	10	7	34*	156	52.00	B. Wood	175	60	381	22	17.32
G.R.J. Roope	16	4	78	620	51.67	P.J. Lewington	319.5	111	721	40	18.03
S.G. Plumb	17	1	116*	796	49.75	W.G. Merry	190	50	515	28	18.39

Knock-out Competition

Final: At Clarence Park, St. Albans, 20 July. NORFOLK beat HERTS by 30 runs (55 overs). Norfolk 223-8 (R.D.P. Huggins 53; D.R. Thomas 46); Herts 193 (50.4 overs). (E.P. Neal 49, D.G. Ottley 41).

Cumberland v Oxfordshire, Minor Counties Championship Play-off
Cumberland won by 2 wickets
Played at the County Ground, Worcester, 13, 14 September (55 overs)
Toss: Cumberland
Umpires: D.B. Harrison and C. Smith

Oxfordshire

G.C. Ford	b Scothern	4
M.D. Nurton	c & b Woods	36
P.A. Fowler	b Scothern	3
P.J. Garner	c Clarke b Woods	36
C.J. Clements	b Halliwell	28
A. Crossley	b Halliwell	1
G.R. Hobbins	run out	27
S.R. Porter	b Reidy	0
R.N. Busby	c Hodgson b Halliwell	17
K.A. Arnold	b Reidy	2
I.J. Curtis	not out	0
Extras		12
	(54.3 overs)	**166**

Cumberland

M.D. Woods	c Fowler b Porter	14
C.J. Stockdale	lbw b Busby	11
G.D. Hodgson	lbw b Hobbins	57
B.W. Reidy	c Hobbins b Porter	23
G.J. Clarke	c Ford b Garner	12
J.R. Moyes	b Garner	17
S. Sharp	b Garner	9
I. Cooper	run out	5
S. Dutton	not out	6
D. Halliwell	not out	0
M.G. Scothern	did not bat	
Extras		15
	(8 wkts, 54.5 overs)	**169**

Cumberland	O	M	R	W
Halliwell	10.3	3	27	3
Scothern	11	4	32	2
Sharp	11	3	34	0
Reidy	11	1	34	2
Woods	11	1	29	2

Oxfordshire	O	M	R	W
Busby	11	6	10	1
Arnold	8	1	31	0
Hobbins	8	2	19	1
Porter	11	0	41	2
Curtis	11	2	34	0
Garner	5.5	1	23	3

Fall of Wickets

Wkt	O	C
1st	15	18
2nd	19	38
3rd	75	94
4th	87	118
5th	89	143
6th	139	157
7th	142	163
8th	154	163
9th	162	–
10th	166	–

England YC v Sri Lanka YC

England Young Cricketers won a remarkable victory over Sri Lanka in the third and last match to taker a series against opponents who had mostly looked stronger. Sri Lanka, who included three Test players — the age qualification was under 19 on 1 September 1985 — had won both one-day matches and had had much the better of the second four-day match.

At Headingley in the first of two rain-affected draws, England earned a first innings lead and eventually set Sri Lanka to make 280 in 285 minutes, Blakey, the Yorkshire opening batsman, having added 101 not out to his first innings 55. The target proved beyond the Sri Lankan batsmen, who were not at their best on a sluggish pitch.

At Bristol, the Sri Lankan captain Gurusinha and Soza put on 291 for the second wicket, but the third day's play was almost entirely lost through rain and Sri Lanka could not exploit the huge lead which they built up.

In the final match at Trent Bridge, Tillekeratne scored his second hundred of the series and Sri Lanka made 406. By the end of the second day they had reduced England to 134 for 6 of which the schoolboy Ramprakash made 46. England were in danger of following on, but next day their later batsmen, led by Smith of Glamorgan, reduced the deficit to 116, after which the Middlesex fast bowler Alistair Fraser, having made 41, had Sri Lanka 41 for 3.

On the final day Sri Lanka were bowled out for 140. England then made light of scoring 257 to win at just over 3½ runs an over and, after two fine innings of controlled aggression by the captain Roseberry and Bartlett, won by 6 wickets.

2, 3, 4, 5 August at Headingley, Leeds. MATCH DRAWN. Toss: Sri Lanka VC. Umpires: C. Cook and B.J. Meyer. EYC 290 (M.W. Alleyne 66, R.J. Bartlett 58, R.J. Blakey 55) and 198-5 dec (R.J. Blakey 101*, R.J. Bartlett 79). SLYC 209 (D.S. Perera 52) and 158-5 (D.S. Perera 54*, C.R. Soza 54).

16, 17, 18, 19 August at County Ground, Bristol. MATCH DRAWN. Toss: SLYC. Umpires: J.H. Harris and A.G.T. Whitehead. EYC 333 (D. Ripley 75). SLYC 576-7 (A.P. Gurusinha 161, C.R. Soza 123, H.P. Tillekeratne 121*, R.C.A. Paulpillai 56).

30, 31 August, 1, 2 September at Trent Bridge, Nottingham. ENGLAND YC beat Sri Lanka YC by 6 wickets. Toss: England YC. Umpires: J. Birkenshaw and N.T. Plews. SLYC 406 (H.P. Tillekeratne 125, R.C.A. Paulpillai 81, C.R. Soza 51) and 140 (A.G.J. Fraser 4-52). EYC 290 (I. Smith 97; D.R. Madena 4-74) and 258-4 (R.J. Bartlett 81, M.A. Roseberry 72).

One-day Internationals

9 August at County Ground, Chelmsford. SRI LANKA YC beat England YC by 139 runs. Toss: England YC. SLYC 254-8 (55 overs) (A.P. Gurusinha 84, B.R. Jurangpathy 54; I. Smith 4-50). EYC 115 (36.5 overs) (M.W. Alleyne 40).

11 August at Lord's. SRI LANKA YC beat England YC by 4 wickets. Toss: England. EYC 158 (54.3 overs). SLYC 162-6 (48.5 overs).

Sri Lanka Young Cricketers won the Agatha Christie Trophy 2-0.

ICC Trophy 1986

Held between 11 June and 8 July, the ICC Trophy enjoyed unprecedented luck with the weather and every match was completed, although the final, in which Zimbabwe beat The Netherlands to retain the Trophy, needed a second day. Zimbabwe, who were stretched only in the final, confirmed their superiority to win a place in the World Cup for a second time.

Final Group Tables

Group One*	P	W	L	Pts	RpO	Group Two	P	W	L	Pts	RpO
ZIMBABWE	6	6	0	24	4.92	THE NETHERLANDS	8	7	1	28	5.03
DENMARK	6	5	1	20	3.68	BERMUDA	8	7	1	28	4.62
Malaysia	6	3	3	12	2.85	United States	8	7	1	28	4.21
Kenya	6	3	3	12	2.73	Canada	8	5	3	20	4.42
East Africa	6	2	4	8	3.07	Papua-New Guinea	8	4	4	16	5.08
Bangladesh	6	2	4	8	2.82	Hong Kong	8	3	5	12	3.58
Argentina	6	0	6	0	2.52	Fiji	8	2	6	8	3.23
						Gibraltar	8	1	7	4	2.58
						Israel	8	0	8	0	2.78

* Singapore & West Africa were unable to take part.

Win = 4 pts. Top two teams in each group qualify for semi-finals. Where points are equal, placings decided by runs per over (RpO).

Semi Finals
2 July. ZIMBABWE beat BERMUDA by 10 wickets at West Bromwich Dartmouth.
Bermuda 201-7 (60 overs) (Gibbons 58). Zimbabwe 205-0 (38.5 overs) (Paterson 123*, Brown 61*).

2 July. NETHERLANDS beat DENMARK by 5 wickets at Mitchells & Butlers.
Denmark 224-8 (60 overs) (Morild 86). Netherlands 225-5 (54.2 overs) (Gomes 127*).

Third-Place Play-Off
4 July. DENMARK beat BERMUDA by 6 wickets at Halesowen.
Bermuda 155 (37.3 overs) (Henriksen 4-26). Denmark 158-4 (26 overs) (From Hansen 78).

Final
Scorecard opposite.

ICC Records set in 1986
Highest Total: 455-9 (60 overs) — Papua-New Guinea v Gibraltar, 18 June
Lowest Total: 46 (25.4 overs) — Gibraltar v Canada, 20 June
Highest Individual Score: 172 — S.D. Myles, Hong Kong v Gibraltar, 11 June
Record Win: 369 runs — Papua-New Guinea beat Gibraltar, 18 June
Hat-Trick: J. Miller — USA v Canada, 11 June
Best Partnership: 251 — 1st wicket, S.R. Atkinson (162) & R. Lifmann (110), Netherlands v Israel, 18 June

20 hundreds were scored; P. Prashad (Canada) scored three. 15 five-wicket hauls were recorded; the best was 6-11 by B. Gohel for Hong Kong v Fiji on 27 June; two bowlers took five wickets twice – P.J. Bakker (Netherlands) and R. Elferink (Netherlands).

The Netherlands v Zimbabwe ICC Trophy Final
Zimbabwe won by 25 runs
Played at Lord's, 7, 8 July (60 overs)
Toss: The Netherlands. Umpires: A. Inman and P. Ogden

Zimbabwe

R.D. Brown	c van Weelde b Lubbers	60
G.A. Patterson	c Visee b van Weelde	11
A. Shah	c Lifmann b van Weelde	12
A.J. Pycroft*	c Schoonheim b Lubbers	30
D.L. Houghton†	b Lubbers	3
A.C. Waller	run out	59
G.C. Wallace	c Schoonheim b Lefebvre	26
P.W. Rawson	run out	1
I.P. Butchart	not out	13
I.E.A. Brandes	b Bakker	6
A.J. Traicos	not out	0
Extras	(LB8, W12, NB2)	22
		243-9

The Netherlands

S.R. Atkinson	c Pycroft b Traicos	31
R. Lifmann	lbw b Shah	41
R. Gomes	c Rawson b Butchart	27
S. Lubbers	not out	35
S. Lefebvre	b Brandes	8
R. Entrop	b Shah	0
D. Visee	b Brandes	5
R. Elferink	b Butchart	31
P.J. Bakker	b Rawson	11
R. Schoonheim†	b Butchart	2
R. van Weelde*	b Butchart	0
Extras	(B1, LB19, W6, NB1)	27
	(58.4 overs)	**218**

The Netherlands	O	M	R	W
Bakker	12	0	58	1
van Weelde	12	1	46	2
Elferink	9	2	31	0
Lefebvre	12	2	34	1
Lubbers	11	0	44	3
Visee	4	1	22	0

Zimbabwe	O	M	R	W
Rawson	11	3	27	1
Butchart	11.4	1	33	4
Traicos	12	2	31	1
Brandes	12	1	52	2
Shah	12	0	55	2

Fall of Wickets

Wkt	Z	TN
1st	18	50
2nd	41	109
3rd	93	109
4th	101	129
5th	170	130
6th	204	139
7th	205	206
8th	229	216
9th	238	218
10th	–	218

Lubbers retired hurt at 182-6 and resumed at 206-7

Village and Club Cricket

Now firmly established, the 'grass roots' weekend at Lord's towards the end of each season continues to grow in popularity. The spectators, admittedly partisan, exceed crowd numbers at average county matches, and the two finals are essentially good-humoured family affairs throughout. The 1986 matches enjoyed splendid weather, close finishes, and perfect pitches. Both, too, produced first-time champions.

William Younger Cup (45 overs). Lord's, 23 August. Stourbridge won toss. Weston-super-Mare 175 (C. Norton 39, N. Evans 32, S. Turner 30; S. Lampitt 5-43, D. Banks 2-34). Stourbridge: 176-6 (43.4 overs) (H. Patel 54, S. Lampitt 42, C. Tolley 24*; D. Hill 3-37). **Stourbridge won by 4 wickets.**

Stourbridge took the senior club event for the first time, although the final was won by a Birmingham League side — Old Hill in 1984 and 1985 — for the third successive year. Lampitt, of whom Worcestershire have great hopes, gave a fine all-round performance. He took 5 wickets at medium pace and made 42, but Bob Willis made fast bowler Dave Hill of the losing club his man of the match.

Weston-super-Mare opened with 73 from Norton and Langford, but off-spinner Smith, the Stourbridge captain, and Brewer, slow left-arm — both men aged 49 — took one wicket each and slowed the scoring rate. Weston struggled against Lampitt, who took the final two wickets with successive balls, and the innings closed at 175. Stourbridge, thanks to a third-wicket partnership of 76 between Patel and Lampitt and an unbeaten 24 from the promising Tolley, got home with eight balls and four wickets to spare. The winners received the William Younger Cup and £1,000, the runners-up £600.

National Village Club Championship (40 overs). Lord's, 24 August. Ynysygerwn won toss. Forge Valley 170-9 (C. Ridsdale 41, A. Grayson 29, M. Wall 24; J. Curtis 4-38, W. Harris 2-47). Ynysygerwn 165-9 (D. Thomas 55, R. Williams 23; S. Glaves 3-34, M. Shepperdson 2-21). **Forge Valley won by 5 runs.**

The competition, started in 1972, was sponsored for the first time by Norsk Hydro Fertilizers of Suffolk, and before a Sunday crowd of 3,000, Forge Valley, from near Scarborough, became the second Yorkshire village to defeat Glamorgan's Ynysygerwn in a Lord's final. The Welsh village had had much pre-match publicity, and sang gallantly in a defeat that might well have been a victory. Forge Valley started slowly but accumulated runs steadily, and the innings closed at 170-9, Curtis, a colliery worker, taking 4-38 in his nine overs. The Welsh, especially Thomas who had played in the 1979 defeat by East Bierley of Huddersfield, had the target well in their sights, though wickets fell regularly. Thomas batted most sensibly until the last ball of the 39th over, when he was bowled for 55. To renewed Yorkshire cheer-ing — Sir Leonard Hutton and Test umpire Dickie Bird were keen onlookers — Ynysygerwn faltered in the final over and ended five short. Mr Jack Davies, President of MCC, presented the trophy and £500 to Forge Valley, the losers getting £350.

Schools Cricket

Out of the stresses of examinations and rain damage to many midweek and traditional fixtures came much good cricket from end-of-term festivals and representative matches. One boy who moved very much to the top was Ramprakash of Gayton HS, at 16 a mature batsman on whom Middlesex are keeping a county paternal eye. He scored hundreds for MCC Schools at Lord's and against Wales and Scotland at England Schools Cricket Association (ESCA) level, so impressing the selectors that he gained a place in the Young England side for the final two of the four-day 'Tests' against the touring Sri Lanka Young Cricketers, who included three players who had appeared in full Tests for their country. In such company the Pinner boy proved well worth his place; he could have two more school seasons ahead, a university place, and a very bright future indeed.

There was sound evidence that youth cricket officials were getting right the formula by which to spot likely boys at early stages of development and to help them progress to higher things. For this the 'festivals season' — born out of examination-hit term-time fixtures — must be given much credit, with especial praise for the MCC Schools Trials held at Oxford over four days. There, ecumenically in the cricket sense of the word, boys from all backgrounds and schools have the chance to prove their worth in matches with their peers and against opponents they would not meet in normal school fixtures. There must always be a risk that schoolmaster 'scouts' fail to feed back talent information to central sources. Happily for the game at school level, though, those teachers who do the scouting do it with complete dedication; the net is close-meshed to ensure the best possible catch.

In mid-July there were festivals galore — at Tonbridge, Bedford, Cheltenham, St Paul's, Ipswich, and Rossall, to name but a few venues; there were ESCA series for all ages and stages. And so to Oxford for four days of intensive trials at the Keble College and St Edward's School grounds, with a starting 'field' of 44 boys from whom would be picked the main body of the MCC Schools XI to play National Association of Young Cricketers in the traditional two-day match at Lord's.

On the first two days at Oxford, ESCA and Headmasters' Conference Schools (HMC) held their own trials:

ESCA North 180-6 dec (S.P. Titchard, Lancs, 87) and 221-9 dec (N. Kendrick, Surrey, 8-83) drew with ESCA South 205-5 dec (M. Ramprakash, Middlesex, 87) and 139-6.
HMC South 225-5 dec (N. Stanley, Bedford Modern, 84, J. Longley, Tonbridge, 53) and 203-4 dec (D. Griggs, Felsted, 105*) drew with The Rest 158-5 and 226-9.

On the third day the 44 boys, regardless of school, formed four sides identified only by the names of the captains. On St Edward's, N.A. Stanley's XI made 205-9 declared, the captain contributing 95, and defeated T.M. Orrell's XI, 171, by 34 runs. At the next field, Keble S.G. Foster's made 189-8 dec and drew with T.G. Twose's, who levelled the totals for two fewer wickets lost when the overs ran out.

The final trial, on 22 July, ended on a high note. MCC Schools East made 213-6, including an elegant 114 from Crawley of Manchester GS. MCC

West, led by a dashing 89 from N.A. Stanley, got to 199-6.

ESCA went off to Rugby and HMC moved to the Christ Church ground for a three-day match with Sri Lanka YC. At first sightings HMC stood little chance against a touring side that included three under-19s who had played full Test cricket. Sri Lanka made 290 in their first innings (D. Perera 100, H. Tillekaratne 70, A. Gurusinha 62) and HMC, bowled out for 136, had to follow on. For most of the school players, a three-day match was a new event, yet, despite having lost Fishpool of Bishop's Stortford with a broken finger on the first morning, the rest of the side rose nobly to their task. Stanley, the captain, and Crawley with 75 and 77, respectively, Speight of Hurstpierpoint, 43, and Yates, Manchester GS, 39, turned defence and survival into attack, and HMC were able to declare their second innings at 330-8, a splendid recovery. Sri Lanka made 77-2, chasing 177.

For the previous two years, MCC Schools had beaten NAYC at Lord's, but rain and bad light doomed the 1986 match to a draw. Ramprakash followed his 117 against Scotland earlier in the week with 116 not out on 6 August. Stanley hit 41 and Atherton of Manchester GS, out of school cricket for some time with a broken thumb, declared at 203-4. NAYC included two sons of famous cricketers in Gary Lloyd (Lancashire) and Mark Ealham (Kent). Lloyd made 59 of NAYC's 132-4 — they declared immediately on avoiding the follow-on — and MCC in their second innings reached 134-3 (Ramprakash 61). The inevitable draw came with NAYC 165-4, 68 runs short of target.

Ramprakash's reputation was counter-productive when Combined Services batted for 65 overs to make 252-5 declared on the Friday; National Cricket Association Young Cricketers (M. Atherton 48, M. Ramprakash 47) were 165-7 from the 50 overs they were allowed.

The MCC Schools XI: M.R. Ramprakash (Gayton HS), S.P. Titchard (Priestley Coll), M.A. Atherton (Manchester GS) (capt), M.A. Crawley (Manchester GS), N.A. Stanley (Bedford Modern), P.N. Gover (Eastleigh Coll), H.R.J. Trump (Millfield), R.J. Turner (Millfield), P.J. Martin (Danum School, Doncaster), M.R. Newton (Peter Symonds), I.J. Houseman (Harrogate GS).

The NCA Young Cricketers XI: M.R. Ramprakash (Middlesex), S.P. Titchard (Cheshire), M.A. Atherton (Lancashire), (capt), G.D. Hodgson (Lancashire), N.J. Speak (Lancashire), G. Lloyd (Lancashire), H.R.J. Trump (Somerset), R.J. Turner (Somerset), P.J. Martin (Yorkshire), I.J. Houseman (Yorkshire), M. Taylor (Middlesex).

The school cricket term began with a wet May and many cancellations. Generally the batting proved stronger than the bowling it had to face, and Stanley (Bedford Modern), Longley (Tonbridge), Speight (Hurstpierpoint), Crawley (Manchester GS), Spiller (Worcester RGS), Morris (Stowe), and young Brown (Caterham), with many another, had aggregates of more than 1,000 runs. Harrow had an unbeaten season, but only heavy rain saved them from crushing defeat by Eton at Lord's. Tonbridge and Millfield were strong, as always. Felsted benefited from their winter tour of Australia, as did Bishop's Stortford from visiting Sri Lanka.

Women's Cricket

The first tour of England by the Indian Women's Cricket team produced two major records – one of note and the other best forgotten. The latter occurred in the first Test. England, in sight of victory and chasing a second innings total of 254, were abruptly halted in the penultimate hour when India succeeded in bowling a record-low 8 overs. With no Special Regulations to enforce a minimum number of overs in a day, England were thwarted, finishing just 25 runs short with 5 wickets standing.

India's tactics included moving *all* cars adjacent to the pavilion, because the fielders (not the batsmen) were being dazzled. They also took an interminable time to set the field, with a left- and a right-handed batsman ever-present.

The abrasive public condemnation of India after the match by England's new chairman, Cathy Mowat, lacked tact, and India threatened to boycott the rest of the tour. Diplomacy won the day, but the animosity among officials of the two governing bodies marred this inaugural tour. The England WCA somewhat pettily reported the Touring Team to the Minister of Sport and the Indian High Commissioner, and have threatened to have India banned from the International Women's Cricket Council.

The record of note was created by Sandyha Aggarwal, India's 'Geoff Boycott'. She scored the world's highest individual score in 52 years of women's Test cricket, making 190 in the third and final Test. The fact that her innings took 9½ hours, facing 523 deliveries, did not perturb Aggarwal. But the overwhelming desire to break Betty Snowball's 51-year-old record of 189 meant that the whole game was killed stone dead.

So the first Test ended with rancour, the third with no prospect of a result. This was also the case in the second Test, in which India, batting first, took a day and two-thirds for their first innings 426-9 declared. Aggarwal took that time to reach 132 — once again condemning the game to oblivion.

On the plus side, England found a good opener in left-hander Lesley Cooke, a sports centre administrator from Cheshire. Her brilliant 117 in the first Test deserved to be a match-winning innings, and coupled with her 72 in the first knock made it a fine debut.

Sarah Potter stamped herself as a capable all-rounder, having overcome her 1984-85 personality clash with selectors and administrators. In the first Test, she picked up 5 wickets and scored 86 not out before running out of partners. In the second Test, she made 49 in her only knock, and then in the third Test scored a well deserved maiden century.

England's new captain, Carole Hodges, was always in the runs, but tended to under-bowl herself. England's newcomers on the bowling scene — Gill Smith (Yorkshire) and Julie May (Kent) — proved very expensive. Hodges' best innings was in the last Test, when she cracked an undefeated 121 not out. She put on a record 207 for the second wicket with Janette Brittin, who, returning after an injury sustained in the first

Test, compiled a sparkling 125. This earned her the Player of the Match award over Aggarwal's pedestrian world record.

Jane Powell, Yorkshire's captain, unlucky to be omitted from the first Test, made her point in the second with a capable 115 not out.

England's opening seamer, Avril Starling, was as consistent as ever. But the bowler who really made her mark was left-arm spinner Gill McConway, who constantly puzzled the touring team. Her 'Phil Edmonds-style' deliveries dominated India's bore-a-minute first knock in the last Test. She bowled 42 overs, 27 maidens, and took a career best of 7 for 34.

England easily took the one-day series for the Micro-Diet Cup 3–0, as India showed their lack of experience at this type of cricket. They were unlucky to bat first on a dreadful wicket in the second one-day match, at the India Gymkhana Club, Osterley, were bowled out for 65, and understandably complained that an international game should never have been staged on such a third-rate track.

Sandyha Aggarwal won the *Sunday Telegraph* Player of the Week champagne for her world record, and was also named Player of the Series. Geoff Boycott must envy her accumulative ability with the bat!

If India are to progress in the world of women's cricket, they must play more positive cricket. They have the ability — in 15 county and representative matches, all one-day affairs, India were unbeaten, winning 12 of them. But the desire not to lose overrules the consideration to occasionally throw caution to the winds. Their total government funding is related to their success in international series, which appeared to be the main reason for their safety-first tactics.

First Test. 26, 27, 29, 30 June at Collingham CC, Leeds. MATCH DRAWN. Toss: India. India 323 (S. Kulkarni 118, M. Desai 54, G. Banerji 38; A. Starling 4-61, S. Potter 3-52, G. McConway 2-56) and 128 (K. Venkatachar 34, S. Gupta 33*; A. Starling 3-26, G. McConway 2-11, S. Potter 2-17, G. Smith 2-30). England 198-9 (J. Brittin absent hurt) (S. Potter 86*, L. Cooke 72; S. Rangaswamy 4-24, S. Gupta 3-57) and 229-5 (L. Cooke 117, C. Hodges 68; S. Rangaswamy 2-72).

Second Test. 3, 4, 6, 7 June at Blackpool. Toss: India. India 426-9 dec (S. Aggarwal 132, G. Banerji 60, S. Kulkarni 78, R. Venugopal 55, R. Punekar 47; G. McConway 2-38, A. Starling 2-69) and 176-2 dec (G. Banerji 75, S. Shah 62*). England 350-6 dec (J. Powell 115*, L. Cooke 64, S. Potter 49, J. Court 42; D. Edulji 3-92, S. Kulkarni 2-97) and 54-2 (C. Hodges 25).

Third Test. 12, 13, 14, 15 July at Worcester. Toss: England. England 332-7 dec (J. Brittin 125, C. Hodges 121*; D. Edulji 4-94, S. Sridhar 2-46) and 253-7 dec (S. Potter 102, C. Hodges 46, J. Court 42; S. Gupta 3-50). India 374 (S. Aggarwal 190, S. Kulkarni 35, M. Singhal 35; G. McConway 7-34, G. Smith 2-68) and 54-1 (S. Aggarwal 24*).

Extras

Test Career Records

The following individual career averages include all official Test matches to the end of the 1986 English season. The India v Australia series, which began on 18 September 1986, is not included.

England

Batting/Fielding	M	I	NO	HS	R	Avge	100	50	Ct/St
C.W.J. Athey	8	15	0	55	233	15.53	–	1	5
M.R. Benson	1	2	0	30	51	25.50	–	–	–
I.T. Botham	85	136	4	208	4636	35.12	13	21	96
G.R. Dilley	22	33	9	56	365	15.20	–	2	6
P.R. Downton	27	43	7	74	701	19.47	–	4	61/5
P.H. Edmonds	41	53	10	64	765	17.79	–	2	37
R.M. Ellison	11	16	1	41	202	13.46	–	–	2
J.E. Emburey	37	56	12	75	686	15.59	–	2	22
N.A. Foster	14	21	3	18*	127	7.05	–	–	3
B.N. French	5	7	2	21	55	11.00	–	–	12
M.W. Gatting	48	83	12	207	2725	38.38	6	13	42
G.A. Gooch	59	105	4	196	3746	37.08	7	21	57
D.I. Gower	86	148	11	215	6149	44.88	13	30	63
A.J. Lamb	46	79	6	137*	2500	34.24	7	10	46
J.K. Lever	21	31	5	53	306	11.76	–	1	11
M.D. Moxon	2	4	0	74	111	27.75	–	1	1
D.R. Pringle	14	25	3	63	413	18.77	–	1	7
N.V. Radford	2	3	1	12*	13	6.50	–	–	–
R.T. Robinson	16	28	3	175	1052	42.08	3	3	6
W.N. Slack	3	6	0	52	81	13.50	–	1	3
G.C. Small	2	2	1	12	14	14.00	–	–	–
C.L. Smith	8	14	1	91	392	30.15	–	2	5
D.M. Smith	2	4	0	47	80	20.00	–	–	–
J.G. Thomas	5	10	4	31*	83	13.83	–	–	–
P. Willey	26	50	6	102*	1184	26.90	2	5	3

Bowling	Balls	R	W	Avge	Best	5wI	10wM
I.T. Botham	19356	9656	357	27.04	8-34	26	4
G.R. Dilley	4059	2073	69	30.04	4-24	–	–
P.H. Edmonds	9903	3516	106	33.16	7-66	2	–
R.M. Ellison	2264	1048	35	29.94	6-77	3	1
J.E. Emburey	8331	2970	97	30.61	6-33	4	–
N.A. Foster	3023	1480	39	37.94	6-104	3	1
M.W. Gatting	344	177	2	88.50	1-14	–	–
G.A. Gooch	1419	546	13	42.00	2-12	–	–
D.I. Gower	36	20	1	20.00	1-1	–	–
A.J. Lamb	24	23	1	23.00	1-6	–	–
J.K. Lever	4433	1951	73	26.72	7-46	3	1
D.R. Pringle	2411	1128	29	38.89	5-108	1	–
N.V. Radford	378	219	3	73.00	2-131	–	–
R.T. Robinson	6	0	0	–	–	–	–
G.C. Small	384	134	4	33.50	3-88	–	–
C.L. Smith	102	39	3	13.00	2-31	–	–
J.G. Thomas	774	504	10	50.40	4-70	–	–
P. Willey	1091	456	7	65.14	2-73	–	–

Australia

Batting/Fielding	M	I	NO	HS	R	Avge	100	50	Ct/St
D.C. Boon	16	29	2	131	930	34.44	2	6	10
A.R. Border	81	143	24	196	6199	52.09	18	31	88
R.J. Bright	22	37	8	33	407	14.03	–	–	11
S.P. Davis	1	1	0	0	0	–	–	–	–
D.R. Gilbert	7	11	4	15	56	8.00	–	–	–
A.M.J. Hilditch	18	34	0	119	1073	31.55	2	6	13
R.G. Holland	11	15	4	10	35	3.18	–	–	5
D.W. Hookes	23	41	3	143*	1306	34.36	1	8	12
M.G. Hughes	1	1	0	0	0	–	–	–	1
R.B. Kerr	2	4	0	17	31	7.75	–	–	1
G.F. Lawson	36	59	10	57*	743	15.16	–	3	7
C.J. McDermott	14	21	1	36	188	9.40	–	–	3
G.R. Marsh	6	11	1	118	380	38.00	1	1	2
G.R.J. Matthews	14	24	2	130	725	32.95	3	2	6
S.P. O'Donnell	6	10	3	48	206	29.42	–	–	4
W.B. Phillips	27	48	2	159	1485	32.28	2	7	52
B.A. Reid	6	8	3	13	29	5.80	–	–	1
G.M. Ritchie	23	42	3	146	1374	35.23	3	7	10
S.R. Waugh	5	9	0	74	113	12.55	–	1	2
K.C. Wessels	24	42	1	179	1761	42.95	4	9	18
T.J. Zoehrer	3	5	0	30	71	14.20	–	–	4/1

Bowling	Balls	R	W	Avge	Best	5wI	10wM
A.R. Border	1607	626	15	41.73	3-20	–	–
R.J. Bright	5025	1887	45	41.93	7-87	3	1
S.P. Davis	150	70	0	–	–	–	–
D.R. Gilbert	1437	724	15	48.26	3-48	–	–
R.G. Holland	2889	1352	34	39.76	6-54	3	2
D.W. Hookes	96	41	1	41.00	1-4	–	–
M.G. Hughes	228	123	1	123.00	1-123	–	–
G.F. Lawson	8405	4250	145	29.31	8-112	10	2
C.J. McDermott	3035	1742	49	35.55	8-141	2	–
G.R.J. Matthews	2281	1005	23	43.69	4-61	–	–
S.P. O'Donnell	940	504	6	84.00	3-37	–	–
B.A. Reid	1407	619	20	30.95	4-90	–	–
G.M. Ritchie	6	10	0	–	–	–	–
S.R. Waugh	324	152	7	21.71	4-56	–	–
K.C. Wessels	90	42	0	–	–	–	–

West Indies

Batting/Fielding	M	I	NO	HS	R	Avge	100	50	Ct/St
C.A. Best	3	4	1	35	78	26.60	–	–	4
P.J.L. Dujon	37	48	4	139	1849	42.02	4	9	124/2
J. Garner	56	65	14	60	661	12.96	–	1	39
H.A. Gomes	54	81	10	143	3032	42.70	9	13	17
C.G. Greenidge	71	117	13	223	5033	48.39	12	27	65
R.A. Harper	16	20	3	60	303	17.82	–	1	21
D.L. Haynes	59	97	10	184	3703	42.56	8	23	36
M.A. Holding	59	75	10	73	910	14.00	–	6	21
M.D. Marshall	45	53	4	92	953	19.44	–	7	23
B.P. Patterson	5	5	3	9	12	6.00	–	–	1
T.R.O. Payne	1	1	0	5	5	5.00	–	–	5
I.V.A. Richards	82	122	8	291	6220	54.56	20	27	79
R.B. Richardson	20	31	3	185	1354	48.35	6	3	25
C.A. Walsh	7	8	4	18*	47	11.75	–	–	2

Bowling	Balls	R	W	Avge	Best	5wI	10wM
J. Garner	12707	5228	247	21.16	6-56	6	–
H.A. Gomes	2221	867	13	66.69	2-20	–	–
C.G. Greenidge	26	4	0	–	–	–	–
R.A. Harper	2776	1021	38	26.86	6-57	1	–
D.L. Haynes	18	8	1	8.00	1-2	–	–
M.A. Holding	12458	5799	249	23.28	8-92	13	2
M.D. Marshall	9880	4639	215	21.57	7-53	13	2
B.P. Patterson	709	426	19	22.42	4-30	–	–
I.V.A. Richards	2932	1052	19	55.36	2-20	–	–
R.B. Richardson	18	5	0	–	–	–	–
C.A. Walsh	1226	610	21	29.04	4-74	–	–

New Zealand

Batting / Fielding	M	I	NO	HS	R	Avge	100	50	Ct/St
T.E. Blain	1	1	0	37	37	37.00	–	–	–
S.L. Boock	26	37	8	37	192	6.62	–	–	13
J.G. Bracewell	20	29	7	110	441	20.04	1	1	16
V.R. Brown	2	3	1	36*	51	25.50	–	–	3
B.L. Cairns	43	65	8	64	928	16.28	–	2	30
E.J. Chatfield	29	36	23	21*	137	10.53	–	–	6
J.V. Coney	49	79	14	174*	2591	39.86	3	16	59
J.J. Crowe	26	42	2	128	1060	26.50	2	5	32
M.D. Crowe	32	52	5	188	1807	38.44	5	5	35
B.A. Edgar	39	68	4	161	1958	30.59	3	12	14
T.J. Franklin	2	3	0	7	9	3.00	–	–	–
S.R. Gillespie	1	1	0	28	28	28.00	–	–	–
E.J. Gray	7	11	0	50	177	16.09	–	1	4
R.J. Hadlee	66	106	13	103	2397	25.77	1	13	33
J.F. Reid	19	31	3	180	1296	46.28	6	2	9
G.K. Robertson	1	1	0	12	12	12.00	–	–	–
K.R. Rutherford	8	13	2	65	151	13.72	–	2	3
I.D.S. Smith	33	45	9	113*	808	22.44	1	2	92/6
M.C. Snedden	11	12	2	32	147	14.70	–	–	2
D.A. Stirling	6	9	2	26	108	15.42	–	–	1
G.B. Troup	15	18	6	13*	55	4.58	–	–	2
W. Watson	2	2	1	8*	9	9.00	–	–	2
J.G. Wright	49	86	4	141	2635	32.13	5	12	33

Bowling	Balls	R	W	Avge	Best	5wI	10wM
S.L. Boock	5620	2102	65	32.33	7-87	4	–
J.G. Bracewell	4216	1732	58	29.86	6-32	2	1
V.R. Brown	342	176	1	176.00	1-17	–	–
B.L. Cairns	10628	4280	130	32.92	7-74	6	1
E.J. Chatfield	6840	2719	88	30.89	6-73	3	1
J.V. Coney	2751	936	27	34.66	3-28	–	–
J.J. Crowe	18	9	0	–	–	–	–
M.D. Crowe	1113	559	12	46.58	2-25	–	–
B.A. Edgar	18	3	0	–	–	–	–
S.R. Gillespie	162	79	1	79.00	1-79	–	–
E.J. Gray	1344	582	13	44.76	3-73	–	–
R.J. Hadlee	17179	7520	334	22.51	9-52	27	7
J.F. Reid	18	7	0	–	–	–	–
G.K. Robertson	144	91	1	91.00	1-91	–	–
K.R. Rutherford	76	56	1	56.00	1-38	–	–
I.D.S. Smith	18	5	0	–	–	–	–
M.C. Snedden	1878	930	24	38.75	3-21	–	–
D.A. Stirling	902	601	13	46.23	4-88	–	–
G.B. Troup	3183	1454	39	37.28	6-95	1	1
W. Watson	437	196	4	49.00	2-51	–	–
J.G. Wright	30	5	0	–	–	–	–

India

Batting / Fielding	M	I	NO	HS	R	Avge	100	50	Ct/St
M. Amarnath	56	95	9	138	3852	44.79	10	22	41
M. Azharuddin	12	20	3	122	821	48.29	3	3	11
R.M.H. Binny	24	37	3	83*	756	22.23	–	4	11
S.M. Gavaskar	115	201	16	236*	9367	50.63	32	40	100
Kapil Dev	77	115	10	126*	3132	29.82	3	17	34
S.M.H. Kirmani	88	124	22	102	2759	27.04	2	12	160/38
Madan Lal	39	62	16	74	1042	22.65	–	5	15
Maninder Singh	18	22	7	15	71	4.73	–	–	6
K.S. More	3	5	2	48	156	52.00	–	–	16
C.S. Pandit	1	2	0	23	40	20.00	–	–	1
L.S. Rajput	2	4	0	61	105	26.25	–	1	1
C. Sharma	12	14	6	54	184	23.00	–	1	3
G. Sharma	2	2	1	10*	11	11.00	–	–	1
R.J. Shastri	43	67	9	142	1998	34.44	5	8	19
L. Shivaramakrishnan	9	9	1	25	130	16.25	–	–	9
K. Srikkanth	17	29	1	116	871	31.10	1	5	12
D.B. Vengsarkar	85	140	16	159	4985	40.20	11	26	58
S. Viswanath	3	5	0	20	31	6.20	–	–	11
N.S. Yadav	26	32	10	43	355	16.13	–	–	8

Bowling	Balls	R	W	Avge	Best	5wI	10wM
M. Amarnath	3467	1698	30	56.60	4-63	–	–
M. Azharuddin	6	8	0	–	–	–	–
R.M.H. Binny	2575	1408	39	36.10	5-40	1	–
S.M. Gavaskar	350	187	1	187.00	1-34	–	–
Kapil Dev	16777	8360	291	28.72	9-83	19	2
S.M.H. Kirmani	19	13	1	13.00	1-9	–	–
Madan Lal	5997	2846	71	40.08	5-23	4	–
Maninder Singh	3772	1459	34	42.91	4-26	–	–
C. Sharma	2160	1244	38	32.73	6-58	3	1
G. Sharma	516	167	3	55.66	3-115	–	–
R.J. Shastri	10129	3764	98	38.40	5-75	2	–
L. Shivaramakrishnan	2363	1145	26	44.03	6-64	3	1
K. Srikkanth	48	21	0	–	–	–	–
D.B. Vengsarkar	47	36	0	–	–	–	–
N.S. Yadav	6199	2670	75	35.60	5-99	2	–

EXTRAS / TEST CAREER RECORDS

Pakistan

Batting / Fielding	M	I	NO	HS	R	Avge	100	50	Ct/St
Abdul Qadir	38	44	4	54	610	15.25	–	2	11
Ashraf Ali	5	5	3	65	206	103.00	–	2	9/2
Imran Khan	57	83	12	123	2140	30.14	2	8	20
Jalaluddin	6	3	2	2	3	3.00	–	–	–
Javed Miandad	74	115	17	280*	5413	55.23	14	28	65/1
Mohsin Kamal	3	4	3	13*	18	18.00	–	–	–
Mohsin Khan	45	73	6	200	2661	39.71	7	9	33
Mudassar Nazar	58	90	7	231	3445	41.50	8	16	40
Qasim Omar	23	37	1	210	1431	39.75	3	5	15
Ramiz Raja	6	9	1	122	264	33.00	1	1	8
Salim Malik	30	40	6	119*	1423	41.85	5	7	31
Salim Yousuf	3	4	1	27	67	22.33	–	–	16/3
Shoaib Mohammad	6	9	1	80	213	26.62	–	1	4
Tausif Ahmed	13	11	5	23*	76	12.66	–	–	4
Wasim Akram	8	10	4	19	48	8.00	–	–	1
Zaheer Abbas	78	124	11	274	5062	44.79	12	20	34
Zakir Khan	1	1	1	0*	0	–	–	–	–
Zulqarnain	3	4	0	13	24	6.00	–	–	8/2

Bowling	Balls	R	W	Avge	Best	5wI	10wM
Abdul Qadir	9785	4455	128	34.80	7-142	9	2
Imran Khan	13971	5857	264	22.18	8-58	17	4
Jalaluddin	1200	538	11	48.90	3-77	–	–
Javed Miandad	1446	672	17	39.52	3-74	–	–
Mohsin Kamal	456	265	8	33.12	3-50	–	–
Mohsin Khan	86	30	0	–	–	–	–
Mudassar Nazar	4512	1947	50	38.94	6-32	1	–
Qasim Omar	6	0	0	–	–	–	–
Salim Malik	134	63	3	21.00	1-3	–	–
Shoaib Mohammad	18	8	0	–	–	–	–
Tausif Ahmed	2816	1145	44	26.02	6-45	2	–
Wasim Akram	1770	688	28	24.57	5-56	2	1
Zaheer Abbas	370	132	3	44.00	2-21	–	–
Zakir Khan	270	150	3	50.00	3-80	–	–

Sri Lanka

Batting/Fielding	M	I	NO	HS	R	Avge	100	50	Ct/St
F.S. Ahangama	3	3	1	11	11	5.50	–	–	1
K.N. Amalean	1	1	0	2	2	2.00	–	–	–
S.D. Anurasiri	2	2	0	8	12	6.00	–	–	–
R.G. De Alwis	7	12	0	28	130	10.83	–	–	17/1
A.L.F. De Mel	16	27	5	34	301	13.68	–	–	9
E.A.R. De Silva	2	3	3	10*	15	–	–	–	1
P.A. De Silva	10	19	2	122	532	31.29	2	1	5
R.L. Dias	16	30	1	109	1144	39.44	3	7	6
A.P. Gurusinha	3	6	2	116*	216	54.00	1	–	2
B.R. Jurangpathy	1	2	0	1	1	0.50	–	–	–
A.K. Kuruppuarachchi	1	1	1	0*	0	–	–	–	–
R.S. Madugalle	18	34	4	103	933	31.10	1	6	8
R.S. Mahanama	2	4	0	41	63	15.75	–	–	1
L.R.D. Mendis	19	35	1	124	1164	34.23	4	7	7
A. Ranatunga	18	33	2	135*	1191	38.41	2	8	8
R.J. Ratnayake	11	18	2	56	195	12.18	–	1	5
J.R. Ratnayeke	14	25	5	38	296	14.80	–	–	1
S.A.R. Silva	8	14	2	111	336	28.00	2	–	30/1
K.P.J. Warnaweera	1	2	0	3	3	1.50	–	–	–
C.D.U.S. Weerasinghe	1	1	0	3	3	3.00	–	–	–
S. Wettimuny	20	38	1	190	1112	30.05	2	5	9
R.G.C.E. Wijesuriya	4	7	2	8	22	4.40	–	–	1

Bowling	Balls	R	W	Avge	Best	5wI	10wM
F.S. Ahangama	801	348	18	19.33	5-52	1	–
K.N. Amalean	110	59	3	19.66	3-59	–	–
S.D. Anurasiri	114	21	0	–	–	–	–
A.L.F. De Mel	3338	2061	58	35.53	6-109	3	–
E.A.R. De Silva	264	75	1	75.00	1-37	–	–
P.A. De Silva	30	22	0	–	–	–	–
B.R. Jurangpathy	24	24	0	–	–	–	–
A.K. Kuruppuarachchi	152	85	7	12.14	5-44	1	–
R.S. Madugalle	72	32	0	–	–	–	–
A. Ranatunga	1023	436	9	48.44	2-17	–	–
R.J. Ratnayake	2243	1196	37	32.32	6-85	2	–
J.R. Ratnayeke	2324	1192	38	31.36	8-83	3	–
K.P.J. Warnaweera	45	26	1	26.00	1-26	–	–
C.D.U.S. Weerasinghe	114	36	0	–	–	–	–
S. Wettimuny	12	21	0	–	–	–	–
R.G.C.E. Wijesuriya	586	294	1	294.00	1-68	–	–

Guide to Newcomers

Record in English First-Class Cricket 1986

Batting/Fielding		M	I	NO	HS	R	Avge	100	50	Ct/St
Derbyshire	M. Jean-Jacques	9	12	3	73	208	23.11	–	1	1
	C.F.B.P. Rudd	1	1	0	1	1	1.00	–	–	–
Essex	N.D. Burns	2	3	0	29	54	18.00	–	–	2/2
Glamorgan	S.J. Base	12	11	4	15*	53	7.57	–	–	3
	M.J. Cann	1	1	1	16*	16	–	–	–	1
	P.A. Cottey	4	5	1	9*	24	6.00	–	–	2
	D.J. Hickey	13	9	5	9*	19	4.75	–	–	3
	S.L. Watkin	1	–	–	–	–	–	–	–	–
Gloucestershire	M.W. Alleyne	10	16	5	116*	336	30.54	1	1	4
Hampshire	P.J. Bakker	3	2	1	3*	6	6.00	–	–	–
Kent	R.P. Davis	1	1	1	0*	0	–	–	–	1
	A.P. Igglesden	5	5	2	8*	22	7.33	–	–	2
	T.R. Ward	1	2	0	29	41	20.50	–	–	–
Lancashire	W.K. Hegg	2	2	0	4	4	2.00	–	–	2/2
Leicestershire	P.D. Bowler	8	11	1	100*	249	24.90	1	1	2
	P. Gill	8	11	4	17	68	9.71	–	–	24
	G.A.R. Harris	1	2	1	6	6	6.00	–	–	–
	L. Tennant	2	2	1	12*	13	13.00	–	–	–
Middlesex	G.K. Brown	1	2	0	14	17	8.50	–	–	1
	A.G.J. Fraser	4	3	2	19*	32	32.00	–	–	–
	M.A. Roseberry	5	8	1	70*	174	24.85	–	2	1
	P.C.R. Tufnell	6	7	1	9	32	5.33	–	–	1
Northamptonshire	A. Fordham	2	3	0	17	26	8.66	–	–	–
	M.R. Gouldstone	1	1	0	35	35	35.00	–	–	–
	G. Smith	2	2	0	4	7	3.50	–	–	1
Somerset	R.J. Bartlett	6	9	2	117*	307	43.85	1	–	4
	R.J. Blitz	5	5	0	18	33	6.60	–	–	8
	D.J. Foster	1	1	0	0	0	–	–	–	–
	M.D. Harman	3	5	2	15	27	9.00	–	–	1
	N.J. Pringle	1	2	0	11	21	10.50	–	–	–
Surrey	M.P. Bicknell	9	10	2	9*	21	2.62	–	–	4
	G.E. Brown	1	2	2	2*	2	–	–	–	4/1
	G. Winterborne	1	–	–	–	–	–	–	–	–

Batting/Fielding (contd)

		M	I	NO	HS	R	Avge	100	50	Ct/St
Sussex	R.I. Alikhan	18	28	4	72	843	35.12	–	7	7
	A.N. Babington	6	3	1	1	1	–	–	–	4
	A.M. Bredin	7	6	2	8*	26	6.50	–	–	1
	C.S. Mays	8	6	2	8*	19	4.75	–	–	2
	M.B. Speight	5	2	0	17	21	10.50	–	–	6
Warwickshire	B.M. McMillan	12	21	4	136	999	58.76	3	6	11
	A.J. Moles	11	18	3	102	738	49.20	2	5	5
Yorkshire	P.J. Berry	1	1	1	4*	4	–	–	–	2
	D. Byas	1	1	0	0	0	–	–	–	1
Cambridge U	A.D. Brown	9	11	1	30	86	8.60	–	–	15/2
	S.D. Heath	1	2	0	10	16	8.00	–	–	–
	T.M. Lord	2	4	0	23	31	7.75	–	–	–
	J.M. Tremellem	1	2	1	4*	7	7.00	–	–	–
Oxford University	J.E.B. Cope	4	5	2	8*	11	3.66	–	–	5
	T.A.J. Dawson	7	9	5	10*	32	8.00	–	–	2
	M.J. Kilborn	7	12	1	59	219	19.90	–	1	3
	A.A.G. Mee	8	14	1	51	183	14.07	–	1	3
	R.A. Rydon	5	9	1	20	64	8.00	–	–	1
	N.V. Salvi	4	7	1	36	126	21.00	–	–	1
	M.R. Sygrove	1	2	0	6	8	4.00	–	–	–
	S. Weale	1	2	0	28	40	20.00	–	–	–

Bowling

		O	M	R	W	Avge	Best	5wI	10wM
Derbyshire	M. Jean-Jacques	159	16	599	22	27.22	8-77	1	1
	C.F.B.P. Rudd	28.3	7	90	0	–	–	–	–
Glamorgan	S.J. Base	222.5	39	774	21	36.85	4-74	–	–
	M.J. Cann	1	1	0	0	–	–	–	–
	D.J. Hickey	281.5	39	1102	24	45.91	5-57	1	–
	S.L. Watkin	16	1	82	2	41.00	2-74	–	–
Hampshire	P.J. Bakker	66.5	20	220	6	36.66	2-15	–	–
Kent	R.P. Davis	59.5	22	121	6	20.16	3-38	–	–
	A.P. Igglesden	125	25	372	11	33.81	4-46	–	–
Leicestershire	P.D. Bowler	25.4	10	57	0	–	–	–	–
	G.A.R. Harris	8	1	34	0	–	–	–	–
	L. Tennant	8	1	35	0	–	–	–	–
Middlesex	A.G.J. Fraser	56.4	15	165	8	20.62	3-46	–	–
	P.C.R. Tufnell	148	32	479	5	95.80	2-47	–	–
Northamptonshire	G. Smith	40	8	132	2	66.00	1-38	–	–

EXTRAS/GUIDE TO NEWCOMERS 237

Bowling (contd)		O	M	R	W	Avge	Best	5wI	10wM
Somerset	D.J. Foster	5	0	29	0	–	–	–	–
	M.D. Harman	67.3	12	149	1	149.00	1-88	–	–
	N.J. Pringle	10	0	48	0	–	–	–	–
Surrey	M.P. Bicknell	197	43	600	27	22.22	3-27	–	–
	G. Winterborne	20	5	47	0	–	–	–	–
Sussex	R.I. Alikhan	10	0	65	0	–	–	–	–
	A.N. Babington	117.5	18	348	15	23.20	4-18	–	–
	A.M. Bredin	115	25	385	7	55.00	2-50	–	–
	C.S. Mays	212.5	45	706	13	54.30	3-77	–	–
Warwickshire	B.M. McMillan	220	34	808	17	47.52	3-47	–	–
	A.J. Moles	64.3	10	198	5	39.60	2-57	–	–
Yorkshire	P.J. Berry	39	13	83	1	83.00	1-10	–	–
	D. Byas	2	0	15	0	–	–	–	–
Cambridge U	S.D. Heath	7	0	39	0	–	–	–	–
	J.M. Tremellem	7	0	32	0	–	–	–	–
Oxford U	T.A.J. Dawson	195	39	649	13	49.92	3-65	–	–
	R.A. Rydon	119	21	471	5	94.20	3-106	–	–
	M.R. Sygrove	17	0	85	2	42.50	1-19	–	–

County caps awarded in 1986

Derbyshire: J.E. Morris, O.H. Mortensen, P.G. Newman, B. Roberts
Essex: J.H. Childs, A.W. Lilley
Glamorgan: H. Morris
Hampshire: R.J. Maru
Kent: S.A. Marsh
Lancashire: C. Maynard, G.D. Mendis
Leicestershire: T.J. Boon, R.A. Cobb, P.A.J. De Freitas, J.J. Whitaker
Northamptonshire: D.J. Capel, R.A. Harper, D.J. Wild
Nottinghamshire: P. Johnson
Somerset: N.A. Felton
Sussex: A.N. Jones, D.A. Reeve, A.P. Wells
Warwickshire: P.A. Smith
Worcestershire: G.A. Hick, R.J. Illingworth, P.J. Newport, M.J. Weston
Yorkshire: P.W. Jarvis, A.A. Metcalfe

A FEAST FOR EVERY FOOTBALL FAN!

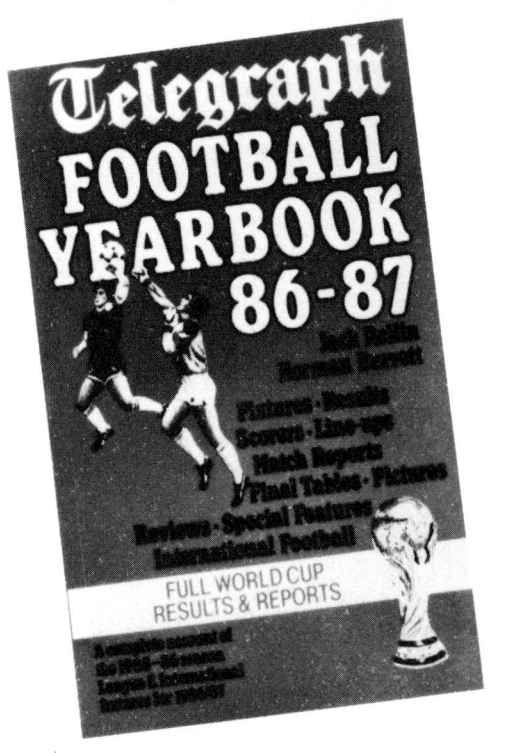

First in the field, and hot on the heels of the World Cup final, this guide covers all aspects of National and International soccer. The authoritative reference work, which with its blend of facts, figures and in-depth analysis, provides a fascinating insight into a dramatic season. Including a day-to-day diary of last season, full match reports, action shots, statistics and forthcoming fixtures.

Available through all leading bookshops, the Telegraph Bookshop at 130 Fleet Street, price £7.95p or by post from Dept. FYB, The Daily Telegraph, 135 Fleet Street, London EC4P 4BL (add 55p p&p). Please allow 28 days for delivery.

FYB 4 28

Obituary 1985-86

The number of deaths among Test cricketers since the last Year Book went to press has been unusually high: 17 in all, headed in fame by *Jim Laker* and *Bill Edrich*, whose careers are covered on pages 242 to 244. *Dick Pollard* and *Laurie Fishlock* were both in their prime when war came: hence they achieved much for Lancashire and Surrey, respectively, one as opening bowler, the other as attacking left-hand bat, relatively little for England.

Colin McCool was the best of four Australian Test casualties, an all-rounder of true quality, a batsman good enough to score a Test hundred, dangerous leg-spinner and superb slip-fielder, who proved a great acquisition to Somerset in the 1950s. *L.J. Nash*, *M.G. Waite*, and *J.W. Wilson* were bowlers who mustered between them only five caps, although the first two were also prominent Australian Rules footballers.

A.J. Bell, known as 'Sandy', was a leading South African bowler of the inter-war years, a great-hearted exponent of fast-medium in-swing. At the same time, *S.H. Curnow* was compiling an average of over 50 for Transvaal in Currie Cup cricket, without once reaching that mark in seven Tests. *J.B. Robertson* was another contemporary, who was three times capped. *E.L.G. Hoad* was the oldest West Indian cricketer when he died aged 90 in his native Barbados, where he had led West Indies in their first-ever home Test in 1929-30. *Lall Singh*, a brilliant fielder, was also in a Test baptism, that of India at Lord's in 1932. The peculiarity of little Lall's selection was that he was Malayan by birth, a native of Kuala Lumpur. *R.B. Kenny* and *K.K. Tarapore* of India and *A.M. Matheson* and *H.D. Smith* of New Zealand also died, the most notable feat of their brief careers being perhaps that the last named took a wicket with his first ball in Test cricket.

MCC mourned the deaths of three former Presidents, *R. Aird*, *W.H. Webster* and *A.H.A. Dibbs*. Ronny Aird (Cambridge and Hampshire) served the Club with singular charm and devotion for all but 60 years, as Assistant Secretary, Secretary, President, and Trustee. 'Tagge' Webster (Cambridge and Middlesex) had a long Committee record besides being also President of Middlesex. Alex Dibbs, a banker by calling and concurrently deputy chairman of both NatWest and British Airways, made a big impact in the councils of Lord's immediately before his untimely death aged 66.

Among other deaths were those of *A.D. (Sandy) Baxter*, a Scot who bowled with success on MCC's New Zealand and Australian tour of 1935-36 but could otherwise spare little time for first-class cricket; another member of that MCC side and Worcestershire wicket-keeper, *J.F. MacLean*; *J. Cutmore*, one of Essex's best inter-war batsmen; the *Rev. J.R. Bridger* who represented Cambridge at five games in wartime and played cricket afterwards for Hampshire; *A.G. Nicholson*, a bowler to be reckoned with in the Yorkshire sides of the 1960s, who died tragically young at 47; *B. Bellamy* and *F. Jakeman*, both stalwarts of Northants; and *S.H. Copley* whose remarkable catching of McCabe when substituting in the England-Australia Test at Trent Bridge in 1930 was one of the turning-points of the match, and who served as coach and/or groundsman for 36 years at King William's College, Isle of Man.

Believed to be the oldest surviving first-class cricketer in the world, *Rupert de Smidt* died in Cape Town at the age of 102. He opened the bowling for Western Province just prior to World War I.

The oldest living English first-class cricketer, *A.G. Pawson*, captain of Oxford in 1910, was 97. He was proud of his seniority among cricketers and of the fact that his son A.H. (Tony) followed him as captain of his university, and was equally successful against Cambridge.

Other Blues who died were *D.H. Macindoe* and *W.H. Bradshaw* of Oxford, and *R.G.H. Lowe* of Cambridge and Kent, who did the hat-trick in the 1926 University Match. David Macindoe played for the Gentlemen as a freshman, led his 1946 side to victory at Lord's, ran the cricket at Eton for many years, and at his sudden death was Vice-Provost. *Giles Baring*, who played for Cambridge without winning a Blue, also died. A fast bowler, he is remembered for his 5 for 121 for Hampshire against the touring Australians in 1934, which included the wickets of Woodfull, Brown, and Bradman in his opening spell for 6 runs.

Finally, here are a few other figures well known in the world of cricket: *A.W. Flower*, the first paid secretary of Middlesex and long-serving officer at Lord's; *W.L. Budd*, a highly regarded Test umpire of the 1970s; *R. Tang Choon*, of Trinidad, a batsman of Test class; *B.J.W. Hill* and *W.R. Genders*, historians respectively of I Zingari and of League cricket; and two local journalists of long service, *Ron Grimshaw* of the *Oxford Mail* and *Dick Williamson*, a free-lance and doyen of Yorkshire cricket and football Press boxes to the time of his death at 85.

E.W. Swanton

Career Details (b-born; d-died; F-c-first-class career)

BELL, Alexander John; b East London, South Africa, 15.4.1906; d Cape Town, 2.8.1985. Western Province, Rhodesia, and South Africa. F-c (1925-26 to 1938-39): 311 runs (9.14); 228 wkts (23.29); 27 ct.

CURNOW, Sydney Harry; b Benoni, 16.12.1907; d Perth, Western Australia, 28.7.1986. Transvaal (1928-29 to 1945-46) and South Africa. F-c: 3,409 runs (42.08), 9 hundreds; 18 ct.

EDRICH, William John; b Lingwood, Norfolk, 26.3.1916; d Chesham, 24.4.1986. Middlesex and England. F-c (1937-58): 36,965 runs (42.39), 86 hundreds; 479 wkts (33.31); 529 ct, 1st.

FISHLOCK, Laurence Barnard; b Battersea, London, 2.1.1907; d 26.6.1986. Surrey and England. F-c (1931-52): 25,376 runs (39.34), 56 hundreds; 11 wkts (45.81); 216 ct.

HOAD, Edward Lisle Goldsworthy; b St Michael, Barbados, 29.1.1896; d Bridgetown, 5.3.1986. Barbados and West Indies. F-c (1921-22 to 1937-38): 3,502 runs (38.48); 53 wkts (36.28); 26 ct.

KENNY, Ramnath Bhaura; b Bombay, 29.9.1930; d Kandivli, 21.11.1985. Bombay (1951-52 to 1960-61), Bengal (1961-62). F-c: 3,079 runs (50.47), 11 hundreds; 15 wkts (31.20).

LAKER, James Charles; b Frizinghall, Bradford (Yorkshire), 9.2.1922; d Putney, 23.4.1986. Surrey (1946-59), Essex (1962-64) and England. F-c: 7,304 runs (16.60), 2 hundreds; 1,944 wkts (18.41); 271 ct.

LALL SINGH; b near Kuala Lumpur, 16.12.1909; d Kuala Lumpur, 19.11.1985. Southern Punjab (1933-34 to 1935-36), Hindus (1934-35 to 1935-36), and India. F-c: 1,123 runs (24.95), 1 hundred; 1 wkt (59.00); 23 ct.

McCOOL, Colin Leslie; b Paddington, Sydney, 9.12.1915; d Woy Woy, New South Wales, 1986. NSW (1939-40 to 1940-41), Queensland (1945-46 to 1952-53), Somerset (1956-60), and Australia. F-c: 12,421 runs (32.85), 18 hundreds; 602 wkts (27.47); 262 ct, 2 st.

MATHESON, Alexander Malcolm; b Omaha, Auckland, 27.2.1906; d Auckland, 31.12.1985. Auckland (1926-27 to 1939-40), Wellington (1944-45 to 1946-47), and New Zealand. F-c: 1,844 runs (23.64), 1 hundred; 194 wkts (28.52); 44 ct.

NASH, Laurence John; b Fitzroy, Melbourne, 2.5.1910; d Heidelberg, Melbourne, 24.7.1986. Tasmania (1929-30 to 1931-32), Victoria (1936-37), and Australia.

POLLARD, Richard; b Westhoughton, Lancashire, 19.6.1912; d 16.12.1985. Lancashire (1933-50) and England. F-c: 3,522 runs (13.29); 1,122 wkts (22.56); 225 ct.

ROBERTSON, John Benjamin; b Wynberg, Cape Town, 5.6.1906; d 5.7.1985.

SMITH, Horace Dennis; b Toowoomba, Queensland, 8.1.1913; d Christchurch, 25.1.1986. Otago, Canterbury, and New Zealand. F-c (1931-34): 404 runs (22.44); 17 wkts (33.52).

TARAPORE, Keki Khurshedji; b Bombay, 17.12.1910; d Pune 15.6.1986. Bombay (1937-38 to 1948-49) and India. F-c: 441 runs (11.30); 148 wkts (28.77).

WAITE, Mervyn George; b Kent Town, Adelaide, 7.1.1911; d Adelaide, 16.12.1985. South Australia (1930-31 to 1945-46) and Australia. F-c: 3,888 runs (27.77), 1 hundred; 192 wkts (31.61); 66 ct.

WILSON, John William; b Albert Park, Melbourne, 20.8.1921; d Melbourne, 13.10.1985. Victoria (1949-50), S. Australia (1950-51 to 1957-58), and Australia. F-c: 287 runs (5.74); 230 wkts (30.51); 17 ct.

Their Record in Tests, page 244

Jim Laker – finest off-spin bowler

JAMES CHARLES LAKER, who died aged 64, was one of the finest off-spin bowlers in the history of cricket, perhaps the finest. Certainly he holds a record never likely to be equalled.

His 19 wickets against Australia in the Old Trafford Test of 1956, for which he will always be remembered, are two more than has ever been taken by anybody else in a first-class match, let alone in a Test match.

Jim Laker's career coincided with an era of uncovered, slow turning pitches, but no one else brought to them the same unrelenting accuracy, allied to considerable powers of spin.

Deceptive appearance

A quiet, reserved thinker on the game with a somewhat flat-footed walk, he did not give the impression of great vitality on the field, but caught many good catches, usually in the gully; he was also a hard-hitting batsman at number eight, good enough to make 63 at Trent Bridge against the 1948 Australians.

His origins will seem strange to present-day cricketers. A Yorkshireman who played in the Bradford League for Saltaire before joining the Army in 1941, he began to make his name later in the war in good-class cricket in the Middle East.

He had been more of a batsman in the League, but now began to concentrate on off-break bowling, and while awaiting demobilization in London in 1946, joined the Catford club. From there it was a short step to the Oval and Surrey — with Yorkshire's permission.

At the end of the 1947 season in which he played his first Championship matches, he was picked for the tour of West Indies under G. Allen and was the most successful bowler despite his lack of experience.

Test trial 8 for 2

He was one of those bowlers who suffered while Australia made their 404 for 3 to win at Headingley in 1948, but in May 1950 he upset a Test trial at Bradford by taking 8 wickets for 2 runs.

In August 1953, his partnership with Tony Lock had much to do with England's recovery of the Ashes at the Oval.

Just over a year later, he was surprisingly left out of Len Hutton's team which retained the Ashes in Australia, but he remained an important part of the strong England bowling side of the 1950s until he retired in 1959 when still a very good bowler.

The publication of Laker's autobiography, including criticisms which he much regretted subsequently, led to the withdrawal of his MCC honorary membership.

New career

However, in another publication he put the record straight, and returned after two years to play for Essex for three seasons. The MCC membership was restored, and he moved on eventually to a new and successful career as a television commentator on cricket.

Though he had not always been in good health in the last few years, his sadly premature death will be a particular shock to viewers who may not remember him when he was a great bowler but who have been long accustomed to his sound, unflappable interpretations of televised matches.

Michael Melford, *The Daily Telegraph* 24 April 1986.

Bill Edrich, man of courage

WILLIAM JOHN EDRICH, DFC, the Middlesex and England cricketer, died suddenly during the night of April 23-24 in his Hertfordshire home aged 70. Unlike his great contemporary Jim Laker, who died a few hours earlier, he had suffered no previous ill-health and had been in his usual robust form at a Middlesex pre-season dinner at Lord's only the previous evening.

Middlesex 'Twins'

Bill Edrich in all that he did on the field and in war was the personification of determination and courage, the very epitome of 'guts'. His name is coupled immortally, of course, with that of Denis Compton in the Middlesex sides for 1937 until 1958, in one of the most fruitful of all partnerships.

Though Compton was as brave a fighter as Edrich when it came to facing Miller and Lindwall, the game came so much more easily to him than to his great friend, and the obvious contrast in method and temperament was part of the fascination to the public of their innumerable partnerships together.

Good cutter

Edrich was never a graceful player. He was a good cutter, but with the bottom hand in control his most telling strokes were the hook and the pulled drive. In a tight corner he was apt to overcome technical limitations with that indomitable spirit.

The Norfolk Edriches were and are steeped in the game, and at one time could raise a formidable family team. Three of Bill's brothers, G.A. and E.H. of Lancashire, B.R. of Kent and Glamorgan, played county cricket, and his cousin J.H. played for both England and Surrey.

Bill opted for Middlesex, qualifying via the MCC ground staff, and when his days at Lord's were over he returned to his roots as captain of Norfolk, for whom he continued to play with all the old zest until the age of 55.

Golden summer

In his first Middlesex season of 1937, Bill scored 2,000 runs, as he was to do eight times more, the climax coming with 3,539 in 1947, a total exceeded only by Compton, who in that same golden summer piled up 3,816.

When in 1938 Edrich (W.J.) scored 1,000 runs (all at Lord's) before the end of May, an early baptism in Test cricket was certain. It came with disastrous results, his six innings against Australia totalling 67 runs and his first five against South Africa the following winter only 21.

Then in the second innings of the last Test at Durban (the 'Timeless' one which lasted 10 days) he at last justified the confidence of his captain, Walter Hammond, by making a dogged 219.

True Test class

As a squadron leader he won the DFC for daylight bombing over Germany, and at the war's end he resumed his cricket as an amateur. Then it was W.J. Edrich who in Australia in 1946-47 established himself as a cricketer of true Test stamp, at No. 3 in the order and also in England's extremity as a fastish bowler propelling that small, tough frame at the enemy as though his lungs would burst.

Tests against Australia continued to bring the best out of him, his crowning moment perhaps being the innings of 55 not out which (with Compton at the other end) at last brought the

Ashes back home at the Oval in 1953. His last Tests were played with Sir Leonard Hutton's winning team in Australia in 1954-55.

In 39 Tests he made 2,440 runs with an average of 40, including six hundreds, and took 41 expensive wickets at 41 runs each. His first-class figures were 39,965 runs, with 86 hundreds, at an average of 42; 479 wickets at 33 runs apiece. They must be seen, of course, as with the rest of his generation in the context of six prime years lost between 1939 and 1945.

His time coincided with an earlier palmy age of Middlesex cricket during which one Championship was won, one shared, and second place was achieved four times.

Joint captains

In 1951 the partnership of Edrich and Compton jointly took over the Middlesex captaincy from R.W.V. Robins, under whose brilliant leadership they had been brought up. Captaincy, as also later committee work, was a sphere which came more naturally to Bill than to Denis, and the latter soon dropped out in favour of his friend.

Bill Edrich stood for all that was best in cricket: Lord's will not be the same without his cheerful presence.

E.W. Swanton, *The Daily Telegraph* 25 April 1986

Their Record in Tests

Batting/Fielding	Career	M	I	NO	HS	R	Avge	100	50	Ct/St
A.J. Bell (SA)	1929-1935	16	23	12	26*	69	6.27	–	–	6
S.H. Curnow (SA)	1930/1-1931/2	7	14	0	47	168	12.00	–	–	5
W.J. Edrich (Eng)	1938-1954/5	39	63	2	219	2440	40.00	6	13	39
L.B. Fishlock (Eng)	1936-1946/7	4	5	1	19*	47	11.75	–	–	1
E.L.G. Hoad (WI)	1928-1933	4	8	0	36	98	12.25	–	–	1
J.C. Laker (Eng)	1947/8-1958/9	46	63	15	63	676	14.08	–	2	12
Lall Singh (Ind)	1932	1	2	0	29	44	22.00	–	–	1
R.B. Kenny (Ind)	1958/9-1959/60	5	10	1	62	245	27.22	–	3	1
C.L. McCool (Aus)	1945/6-1949/50	14	17	4	104*	459	35.30	1	1	14
A.M. Matheson (NZ)	1929/30-1931	2	1	0	7	7	7.00	–	–	2
L.J. Nash (Aus)	1931/2-1936/7	2	2	0	17	30	15.00	–	–	6
R. Pollard (Eng)	1946-1948	4	3	2	10*	13	13.00	–	–	3
J.B. Robertson (SA)	1935/6	3	6	1	17	51	10.20	–	–	2
H.D. Smith (NZ)	1932/3	1	1	0	4	4	4.00	–	–	–
K.K. Tarapore (Ind)	1948/9	1	1	0	2	2	2.00	–	–	–
M.G. Waite (Aus)	1938	2	3	0	8	11	3.66	–	–	1
J.W. Wilson (Aus)	1956/7	1	–	–	–	–	–	–	–	–

Bowling	Balls	R	W	Avge	Best	5wI	10wM
A.J. Bell (SA)	3342	1567	48	32.64	6-99	4	–
W.J. Edrich (Eng)	3234	1693	41	41.29	4-68	–	–
J.C. Laker (Eng)	12027	4101	193	21.24	10-53	9	3
C.L. McCool (Aus)	2504	958	36	26.61	5-41	3	–
A.M. Matheson (NZ)	282	136	2	68.00	2-7	–	–
L.J. Nash (Aus)	311	126	10	12.60	4-18	–	–
R. Pollard (Eng)	1102	378	15	25.20	5-24	1	–
J.B. Robertson (SA)	738	321	6	53.50	3-143	–	–
H.D. Smith (NZ)	120	113	1	113.00	1-113	–	–
K.R. Tarapore (Ind)	114	72	0	–	–	–	–
M.G. Waite (Aus)	552	190	1	190.00	1-150	–	–
J.W. Wilson (Aus)	216	64	1	64.00	1-25	–	–

Looking forward

England on Tour 1986-87

Tour Party to Australia

	Age	Caps		Age	Caps
M.W. Gatting, captain (Middx)	29	48	N.A. Foster (Essex)	24	15
C.W.J. Athey (Glos)	28	8	B.N. French (Notts)	27	5
I.T. Botham (Somerset)	30	85	D.I. Gower (Leics)	29	86
B.C. Broad (Notts)	28	5	A.J. Lamb (Northants)	32	46
P.A.J. De Freitas (Leics)	20	0	C.J. Richards (Surrey)	28	0
G.R. Dilley (Kent)	27	22	W.N. Slack (Middx)	31	3
P.H. Edmonds (Middx)	35	41	G.C. Small (Warwicks)	24	2
J.E. Emburey, vice-capt (Middx)	34	37	J.J. Whitaker (Leics)	24	0

Tour Manager: P.M. Lush. Assistant Manager: M.J. Stewart. Physiotherapist: L. Brown. Scorer: S.P. Austin.

Tour Itinerary

October	18-20	Queensland Country XI (Bundaberg)
	22	SE Queensland Country (Lawes)
	24-27	Queensland (Brisbane)
	29	S. Australia Country XI (Wudinna)
	31-3 Nov	South Australia (Adelaide)
November	5	WA Country XI (Kalgoorlie)
	7-10	Western Australia (Perth)
	14, 15, 16, 18, 19	**Australia** (Brisbane) 1st B+H Test
	21-24	New South Wales (Newcastle)
	28, 29, 30, 2, 3, Dec	**Australia** (Perth) 2nd B+H Test
December	6-9	Victoria (Melbourne)
	12-16	**Australia** (Adelaide) 3rd B+H Test
	18-21	Tasmania (Hobart)
	23	Prime Minister's XI (Canberra)
	26-30	**Australia** (Melbourne) 4th B+H Test
January	10, 11, 12, 14, 15	**Australia** (Sydney) 5th B+H Test

B+H Challenge (at Perth)

December	30	West Indies v Pakistan
January	1	Australia v England
	2	Australia v Pakistan
	3	England v West Indies
	4	Australia v West Indies
	5	England v Pakistan
	7	Final

B+H World Series Cup

January	17	West Indies (Brisbane)
	18	Australia (Brisbane)
	22	Australia (Sydney)
	24	West Indies (Adelaide)
	26	Australia (Adelaide)
	30	West Indies (Melbourne)
February	1	Australia (Melbourne)
	3	West Indies (Devonport)
	8	First Final (Melbourne)
	11	Second Final (Sydney)
	13	Third Final (Melbourne)

The 1987 season

As will probably be frequently recalled during the coming year, it was 1787 when a few members of the White Conduit Club, who played in Islington Fields, instructed Thomas Lord to find them a private ground for a new club. When he did so, in what is now Dorset Square, the club became the Marylebone Cricket Club and the ground Lord's. The bicentenary of these events will be celebrated in 1987 with various jollifications, including a ball at the Nursery end of Lord's, and with a five-day match in August between an MCC side drawn from players of all nations currently representing English counties and one of players based overseas. Three places are to be left open in the latter side in case some outstanding players cannot be fitted into the home-based XI.

The international flavour of the match is a sign of the times, contrasting with the 150th celebration in 1937 when two matches were played in late May before a total of only 27,000 people, there being at the time a bus strike. One was North v South, the other between the MCC team recently returned from Australia and the Rest of England.

Before the MCC bicentenary match, England, in addition to the Ashes series in Australia, will have played a five-match Test series against Pakistan. There were few illusions about the strength of India and New Zealand before the 1986 season and there will be fewer still about Pakistan, for in 1982 England were lucky to win 2-1. Since then they have been to Pakistan in 1983-84 and lost there 1-0.

By the end of 1987 England should have had their fill of Pakistan and vice versa. The MCC bicentenary match is not the only historic event of the year. Another is the first World Cup tournament to be staged jointly — in India and Pakistan — beginning in the second week in October and continuing into November. When it is over, England will tour Pakistan and then New Zealand.

One sentiment likely to be expressed often during the coming season may be apprehension about the World Cup arrangements. India and Pakistan do not have the advantages which England possesses as a stage for such a jamboree — the relatively short distances, the easy communications, the free movement of currency and the all-round experience. Yet their enterprise and enthusiasm are to be respected. It may be fashionable to forecast muddles of classical proportions, but it is very often the case that where confusion is foreseen, the actuality is smoother than if it had all been taken for granted.

As for the rest of the domestic season, the bad news — a matter for only passing gloom, fortunately — is that this is the season when the fixture cycles of the Championship and the Sunday League do not marry. What this means is that counties will find that only four of their home Sunday matches will fit neatly into the middle of their home championship matches against the same opponents. As a result, there may be some dodging about on Saturday and Sunday evenings. The computer is sorry about it, but apparently it can't be helped.

Fixtures 1987

Duration of Matches (*including play on Sunday)			
Cornhill Tests	5 days	One-day Internationals	1 day
Britannic Assurance		Benson & Hedges Cup	1 day
County Championship	3 days	NatWest Bank Trophy	1 day
Tourist matches	3 days or as stated	Sunday League	1 day
University matches v Counties	3 days	Other matches	as stated

APRIL 18, SATURDAY
Fenners — Cambridge U v Essex

APRIL 22, WEDNESDAY
The Parks — Oxford U v Kent
Fenners — Cambridge U v Lancashire
Lord's — MCC v Essex (3 days)

APRIL 25, SATURDAY
Britannic Assurance Championship
Chesterfield — Derbyshire v Sussex
Bristol — Glos v Essex
Southampton — Hampshire v Northants
Lords* — Middlesex v Yorkshire
Trent Bridge — Notts v Surrey
Taunton* — Somerset v Lancashire
Edgbaston* — Warwickshire v Glamorgan
Worcester* — Worcs v Kent

Other Match
Fenners — Cambridge U v Leics

APRIL 29, WEDNESDAY
Britannic Assurance Championship
Chelmsford — Essex v Warwickshire
Canterbury — Kent v Glamorgan
Old Trafford — Lancs v Middlesex
The Oval — Surrey v Derbyshire
Hove — Sussex v Glos

Tourist Match
Arundel — Lavinia Duchess of Norfolk's XI v Pakistan (One day)

Other Matches
The Parks — Oxford U v Hampshire
Fenners — Cambridge U v Northants

MAY 2, SATURDAY
Benson & Hedges Cup
Derby — Derbyshire v Northants
Swansea — Glamorgan v Sussex
Bristol — Glos v Notts
Canterbury — Kent v Minor Counties
Taunton — Somerset v Essex
Edgbaston — Warwickshire v Yorkshire
Worcester — Worcs v Lancashire
The Parks — Combined Univ v Hampshire

Tourist Match
The Oval* — Surrey v Pakistan

MAY 3, SUNDAY
Sunday League
Derby — Derbyshire v Northants
Cardiff — Glamorgan v Sussex
Leicester — Leics v Hampshire
Trent Bridge — Notts v Kent
Taunton — Somerset v Essex
Edgbaston — Warwickshire v Yorkshire
Worcester — Worcs v Lancashire

MAY 6, WEDNESDAY
Britannic Assurance Championship
Swansea — Glamorgan v Lancashire
Leicester — Leics v Essex
Lord's — Middlesex v Northants
Taunton — Somerset v Surrey
Worcester — Worcs v Sussex
Headingley — Yorkshire v Hampshire

Tourist Match
Canterbury — Kent v Pakistan

Other Match
Fenners — Cambridge U v Derbyshire

MAY 9, SATURDAY
Benson & Hedges Cup
Bristol — Glos v Leics
Southampton — Hampshire v Middlesex
Trent Bridge — Notts v Derbyshire
Taunton — Somerset v Combined Univ
The Oval — Surrey v Kent
Hove — Sussex v MCCA
Headingley — Yorkshire v Lancashire
Perth — Scotland v Warwickshire

Tourist Match
Chelmsford* — Essex v Pakistan

MAY 10, SUNDAY
Sunday League
Southampton — Hampshire v Surrey
Canterbury — Kent v Worcs
Old Trafford — Lancashire v Glamorgan
Hove — Sussex v Derbyshire
Headingley — Yorkshire v Northants

LOOKING FORWARD/FIXTURES 1987

MAY 12, TUESDAY
Benson & Hedges Cup
Chelmsford	Essex v Middlesex
Southampton	Hampshire v Somerset
Canterbury	Kent v Sussex
Southport	Lancashire v Scotland
Leicester	Leics v Notts
Northampton	Northants v Glos
The Oval	Surrey v Glamorgan
Headingley	Yorkshire v Worcs

Tourist Match
Derby	Derbyshire v Pakistan (One day)

MAY 14, THURSDAY
Benson & Hedges Cup
Chelmsford	Essex v Hampshire
Old Trafford	Lancashire v Warwickshire
Leicester	Leics v Derbyshire
Lords	Middlesex v Combined Univ
Trent Bridge	Notts v Northants
Hove	Sussex v Surrey
Worcester	Worcs v Scotland
Oxford (Christchurch)	MCCA v Glamorgan

Tourist Match
Taunton	Somerset v Pakistan (One day)

MAY 16, SATURDAY
Benson & Hedges Cup
Derby	Derbyshire v Glos
Cardiff	Glamorgan v Kent
Lord's	Middlesex v Somerset
Northampton	Northants v Leics
Edgbaston	Warwickshire v Worcs
Oxford (Christchurch)	MCCA v Surrey
Fenners	Combined Univ v Essex
Glasgow (Hamilton Cres)	Scotland v Yorkshire

Tourist Match
Hove*	Sussex v Pakistan

MAY 17, SUNDAY
Sunday League
Chelmsford	Essex v Leics
Swansea	Glamorgan v Kent
Bristol	Glos v Warwickshire
Lord's	Middlesex v Somerset
Northampton	Northants v Hampshire
The Oval	Surrey v Lancashire

MAY 20, WEDNESDAY
Britannic Assurance Championship
Chelmsford	Essex v Glamorgan
Bournemouth	Hampshire v Notts
Dartford	Kent v Sussex
Leicester	Leics v Lancashire
Edgbaston	Warwickshire v Surrey
Worcester	Worcs v Derbyshire
Headingley	Yorkshire v Somerset

Other Matches
The Parks	Oxford U v Glos
Fenners	Cambridge U v Middlesex

MAY 21, THURSDAY
Texaco Trophy (1st 1-day international)
The Oval	England v Pakistan

MAY 23, SATURDAY
Texaco Trophy (2nd 1-day international)
Trent Bridge	England v Pakistan

Britannic Assurance Championship
Derby	Derbyshire v Warwickshire
Cardiff	Glamorgan v Yorkshire
Old Trafford	Lancashire v Worcestershire
Northampton	Northants v Leics
Taunton	Somerset v Glos
The Oval	Surrey v Essex
Hove	Sussex v Middlesex

Other Match
The Parks	Oxford U v Notts

MAY 24, SUNDAY
Sunday League
Derby	Derbyshire v Worcestershire
Cardiff	Glamorgan v Yorkshire
Canterbury	Kent v Middlesex
Old Trafford	Lancashire v Hampshire
Taunton	Somerset v Glos
The Oval	Surrey v Essex

MAY 25, MONDAY
Texaco Trophy (3rd 1-day international)
Edgbaston	England v Pakistan

MAY 27, WEDNESDAY
Benson & Hedges Cup
Quarter-finals

Tourist Match
Yorkshire or Ireland v Pakistan

MAY 30, SATURDAY

Britannic Assurance Championship
Chesterfield	Derbyshire v Glamorgan
Southampton	Hampshire v Glos
Leicester	Leics v Somerset
Northampton	Northants v Kent
Worcester	Worcs v Essex
Middlesbrough	Yorkshire v Notts

Tourist Match
Lord's*	Middlesex v Pakistan

Other Match
The Parks	Oxford U v Warwickshire

MAY 31, SUNDAY

Sunday League
Southampton	Hampshire v Glos
Old Trafford	Lancashire v Somerset
Northampton	Northants v Sussex
Trent Bridge	Notts v Leics
Edgbaston	Warwickshire v Derbyshire
Worcester	Worcs v Essex
Middlesbrough	Yorkshire v Kent

JUNE 3, WEDNESDAY

Britannic Assurance Championship
Swansea	Glamorgan v Hampshire
Bristol	Glos v Lancashire
Tunbridge Wells	Kent v Surrey
Lord's	Middlesex v Essex
Taunton	Somerset v Notts
Edgbaston	Warwickshire v Leics
Sheffield	Yorkshire v Worcs

JUNE 4, THURSDAY

First Cornhill Test
Old Trafford	ENGLAND v PAKISTAN

JUNE 6, SATURDAY

Britannic Assurance Championship
Swansea*	Glamorgan v Somerset
Tunbridge Wells	Kent v Essex
Leicester	Leics v Worcs
Lord's	Middlesex v Glos
Northampton	Northants v Surrey
Trent Bridge	Notts v Lancashire
Horsham	Sussex v Hampshire
Harrogate	Yorkshire v Derbyshire

JUNE 7, SUNDAY

Sunday League
Leicester	Leics v Worcs
Lord's	Middlesex v Glos
Northampton	Northants v Notts
The Oval	Surrey v Warwickshire
Horsham	Sussex v Hampshire
Sheffield	Yorkshire v Derbyshire

JUNE 10, WEDNESDAY

Benson & Hedges Cup
Semi-finals

Tourist Match
Glasgow (Titwood)	Scotland v Pakistan

Other Matches
Harrogate	Tilcon Trophy (three days)

JUNE 13, SATURDAY

Britannic Assurance Championship
Ilford	Essex v Kent
Cardiff	Glamorgan v Warwickshire
Old Trafford*	Lancashire v Yorkshire
Bath	Somerset v Middlesex
The Oval	Surrey v Hampshire
Worcester	Worcs v Leics

Tourist Match
Bletchley*	Northants v Pakistan

JUNE 14, SUNDAY

Sunday League
Ilford	Essex v Kent
Ebbw Vale	Glamorgan v Notts
Swindon	Glos v Sussex
Southampton	Hampshire v Derbyshire
Leicester	Leics v Surrey
Bath	Somerset v Warwickshire
Worcester	Worcs v Middlesex

JUNE 17, WEDNESDAY

Britannic Assurance Championship
Derby	Derbyshire v Lancashire
Ilford	Essex v Northants
Basingstoke	Hampshire v Yorkshire
Bath	Somerset v Kent
Hove	Sussex v Glamorgan
Edgbaston	Warwickshire v Notts
Worcester	Worcs v Glos

Other match
Fenners	Cambridge U v Surrey

JUNE 18, THURSDAY

Second Cornhill Test
Lord's	ENGLAND v PAKISTAN

JUNE 20, SATURDAY

Britannic Assurance Championship
Southampton	Hampshire v Middlesex
Liverpool	Lancashire v Kent
Hinckley	Leics v Sussex
Luton	Northants v Warwickshire
Trent Bridge	Notts v Worcs
Headingley	Yorkshire v Essex

Other Match
The Parks	Oxford U v Glamorgan

LOOKING FORWARD/FIXTURES 1987

JUNE 21, SUNDAY
Sunday League
Ilkeston	Derbyshire v Glos
Basingstoke	Hampshire v Middlesex
Old Trafford	Lancashire v Kent
Luton	Northants v Glamorgan
Trent Bridge	Notts v Worcs
Bath	Somerset v Sussex
Edgbaston	Warwickshire v Essex
Headingley	Yorkshire v Surrey

JUNE 24, WEDNESDAY
NatWest Bank Trophy (1st round)
	Bucks v Somerset
	Cambs v Derbyshire
	Durham v Middlesex
Cardiff	Glamorgan v Cheshire
	Hampshire v Dorset
Old Trafford	Lancashire v Glos
Leicester	Leics v Oxfordshire
Northampton	Northants v Ireland
Jesmond	Northumberland v Essex
Trent Bridge	Notts v Suffolk
Myreside (Edin.)	Scotland v Kent
Burton-on-Trent	Staffs v Warwickshire
	Surrey v Hertfordshire
	Sussex v Cumberland
	Wiltshire v Yorkshire
Worcester	Worcs v Devon

Tourist Match
	Combined Univ v Pakistan

JUNE 27, SATURDAY
Britannic Assurance Championship
Chelmsford	Essex v Somerset
Gloucester	Glos v Worcs
Canterbury	Kent v Notts
Old Trafford	Lancashire v Derbyshire
Lord's	Middlesex v Glamorgan
Northampton	Northants v Yorkshire
Guildford	Surrey v Sussex
Edgbaston	Warwickshire v Hampshire

Tourist Match
Leicester*	Leics v Pakistan

JUNE 28, SUNDAY
Sunday League
Gloucester	Glos v Worcs
Canterbury	Kent v Somerset
Old Trafford	Lancashire v Derbyshire
Lord's	Middlesex v Glamorgan
Guildford	Surrey v Northants
Hove	Sussex v Notts
Edgbaston	Warwickshire v Hampshire

JULY 1, WEDNESDAY
Britannic Assurance Championship
Swansea	Glamorgan v Northants
Gloucester	Glos v Hampshire
Canterbury	Kent v Yorkshire
Old Trafford	Lancashire v Essex
Leicester	Leics v Derbyshire
The Oval	Surrey v Middlesex
Edgbaston	Warwickshire v Somerset
Kidderminster	Worcs v Notts

Other Match
Lord's	Oxford v Cambridge

JULY 2, THURSDAY
Third Cornhill Test
Headingley	ENGLAND v PAKISTAN

JULY 4, SATURDAY
Britannic Assurance Championship
Heanor*	Derbyshire v Hampshire
Swansea	Glamorgan v Glos
Northampton	Northants v Lancashire
Trent Bridge	Notts v Yorkshire
The Oval	Surrey v Leics
Hove	Sussex v Kent
Worcester	Worcs v Warwickshire

JULY 5, SUNDAY
Sunday League
Chelmsford	Essex v Sussex
Lord's	Middlesex v Leics
Tring	Northants v Lancashire
Trent Bridge	Notts v Yorkshire
Worcester	Worcs v Warwickshire

JULY 8, WEDNESDAY
NatWest Bank Trophy (Second Round)
Leics or Oxon v Hampshire or Dorset
Scotland or Kent v Cambridgeshire or Derbys
Sussex or Cumberland v Lancashire or Glos
Wiltshire or Yorkshire v Glamorgan or Cheshire
Durham or Middlesex v Notts or Suffolk
Northants or Ireland v Surrey or Hertfordshire
Staffs or Warwickshire v Bucks or Somerset
Northumberland or Essex v Worcs or Devon

Tourist Match
Burton-on-Trent Minor Counties v Pakistan

JULY 11, SATURDAY
Benson & Hedges Cup
Lord's	Final

Tourist Match
Old Trafford,	Notts, Lancashire or
Trent Bridge or	Warwickshire v Pakistan
Edgbaston	

LOOKING FORWARD/FIXTURES 1987

JULY 12, SUNDAY
Sunday League
Cheadle	Derbyshire v Glamorgan
Chelmsford	Essex v Glos
Southampton	Hampshire v Worcs
Old Trafford	Lancashire v Leics
The Oval	Surrey v Somerset
Edgbaston	Warwickshire v Notts
Scarborough	Yorkshire v Middlesex

JULY 15, WEDNESDAY
Britannic Assurance Championship
Derby	Derbyshire v Kent
Southend	Essex v Hampshire
Bristol	Glos v Middlesex
Trent Bridge	Notts v Leics
Taunton	Somerset v Worcs
The Oval	Surrey v Yorkshire
Nuneaton	Warwickshire v Sussex

Tourist Match
Cardiff	Glamorgan v Pakistan

JULY 18, SATURDAY
Britannic Assurance Championship
Southend	Essex v Derbyshire
Cardiff	Glamorgan v Surrey
Bristol	Glos v Northants
Bournemouth*	Hampshire v Warwickshire
Lord's	Middlesex v Notts
Taunton	Somerset v Leics
Hastings	Sussex v Yorkshire

Tourist Match
Worcester*	Worcs v Pakistan

JULY 19, SUNDAY
Sunday League
Southend	Essex v Derbyshire
Cardiff	Glamorgan v Surrey
Bristol	Glos v Yorkshire
Canterbury	Kent v Northants
Trent Bridge	Notts v Middlesex
Taunton	Somerset v Leics
Hastings	Sussex v Lancashire

JULY 22, WEDNESDAY
Britannic Assurance Championship
Derby	Derbyshire v Notts
Portsmouth	Hampshire v Sussex
Folkestone	Kent v Glos
Southport	Lancashire v Warwickshire
Leicester	Leics v Middlesex
Northampton	Northants v Somerset
The Oval	Surrey v Worcs
Headingley	Yorkshire v Glamorgan

JULY 23, THURSDAY
Fourth Cornhill Test
Edgbaston	ENGLAND v PAKISTAN

JULY 25, SATURDAY
Britannic Assurance Championship
Bristol	Glos v Derbyshire
Portsmouth	Hampshire v Essex
Old Trafford	Lancashire v Notts
Leicester	Leics v Yorkshire
Lord's	Middlesex v Kent
Northampton	Northants v Sussex
Worcester	Worcs v Somerset

JULY 26, SUNDAY
Sunday League
Swansea	Glamorgan v Warwickshire
Portsmouth	Hampshire v Essex
Old Trafford	Lancashire v Notts
Leicester	Leics v Yorkshire
Lord's	Middlesex v Derbyshire
Finedon	Northants v Glos
Worcester	Worcs v Somerset

JULY 29, WEDNESDAY
NatWest Bank Trophy
Quarter Finals

Tourist Match
Ireland or Yorkshire v Pakistan

AUGUST 1, SATURDAY
Britannic Assurance Championship
Cheltenham	Glos v Leics
Canterbury	Kent v Derbyshire
Lord's	Middlesex v Surrey
Weston-s-Mare	Somerset v Glamorgan
Eastbourne	Sussex v Notts
Edgbaston	Warwickshire v Northants
Headingley	Yorkshire v Lancashire

Tourist Matches
Southampton*	Hampshire v Pakistan
Worcester	England v Australia
	(4 days, Women's Test)

AUGUST 2, SUNDAY
Sunday League
Cheltenham	Glos v Leics
Canterbury	Kent v Derbyshire
Lord's	Middlesex v Surrey
Weston-s-Mare	Somerset v Glamorgan
Eastbourne	Sussex v Worcs
Edgbaston	Warwickshire v Northants
Scarborough	Yorkshire v Lancashire

LOOKING FORWARD/FIXTURES 1987

AUGUST 5, WEDNESDAY
Britannic Assurance Championship
Chesterfield	Derbyshire v Yorkshire
Abergavenny	Glamorgan v Leics
Cheltenham	Glos v Surrey
Canterbury	Kent v Middlesex
Old Trafford	Lancashire v Northants
Worksop	Notts v Warwickshire
Weston-s-Mare	Somerset v Hampshire
Eastbourne	Sussex v Essex

AUGUST 6, THURSDAY
Fifth Cornhill Test
The Oval	ENGLAND v PAKISTAN

AUGUST 8, SATURDAY
Britannic Assurance Championship
Chesterfield	Derbyshire v Surrey
Cheltenham	Glos v Kent
Southampton	Hampshire v Lancashire
Leicester	Leics v Warwickshire
Lord's	Middlesex v Worcs
Northampton	Northants v Essex
Trent Bridge	Notts v Somerset
Sheffield	Yorkshire v Sussex

AUGUST 9, SUNDAY
Sunday League
Chesterfield	Derbyshire v Surrey
Cheltenham	Glos v Kent
Bournemouth	Hampshire v Glamorgan
Leicester	Leics v Warwickshire
Lord's	Middlesex v Lancashire
Northampton	Northants v Essex
Trent Bridge	Notts v Somerset
Hull	Yorkshire v Sussex

Other Matches
Warwick	Under 25 Semi-finals (1-day) (or 16 August)

AUGUST 12, WEDNESDAY
NatWest Bank Trophy
Semi-finals

Tourist Match
Trent Bridge, Old Trafford or Edgbaston	Notts, Lancashire or Warwickshire v Rest of World XI (Three days)

AUGUST 15, SATURDAY
Britannic Assurance Championship
Derby	Derbyshire v Leics
Chelmsford	Essex v Middlesex
Trent Bridge	Notts v Northants
Taunton	Somerset v Yorkshire
The Oval	Surrey v Kent
Hove	Sussex v Warwickshire
Worcester	Worcs v Glamorgan

Tourist Match
Bristol*	Glos v Rest of World XI (Three days)

AUGUST 16, SUNDAY
Sunday League
Derby	Derbyshire v Leics
Chelmsford	Essex v Middlesex
Llanelli or Swansea	Glamorgan v Worcs
Trent Bridge	Notts v Hampshire
Taunton	Somerset v Yorkshire
The Oval	Surrey v Kent
Hove	Sussex v Warwickshire

Other Matches
Warwick	Under 25 Semi-finals (1-day) (if not played on 9 August)

AUGUST 19, WEDNESDAY
Britannic Assurance Championship
Chelmsford	Essex v Notts
Cardiff	Glamorgan v Middlesex
Bournemouth	Hampshire v Kent
Lytham	Lancashire v Sussex
Northampton	Northants v Worcs
The Oval	Surrey v Somerset
Edgbaston	Warwickshire v Glos
Scarborough	Yorkshire v Leics

AUGUST 20, THURSDAY
MCC Bicentenary Match (Five days)

AUGUST 22, SATURDAY
Britannic Assurance Championship
Derby	Derbyshire v Essex
Neath	Glamorgan v Worcs
Bournemouth	Hampshire v Somerset
Wellingborough	Northants v Middlesex
Trent Bridge	Notts v Glos
Hove	Sussex v Surrey
Edgbaston	Warwickshire v Lancashire

254 LOOKING FORWARD/FIXTURES 1987

AUGUST 23, SUNDAY
Sunday League
Neath	Glamorgan v Essex
Moreton-in-Marsh	Glos v Notts
Bournemouth	Hampshire v Somerset
Leicester	Leics v Kent
Wellingborough	Northants v Middlesex
Hove	Sussex v Surrey
Edgbaston	Warwickshire v Lancashire
Worcester	Worcs v Yorkshire

AUGUST 26, WEDNESDAY
Britannic Assurance Championship
Maidstone	Kent v Lancashire
Leicester	Leics v Notts
Uxbridge	Middlesex v Warwickshire
Northampton	Northants v Derbyshire
The Oval	Surrey v Glamorgan
Hove	Sussex v Somerset
Worcester	Worcs v Hampshire
Headingley	Yorkshire v Glos

AUGUST 29, SATURDAY
Britannic Assurance Championship
Colchester	Essex v Surrey
Maidstone	Kent v Hampshire
Old Trafford	Lancashire v Glos
Leicester	Leics v Northants
Uxbridge	Middlesex v Sussex
Trent Bridge	Notts v Derbyshire
Edgbaston	Warwickshire v Worcs

AUGUST 30, SUNDAY
Sunday League
Derby	Derbyshire v Notts
Colchester	Essex v Yorkshire
Maidstone	Kent v Hampshire
Old Trafford	Lancashire v Glos
Leicester	Leics v Northants
Lord's	Middlesex v Sussex
Worcester	Worcs v Surrey

Other Matches
Edgbaston	Warwick Under-25 Final (one day)
Llanelli	Glamorgan v Somerset (Buckleys Brewery Trophy)

SEPTEMBER 2, WEDNESDAY
Britannic Assurance Championship
Colchester	Essex v Worcs
Cardiff	Glamorgan v Derbyshire
Bristol	Glos v Somerset
Southampton	Hampshire v Leics
Trent Bridge	Notts v Sussex
The Oval	Surrey v Northants
Edgbaston	Warwickshire v Kent

SEPTEMBER 5, SATURDAY
NatWest Bank Trophy
Lord's	Final

Other Match
Scarborough	Yorkshire v MCC

SEPTEMBER 6, SUNDAY
Sunday League
Canterbury	Kent v Sussex
Leicester	Leics v Glamorgan
Trent Bridge	Notts v Essex
Taunton	Somerset v Northants
The Oval	Surrey v Glos
Edgbaston	Warwickshire v Middlesex
Headingley	Yorkshire v Hampshire

Other Match
Scarborough	Derbyshire v Lancashire (ASDA Trophy, one day)

SEPTEMBER 7, MONDAY
	Bain Dawes Trophy Final (one day)
Scarborough	Yorkshire v Hampshire (ASDA Trophy, one day)

SEPTEMBER 8, TUESDAY
Scarborough	ASDA Final (one day)

SEPTEMBER 9, WEDNESDAY
Britannic Assurance Championship
Old Trafford	Lancashire v Surrey
Leicester	Leics v Glos
Lord's	Middlesex v Hampshire
Trent Bridge	Notts v Glamorgan
Taunton	Somerset v Derbyshire
Hove	Sussex v Northants
Scarborough	Yorkshire v Warwickshire

SEPTEMBER 12, SATURDAY
Britannic Assurance Championship
Derby	Derbyshire v Middlesex
Chelmsford	Essex v Lancashire
Bristol	Glos v Glamorgan
Canterbury	Kent v Leics
Worcester	Worcs v Northants

SEPTEMBER 13, SUNDAY
Sunday League
Derby	Derbyshire v Somerset
Chelmsford	Essex v Lancashire
Bristol	Glos v Glamorgan
Canterbury	Kent v Warwickshire
The Oval	Surrey v Notts
Hove	Sussex v Leics
Worcester	Worcs v Northants

Fixtures are the copyright of the Test and County Cricket Board 1986